Business in Europe

Sonia El Kahal

Principal Lecturer
Sheffield Hallam University

135663X

CHESTER COLLEGE

ACC No. 0107854   DEPT

CLASS No. 337.142 ELK

LIBRARY

The McGraw-Hill Companies

London · New York · St Louis · San Francisco · Auckland · Bogotá · Caracas
Lisbon · Madrid · Mexico · Milan · Montreal · New Delhi · Panama · Paris
San Juan · São Paulo · Singapore · Sydney · Tokyo · Toronto

Published by
McGraw-Hill Publishing Company
Shoppenhangers Road, Maidenhead, Berkshire, SL6 2QL, England
Telephone 01628 502500
Facsimile 01628 770224

The LOC data for this book has been applied for and may be obtained from the
Library of Congress, Washington, D.C.

A catalogue record for this book is available from the British Library.

Further information on this and other McGraw-Hill titles is to be found at
http://www.mcgraw-hill.co.uk

Copyright © 1998 McGraw-Hill International (UK) Limited. All rights reserved. No part of this
publication may be reproduced, stored in a retrieval system, or transmitted, in any form or by any
means, electronic, mechanical, photocopying, recording, or otherwise, without the prior permission of
McGraw-Hill International (UK) Limited.

McGraw-Hill

A Division of The McGraw·Hill Companies

Typeset by Mackreth Media Services, Hemel Hempstead

Printed and bound in Great Britain at the University Press, Cambridge
Printed on permanent paper in compliance with ISO Standard 9706

For my sister Raghda Hamzawi,
in admiration of her courage

CONTENTS

PREFACE

The Single European Market represents the third largest trading bloc in the world, after North America and Far Asia. It has captured the attention of politicians, business people and academics and led to a considerable increase in publications and academic research. Topics now include key aspects of the economics and politics of European integration, the structure and functions of Community institutions and comparative analysis of European markets. Various models and techniques for direct application in the Single European Market have also been developed, as well as detailed guides for conducting business. Together, these descriptive and prescriptive studies constitute a significant expansion of empirical knowledge about the Single European Market. It is therefore understandable that there may be some hesitation in writing yet another book in this area. Some might argue that the Single Market is failing in most of its objectives, that it is old, static, and high cost. Others would regard European growth as relatively slow compared to global markets and therefore as not necessarily presenting any serious challenge to global competition. However, as the European Community develops, the Single Market in Europe already has had wider implications for business than expected both within the European Union and in the rest of the world. The changes so far engendered are so large that the repercussions are global and not just internal to the Community. A *Fortune* special report describes the social, political and economic turmoil in Europe since 1992, and its global impact as follows:

> ... This bad news for Europeans also touches Americans and Asians – and anybody who does business on a global basis. Without continued progress towards closer political and economic unity, trade barriers in Europe will no longer keep falling – protectionism is bound to rise, particularly against Japan. Development of new markets such as Portugal and Greece will lag. The troubled economies of Eastern Europe could flame out entirely, sending more refugees West, stoking nationalist sentiments and more violence for skinheads and other latter-day fascists
>
> (*Fortune*, 14 December 1992)

At the national level more and more managers, besides those employed in already established European firms, are now realizing that their customers and interests cannot be located in and conceived of as operating within national boundaries only. Domestic firms and local authorities are increasingly facing European competition within their own domestic markets. To compete successfully or simply to survive in such a challenging and dynamic new environment, firms are realizing the need for their managers to look for opportunities in the Single Market as well as in local domestic markets, while local and regional political authorities increasingly turn to the EU for realization of their development needs. European Community legislation about companies, rules on company take-overs, mergers and acquisitions, joint ventures, licensing arrangements, European technical standards, training and so on, are becoming in many ways too complicated and technical. Yet, companies and their managers are expected to cope with these dynamic changes in their business environment, as well as the challenges imposed by the openness to world competition, particularly from US firms which are already based in Europe, and Japanese firms which are pouring funds into Europe in an effort to establish a predominant base within the EU. It is important therefore to try to understand how the dynamic process of change and competition created by the single European Market has taken place, what the underlying processes are that drive it, how it is developing in contemporary Europe and most importantly how to cope within it in order to succeed or simply to survive.

The main distinguishing feature of this book is its interdisciplinary and practically oriented approach. It aims at training students and managers in acquiring practical skills and techniques to compete successfully in the 'new' European business environment, by providing them with a series of practical frameworks that facilitate analysis and understanding.

Another distinctive feature of this book is its practical relevance. By focusing mainly on contemporary developments and changes occurring in the 'new' Europe, particular attention is given throughout to the impact of the 1992 programme on industry and the responses of firms to the Single European Market. The book does not cover every issue but it addresses the core business questions and themes that students, and managers in Europe need to be aware of.

Detailed and practical examples of western and US and Japanese multinationals operating in the 'new' European Single Market represent another distinctive feature of the book. These cases are useful in illustrating more concretely industry's response to the changing European business environment.

A further feature of this book is that it aims to provide a wider understanding of the dynamic process of change and competition created by the Treaty of European Union. Operating in Europe cannot be fully abstracted from global competition. In this modern globalized world the content of what can be seen as relevant to European business has hugely widened. Firms are continuously under pressure to change and innovate if they want to secure competitive advantage. This book deals with contemporary issues such as the globalization of markets, the rise and development of strategic alliances, green environmental issues, the demand for broader social responsibilities from business, marketization efforts in central and eastern Europe, and assesses their direct implications for European business.

The recent growing awareness of, and demand for, European business knowledge has pushed many universities and colleges to introduce general and specialized courses in 'European business' and 'European management'. This book will be useful as a comprehensive yet accessible introductory text on business in the 'new' Europe. It provides useful resources for introductory courses on European business in the undergraduate curriculum and for post experience diplomas Certificate in Management Studies (CMS) and Diploma in Management Studies (DMS). The issues or topics-driven level 3 undergraduate business module would derive considerable benefit from this text. Students on language programmes taking social science or business units would find this complementary to their studies at level 3. MBA programmes would find plenty of 'meat' in the text, and useful insights and 'titbits' of information relating to culture and business practice that could help them with European business-related activities. From a teaching perspective, this text should appeal to teachers on specialized European courses, as it is a source of institutional detail, and of legal changes and practices, which are hard to keep abreast. It covers a wide range of political, economic, cultural and business issues that do not require a high level of analytical skills derived from a single discipline, such as economics, politics, or business.

The book should also be valuable to senior executives wishing to update their European business knowledge and enhance their managerial skills in Europe. It should also be of interest to managers of companies planning to remain national or local, but who wish to know what developments can be expected in their own markers as a result of the closer economic and political integration in Europe.

OVERALL STRUCTURE OF THE BOOK

The book is organized into three main parts, subdivided into 14 chapters. Key concepts and substantive subject areas in the field are introduced in a way that makes them accessible, understandable and thought-provoking to students and managers who may be encountering this subject for the first time. Each chapter has a carefully selected up-to-date list of recommended further reading to guide readers' next steps in European business should they wish to study further. Short case studies taken from existing multinational firms operating in Europe are also included to illustrate the challenges faced by business in the Single European Market. Seminars and suggestions for group projects at the end of each chapter have been specifically designed to assist students in testing their understanding of the material covered, and its relevant practical applications.

Part One (Business Environment of the New Europe) aims to present an understanding of the politics and economics of European integration and their implications for doing business in the European Union. The early concept of 'Europe without frontiers' and the contemporary Treaty on European Union are closely examined as well as the main Community policies and decision-making processes that influence business in the Single European Market. An introductory knowledge of the 15 EU member states is also included providing useful and insightful material related to each member state.

Part Two (Business Operations in the New Europe) explains and illustrates how Europe's industrial structure is adjusting to the new European environment. West European, US and Japanese firms' reactions to the new challenges of the Single European Market are closely examined. Particular attention is made to European business policy and strategy, European marketing and European management.

Part Three (Contemporary Trends and Issues in European Business) considers recent trends towards the globalization of markets, the rise and development of strategic alliances in Europe and the European Green movement. The European Union's developing relationship with Central and Eastern Europe is also examined as well as the recent restructuring of Eastern European firms in their attempt to face west European and global competition. Finally a comparative study of the role of women in European business is provided.

ACKNOWLEDGEMENTS

First of all I am grateful to my dear husband for his thorough review of the manuscript. I could not have completed it without his continuous and consistent support and encouragement, particularly when deadlines were getting tight.

I would also like to thank my daughter Diala for her valuable research assistance and my son Khaldoun for his patience, understanding and forbearance.

Special thanks also go to the internal reviewers at McGraw-Hill for their helpful comments which helped improve the text.

Finally, I am grateful to all staff at Sheffield Hallam University Library for their professional and invaluable assistance, and to Suzanne Tieze, senior lecturer at the Business and Management School for contributing Chapter 14 "Women in the European market".

BUSINESS ENVIRONMENT OF THE NEW EUROPE

J. VanderMerwe recounts a conversation he overheard in the departure lounge of Heathrow Airport that highlights in a small way the problematic nature of the European's Single Market (Calori and Lawrence, 1991, p. 3). The discussion was between an American, an Englishman and a German manager, all working for the same US company:

American: We just spent three days at Headquarters in Colorado. Fantastic! The Board revealed a fully integrated European strategy for our business over here. What is more, further penetration into the German market is a priority.
Englishman: That is very nice. When you discussed the European strategy, how exactly did you define Europe?
American: Hell, you ought to know, you are European.
Englishman: Well, I am English actually. I come from Hereford.
American: Sure, but don't you think that many problems will be resolved by 1992, with the United States of Europe.
Englishman: No exactly. Europe will remain what it is, a collection of countries each with different customs, sometimes even within a particular country. Jolly hard to build a fully integrated European Strategy.
German: And there are other questions. You implied that Europe is the EC, but it now also includes the former Eastern Bloc countries. As to the further penetration of the German market, you must recognise that it is both a mature and a fragmented market, with regional differences as well. The characteristics of distribution in Schleswig-Holstein differ importantly from those in Bavaria. Then we don't even speak about the completely different situation on the East German market.
Englishman: Also, you must take account of the entirely different conditions we face in the premium and middle-range segments of the market, where the internal cultural differences will be more critical.
American: You Europeans sure want to make everything complicated.

This story clearly illustrates the different perceptions of Europe that exist. The countries of Europe may have a number of broad features in common such as good transport systems, good retailing systems, effective media and a considerable degree of technological and financial development. They may appear similar on the face of it, apart from language and social considerations. Differences between countries in Europe will continue to persist, despite the efforts in Brussels to create a homogeneous market through increased harmonization and common legislation, but the relationship between these tendencies is dynamic, and further affected by changes and restructuring in the global political economy. In order to succeed, business managers will need to develop an awareness of such issues.

Chapter one provides an overview of integration theories in an attempt to explain the economic and political motives behind the creation of the EEC. An examination of the Single European Act itself, its aims, objectives and the philosophy of 'Europe without frontiers' are provided in Chapter Two. Chapter Three considers the pressures towards closer political union in Europe and provides a detailed analysis of the Treaty on European Union. Business in the Single Market does not operate in a vacuum, but is heavily influenced by EU legislation and policies. Chapter Four describes the Community institutions, their functions and power and explains the decision-making processes involved. It also provides practical advice on how to influence EU policy-makers, and how to develop an active role in determining key policies affecting business in Europe. Finally, Chapter Five examines in detail EU policies and discusses their implications for companies doing business in Europe.

INTEGRATION THEORIES AND THE MOVEMENT TOWARDS A SINGLE MARKET IN EUROPE

Knowledge about the European Community (EC) is generally limited, and while students should become better informed with recent events and changes in the European Union (EU), the aim of this chapter is to provide a framework for understanding European integration and the issues and principles that underlie the various sectors of European integration, and to understand why and how the recent interest and revival in completing the Single Market in the 1990s arose.

LEARNING OBJECTIVES

- To understand what is meant by European integration and be able to consider the issues arising from European regionalism
- To identify the initial political and economic motives behind the creation of the European Economic Community (EEC)
- To provide a brief overview of the Treaty of Rome: its aims, objectives and limitations

THE FOUNDATIONS OF EUROPEAN INTEGRATION

Facts means nothing without some idea of which are more relevant than others, and how they relate to each other. Integration theories can shed some light on the dynamics behind European integration, and the recent push towards greater economic and political union.

A sharp distinction is often drawn between theory and practice, especially in the business and political worlds. Many business and political practitioners deny the relevance of theory altogether. They often consider practice as the real and central consideration, while theory is seen as something fanciful, abstract or ideal, and contrary to experience. Theory, in this view, is speculative thought and a set of statements on how things ought to be. In other words, theory is nothing but a guide to action. According to them, nothing in theory can substitute for experience, commonsense and intuition, upon which practice must ultimately rely.

It is self-delusion on the part of decision makers or business people to believe that they can operate without theoretical propositions. All our actions are based on some kind of theory, or a set of preconceived assumptions although usually implicitly. Theory in fact provides the basic principles of practice. Theory is a guide for action, a set of statements either about how things ought to be or about how they are. Theory can be used for several purposes: as a basis for legitimation, a framework for organizing facts, or a basis for the explanation of events and historical developments.

Theory as a guide for legitimation

Theory can be used for political purposes. Politicians and diplomats often rely on theoretical arguments in their briefs to legitimize their actions and to gain public approval and consent. They will often refer to theory as a convenient and often convincing explanation of their actions by relating them to broader considerations that they feel are relevant, such as those pertaining to the domestic environment, or to the national interest, or involving suitable comparisons with other states.

Theoretical arguments play a crucial role in the context of the European Union particularly in dealing, for example, with conflicts between different national interests, national sovereignty and national identity. It is, for example, much more powerful to explain the reasons why the UK opted out of the European Exchange Rate Mechanism and the Social Charter at the Maastricht Conference not only in terms of the issue itself but by relating it to the wider context of a country's power status, national sovereignty and identity, and other more general foreign policy interests.

Theory as a guide for action

By stating how things ought to be, linked to an analysis of how things have developed in the way they have, theory can be used as a guide for action that can provide us with a 'prescription for change', to make the world a better place to live in (Waltz, 1979), or shift developments towards our own particular interests, or to take better advantage of opportunities as they arise.

Theory as an analytical framework for organizing facts

Theory can help us to organize the storage of data, their classification and their retrieval. It enables us to proceed with clarity in the process of identifying relevant values and appropriate variables, and in determining the most rational course of action. Theory can therefore help us to separate and identify more clearly the relevant factors of an issue, thus allowing a more comprehensive understanding of its complexity and of different ways of analysing the issue.

INTEGRATION THEORIES

Before considering the various approaches towards explaining European integration it is useful first to define what is meant by 'integration'. Integration is generally defined as 'a process whereby a group of people organized initially in two or more independent national-states, come to constitute a political whole which can be described as a Community' (Pentland, 1973, p. 29). Such a general definition is essentially a political, state-centric one. It identifies integration as a consequence or an effect of governments, two or more intending to integrate and assumes integration as a future outcome. This conception of integration is rather narrow, and institutionally based. In particular, it focuses overwhelmingly on states, consequently referring only to the role of firms – national, multinational, and global – to the extent to which they affect state policies, or European Union policies, positively or negatively.

Although states are indeed the only units capable of formal membership of the European Union, this does not mean that business is not central to understanding the development, progress, and future possibilities of European integration. Furthermore, the concept of integration is normally taken to refer only to specific observable attempts at regional integration, for example, in Africa (Economic Community of West African States – ECOWAS), the Caribbean (Caribbean Community and Common Market – CARICOM), and more recently in Far Asia (Asia Pacific Economic Cooperation – APEC) as well as Europe. The argument in this book, developed more fully below and in Part Three, is that formal regional integration can only be properly understood if placed in the context of recent important developments within the global political economy, for example, global financial integration, and regional trading blocs.

There are various general approaches that have been developed in order to explain European integration. These are known as the Federalist, Functionalist, Pluralist, or Neo-functionalist and Marxist theories (Harrop, 1989, Chapters 7–10).

The Federalist theory

The aim, and means, of integration for the Federalists is to create a political community based upon strong, rule-bound central political institutions, superimposed upon autonomous nation states to keep order and control among them. Federalism was the main focus of the debates over the future of Europe at the Maastricht Conference, and caused major concern and worry about the idea of supranationality, especially to the UK and Danish governments.

The Functionalist theory

The Functionalists claim that there is a concrete distinction between activities that are political and those that are economic or technical. Technical/economic decisions are seen as less controversial than political ones. By separating economics from politics, increased technological cooperation, for the Functionalist, will necessarily lead to political cooperation. The Functionalist theory of integration basically claims that only activities concerned with national security are political, while areas such as public health, transport and agriculture are non-political. Cooperation in these areas is therefore easier to reorganize and institutionalize, they argue, since it is beneficial to all. Functionalism has contributed greatly to the recent development of and increase in mergers and acquisitions, joint ventures and strategic alliances in Europe, and it is important for students of business, and business managers, to understand the dynamics underlying them.

The Pluralist theory

According to the Pluralists, integration is seen as the formation of a 'Community of States' defined by a high and self-sustaining level of diplomatic, economic, social and cultural exchange between member states. This conception is popular among statesmen because the major concern of the Pluralists is the problem of developing peaceful relations among states, while maintaining national sovereignty and state security. According to them, peaceful change can be achieved without the need for recourse to arms. Integration, they claim, will be enhanced not by the elimination of state borders, but by the development and improvement of the conduct of relations between states by developing their capacities to handle information about their political environment and to adjust to each other's behaviour through increased social communications. To be fully integrated in a Pluralist sense, states would have to form a 'Community of States'. This was the Gaullist vision of Europe – *L'Europe des Patries* – also known as political union.

The UK's view on European integration provides a classic example of a Pluralist view of the creation of a single market, and encourages European political and economic cooperation only so long as they take the form of intergovernmental organization, without causing loss of national identity or national sovereignty.

The Neo-functionalist approach

Integration, for the Neo-functionalists, is 'the process whereby political actors in several distinct national settings, are persuaded to shift their loyalties, expectations and political activities towards a new centre, where institutions possess and demand jurisdiction over the pre-existing national state'. To this extent, it is close to the Pluralist view.

The end result of political integration, in this view, is a new political community, superimposed on the pre-existing states, leading to the development of a new supranational state. Integration for the Neo-functionalist is therefore more concerned with why and how states cease to be wholly sovereign, how and why they voluntarily mingle, merge and mix with their neighbours so as to lose the factual attribute of sovereignty while acquiring new techniques for resolving conflicts between them. Theories developed about the working of the Community in Brussels, the decision-making processes, and the dialogue between the Commission, the Council and the Parliament, all provide good illustrations of a Neo-functionalist approach to integration. The Single European Act, the removal of physical, trade and monetary barriers, the ratification and debates before, during and after Maastricht, especially the French referendum – during which every household in France received a detailed copy of the European Union Treaty, including the proposed ratifications – is a triumph of and for Neo-functionalist thinking.

The Marxist theory

For the Marxist, in order to understand European integration one must seek to understand the present as history. Integration for the Marxists is a response to interdependence. European integration, in their view, emerged as a policy response to the necessary expansion of capitalism. The way to achieve and sustain economic growth is by taking advantage of economies of scale. This explains, for example, why European nations came together to counterbalance US hegemony, and why mergers are increasingly encouraged in order to create firms large enough to compete against US and Japanese multinationals. The state, in this view, plays an important role in both economic and political integration. It must ensure the creation of a secure environment for industry and commerce, complete with legal systems protecting private property contracts and the provision of a cooperative labour force. It must also construct an ideological climate favourable to capitalism (Pentland, 1973, pp. 29–136; Cocks, 1980). Of these theories, it can be seen that all but the Marxist approach conceive of integration as mainly a political process or condition.

(This section taken from El Kahal, 1994, pp. 147–150)

THE CREATION OF THE EUROPEAN COMMUNITY

Economic and political motives

To understand the recent pressures towards demanding closer integration in Europe, it is important to identify what the initial political and economic motives behind the creation of the EEC were, without which the Single Market cannot be fully understood.

The idea of creating a 'Unified Europe' to maintain peace and to create a common European culture dates back to the fourteenth century, when Pierre Dubois proposed a

European Confederation to be governed by a European Council. However, movements to unite Europe politically only emerged after the First World War to end the destructive antagonistic rivalry of European nation states.

Count Richard Coudenhove-Kalergi established the Pan-European Union in 1923 as a non-party mass movement for the unification of Europe. In 1926, another organization, the Association for European Co-operation was started. The interwar years also saw the early advocacy of a European Customs Union and a recommendation for a single market from 1920 in the face of increasing Japanese and US exports, economic stagnation, economic nationalism and tariff protectionism in Europe (Dedman, 1996, p. 16). In September 1929, Aristide Briand proposed the creation of a European Federal Union at the Assembly of the League of Nations. However, interest in such movements and proposals had no effect on the realities of European economic and political affairs and such organizations never achieved a mass following but remained a minority preoccupation of certain intellectuals (Lipgens, 1982, pp. 35–42).

It was only in 1945, following the end of the Second World War, that concrete efforts were made to create a secure union of countries in western Europe. The end of the Second World War did not automatically result in peace and improved economic and social conditions. Until the late 1940s, most of Europe was still in economic and political chaos. Agricultural output between 1946–47 was only 75 per cent of the 1938 level; a UN Commission estimated in 1946 that 100 million Europeans lived on less than 1500 calories per day (i.e. they were going hungry). In 1947, industrial production in Belgium, the Netherlands, and France was still 30–40 per cent lower than in 1939. European conditions were made worse in 1946–47 by a wet summer and a severe winter leading to poor harvests and a fuel crisis as snow disrupted coal supplies. These massive shortages of fuel, food and industrial capital goods led to a large trading deficit with the USA as the alternative supplier, and a dollar shortage (Dedman, 1996, p. 34). European governments were faced with a severe fall in foreign trade, and were threatened with high inflation. In addition to the loss of many colonies, the territorial realignment and the reshaping of national boundaries increased the number of separate Customs Unions and created massive problems by dislocating industrial links.

Massive borrowings were undertaken by the European states, far exceeding their capacity to repay, thus leading to the intense pressures upon the international financial system. There were also massive losses of labour and capital, which resulted in the collapse of industry and trade. A great depression set in all over Europe. The division of Europe into east and west as a result of the Cold War also resulted in the Soviet Union consolidating its position and control over eastern European countries, which was seen as posing the major security threat to the west.

In the face of this deep economic and political chaos, there was a strong desire in Europe to create a unified Europe to achieve peace and stimulate recovery. The attempt to achieve integration by military aggression had failed under Hitler, as it had earlier under Napoleon. An attempt to establish a political community based upon integrated defence forces was also defeated in the French National Assembly. The idea of a political union was then transferred into the economic field. Jean Monnet 'the father of European integration' as early as 1945 asserted:

> The nations of Europe are too circumscribed to give their people the prosperity made possible, and hence necessary, by modern conditions. They will need larger markets ... Prosperity and vital social progress will remain elusive until the nations of Europe form a federation for a 'European Entity' which will force them into a single economic unit
>
> (Monnet, 1988, p. 41)

Robert Schuman, the French Foreign Minister (1948–1952) supported by Monnet, proposed the Schuman Plan of May 1950, which led to the signing of the Treaty of Paris one year later and resulted in the creation of a common market for coal, steel, coke, iron ore and scrap between France, Germany, Belgium, the Netherlands, Luxembourg and Italy, the European Coal and Steel Community (ECSC) in 1954. Coal and steel were of central importance to nation states' economic and military power during that period. They had provided both the military capacity for invasion as well as being a motive for German and French territorial acquisitions (Dedman, 1996, p. 57). Steel was the major element in states' post-war economic reconstruction, and was needed for railways, buildings, ships, vehicles, and machinery. Shuman's original announcement on 9 May 1950 proposed that 'the entire French and German production of coal and steel by placed under a joint High Authority within an organization open to the participation of other European nations. The High Authority was to ensure the supply of coal on equal terms inside a common market.' (Milward, 1984, pp. 378–9). The Treaty of Paris 1951 was therefore a commercial treaty establishing the ECSC as a regulated market-sharing arrangement under supranational control. It was designed to balance the six states' particular vested interests in coal and steel and to facilitate achievement of national objectives in these two sectors.

The possibility of further integration was later developed in the Spaak Report which led to the Treaty of Rome in 1957, thus creating the European Economic Community. The Spaak Report of 1955 was originally suggested at the Messina Conference, held in Sicily. It called for the integration of atomic energy, the establishment of a common market, the creation of a European Fund and a European Investment Bank, and the harmonization of conditions of work and pay (Jensen, 1967, pp. 46–69; Dedman, 1996, pp. 129).

The Treaty of Rome

The Treaty of Rome was signed in March 1957 by the six founding European states: Belgium, France, Germany, Italy, Luxembourg and the Netherlands. It took effect from January 1958, thereby creating the EEC with completion date set for full operation on 31 December 1969. The general objectives of the creation of the EEC are summarized in Article 2 of the Treaty:

> The Community shall have as its task, by establishing a common market and progressively approximating the economic policies of member states, to promote throughout the Community a harmonious development of economic activities, a continuous and balanced expansion, an increase in stability, an accelerated saving in standard of living and a closer relation between the states belonging to it.

These objectives it was claimed could be achieved through:

1 the establishment of a Common Customs Tariff. All tariff and other barriers to trade among the member states were to be eliminated, and common external tariffs are to be formulated between the six
2 a common commercial policy towards Third World countries
3 a common agricultural policy
4 the free movement of people, goods, services and capital, and the equal treatment of all workers with respect to wages and conditions, entitlements to welfare benefits
5 the creation of a European Social Fund and a European Investment Bank

The substantive material of the Treaty can be seen in terms of three economic axes: (a) liberalization, (b) normalization, and (c) development. The liberalization axis dealt specifically with the unification of the markets and consisted of the establishment of the

Customs Union, the special provision for agriculture and transport, and the provision for the free circulation of persons, goods, services and capital. Normalization of competition was to be achieved by attempting to control monopolies, controlling state aids and subsidies, and correcting distortions that might arise from legislation on regulations imposed on industries. Finally economic development was to be achieved through the creation of the European Investment Bank and the European Social Fund.

The Treaty of Rome, none the less was as Dedman (1996, pp. 93–94) argues

a statement of intent, a programme of action, a timetable. It was not a detailed comprehensive blueprint of regulations .... The Treaty's actual provisions often consisted of general statements concerning objectives and intentions where the detail would have to be worked on and agreed in the future... The Treaty of Rome, actually left virtually everything to be done and relied on governments to reach agreement later.

Member states' interests in and enthusiasm for cooperation and integration have varied. For the three Benelux countries, the experience of the war re-emphasized their vulnerability to hostile and more powerful neighbours due to their relative small size. They realized that the only real prospect of being able to exercise any sort of influence in Europe was through a more unified interstate system.

Italy had a fascist regime for over 20 years and was suffering economic difficulties with employment, inflation, balance of payments and poverty in the south. According to Romero (1993), Italy's main objective in the EEC was to encourage 'rational productive emigration'. It needed to export its unemployment, particularly from the underdeveloped south. Italy wanted and tried to win acceptance for the 'free circulation of labour' inside the EEC to complement the principle of a 'free movement of goods'. The government's main goal was an open European labour market to drain off Italy's massive unemployment (Romero, 1993, pp. 38–39; Dedman, 1996, pp. 105–106).

France wanted mainly to contain German economic growth and gain access to German coal and markets. Germany had big reserves of coking coal, used in steel production, and France depended on German coal supplies.

What did West Germany hope to gain from the Treaty of Paris? Political considerations were of upmost importance in negotiating the Treaty of Paris for Germany. When the Federal Republic emerged in May 1949 made up of the UK, US' and French zones, Germany was still subject to numerous restrictions and controls. The Occupation Statute prohibited full responsibility for foreign affairs, defence or foreign trade, and ownership and decartelization of the Ruhr industries. The International Authority of the Ruhr 1948 undertook the compulsory allocation of coal between domestic and export markets. Konrad Adenauer, Federal Chancellor (1949–1963), wanted to remove these constraints. He was also keen to obtain full sovereignty for his state. (Dedman, 1996, p. 63). Germany therefore thought that through European unification, it could re-establish itself in the world and regain its self-respect.

Austria, Sweden and Switzerland's neutrality at that time posed a major obstacle to economic, monetary and political union. Finland had special relations with the Soviet Union, and Iceland did not like the EEC fishing policies.

Britain was originally reluctant to join the EEC for different reasons. The war experience appeared at first to strengthen rather than weaken Britain. It was generally claimed that 'Britain won the War' and there was a strong national pride and sense of achievement. The British saw themselves not only as Europeans but as a world power. Britain was still the third greatest global power in 1945 with 1.5 million men in its armed forces around the world. Atomic bomb tests in 1952 reinforced Britain's self-image as one of the Big Three globally and not as one of the Big Three in Europe (Dedman, 1996, p. 107). 'We are in Europe, with Europe, but not part of it' was the general attitude. In 1945, Britain not only possessed the largest empire in the world but also played a major role at the United Nations. It was one of the five permanent members of the Security Council with a veto power. Britain joined the EEC in January 1973 not out of enthusiasm or strong economic interests but for lack of visible alternatives following the trends towards decolonization and its withdrawal from the Indian subcontinent in 1947, its inability to impose its will at the Suez crisis of 1956, the accelerated tariff reductions within the EEC in the first three years which posed a challenge to British trade, South Africa leaving the Commonwealth in 1961, and the bilateral meeting between Presidents Khrushchev and Kennedy in June 1961 which excluded France and Britain. Britain first applied under the Macmillan government but its application was vetoed by Charles De Gaulle, the French president in 1963. Realizing that it had no influence outside Europe, Britain applied again for membership in 1973.

The first enlargement of the Community took place in January 1973 with the accession of the United Kingdom, Denmark and Ireland. Greece joined in 1981, Spain and Portugal in 1986. A set of four criteria were set at the mid-1993 Copenhagen summit as prerequisites for further membership:

- acceptance of the obligations of economic and political union
- stability of institutions guaranteeing democracy, the rule of law, human rights and the rights of minorities
- the existence of a functioning market economy
- and the capacity to cope with competitive pressures and market forces within the EU

Austria, Finland and Sweden are the three new entrants that joined in January 1995. Following the dramatic collapse of the former USSR, and the consequent demise of socialist, centrally planned economies throughout East and Central Europe in the early 1990s, Poland and Hungary have formally applied for membership, while the Czech Republic, Slovakia, Romania, Bulgaria and Slovenia are likely to apply after the 1996 intergovernmental conference. Estonia, Latvia and Lithuania would probably not be ready for membership for at least another 10 years, while Malta and Cyprus are first in line in the next phase of enlargement. What is not in doubt is that the European Union has enlarged rapidly since the 1980s, and is set to increase its membership even further during the coming decade.

THE CALL FOR CLOSER EUROPEAN INTEGRATION IN THE 1980S AND 1990S

The dynamics behind the contemporary revival of interest in closer economic and political integration in the European Community, is in part a reflection of large-scale economic and political problems in the global system as a whole (Palmer, 1988). The oil recession in the 1970s made Europeans increasingly aware of their dependence upon the international monetary system. Many large firms became insolvent due to the rising price of oil. As a result, a recession gripped Europe, with high levels of unemployment and inflation rates rising sharply.

By the 1980s there was a real fear in Europe of a breakdown of the international monetary system, due to large US deficits and the inability of the USA to continue financing them. There was a major concern that these deficits might lead to an increase in international interest rates by the end of the decade. As a result, it was feared that those Third World countries with the greatest levels of indebtedness to western banks would be obliged to default on their debt payments, which would lead to a collapse of the international monetary system and to worldwide economic depression. The stock-market crash of October 1987 in London, for example, seemed to confirm the worst apprehensions of western European governments. Additionally, the economic recession in the early 1980s in Europe resulted in industrial decline and decay of social provision. Europe was increasingly unable to counter the growing commercial challenge from the USA, Japan and the Pacific Rim.

Another dynamic force behind the push towards closer economic integration in Europe in the 1980s was the worsening of transatlantic relations between Europe and the USA, which started to sour as early as 1973, due mainly to the deficit in the US trade balance under presidents Ford, Carter and Reagan. Throughout the 1970s, both the USA and the EC had several conflicts over international trade protectionism, such as when the USA sought to protect its steel industry through triggering prices designed to ward off European and Japanese competition. OPEC prices were also cut to help US chemical and synthetic textile manufacturers to undercut foreign competition. Additionally, in 1985 the USA spent billions of dollars to develop its Strategic Defense Initiative. Europe complained that this would give an indirect boost to the USA's competitive edge in advanced information technology, and reinforce Europe's relative technological backwardness and dependence on the USA.

The challenge of an increasingly competitive external world also provided much of the incentive for increased European integration. The information technology revolution of the 1980s posed a threat to Eruope. US and Japanese firms were evidently superior in this area of new technology, and EC competitiveness was at stake. Europe became unable to counter the growing commercial challenge from the USA and Japan and the developing Pacific Rim competition. European states and firms realized that a major cause of their lack of growth and competitiveness was due to the fragmentation of the EC into national markets. After the 1970s' recession, although non-tariff barriers were removed, each nation imposed its own barriers to protect its industry against outside competition, whether from within the EC or outside.

Another factor which stimulated the need for the creation of a Single European Market was the increasing internationalization of capital, labour and production, which was made easier by new developments in information technology (IT). The past 30 years have seen an extraordinary expansion, not only in world trade, but also in the deployment of international finance and new forms of international production, due to developments in computer technology and international communications which facilitated the internationalization of production, distribution and consumption. Subcontracting and franchising grew rapidly. With the increased ease of international capital movements and production dispersal, multinational firms established factories in countries where labour was cheaper.

Finally the rise of Japanese competition, through economic development and emergence as a leading world economic power, placed a serious strain on European performance. The European Community began to look for new ways of shielding their domestic industry from the new competitive threat.

REVIEW QUESTIONS

1. To what extent do theories of integration help us to understand the dynamics behind European economic and political integration?
2. What were the economic and political motives behind the creation of the EEC following the Second World War?
3. What factors have stimulated the recent push towards greater economic and political integration in the European Union?

4. Is the EEC a structure for peace or an alliance for economic defence?
5. Why did Austria, Finland and Sweden recently apply for membership in the European Union?
6. What are the economic and political challenges or benefits of a further enlargement of the EU?

EXERCISE 1.1: The enlargement of the EU: problems and future prospects

Aim   This exercise is designed to illustrate the complexity of the enlargement of the European Union. It aims to improve students' awareness and analytical skills in analysing economic, political, social and cultural factors and assessing their implications for European business.

Assignment   Poland and Hungary have formally applied for membership in the European Union. The Czech Republic, Slovakia, Romania, Bulgaria and Slovenia are expected to apply soon. Students are asked to discuss the economic, political, social and cultural consequences of a further enlargement of the European Union.

Format   The class should be divided into two groups. Each group has a specific assignment.

● Group 1 should explain the benefits of a future enlargement to the EU as a whole
● Group 2 should argue against a further enlargement and highlight its negative implications for business, the economy, and society

Each group should develop arguments to present to the class, and seek to persuade them either of the benefits of further enlargement or its negative implications.

Each group will have 15 minutes to discuss its position internally and develop its arguments into a coherent and presentable form. In their presentation, students should use relevant economic, political, social and cultural data about the new applicants to support their point of view.

Sources

In researching their country profiles students are encouraged to consult the following documentation:

● United Nations
  – *East West Business Directory*   This directory provides detailed information on the activities for the 1990s of hundreds of affiliates which have been established in the OECD economies by direct investment enterprises in Bulgaria, Hungary, Czech Republic, Poland, Romania, the former USSR and Yugoslavia.
  – *Economic Bulletin for Europe*   This bulletin reviews current economic developments in western Europe, North America and the transition economies of eastern Europe and the former Soviet Union. It also provides an economic outlook.
  – *Economic Survey of Europe*   This publication provides an account of the principal macro-economic developments in the European region. It offers a framework for viewing the reform process in eastern Europe and in Europe as a whole and analyses the optimal framework for western support to economic reforms in eastern countries. The Survey includes statistical appendices and a list of over 50 tables and charts quantifying the evaluation.

- ⊙ OECD
  - – Country profiles
  - – Economic surveys
  - – Eurostat
- ● Economic Intelligence Unit
  - – publishes annual country profiles and quarterly reports

FURTHER READING

Dedman, M.J., *The Origins and Development of the European Union 1945–1995: A History of European integration,* Routledge, 1996.

Haas, E.B., *The Uniting of Europe: Political, Social and Economic Forces, 1950–1957*, Stanford University Press, Stanford, 1958.

Harrop, K., *The Political Economy of Integration in the European Community*, Edward Elgar, Aldershot, 1989.

Lipgens, W., *A History of European Integration, 1945–1947*, **1**, Clarendon Press, Oxford, 1982.

Pentland, C., *International Theory and European Integration,* Faber and Faber, London, 1973.

Schmitt, H.A., *The Path to European Union: From Marshall Plan to the Common Market*, Louisiana State University Press, Baton Rouge, 1962.

TWO

THE CREATION OF A SINGLE MARKET IN EUROPE

The aim of this chapter is to explain the background to the Single Market programme, to outline the measures being taken at Community level to improve it and ensure its proper functioning, and to highlight issues directly affecting business, such as institutional reforms. Treaty provisions, new legislations, competition policy, consumer policy, environmental policy, social policy, and so on.

LEARNING OBJECTIVES

- To introduce the background to the creation of a Single Market in Europe and its relevance for business
- To explain the philosophy behind 'Europe without frontiers'
- To provide an overall assessment of the '1992' programme

BACKGROUND TO THE DYNAMICS BEHIND THE CREATION OF A SINGLE MARKET IN EUROPE

The awareness in business of the relevance of the opening up of the Single Market is steadily increasing. However, business is finding it difficult to work out how best to select and address the issues that are the most relevant. Most trade associations and individual companies do not have the necessary intellectual and financial resources available, and there are very few European-level think-tanks. It is therefore important for business to identify the impact of the changing European business environment, and to prioritize its activities to take advantages of the opportunities offered. Can business afford to ignore the changes brought about by the Single European Market?

- **The free movement of goods, people, services and capital**   The elimination of obstacles to the free movement of goods and services makes it easier for business to offer products or services on a Community-wide basis. The principle of freedom of establishment also ensures the right for businesses to set-up an agency, branch or subsidiary anywhere in the Community. Operating throughout the Community may become much easier and expansion into new markets more feasible. However, a free internal market may also lead to increased competition in national markets.
- **Standards**   The free circulation of goods across borders requires them to be EC-marked.

The marking is an indication that your product complies with the 'essential requirements' that a product must meet in order to be sold in the Community. Businesses are required to affix the identification number of the organization that tested or certified their product. It is therefore important to keep abreast of developments in new technical regulations to ensure that you comply.

- **Value-added tax (VAT)**   The abolition of border controls leaves consumers free to shop cross-border to take advantage of lower tax rates in neighbouring member states. This may affect regional sales for some products, depending on differences in national VAT rates and access to products (DTI, *European Manual*, 1996, p. 10). Since some member states had to raise the level of VAT on certain products to bring them near to, or in line with, the agreed minimum standard rate of 15 per cent, this may reduce demand and may affect regional sales for some products.
- **Free movement of people**   Under the 'mutual recognition' of professional qualifications, businesses will be able to transfer their personnel easier in other member states in order to provide services there, but this also means that professionals from other member states will also be able to set-up businesses in national markets which means greater competition in national markets.
- **Environment policy**   This is mainly concerned with the award of eco-labels for environmentally less-damaging products. The introduction of the eco-label means achieving a greater competitive advantage if businesses are awarded an eco-label. It is therefore important to find out more about the criteria for eco-labelling and the application procedure.

EUROPE WITHOUT FRONTIERS: THE PHILOSOPHY

The Single Market was officially 'open for business' on 1 January 1993. It was a huge market of 345 million consumers, covering the then 12 member states of the EC. The Agreement on the European Economic Area (EEA), entered into force on 1 January 1994, and extended the principles of the Single Market to five of the seven countries of the European Trade Association (EFTA) – Austria, Finland, Iceland, Norway and Sweden – thus increasing the size of the Single Market to 370 million consumers, as compared with a US population of 252 million and a Japanese population of 124 million, and creating the world's largest free trade zone.

The Single Market objective

At the request of heads of states and governments of all member states, the Commission published a White Paper in June 1985 setting out a legislative programme for completing the Single Market. The White Paper attempted to identify all the existing physical, technical and fiscal barriers that prevented the free functioning of the market, and put forward 300 legislative proposals required for their removal (Commission of the EC, 1989). The aim of the programme was:

- To remove all remaining physical, technical and fiscal barriers between the member states in order to achieve the establishment of the four freedoms of movement:
  - Free movement of goods
  - Free movement of people
  - Free movement of services
  - Free movement of capital

- To abolish systematic controls at the borders between the member states through:
  - The removal of physical barriers
  - The removal of technical barriers
  - The removal of fiscal barriers
  - The liberalization of internal competition through strict competition policies.

The Single Market objective was embodied in Community law by the Single European Act (SEA) which was signed in February 1986 and entered into force on 1 July 1987. The SEA defined the internal market as: 'An area without internal frontiers in which the free movement of goods, persons, services and capital is ensured' (Department of Trade and Industry, September 1994a, p. 16).

The Single Market programme

The Single European Act covers a broad spectrum of Community law, and contains several amendments to the original Treaty of Rome. It can be argued that the importance of the SEA did not lie so much in the institutional Act itself, but more in its rather intangible role in the development of a momentum for the deepening and extension of regional integration. It certainly added a great deal to the credibility of the 1992 objective and thus helped to create a virtuous circle, involving both governments and the marketplace (Tsoukalis, 1993, p. 45).

Free movement of goods

Frontier controls, delays, customs red-tape, bureaucracy, divergent standards and technical regulations, conflicting business laws and protectionist procurement practice, and the weight of documentation have been for a long time both frustrating and costly to the movement of goods within the Community. The size of the costs was estimated as exceeding Ecu 200 billion in 1985 (Cecchini Report, 1989, p. xviii).

To ensure the speedier movement of goods across national borders, the SEA introduced the Single Administrative Document in January 1988. This document replaces some 70 different administrative forms previously used for transporting goods within Europe. The SEA also proposed the approximation of VAT and excise duty rates.

According to the proposal, member states will have two VAT rates, a standard rate in the band 14 per cent – 20 per cent and a lower rate in the band four per cent – nine per cent on certain basic items such as food, domestic energy, public transport, books and periodicals (Duddley, 1990, p. 34).

To ensure free movement of goods according to the SEA, any product which can be sold in any member state, should also be freely marketable in all other parts of the Community, unimpeded by different national rules, standards, tests or certification practices. To achieve this, all technical barriers to the free movement of goods in the Community had to be removed, including differences in national industrial standards, differences in national regulations and differences in testing and certification procedures (European File, 1988).

Due to the existence of different national production standards and regulations which meant that many products had to be separately manufactured to separate standards for each separate country, the Commission proposed the harmonization of technical standards, and adjustment of national regulations to conform to an agreed Community standard. This 'new approach to the harmonization' of technical conditions and standards was adopted on 7 May 1985. It stated that once minimum standards in respect of safety and compatibility are reached, individual variations can be tolerated. There were four main elements to the 'new approach':

1. Harmonization should be limited to essential safety requirements.
2. The task of drawing up technical specifications in relation to the essential safety requirements established by the Council should be left to European standardization organizations. These standards are formulated in the three European standards bodies: CEN, CENELEC (which specializes in electrotechnical standards) and ETSI (which deals with telecommunications standards).
3. The new European standards should be voluntary.
4. Governments would be obliged to presume that products manufactured according to those standards are in conformity with the essential requirements set out in the relevant directives. If producers chose not to manufacture according to European standards, they would need a certificate of conformity from designated bodies (Tsoukalis, 1993, p. 142).

A Joint European Standards Institution was consequently established to produce European standards essential for safety in use, health, consumer protection and the environment. Products complying with these requirements are issued with a CE marking to show that they conform with the essential requirements and which will guarantee their legitimate and free access to all markets in the Community.

Another possibility is to attain a BS 5750 standard. BS 5750 lists the key requirements of a quality management system, which can be applied to almost any type of organization. These are identical to the international ISO 9000 standards and the European EN 29000 standards. They include the need to establish a quality policy, to allocate responsibility clearly, to give authority to those allocated responsibility, to document each state of the production process, and to establish systems for identifying, remedying and preventing defects in quality (DTI, *Euro Manual*, 1995, pp. 5–6).

The free movement of goods also required stronger measures to strengthen the protection of intellectual and industrial property rights. A Single Community Patent and a Single Community Trade Mark were proposed. Previously, each member state had its own national patent system. Any inventor who wished to obtain patent protection across the whole Community had to apply for a patent in each country individually, and the procedures involved tests to establish what is patentable. This was a formidable task, considering the differences in standards regulations between member states. The Single Community Patent Convention (CPC) was signed in December 1989, making it possible to obtain patent protection in some or all of the Community to which it applies through a single application. The Community Patent will be valid for 20 years, but the high costs of translation into all the EU's 11 official languages may be a deterrent to its wide use (EIU, 1995a, p. 55). To date only six EU member states have taken the necessary action (Denmark, France, Germany, Greece, Italy and Luxembourg), but all the others except Portugal have at least started their ratification procedures. A regulation granting up to five years' supplementary protection for medical products, to compensate for the proportion of patent life expanded on pre-market testing, was adopted in 1992 and came into force in 1993.

As far as trade marks are concerned, prior to the Single European Act there were 10 separate systems for registering trade marks in the European Community. This meant that anyone wishing to protect a trade mark throughout the EC had to meet the criteria laid down by each of the separate national systems. Against this, the Commission proposed that there should be a Community trade mark. This would operate in parallel with national systems, and would enable business to secure Community-wide protection through a single application to a Community Trade Mark Office set-up for this purpose and which confers the same rights in all member states. Member states would also designate some of their courts as Community trade mark courts. A Community trade mark owner who considers that another business is infringing its trade mark in other member states would be able to go to one of these courts and obtain a judgment valid for the whole of the EC. A first directive on trade marks, was adopted in 1989 and sought to harmonize the requirements of national trade marks laws. In December 1993, after 13 years of discussions, the Council finally approved the important regulation on Community trade marks. The Community Trade Mark Office will be located in Alicante (Spain) as part of the Office for Harmonization in the Internal Market.

A Directive has also been adopted to harmonize software copyright laws in the member states to ensure a common standard of protection for computer programs. The Software Directive ensures that computer programs are protected under copyright as literary works throughout the Community and that the unauthorized copying of a program is an infringement of copyright in the program. Ideas and principles underlying a program, however, including those underlying its interface, are not protected (DTI, *Euro Manual*, 1995, p. 27).

In July 1995, the Council of Ministers approved a reinforcement of a 1988 regulation that expands customs authority to seize and destroy counterfeit goods on import, export or in transit. The amended regulation, which took effect in July 1995, extends the regulation to cover products infringing copyright and design protection as well as trade marks (EIU, 1995a, p. 57).

Free movement of people

To ensure the free movement of people the Commission proposed the abolition of systematic customs checks on intra-Community travellers at the internal borders. Under the 1990 Schengen agreement, all EU member states except the UK, Ireland and Denmark were pledged to eliminate frontier formalities, but their timetable has repeatedly slipped. The Schengen accord also envisages harmonization of visa requirements and procedures for granting political asylum. External border checks, however, will remain to protect the Community from illegal immigration, crime, drugs, terrorism and the carrying of firearms.

Individuals are no longer subject to value-added tax (VAT) on goods brought back from another member state, provided they have paid VAT (and excise duty) in the country of origin. Specific tax arrangements for new vehicles will continue to ensure that these are taxed in the country of destination, but without this giving rise to frontier controls or formalities. The Council has agreed to the retention until 1999 of duty-free shops, particularly at airports (EIU, 1995a, p. 37).

As far as non-EU citizens are concerned, the Commission in July 1995 presented its proposed format for a common model visa for non-EU citizens, which is intended to enter into force in 1996. The standard format visa will initially be a national visa, and will allow free movement of non-EU citizens only when mutual recognition of visas has been established in the EU (EIU, 1995a, p. 39).

To ensure an effective operation of the Single Market, people within the Community must have the right to live and work where they can find suitable employment. Companies must also be allowed to recruit the people they need anywhere in the Community without restriction. To eliminate previous frustration caused by administrative procedures concerned in obtaining residence permits, taxation, social security arrangements, or discrimination against qualifications from non-national institutions, the Commission proposed to extend the right of residence in any member state to all citizens of the European Union, as well as the freedom to work anywhere in the Community. Under the current regulations and directives, an EU worker who establishes himself in another member state is entitled to have his immediate family admitted to that state (EIU, 1995a, p. 38).

The need for mutual recognition of professional qualifications was also seen as necessary to remove further restrictions on Community citizens' movement. In practice, freedom to work in other member states was restricted in the past by differing professional qualifications. Academic qualifications of students or vocational training and professional qualifications were not always equally recognized in all member states. Professionals often had to requalify before they could pursue their profession in other member states. Accountants, for example, had to spend nearly 50 years to qualify and requalify in order to be qualified to audit throughout the Community (Department of Trade and Industry, 1991, p. 3).

To overcome these difficulties, the Commission put forward proposals for the mutual recognition of academic diplomas and the mutual acceptance of vocational training qualifications for apprentices. Decision 85/368 requires that all member states take common action to achieve comparability of vocational training qualifications. According to this system, provided that professional people meet certain minimum requirements of qualification, experience and supervised training, their qualifications will be recognized in all member states and they are allowed to practice without any further restriction. This proposal was agreed by the Council in December 1988, and implemented with effect from 4 January 1991. The directive clearly stipulates that if an EU citizen is fully qualified in one member state, he or she has a right to be recognized as a professional in another member state, including the right to use the relevant professional title or designatory letters. The directive also allows a professional from one member state to become a member of the equivalent profession in another without having to requalify, based on the principle of mutual recognition. This directive applies only to professions whose practice is regulated by law or administrative rules, and involving at least three years of higher education. Unlike the approach of the harmonization directives, there are no minimum criteria for curricula, but host states may require foreigners to complete an adaptation period or aptitude test. Another directive was passed in 1992 to cover workers with fewer than three years' vocational training (EIU, 1995a, p. 38). So far, the greatest progress has been achieved in the health sector. Doctors, nurses, dentists, veterinarians and midwives have had all their basic training harmonized, and now have the right of establishment and the right to practice in all Community countries. This has led to the introduction of a European 'Vocational Training Card' which aims to provide proof that the holder has reached a generally accepted standard.

Free movement of services and capital

According to the SEA, businesses in the Community should have free access to efficient financial services. They should be able to choose the services most appropriate to their requirements, which are also the most reliable and the least costly, notably in the banking, insurance and investment services sectors. In addition, business firms should be able to exercise their activities throughout the Community without having to fragment their financial dealings, which can be caused by disparate national regulations. To overcome these fiscal barriers, a directive for the full liberalization of capital was adopted in 1988, requiring member states to implement it.

The main features of the directive were: first, all restrictions on the transfer of cash were to be abolished. Second, discriminatory measures such as the taxation of certain types of investment, must also be eliminated. Third, consumers in one area should have access to the full range of insurance, unit trusts, banking, mortgage and securities options available in all member states.

A second Banking Coordination Directive was adopted in 1988. It provided the right of a credit institution that is authorized in any one member state to provide services and to establish a branch in any other member country, without having to obtain further authorization. This directive also put forward the idea of a single banking licence valid throughout the European Community, and a proposal for the creation of an integrated European securities market was expected to make it easier for companies to treat the Community as a Single Market for the issue of shares and bonds, and for obtaining stock-exchange listing.

The directive for a full liberalization of activities and services in transferable securities was adopted in 1985, and came into force in 1989. According to this directive, unit trusts, which are authorized by their own member state, will be allowed to market their units to investors in any other member state. Financial services and banks will be able to offer the full range of their services throughout the entire Community, and set up branches in other member states as easily as in their own country. Insurance too can be bought, and is valid throughout the Community (*European File*, 1988b).

As far as VAT payments are concerned, agreement was reached on the VAT rates in Directive No. 92/77/EEC establishing a time-limited minimum standard rate of VAT, and one or two optional reduced rates which could be applied to an agreed list of goods and services. (VAT is a tax on consumption within a national territory. In theory when goods cross a frontier VAT comes off on one side, and goes on the other.) Agreement was also reached on the administration of VAT after the abolition of frontier VAT controls. From 1 January 1993 most cross-border commercial VAT transactions continue to be based on the destination principle. This means that intra-Community sales continue to be zero-rated by the seller, and VAT is paid by the VAT-registered customer at the rate in force in the country of consumption. Goods will no longer be stopped at the frontier for VAT checks. According to the Commission and effective from January 1993:

1. There would be no convergence of rates.
2. There would be no change to the present system of relieving VAT on goods exported from one Community country to another, and of imposing VAT on goods imported from another Community country (named the 'destination system', as distinct from the Commission's proposed 'origin system').
3. Customs checks at borders would, however, cease: traders would themselves include or exclude VAT on their invoices, and would enter this or their normal VAT returns to their home authorities. These returns would be subject to the usual checking and audit procedures. This procedure is known as the Postponed Accounting System (PAS).
4. Individual's imports of tax-paid goods from other member countries would pay no further tax as from 1 January 1993 in conjunction with an adequate approximation of VAT and excise duty rates.

The above was denoted a 'transitional arrangement' by the Commission, and in 1996 consideration is to be given to installing the original system on 1 January 1997 (Manser, 1994, pp. 47–48).

The abolition of VAT controls at frontiers prevents delays caused by goods being held at borders prior to payment of VAT. Exporters and importers must record their own VAT information and compile their own trading records, filing regular returns to the authorities. While the new system has reduced costly border delays, many firms had to upgrade their computer systems at considerable expense (EIU, 1995a, pp. 76–77).

ASSESSMENT OF THE 1992 PROGRAMME

In 1986, on behalf of the European Commission, Lord Cockfield, Commission vice-president responsible for the internal market, invited Mr Cecchini, special advisor to the Commission, to organize a comprehensive enquiry into the likely economic impact of completing the action programme set out in the 1985 White Paper on the internal market, and to evaluate the costs and benefits of the proposed Single Market (Cecchini, 1992). A large number of independent economic experts, consultants and research institutions contributed to this project and the main conclusions of the study are summarized as follows.

> The completion of the European internal market planned for the end of 1992 will help generate industry and services; it will give a lasting boost to the prosperity of all Europeans with savings of some 200,000 million ECU for firms, and in the medium term 2 to 5 million new jobs as well as 5 to 7 per cent extra non-inflationary economic growth.

The Cecchini Report concluded that the economic gains of EC market integration in the short term would trigger a major relaunch of economic activity, adding on average 4.5 per cent of GDP for the Community as a whole. It was also assumed to simultaneously cool the economy by deflating consumer prices by an average of 6.1 per cent. This in turn was expected to lead to a relaxation of budgetary and external constraints, thus improving the balance of public finance by an average equivalent to 2.2 per cent of GDP, and boosting the EC employment and reducing unemployment by 1.5 per cent by creating 1.8 million new jobs (Cecchini, 1992, p. 97). The long-term benefits of the removal of trade barriers, according to the Report, would be improved conditions of supply by industry, lower unit production costs and therefore lower prices, thus ensuring long-term job creation. The opening up of public contracts was expected to result in cuts in public deficits and a general cooling of inflationary pressures.

According to the Cecchini Report, consumers would benefit from a Europe without frontiers in several ways. They will be able to pay similar prices for the same item and items will be cheaper because they will be produced in the cheapest way. Also, there would be greater consumer choice, due to market integration and increased internal competition (Cecchini, 1992, p. 73).

Four major consequences were expected from the combined impact of the elimination of barriers and the subsequent boost to competition:

- significant reduction in costs, thanks to improved exploitation by companies of economies of scale in production and business organization
- improved efficiency within companies, widespread industrial reorganization, and a situation where prices move downward toward production cost under the pressure of more competitive markets
- new patterns of competition between entire industries and reallocation of resources as, in home market conditions, real comparative advantages play the determining role in market success
- increased innovation, new business processes and products generated by the dynamics of the internal market

(Cechini Report, 1992, p. 73)

The Report states further that companies would have greater opportunities for success. Competition, the Report argues, would lower input cost by removing non-tariff barriers, thus leading to direct reductions in the cost and price of goods and services for final consumption. Consequently, companies would be able to cover their basic requirements of labour, capital, plant and components more cost effectively. Competition would also trigger increased efficiency and innovation, with EC integration offering management the opportunity to optimize existing resources, modernize plant, and promote new activities and new ways of organizing work, and to introduce new business processes and products (Cecchini, 1992, p. 74).

However, some criticisms of Cecchini's figures have been noted as follows (Piggot, 1993, p. 176):

1. They are very optimistic. It is assumed that all the proposals will be carried out on time and in a world and European economy which is expanding, not one of recession.
2. They also assume labour made redundant by rationalization due to restructuring will be successfully re-employed – again, a very optimistic view.
3. They ignore the distributional aspect. Estimates are aggregated for the EC as a whole, and do not look at the possible detrimental effects on some states compared to others. No account is made of the adjustment costs of firms, regions and even governments to the single market.
4. It is assumed that states will adopt similar economic policies and trade policies.
5. Such estimates are complex and it must be remembered that they are only approximate.
6. It was a report commissioned by the EC and one has to question its neutrality.

Anticipated business advantages and disadvantages of the single European Market for firms
- **Advantages for business**
  - falling unit costs as production runs are lengthened
  - Community-wide registration and protection of trade marks
  - EC-wide protection of patents enabling innovations to be marketed more easily, more quickly and more cheaply
  - removal of distortions of competition in the form of divergent tax rate and types
  - lower R&D costs as production runs are lengthened
  - opportunity for longer product life-spans
  - simplified inventory management as special products meeting separate national standards are no longer necessary
  - shorter border waiting times
  - simplification of formalities through mutual recognition of type approval procedures
  - falling cost through freedom to choose insurers
  - assumption that costs will come down with freedom of capital movement

- **Disadvantages for business**
  - rapidly expanding demand might generate bottlenecks in capital supply
  - heavier capital needs in creating and expanding new markets
  - shortfalls in staff available for international business
  - difficulties in operating EC wide after sales service
  - language barriers
  - higher cost of providing information throughout the EC
  - greater costs of managing and controlling international business, especially establishing foreign branches
  - need to take account of different mentalities, cultures

The Edinburgh European Council meeting in December 1992 noted that since 1985 over 500 internal market measures had been agreed, including 90 per cent of those in the original

White Paper, and concluded that the White Paper programme for creating the Single Market had been successfully completed in all essential respects, and that internal border controls on capital, goods, services and customs controls on persons had been removed. As far as the free movement of goods is concerned, most goods in the Community are now covered by the New Approach to Technical Harmonization. Conformity to the directive laying down the essential requirements, relating to, for example, health and safety, to be met by a product falling within the directives are now being tested to European harmonized standards. The standards are formulated in the three European standards bodies: CEN, CENELEC and ETSI. All products sold in the Community now bear the EC marking to show that they conform with the essential requirements. The principle of mutual recognition of testing and certification is now accepted by all member states. It has resulted in the setting-up of the European Organization for Testing and Certification (EOTC) which seeks to further mutual recognition in the non-regulated area through agreement groups in product sectors or in cross-sectoral fields such as testing and certification (DTI, 1994a, p. 21). Examples of EC directives in the field of harmonization are those dealing with pressure vessels, toys, building products and machines. Serious progress has also been achieved with respect to the food sector, dealing with labelling and additives. However, considerable work has still to be undertaken to establish a Single Market in the energy and telecommunications services sectors. The Council adopted a resolution on 16 June 1993 stating the aim of opening up the public voice telephone services sector to competition by 1 January 1998 (DTI, 1994a, p. 19).

REVIEW QUESTIONS

1. Account for the relaunch of the EC since the 1980s and what challenges lie ahead for the EU as far as business is concerned.
2. What is meant by 'Europe without Frontiers'?
3. Should the European Single Market be simply considered in economic terms as a market to restore European competitiveness and raise European income, or as 'Fortress Europe' to reassert itself as a world power as the USA and Japan?
4. As a European business consultant working for the Department of Trade and Industry, you have been approached by a local company for your advice. Write a consultancy report to the director general highlighting the opportunities and challenges created by the Single Act. What recommendations can you make for change to meet the challenge of the Single European Market?
5. What problems lie in eliminating the three types of barriers: physical, fiscal and technical. Illustrate your answer with examples from any particular industry of interest to you.

EXERCISE 2.1: The creation of the Single European Market and its implications for business

Aim   This exercise is designed to illustrate the complexity of the Single European Market and its implications for business. It aims to improve students' skills in conducting a debate, in choosing the main issues to be discussed, and in reaching an acceptable position between the different points of view involved.

Assignment   The class is divided into two groups. Each group has a specific assignment:

● *Group 1: The protagonist view of 1992*   This group should explain the benefits of European economic and political integration and its positive contribution to business.

- *Group 2: The antagonist view of 1992* This group should argue against European economic and political integration, highlighting its negative implications for business, the economy, national identity and sovereignty.

Each group should develop arguments to present to the class, and seek to persuade them either of the benefits of the Single Market or of its negative implications.

FURTHER READING

Cecchini, P., *1992: The European Challenge. The Benefits of the Single Market*, The Cecchini Report, Wilwood House, Aldershot, 1989.

Dudley, J., *1992. Strategies for the Single Market*, Kogan Page, London, 1990.

Economist Intelligent Unit, *The EIU European Yearbook 1994–1995*, Research Report, EIU Ltd, London, March 1995.

European File, The removal of technical barriers to trade, Commission for the European Communities, European Documentation, November 1988.

Harris, N., *European Business*, Macmillan, London, 1996.

Manser, W., Control from Brussels, Adison-Wesley, London, 1994.

Tsoukalis, L., *The New European Economy: The Politics and Economics of Integration*, Second revised edition, Oxford University Press, Oxford, 1993.

THREE

FROM ECONOMIC UNION TO CLOSER POLITICAL UNION: THE TREATY ON EUROPEAN UNION

While the removal of barriers across Europe is designed to promote increased business, cost savings and greater efficiency, liberalization of this kind would be impossible without considering the political requirements and implications involved. Reconciling economic gains with political considerations is essential to the successful development of the Single Europe Market, and business students and managers need to be aware of these aspects if they are to succeed in the 'New' Europe. The aim of this chapter is to provide an overall view of the main issues covered in the Treaty on European Union and to explain their implications for business in general.

LEARNING OBJECTIVES

- To introduce the Maastricht Treaty and explain its aims and objectives
- To examine closely the three central pillars of the Treaty on European Union, and its three central pillars
- To explain the main issues related to the European Monetary Union and the European central currency (Euro)

THE MAIN FEATURES OF THE MAASTRICHT TREATY

The major difference between the Single European Act and the Maastricht Treaty is that while the Single European Act represented precise guidelines on how to achieve the Single Market, including a timetable for implementation, the Maastricht Treaty provided greater scope for views about what the European Community is or should be concerned with. The Maastricht Treaty does not restrict itself to the 10 activities of the Treaty of Rome, which were mainly economic and designed to promote closer relations between states. It cites just about every goal and policy with which a modern national government should concern itself. It deals for example with joint foreign and security policy and common defence policy, health, education, the environment, industrial policy and consumer protection, cooperation on immigration policy, the establishment of common law for the treatment of workers, economic and monetary union, the future role of the European Central Bank in continually assessing the economic policy of each member, and so on (*Economist*, 11 July 1992, pp. 12–39).

The Maastricht Treaty comes in two distinct parts: first, political union and second, economic and monetary union. The structure of the Treaty is complicated as well as highly technical. It involves not just new proposals but a host of amendments and changes to existing treaty provisions. The Treaty has been very harshly criticized in Britain and beyond. One former Commissioner official said it had 'all the readability of a railway timetable'. A French member of the European Parliament said that the Vatican would have drafted it better, and a member of the UK House of Lords castigated it as 'a shambles with which no lawyer or accountant would wish to be associated'.

The central concern of the Maastricht Treaty was to create a new entity: a European Union going beyond mere cooperation and the Single Act, and it is this which has made it so contentious an issue, especially for politicians, local and national.

AIMS AND OBJECTIVES OF THE MAASTRICHT TREATY

According to Article B of the Treaty, the European Union will set itself the following objectives:

- To promote economic and social progress which is balanced and sustainable, in particular through the creation of an area without internal frontiers, through the strengthening of economic and social cohesion and through the establishment of economic and monetary union, ultimately including a single currency.
- To assert the European identity on the international scene, in particular through the implementation of a common foreign and security policy including the eventual framing of a common defence policy which might in time lead to a common defence.
- To strengthen the protection of the rights and interests of the nationals of member states through the introduction of a citizenship of the Union.
- To develop close cooperation on justice and home affairs.
- To maintain the *acquis communautaire* and build on it with a view to considering to what extent the policies and forms of cooperation introduced by this Treaty may need to be revised with the aim of ensuring the effectiveness of the mechanisms and the institutions of the Community (European Commission, 1994, p. 9).

In order to achieve these objectives, the Treaty of European Union called for:

1. The convergence of monetary and fiscal policy among the EC hardliner member states and a common European currency by 1999 at the latest.
2. Political union, with more rights for the European Parliament by making the Commission more accountable to the Parliament while extending the latter's role in European Community legislation, and the introduction of closer intergovernmental cooperation on common foreign and security policy and justice/home affairs.
3. New rights for European citizens (with people being citizens of the European Union), without affecting national citizenship.
4. A new strategy regarding the future enlargement of the EC with the eventual admission of a dozen new nations.
5. The European Community's field of responsibility is to expand to cover increased consumer protection, public health policy, the issuing of visas, the creation of major transport cooperation, industrial policy, education, training and increased activities in the field of environmental protection, research and development and social policy (except in the UK), and cooperation on domestic and criminal policy.

The Maastricht Agreement of December 1991, was signed in February 1992 in Maastricht and entered into force on 1 November 1993.

The Treaty is based on three central pillars. The first (Titles I, II, III and IV) amends the EEC, ECSC and Euratom Treaties, as revised most recently by the Single Act, formally substituting the term 'European Community' for 'European Economic Community' in the Treaty of Rome, reflecting the fact that the Community deals with more than just economic issues. The second pillar (Title V) concerns foreign and security policy and is built upon the existing intergovernmental procedures of European Political Cooperation. The third (Title VI) covers justice and home affairs.

First pillar: internal common policies and economic and monetary union

Title I of the Treaty of Maastricht lays out the aims of the Treaty in establishing the European Union and stresses the objective of economic and monetary union. Article A of the Treaty states that the European Economic Community will in future officially be called the European Union. 'By this Treaty, the High Contracting Parties establish among themselves a European Union, hereinafter called the 'Union'. The 'Union shall be served by a single institutional framework which shall ensure the consistency and the continuity of the activities carried out, in order to attain its objectives'. The Council, the Commission and the European Parliament shall be responsible for implementation of EC policies, each in accordance with its respective powers.

Internal Community policies
The Maastricht Treaty transfers new responsibilities to the Community in a number of areas.

Visa policy   In the European Single Market, there are no longer any borders between the member states. Individual countries can no longer carry out checks on people crossing borders within the Community. Such checks will only be possible at the Community's external frontiers. This possibility of an influx of people from outside the Community is becoming seen as an increasingly serious problem for member states. The Treaty on European Union transfers the responsibility for visa policy to the Community. The principle is that the Council, acting unanimously – as of January 1996 the decision is by qualified majority – decides whether nationals of non-member countries must be in possession of a visa to cross the Community's internal frontiers. When a situation in a non-member country threatens to cause a sudden influx of its nationals into the Community, the Council can, by qualified majority, immediately impose a visa requirement for a maximum of six months. Any extension must be by unanimous decision. It is intended that by the end of 1997 the Council will also decide by a qualified majority, on a uniform design for visas (European Commission, 1994, p. 14).

European citizenship   Article 8 of the Treaty establishes the basis for citizenship of the Union. Citizenship of the Union is not intended to weaken existing national identities, but to bring new rights and benefits to the people of the Union. According to Article 8b for example:

> every citizen of the Union residing in a member state of which he is not a national shall have the right to vote and to stand as a candidate at municipal elections in the member state in which he resides, under the same conditions as nationals of that State. As far as local and European elections are concerned, an EC citizen living in another EC country will be treated as a national of that country. This means that community citizens will be able to stand as candidates and vote in these elections (but not general elections) even if they live in an EC country other than their own.

Article 8c grants citizens of the Union the right to use the diplomatic and consular facilities of another EC country if travelling, working or living in a part of the world where his own country is not represented. Additionally, every citizen of the Union, according to Article 8d, will be able to raise any cases of alleged maladministration, by any EC institution in the course of its activities, with a Community ombudsman. The ombudsman will investigate the complaint and publish his findings. However, the Treaty makes no provision for ensuring the ombudsman's report is acted upon.

Economic and monetary policy   Much of the Treaty is taken up with a detailed explanation of how Europe would follow the path to a single currency. A three-stage monetary union process is envisaged by the Treaty. Before going into detail about the three stages a brief introduction to the structure, function and operation of the European monetary system is necessary.

The first steps towards monetary union in Europe were made in 1969 with the Barre Plan, which required member states to consult before making changes to their domestic economic policy. Early attempts at linking currencies were unsuccessful. In 1977, Roy Jenkins, then president of the Commission again raised the issue of monetary union. In 1988, Jacques Delors was asked by the Council of financial ministers to investigate more closely the process of monetary policy links and the issues involved in achieving European monetary union.

Monetary union, simply stated, is an agreement between member states in terms of which internal exchange rates are permanently fixed, and with no institutional barriers to the free movement of capital or to the circulation of currencies. The dynamics behind a closer European Community are not simply a response to internal changes within the Single Market after 1992. Several factors operating at the global level have influenced this recent push towards greater monetary integration in the European Community. Some of these are: globalization of markets, globalization of international communications and technology, globalization of the international financial system and global competition from international financial markets mainly the USA and Japan.

The European Monetary System (EMS) was created in 1979. It is a system of fixed but adjustable exchange rates, designed to create a zone of monetary stability in Europe. The main objectives of creating the EMS were described in 'The European Monetary System: Origins, Operation and Outlook' (European Perspectives Series, 1985):

- To attain and ensure a zone of internal and external monetary stability, with both low inflation and stable exchange rates.
- To improve economic policy coordination, and therefore ensure a high level of employment and boost in growth.
- To provide a pool of stability in world currency markets.

The European Monetary System was based on three main elements: the ERM, the ECU, the financial support mechanisms and agreement to coordinate monetary policy.

The Exchange Rate Mechanism (ERM) was introduced in 1979. The main impetus for the ERM was the general dissatisfaction with the floating exchange rate system which came to replace the fixed rates of the Bretton Woods system in the early 1970s. There was a general concern in the Community with the high level of exchange rate volatility, which prevented European business from reaping the full benefits of the Common Market. The ERM is the exchange rate pegging arrangement by which bilateral exchange rates between member countries are stabilized (Emerson and Huhne, 1991).

Under the ERM, each currency has a central rate against the ECU (this will be discussed in the next section) called the 'central rate'. Membership of the ERM obliges each country to keep its exchange rate against other currencies within 2.25 per cent above or below a predetermined central target rate (set between six per cent to 15 per cent for new members for a transitional period). The ERM is a flexible system of exchange cooperation where the central rate can be changed allowing a currency to depreciate or appreciate against other currencies within the mechanism (subject to the mutual agreement of all members). There were no realignments in the ERM from January 1987 to mid-September 1992. Until then, all currencies were included in the ERM with the exception of the Greek drachma and the Portuguese escudo. However, at the beginning of September 1992, a currency crisis in Europe led to several realignments within the EMS, which led to the partial disintegration of the ERM. The UK and Italy were forced to leave the ERM; Spain devalued twice; and Portugal devalued once. The French franc escaped devaluation in September and managed to stay in the ERM, after drawing down half its reserves and receiving massive German assistance to prop up the franc (Goldstein, 1993, pp. 117–132). The Danish krone has also been threatened in part because Finland, Sweden and Norway have had to cut loose their unilateral pegs to the EMS; and the Irish punt was very weak (Portes, 1993, pp. 1–5). The collapse of the ERM in 1993 shows how difficult it was to achieve European monetary union and puts into question the desirability or even viability of such a plan.

The second main element of the EMS is the European currency unit (discussed in the next section). The third element of the EMS is the credit mechanism, or financial support mechanism, which was intended to provide short- and medium-term support for member states with balance of payments difficulties via the granting of credit. However, this system has not been used since 1979.

Although the EMS did provide a useful framework for monetary stability, exchange rates under the system were still permitted to fluctuate within 2.25 per cent of the target rate, which meant that monetary policies and inflation rates consequently could still diverge significantly in the short term. Since central rates could also be periodically realigned, exchange rate uncertainty still remained. In June 1988, at the Hanover Summit, EC heads of state directed the Commission to prepare a report into how an economic and monetary union could be achieved. The EC president, Jacques Delors, with the assistance of Europe's central bankers and some independent monetary experts, proposed a three-stage transition to full European Monetary Union (EMU) which was to become known later as the 'Delors Plan' (Delors, 1989).

European Monetary Union (EMU) is an irrevocable commitment to fix bilateral exchange rates against each other by eliminating exchange rate uncertainty and transaction costs. The EMU is achieved through three stages as outlined below.

The changeover to the single currency in Europe: chronological sequence

- **Stage 1** – July 1990
    - completion of Single European Market
    - currency linkage through EMS
    - liberalization of capital movements
    - initiation of convergence programme

- **Stage 2** – 1 January 1994
    - establishment of European Monetary Institute to monitor progress
    - strict monitoring of convergence progress by member states
    - progress report by December 1996

- **Stage 3** – January 1998
    Preparation – Early 1998
    - decide which countries qualify for monetary union on the basis of economic performance for 1996–97
    - establish the European Central Bank (ECB) and the network of national central banks
    - ECB to start production of Euro banknotes
    Launch – January 1st 1999
    - fix national exchange rates against the Euro 'irrevocably'
    - definition and execution of the single monetary policy in Euros
    - central banks begin to use Euro, as do inter banks and markets
    - issue new government debt in Euros
    Completion – January 1st 2002
    - start circulation of the Euro banknotes and withdrawal of national banknotes
    - start circulation of the Euro coins and withdrawal of national coins
    - convert retail payment systems to Euros
    1 July 2002
    - cancel the legal tender status of national banknotes and coins
    - Euro becomes sole legal tender
    - Official foreign exchange reserves to be managed by ECB

    (*Sources*: Adapted from European Council, *The changeover to the single currency: chronological sequence of events*, European Council, Madrid, December 1995: ANNEX; *The Economist*, Volume **338**(7949), 20 January, 1996; and Williams, A., 1994, p. 138)

Stage 1, including the completion of the internal market is now largely completed. At the moment economic indicators vary widely for each country. The plan is that these differences would slowly begin to vanish. In each country inflation, interest rates, exchange fluctuations, budget and public deficits should begin to fall in line with each other and converge with the record of the best performing economies. If this process is successful, then there is the possibility of locking fixed rates, and merging all currencies in one. According to the Treaty, heads of government must begin to put in place programmes to achieve convergence. The Council is to keep an eye out for any sign that an economy is getting in a mess. The idea is that if this happens, the Council can step in and reprimand the country concerned. Conversely, if a country has other difficulties, financial assistance can be offered. It is up to the Commission to monitor each government's debt. If one country is in the red, the Commission should report it to the Council. EC finance ministers can then require that remedial action is to be taken. The European Investment Bank would then reconsider its lending policies to that country, or call in an interest-free loan, or impose draconian fines, decided by two-thirds qualified majority.

Stage 2, began in January 1994 and involved preparatory work and monetary policy coordination. Under the Treaty, each government must begin to put in place programmes to achieve convergence. The Treaty also states that during Stage 2 member states 'shall endeavour to avoid excessive budgetary deficits'. The Commission will monitor member states' budgetary situations and their stock of government debt with a view to identifying gross errors. If it considers that there is an excessive budget deficit in a member state, it can submit an opinion to the Council. The Council will decide whether an excessive deficit exists, and if so, it can make non-binding recommendations to the member state concerned. If a member state fails to reduce the deficit, the Council may decide to give notice to the state to take measures to do so. If the state still fails to comply with the Council's decision, the Council will be able among other measures, to impose a fine and invite the European Investment Bank to reconsider its lending policy towards the state. The Treaty also deals with the problem of member states which have serious balance of payments problems which threaten to jeopardize the working of the Single Market during Stage 2. The Commission reports to the Council of the European Union on the progress made by member states towards economic and monetary union. The Council has to assess which member states meet the necessary conditions for a single currency, and will recommend its findings to the European Council while the European Parliament will be consulted.

Four convergence criteria are set out by the Maastricht Treaty in order to assess countries qualifying for EMU. These are: inflation, budgetary deficit, interest rates and exchange rates.

1. Average rate of inflation over one year should not be more than 1.5 per cent above the rates in the three member states where it is lowest.
2. Average long-term interest rates over one year to be within two percentage points of the rates prevailing in, at most, the above three countries.
3. No member state should have a budget deficit which the Council has formally designated as excessive; and
4. A member state's currency would have to demonstrate successful membership for two years of the normal fluctuation band of the ERM without being devalued on that state's own initiative

> (Article 109j and Article 104c; see also European Commission, 1994, pp. 25–26)

Article 109j includes other important factors such as the integration of markets, deficits and surpluses in the current account of the balance of payments, changes in unit labour costs and other price indicators.

The European Council, acting by qualified majority, confirmed that the **third stage** of EMU will begin on 1 January, 1999, as scheduled by the Maastricht Treaty. Stage 3 comprises a move to fixed exchange rates, a single currency and the establishment of a European Central Bank. When stage 3 begins a new single currency (now called the Euro) will become a currency in its own right and will no longer be defined as a basket of currencies as is the ECU currently (Article 1091). The actual introduction of single currency notes and coins is not expected until the year 2002. All the participating states will agree the conversion rates at which their currencies will be irrevocably fixed and will be exchanged for the single currency, with the exception of the UK, which according to the Treaty, shall not be obliged, or committed, to move to the third stage of economic and monetary union without a separate decision to do so by its government and parliament (Article 189j (2)). Denmark was also granted exemption from participation in the third stage of economic and monetary union. Under Article 109j (2), the Danish Government is to notify the Council of its position concerning participation in the third stage before the Council makes its assessment (of whether Denmark has satisfied the 'convergence' criteria). The German government has also announced, since the agreement at Maastricht, that any decision to proceed to EMU would require majority support in a separate vote in the *Bundestag*.

The changeover to the single currency will take place through three periods:

- The first period known as the interim period will end on 1 January, 1999. During this period a selection of qualifying countries should take place, based on 1997 actual data with regard to the convergence criteria. During this period, the European Central Bank will also be created, in order to be fully operational on 1 January, 1999.

- The second period will begin on 1 January, 1999 with the start of the third stage of EMU. During this period, the conversion rates between national currencies of participating countries will be irrevocably fixed against the Euro. The European monetary policy and the foreign exchange policy will be carried out in Euros. Operations in foreign exchange markets will be executed in Euros and new tradeable public debt will be issued by EMU countries in Euros.

- The third period will begin on 1 January, 2002. During this period, Euro banknotes and coins will circulate alongside national currencies. By 1 July, 2002, national currencies, it is expected, will cease to be legal tender and will be completely substituted by the Euro in participating countries

(Mazio, 1996, pp. 178–184)

'ECU' or 'Euro'?

The 'ECU' or European Currency Unit is and will be up to 1 January, 1999 the official currency of the European Community. Its value is defined in terms of a 'basket' of all of the Community member states' currency (*The ECU*, European Documentation Series, 1987). The basket is composed of fixed proportions of Community currencies. The ECU has no independent value on its own, but its value is calculated from the value of all 12 currencies, each reflecting its economic and financial strength and the relative economic importance of each member state within the Community. The value of the ECU is revised every five years, or on request if the external value of a currency has changed by 25 per cent in accordance with Section 2.3 of the European Council Resolution of 5 December 1978.

Since the ECU is based on a mixture of currencies the value of the ECU against any particular EU currency does not alter much over time. The Maastricht Treaty will not allow any new currency to join before the transformation, in other words until the establishment of a single currency in Europe, even if the EU were enlarged. This explains why, for example, the Austrian, Finnish and Swedish currencies cannot be included.

The ECU has actually existed for many years. Until now, however, it has only been used for non-cash transactions, such as cheques or bank transfers, for deposits on savings accounts, the purchase of bonds or other forms of investment. The ECU is mainly used for loan issues on the international capital market by the Community authorities, governments and multinational companies, by large-scale investors and in credit transactions between banks. The ECU is the official unit of account of Community institutions. The EC budget is now drawn up in ECUs and all accounts are in ECUs. Financial aid and Community loans are also expressed in ECUs. The Commission uses the ECU for billing and as an instrument of payment.

The ECU has also developed a 'private' market. It has recently become a major currency unit, an important instrument for international financial transactions in Europe, the USA, Japan and the Far East. It is now being used increasingly for settling international transactions. A growing number of companies are now invoicing and carrying out their international accounting in the ECU (Drew, 1992, p. 174).

According to the Treaty on European Union, the name of the single EU currency will also be 'ECU', written in three capital letters. Discussions on whether this name 'ECU' was appropriate for the new currency was raised during the ratification of the Treaty. First of all the name as proposed in the Maastricht Treaty the 'ECU', very closely resembles the name of the existing 'ECU' which itself was derived from the acronym of 'European Currency Unit'. Second, the name has some historic connotations as 'ecu' was the name of gold and silver coins issued mainly in France between the 13th and 18th centuries. These first ecus were gold coins minted under Louis IX of France in 1266. On their obverse, they depicted a shield of arms known in Latin as '*scutum*' which gave the coin its initial name. The French, having difficulties in pronouncing the 'sc', added an 'e' and changed the name to 'escutum', later to 'escu' and then to 'ecu'. During the 15th and 16th centuries, the ecu was virtually the only gold coin struck in Europe. In 1576, Charles V combined the ecu and the franc, the two most important coins in France (Mehnert-Meland, 1994, pp. 98–99). Third, except for the French, the name 'ECU' will be a foreign word in any other EU language. Arguments were made that the new currency should indicate its pan-European nature with a name free of ties to any given EU member state and a number of proposals were made in this respect (Mehnert-Meland, 1994, p. 99). Finally, in Article 1091 of the Treaty on European Union, it was agreed that the 'Euro' will replace the generic name 'ECU' indicating the European Single Currency. The 'ECU' will cease being a basket currency and will become a currency in its own rights, while its external value will remain unchanged.

Benefits and costs of the European single currency (EURO)

As far as the benefits of the adoption of a European single currency, now called the 'Euro', Michael Emerson and Christopher Huhne argue that first, business people would be able to quote to provide goods and services in the same currency, knowing that what they receive in cash would be exactly what they had planned, rather than a different amount determined by the movements of foreign exchange rates (Emerson and Huhne, 1991). Traders, they argue could take advantage of price differences to buy and sell much more easily and make profits, because goods and services would be priced in the same currency. They would be able to notice price differences more easily, which would encourage trade and competition. Bankers, in their view, would also benefit from the adoption of a single currency in Europe. They would be able to borrow and lend throughout the Community in a much easier way. A European single currency would also assist investors in avoiding the risk of a sharp rise in currency, and in avoiding the risk that exchange rate changes might wipe out the value of their future profits (Emerson and Huhne, 1991, Chapter 2). Quoting a price in Euros for example, will remove many of the trading risks connected with currency fluctuation. The Euro will be invaluable for certain international industries where direct, instant and meaningful price comparisons are necessary (Bennett, 1994, p. 35). Valuations in Euros could also be valuable as a means for invoive settlement especially in countries where national currencies are not widely acceptable abroad, as an alternative to the US dollar.

A European single currency furthermore removes entirely the currency exchange risk associated with international transactions for firms in countries within the scheme. Share prices in European companies will be quoted in the same currency units everywhere, facilitating pan-European share trading and access to all European stock exchanges by investors and companies through the Union. This constitutes a major advantage to businesses seeking external finance (Bennett, 1994, p. 38). Wages, national insurance contributions and social security benefits will be payable in the same currency through the Union, enabling instant and meaningful comparison of reward packages. This should encourage harmonization of wages across national frontiers. Employees doing identical work in firms using the same level of technology in various EU regions will be able to compare their earnings and living costs against a standard and understandable yardstick (Bennett, 1994, p. 38). A single European currency will enable cash received from several different countries to be lumped together instantly and without conversion, and deposited in the highest interest earning country. Less book-keeping will be necessary for firms with transactions since no foreign exchange calculations will be required. Businesses will be able to record and compare all accounting values in one unit, making for easy identification of the most costly and the most profitable activities in various markets. The creation of a single European currency, with the abolition of currency exchange rates and fluctuations will automatically remove from businesses this substantial cost.

Absence of exchange rate fluctuations will facilitate long-term planning and strategy formulation as there is less uncertainty concerning prospective returns on foreign EU activities.

EMU will benefit the money and capital markets. There will be only a single money market and a single currency the Euro. Under the European system of central banks the banking system will have access to money in Euros only and only at similar interest rates. Hence, interest rates in the interbank market of member states will be harmonized from the start (Schlesinger, 1996).

Advantages of the Euro
- prices quoted in a common unit
- pan-European price labelling and packaging
- removal of currency exchange risk
- share prices in European companies will be quoted in the same currency units
- wages, national insurance contributions and social security benefits will be payable in the same currency
- reduction of transactions' costs for business
- less book-keeping for companies operating in several EU member states
- better information on input costs and competitors' prices
- economic stability
- consumers will be able to compare easily prices of similar items
- fast cross-border cash transactions
- transparency of pricing
- assessment of potential customer's creditworthiness should be facilitated
- abolition of exchange rates and fluctuations: facilitating long-term planning and strategy formulation
- transaction costs will fall because of the creation of a joint European payment system (called TARGET)

Adopting the Euro, however, carries with it many disadvantages. For retailers, the changeover to the Euro would mean re-equipping with new cash tills, slot machines, money handling systems. Most firms' accounting systems are now computerized and based on software packages that calculate values in a company's domestic currency. Time and money will be involved in changing these systems. Further costs and transitional problems will also be required for staff training, to familiarize employees with new cash tills and money handling arrangements. Other difficulties will include labelling expenses, and redrafting documentation (Bennett, 1996b, pp. 76–77).

How to prepare your business for the Euro
Mehnert-Meland identified four main issues related to the conversion of the national

currencies into the Euro which need to be addressed by any business or individual transacting with parties in the EU. These are:

1. *Information* Business must keep informed about the events in the EU leading to the introduction of the Euro. Good sources for information include the media in general, banks and other financial institutions, accounting firms, brokers and the legal profession.
2. *Preparation* It is estimated that large companies and institutions will require up to three years to prepare for the conversion to the Euro. It is therefore essential for businesses to start adjusting their business operations.
3. *Adjustment of existing and interim contracts* Business should start amending contracts denominated in existing currencies of the EU member states if such contracts may be in existence past the conversion of the underlying currency. This process may require significant amounts of time and resources and should be initiated as soon as possible. In addition, business should include provisions in any new contract negotiated between now and the actual conversion date related to the currency of the contract, and the resulting contractual obligations into the Euro.
4. *Development of infrastructure* Business should also provide for the necessary external infrastructure including communications with banks, accountants and attorneys for the establishment of bank relations in the new currency, conversion of assets, accounting changes resulting from the redenomination of assets and liabilities, and the general legal requirements associated with the conversion.

(*Source*: Mehnert-Meland, 1994, pp. 138–141)

The adoption of a single currency in Europe will also have dramatic effects on personnel and human resources management. Employees will be able to compare their own Euro wages, national insurance and superannuation contributions with those of workers in other EU member states, which might lead to a serious migration of labour from the less prosperous to more affluent areas. On the other hand, it could also be argued that this transparency of labour costs might also induce a large number of businesses to relocate in low-wage regions, thus creating unemployment in high-wage regions, which itself will exert downward pressure on pay (Bennett, 1996b, pp. 27–34).

Finally, it is important to note that the debate over the benefits and costs of the Euro is not a mainly economic one. The goal, a single European currency, the Euro is also politically driven (*Economist*, 20 April, 1996). A summary of the arguments presented by Kenneth Clarke (see below), Britain's former chancellor of the exchequer on whether Britain should join economic and monetary union, if it goes ahead in 1999 is quite illustrative.

Britain and the EMU: Potted guide to the arguments presented by K. Clarke (quoted in *The Economist*, 9 March, 1996)

Pro-EMU

- Because Britain's long-term commitment to anti-inflationary discipline is in doubt, the country pays an interest-rate premium over German rates, which is costly for industry and the government – and which EMU would eliminate.
- If Britain did not join EMU, the position of the City of London as Europe's predominant financial capital would be undermined, threatening the City's £19.9 billion ($30 billion) overseas earnings.

- Similarly, staying out of EMU would make Britain less attractive to overseas investors, cutting its 23 per cent share of total inward investment in the EU.
- EMU would eliminate transaction costs for firms, estimated by the European Commission in 1990 at 0.4 per cent of European GDP. And Britons would save about 10 per cent of what they spend because they would not have to change their money.
- Without a single currency, European countries would be prone to competitive devaluation. This could undermine support for the single European market in goods and services.
- If Britain stays out, she will be isolated.
- A single European currency is a vital step towards European Union, which alone can prevent Europe from disintegrating into warring nation states.

Anti-EMU

- European monetary union would undermine flexibility in responding to 'asymmetric shocks' – economic quakes that hit one country harder than another. A country suffering from such a shock can at present absorb it be devaluing its currency. Deprived of that option, the impact would fall entirely on unemployment and output.
- Britain's interest rates tend to move with the rate set by the central bank, whereas elsewhere in the EU many rates (e.g., for home loans) are fixed.
- A Europe-imposed hike in interest rates would hit Britain hard.
- EMU would lead to pressure for more aid to less-developed countries and regions of the community. As Britain already pays £934 million net to the EU budget, more aid would mean higher taxes.
- Consumers would be baffled by the changeover from familiar pounds to unfamiliar Euros. Firms would take advantage of the confusion to raise prices.
- There would be strong pressure for stable countries (Britain, for instance) to bail out any European Union government (not-Britain, for instance) that got into difficulties by borrowing too much.
- Britain's refusal to join would lead to a more flexible, multi-speed Europe.
- EMU would lead to a federal Europe.

Second pillar: common foreign and security policy

There is no references to common foreign and security policy in the Treaty of Rome. The initial position was that the European Economic Community should concern itself exclusively with trade and not foreign affairs. However, the advantages of member states acting together in the foreign policy field became increasingly apparent, particularly in those areas where commercial policy and foreign affairs overlapped. The European Political Cooperation (EPC) was thus established in 1970. This allowed foreign ministers of the six founding members to meet regularly, outside the framework of the Treaties, to examine issues of common concern and coordinate foreign policy.

Although the EPC operated by consensus, its relative ineffectiveness was soon revealed following the Soviet invasion of Afghanistan in December 1979, the Iraqi occupation of Kuwait in August 1990, the collapse of the USSR in 1991, the crisis in former Yugoslavia which broke out in June 1991 and the Community's attitude to the central and eastern European countries since their transition to market economy. In each crisis, the Community was not able to sustain a common position and lacked the political determination to enforce the collective will of its members. These experiences, coupled with the unification of Germany, reignited the demand for political union (Welsh, 1996, pp. 108–119). The main question was whether the common foreign and security policy should remain intergovernmental or be brought within the conventional institutional structure and to what extent policy and action should be determined by majority voting (Welsh, 1996, p. 118). The text that finally emerged in Title V of the Treaty of European Union constructed the common foreign policy and security alongside the European Community itself as a second 'pillar' of the European Union. According to Article J.1 the objectives of the common foreign and security policy are:

- to safeguard the common values, fundamental interests and independence of the Union
- to strengthen the security of the Union and its member states in all ways
- to preserve peace and strengthen international security, in accordance with the principles of the United Nations Charter as well as the principles of the Helsinki Final Act and the objectives of the Paris Charter
- to promote international cooperation
- to develop and consolidate democracy and the rule of law, and respect for human rights and fundamental freedoms

According to Article J.1(4)

> The member states shall support the Union's external and security policy actively and unreservedly in a spirit of loyalty and mutual solidarity. They shall refrain from any action which is contrary to the interests of the Union or likely to impair its effectiveness as a cohesive force in international relations. The Council shall ensure that these principles are complied with, by the introduction of a new concept of 'joint action' (under Article J.3).

The Council is thus given the responsibility for deciding in principle on 'joint action', according to general guidelines laid down by the European Council, and agreeing on the means to be employed to achieve it. Once a 'joint action' is decided, member states are committed to support it and consult with the Council before any national action is taken in the context of 'joint action' other than the simple implementation of Council decision. Article J.3(7) clearly states:

> Should there be any major difficulties in implementing a joint action, a member state shall refer them to the Council which shall discuss them and seek solutions. Such solutions shall not run counter to the objectives of the joint action or impair its effectiveness.

This means that if the 15 member states unanimously agree a joint stance would be helpful, they meet and vote. In other words, as Welsh argues, once a joint action is decided upon, member states who disagree with it or the way in which it is implemented must remain passive (Welsh, 1996, p. 120). Britain negotiated an opt-out clause, so that where circumstances change or national interest is at stake, it can be set free from an EC decision.

Cooperation on defence is clearly stipulated in Article J.4 under which

> the union requests the Western European Union (WEU), which is an integral part of the development of the Union, to elaborate and implement decisions and actions of the Union which have defence implications. The Council shall, in agreement with the institutions of the WEU, adopt the necessary practical arrangements.

Third pillar: justice and home affairs

Maastricht for the first time made justice and home affairs a matter for intergovernmental cooperation between the then 12 member states. Considering serious problems of drugs, refugees, and terrorism, it was believed that only coordinated action and intergovernmental cooperation could bring together police and judicial authorities across borders to cope with these threats. The major impetus for such an initiative is first the realization that relaxing internal community frontiers made cross-border cooperation more imperative in order to tackle a possible growth in international crime. The second factor was the increasing waves of immigrants entering the Community from the south and the east.

Provisions for intergovernmental cooperation on justice and home affairs in the European Union as set out in the Maastricht Treaty cover: asylum policy, rules governing the crossing by people of the member states' external borders, immigration policy, combating drug addiction, combating international fraud, judicial cooperation in civil matters, judicial cooperation in criminal matters, customs cooperation; and police action to prevent and combat terrorism, drug trafficking and other serious forms of international crime, including fraud. The Maastricht Treaty also involves the creation of a European Police Office (EUROPOL) providing a Community-wide information exchange system on serious international crime. EU governments and the European Commission are expected to report annually to the European Parliament on their activities in this area.

SOCIAL POLICY

Social policy, as well as monetary policy is of vital importance to business. In addition to the three pillars, a Social Agreement was also appended to the Maastricht Agreement. It reflects the determination of member states, with the exception of the UK, to implement the 1989 Social Charter declaration to improve living and working conditions (Article 1), terms of employment, equality between men and women with regard to labour market opportunities and treatment at work (Article 2), equal pay for equal work for male and female (Article 6), employee consultation and dialogue between management and labour (Article 3), social security and social protection of workers, and sets out areas for action.

The aim of the Social Charter is to achieve a standardized minimum level of working conditions so that companies and countries in the Community cannot compete unfairly at the expense of working people. The Social Agreement was introduced to provide necessary protection for workers when the competitive pressures of the Single Market tempt employers and governments to depress working conditions (the Social Policy is discussed further in Chapter 5).

Other important issues embodied in the Maastricht Treaty are the subsidiarity principle, and the development of the co-decision, cooperation procedures in decision making (discussed in Chapter 4).

SUBSIDIARITY

Jacques Delors found the task of defining subsidiarity so daunting that during an emotional speech to the European parliament he offered a job and ECU 200 000 to anyone who could define subsidiarity on one page. Subsidiarity is the principle that decisions should be taken at the lowest level possible. The Committee of the Regions gives regions a voice in the Community's decision-making process. On 25 October, 1993, Parliament, the Council and the Commission concluded an Inter-institutional Agreement on the procedures for implementing the subsidiarity principle. Clause 3b of the Maastricht Treaty states that:

... in areas which do not fall within its exclusive competence, the Community shall take action, in accordance with the principle of subsidiarity, only if and in so far as the objectives of the proposed action cannot be sufficiently achieved by member states and can therefore, by reason of the scale of the effects of the proposed action, be better achieved by the Community.

The subsidiarity principle further means that decisions (by parliaments, governments and other authorities) are to be taken as close as possible to the citizen, in other words at the lowest possible level of local or regional authority; they are to be taken at higher levels that is central government or the Community only if there is good reason. Article 3b stipulates that '... subsidiarity does not apply only to legislative powers'. The Union treaty claims to mark 'a new stage in the process of creating an ever closer union among the peoples of Europe, in which decisions are taken as closely as possible to the citizen'.

Subsidiarity has two aspects:

1. A very careful examination of the justification for legislation. If it is justified, there is no legislation at Community level.
2. The second aspect is when EC institutions and member states are all convinced that it is justified, then you have to make it absolutely clear: that it is a good legislation and that is why it is needed.

In practice the principle of subsidiarity is very difficult to implement. Each member state has its own view of what subsidiarity is all about. They do not have the same concept of what subsidiarity means, and the position is different in different areas of endeavour.

REVIEW QUESTIONS

1. List the main innovations brought about by Maastricht, and discuss their implications for business in Europe.
2. Provide a brief overview and discuss the implications of monetary union, european citizenship, justice and home affairs, social policy, and the extension of a regulated business environment, for business in the new Europe.
3. List the main objections that have been voiced against the adoption of a single currency known as the Euro. Are they justified?
4. The goal of the Euro is not mainly an economic one, but is also politically driven. Discuss.
5. Motives of member states for supporting subsidiarity were different. Germany, for example, saw subsidiarity as synonymous with federalism in distributing power between local communities while Britain considered it as a straightjacket on Brussel's powers. Discuss the basis of these differences, and how, if at all, they might be reconciled.

EXERCISE 3.1: Maastricht Treaty: advantages and problems of implementation

Aim   This exercise aims to improve students' skills in researching, writing and presenting a discussion paper.

Assignment   Dr Sked, chairman of the Anti-Federalist League argues that the Maastricht Treaty 'represents a bad dream that will turn into a nightmare ... It will ruin large parts of Europe and create tensions with America and Japan.' Students are expected to develop their own ideas and support them with empirical evidence. Each paper should be presented in no more than 10 minutes, followed by group discussion.

Sources

In addition to the list of further reading provided below, students are strongly recommended to consult current newspapers and journals. The following electronic databases containing full text of the newspapers will be useful:

- *The Economist*
- *The Financial Times*
- *The Guardian and Observer*
- *The Independent*
- *The Times*

FURTHER READING

Banca Nazionale del Lavoro, Quarterly Review, *European Monetary Union: The Problems of the Transition to a Single Currency*, Special Issue, BNL Edizioni, Roma, March, 1996.

Bennett, R., *Prospects for Business in the European Union,* Croner Publications Ltd, London, 1994.

Furlong, P. and Cox, A. (eds), *The European Union at the crossroads. Problems in Implementing the Single Market Project,* Earlsgate Press, Lincolnshire, 1995.

Mehnert-Meland, R., *ECU in Business. How to Prepare for the Single Currency in the European Union*, Graham and Trotman, London, 1994.

Welsh, M., *Europe United?* Macmillan, London, 1996.

Williams, A., *The European Community*, second edition, Blackwell, Oxford, 1994.

COMMUNITY INSTITUTIONS AND THE DECISION-MAKING PROCESS

All Single Market proposals have to go through the European Community before becoming directives to be implemented in the European Union. Since most of these decisions affect all areas of business in the Community, it is important for business managers to understand how these decisions are taken, and how to influence the process in Brussels. For years, one of the most regular criticisms of the EC institutions had been their lack of democratic accountability. In order to make the decision-making process in the Union more efficient and understandable, the Maastricht Treaty introduced some changes to the existing decision-making procedures in order to improve and simplify it. The aim of this chapter is to examine these changes and discuss their implications for the overall decision-making in the European Union.

LEARNING OBJECTIVES

- To introduce the five main Community institutions and describe their functions and powers
- To explain the overall decision-making process and the changes introduced by the Maastricht Treaty
- To provide guidance on how to influence the decision-making process in Brussels

Under the Maastricht Treaty, the Council and the Commission may make Regulations, issue Directives, take Decisions and make Recommendations or deliver Opinions.

- *Regulations* have general application and are directly applicable in all member states. They do not have to be confirmed by national Parliament in order to have binding legal effect. If there is a conflict between a Regulation and existing national law, the Regulation prevails.
- *Directives* are binding on member states as to the result to be achieved within a stated period but leave the method of implementation to national governments.
- *Decisions* are specific to particular parties and are binding in their entirety on those to whom they are addressed, whether member states, companies or individuals. Decisions imposing financial obligations are enforceable in national courts.
- *Recommendations and Opinions* have no binding force but merely state the view of the institution that issues them.

Before going into detail about the changes introduced by the Maastricht Treaty to the decision-making process in an attempt to make it more transparent, democratic and efficient, an understanding of the role and functions of the European Union decision-making bodies is necessary.

THE EUROPEAN UNION DECISION-MAKING PROCESS

There are five main EU decision-making bodies: the Commission, the Council of Ministers, the European Parliament, the Economic and Social Committee, and the Court of Justice. The Treaty of European Union has also added the Committee of the Regions which is served by staff of the Economic and Social Committees.

The Commission

The Commission is sometimes called the European Commission and more formally the Commission of the European Union. The European Commission headquarters are in Brussels. It has offices in Luxembourg, information offices in each of the members states and delegations in many of the world's capitals. The Commission is currently divided into 23 directorates general, formally responsible for the technical preparation of legislation and its implementation. Each directorate covers a particular area of policy and there is a number of specialist units and support services. The Commission is headed by 20 civil servants representing the 15 member states who are chosen to represent the interest of the EU rather than individual countries. Prior to the Treaty of European Union, commissioners were appointed by the Community governments, two from each of the larger member states and one from each of the smaller states. France, Germany, Italy, Spain and the UK have two each, while The Netherlands, Denmark, Portugal, Luxembourg, Ireland, Belgium and Greece have one each. Commissioners were appointed to serve a four-year term, which was renewable. In The Treaty on European Union the term has now been changed to five years with effect from 1994 in order to bring the renewal of the Commission roughly into line with the life of the Parliament (Nicoll and Salmon, 1994, p. 62). Commissioners are chosen on the basis of their general competence in their own established careers, with lawyers, economists, ex-ministers and ex-diplomats dominating. Commissioners are not appointed as national delegates, but are required to act in the interests of the Community as a whole. Once appointed, each commissioner takes an oath in which he or she pledges not to seek or accept instructions from national governments or political parties, but to serve the interests of the European Union as a whole. When commissioners travel abroad they do so as representatives of the Community and not of the member state to which they belong. The president and the vice-president of the Commission are appointed by common accord of the governments for a period of two years, renewable. The European Parliament has to be consulted on the choice of the president, and must then officially approve the Commission membership before it can take up its duties. This new procedure was applied for the first time on 21 July 1994. Until 1989, when Greece appointed Madame Panpandereou and France Madame Scrivener (re-appointed in 1993) all the Commissioners had been men (Nicoll and Salmon, 1994, p. 62).

Although each Commissioner has a portfolio of subjects for which he or she is responsible, decisions are collegiate. Commissioners are assisted by a group of political officials (a Cabinet) who perform an advisory and coordinating function. The Cabinet, each with a *chef de cabinet* usually comprises six members of fellow nationals, with at least one coming from another member state. These are called the 'Services', and are staffed mainly by career officials recruited by competitive examination from member states. These are normally the first port of call to find out the basis of Commission thinking and to seek to influence it. Commissioners discuss proposals made to the Community and then decide on the nature of the final proposal collectively. Cabinet chefs have regular weekly inter-Cabinet committees, under the Commission, which are designed to identify those issues upon which Commissioners need to focus at their weekly meetings.

Functions and Powers of the Commission

The Commission is responsible for the initial preliminary design of Community policy, proposals and legislation. It is also responsible for implementing decisions taken by the Council of Ministers. As the Community 'watchdog', the Commission sees that decisions of the EU institutions are properly implemented. It has a direct role in the supervision of the daily operation the of major policies upon which agreement at the 15-nations' level has been reached.

The Commission is also the 'guardian' of the Treaties. It can initiate action against member states, institutions and firms which do not comply with EU rules, if necessary with the aid of the European Court of Justice. The Commission is thus in a position not only to effect EU policy, but to affect it also. It has for example, the power to fine firms that break certain operational rules. The Commission is also responsible for the administration of Community funds, such as the European Social Fund, the Regional Development Fund and the Agricultural Guarantee and Guidance Fund. Finally, the Commission liaises closely with member states and firms in order to keep them up to date with the latest developments, such as new legislation and new policies associated with the Treaty of European Union.

At the Essen Summit at the end of 1994, the EU heads of state or government laid out a clear agenda for the Commissioners appointed at the beginning of 1995. These were as follows:

- To continue to follow through a strategy of growth, competitiveness and employment set out in the recent White Paper, in particular, aiding structural changes to facilitate improved competitiveness and employment conditions.
- Monitoring convergence between the member states as a means of improving the potential for monetary union.
- To prepare for further expansion of the EU, in particular the inclusion of central and eastern European countries.
- To identify areas where eastern neighbours can align their policies and agenda for achieving inclusion.
- To participate in the preparation for the 1996 intergovernmental conference which has been charged with revising the Maastricht Treaty to define the future development of the EU which could include as many as 25 member states 10 years from now (Welford and Prescott, 1996, p. 27).

The Maastricht Treaty introduced some innovations concerning the Commission's role and functions. The Commission was granted an additional right of initiative, shared with the member states, in the fields of common foreign and security policy and in certain matters covered by justice and home affairs. However, the exclusive right of initiative in Community matters has been confirmed in the Treaty on the understanding that, in line with the principle of subsidiarity, it is answerable for how it exercises that right.

The Council of Ministers

Until 1986, the Council of Ministers had no legal standing in terms of the Community's Treaties. It was set up by the heads of state themselves in 1974. The Council's headquarters and General Secretariat are in Brussels, but in April, June and October, meetings of the Council are held in Luxembourg. Originally, the Council of Ministers met four times a year to offer top-level guidance, and to review progress over the previous months. In addition to the normal Council meetings the European Council, often referred to as the European Summit, comprising heads of state and heads of government, now meets twice a year to discuss broad areas of policy.

The Council of Ministers is made up of one representative from each member state, normally ministers. The presidency rotates among the member states for a six-month period in alphabetical order of the countries' names. Each presidency plans for and proposes the decisions to be taken at the European Council meeting which it will host and which have now become major political and media events. Each government delegates to the Council one of its members. Members of the Council are therefore representatives of their own states, and they act on the basis of instructions received from their own governments.

The Foreign Affairs Council, the Agriculture Council and the Economic and Finance Council (ECOFIN) meet monthly. The Internal Market Council meets four or five times a year. The Fisheries and Budget Councils meet three or four times, Councils such as Industry, Research, Steel, Transport, Energy, Education, Development, Environment, Culture and Social Affairs meet two or three times, and those such as Consumer Affairs, Tourism, Health, Telecommunications once or twice a year (Nicoll and Salmon, 1994, p. 67).

Functions and powers of the Council
The Council is the Community's central decision-making body. The main function of the Council is to formulate Community law. The Council acts at the request of the Commission by adopting or modifying proposals from the Commission. It may occasionally issue opinions and initiate proposals, but these are not binding.

The Council role in the Community decision-making process has been extended by the Treaty of European Union to cover the fields of common foreign and security policy and cooperation on justice and home affairs.

The work of the Council is prepared by a committee of Permanent Representatives (COREPER) whose function is to filter through the proposals before passing them on to the council for a final decision.

The European Parliament

The European Parliament is a directly elected body. Any citizen of the European Union can stand for election. Members of the European Parliament are elected to serve for a five-year term of office. European members of the Parliament, once elected, sit in political groupings regardless of nationality and not in national blocks as representatives of member states. They choose which of the various political groupings they wish to join. Virtually all members play an active part in one or more of the 19 Committees, which deal with foreign affairs and security; agriculture, fisheries and rural development; budgets, economic, monetary affairs and industrial policy; energy, research and technology; external economic relations; legal affairs and citizen's rights; social affairs, employment and the working environment; regional policy, regional planning and relations with local and regional authorities; transport and tourism; environment, public health and consumer protection; youth, culture, education and the media; development and cooperation; civil liberties and internal affairs; budgetary control; institutional affairs; rules of procedure, verification of credentials and immunities;

CHESTER COLLEGE LIBRARY

women's rights; and petitions (Nicoll and Salmon, 1994, p. 88). These divisions of issue areas are not identical with the distribution of functions among the Commissioners, but they do loosely shadow the latter.

Functions and power of the European Parliament

The European Parliament works by means of these Committees which report to plenary sessions and submit draft resolutions. Outside the formal committee structure there are a number of inter-party groups. Parliament has also appointed specific Committees of Enquiry, for example, into drug trafficking, alleged irregularities at a nuclear power station, and trade in cattle illegally dosed with hormones. The Committees of Enquiry produce reports, which are their property and cannot be amended in debate on the floor of the House. The Committee of Enquiry usually produces a draft resolution, which sets out what should be done to remedy a particular evil, which the House votes upon. (Nicoll and Salmon, 1994, p. 330). Members join Committees according to their interests. For each Committee, there is a *rapporteur*, who writes the report and draft resolution. When approved by the Committee by simple majority vote and amended by the same, the resolution is sent forward to the plenary for inclusion in an agenda for debate and vote on the resolution.

Until 1987, the powers of the European Parliament (EP) were limited, and consisted of budgetary, consultative and supervisory powers only. The EP can reject the Council's draft budget with an absolute majority. The EP also has the right to propose amendments to non-compulsory expenditure in the budget, but it has no say over compulsory expenditure, which accounts for 70 per cent of total expenditure. The EP can also dismiss the Commission by a two-thirds majority vote, but only through *'en bloc'* dismissal. It has no say, however, over its reappointment, and in principle the same Commission could be reappointed by national governments. The EP has the right to issue an opinion on draft legislation, but these opinions, until 1987, were not binding on either the Commission or the Council. Finally, the EP has a delaying power. The Court of Justice ruled that any legislation adopted by the Council without receiving an EP opinion was invalid.

The Single European Act gave the European Parliament additional powers in 1987, such as the 'Assent Procedure'. Since 1987, the EP is required to give its assent to any new application for membership in the EC, giving the EP additional veto power over EC enlargement in the future. EP assent is also required for any new association agreements with Third World countries, including the renewal of existing agreements. An additional competence given to the EP by the Single Act is that known as the 'Cooperation Procedure'. Until 1987, the EP gave only its opinions and proposed amendments to draft legislation, however, neither the Council nor the Commission were under any obligation to act upon EP recommendations. The Council could overturn the Parliament's amendments by unanimous vote. Article 149 of the Single European Act, introduced the 'Cooperation Procedure', according to which all legislation necessary for the Single European Market must return to the EP for a second reading. The EP has two or three months to either accept, amend or reject it. If rejected, the Council can only adopt such legislation after a second reading and by unanimous vote.

The tasks of the European Parliament have been very substantially increased under the Treaty of European Union, both through its power to approve the Commission and through the greater part it now plays in the legislative process. The Parliament also has to be consulted on the appointment of the president of the European Monetary Institute and of the president and executive board members of the European Central Bank. It has also acquired the right to ask the Commission to make proposals.

Article 138c of the Treaty provides the Parliament with the power to set up Temporary Committees of Inquiry. As far as legislation is concerned, the Treaty increases the Parliament's role in common foreign and security policy and in the fields of justice and home affairs. The Parliament has to be consulted on the main aspects, it has to be kept regularly informed and it may ask questions of the Council or make recommendations to it (Article J.7).

The powers of the Parliament were also increased in particular by introducing the 'Co-decision Procedure'. Prior to Maastricht, EC law was made by two kinds of procedure: Consultation Procedure (Treaty of Rome), and Cooperation Procedure (Single Act). Maastricht proposed a third procedure: Co-decision Procedure by giving more power to the Parliament and less to the Commission.

The **Consultation Procedure** is the oldest procedure whereby the Commission makes a draft proposal which is sent to be debated in the European Parliament in consultation with the Economic and Social Committee. The Commission then reacts to what the Parliament and Economic and Social Committee have to say, and may amend the proposal. The proposal is then send to the council who after discussion and compromise must agree unanimously on it before they can ratify it, and becomes law.

The **Cooperation Procedure** was introduced in 1987 by the Single Act. The Cooperation Procedure is illustrated in Fig. 4.1.

Under the Cooperation Procedure, the Parliament gives its opinion twice: first, when the Commission proposal is submitted to the Council, and again after the Council has reached an agreement in principle – a 'Common position'. At both stages it can propose amendments. If the Council fails to agree unanimously on a proposal which is almost always, they agree on a Common position by qualified majority. The proposal is then sent back to the Parliament for a second reading. If the Parliament agrees, the Council will act and turn it into law. Parliament may also reject/amend by absolute majority. The Commission then has to add its opinion and the issue is passed back to the Council. If the Commission rejects Parliament's amendment, the Council may act only unanimously. The Commission, therefore, an unelected body does have heavy weight in what becomes law and what does not.

The **Co-decision Procedure** was introduced by Maastricht in November 1993.

As illustrated in Fig. 4.2, the Co-decision Procedure extends the power of the Parliament by allowing it to veto a measure by absolute majority, thus overriding the Council for the first time. The Commission is excluded from the Co-decision Procedure, and will be thus subject to Parliament approval. The procedure is the same as for the Cooperation Procedure up to the adoption of a Common position. If the Parliament proposes amendments to the Common position, these must be presented to the Commission for their opinion. The Council can approve all the Parliament's amendments by a qualified majority, or by unanimity where the Commission has given a negative opinion. A Conciliation Committee is called in if Parliament amendments are rejected by Council, or if Parliament rejects a Common position. This committee is made up of 12 representatives of the Council together with an equal number of MEPs. They have six weeks to reach an agreement: simple majority in Parliament, qualified majority in Council. If either institutions fails to approve the proposal, it will not be adopted as Community law.

The Co-decision Procedure affords ample opportunity for lobbying of MEPs by business.

The Committee of the Regions

Articles 198a to 198c of the Treaty of European Union set up the Committee of the Regions as a body responsible for representing regional and local authorities in the Union. Members of the Committee of the Regions are local or regional elected representatives. The Committee of the Regions must be consulted on matters involving education, culture, public health, trans-European networks and economic and social cohesion. Consultation is optional in all other

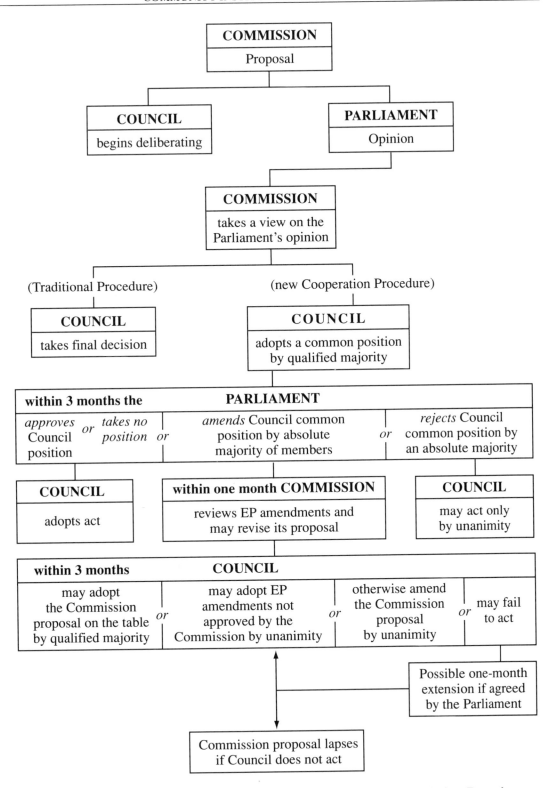

Figure 4.1 The New Co-operation Procedure (*Source*: DTI, The Single Market: Brussels can you hear me?, 1991)

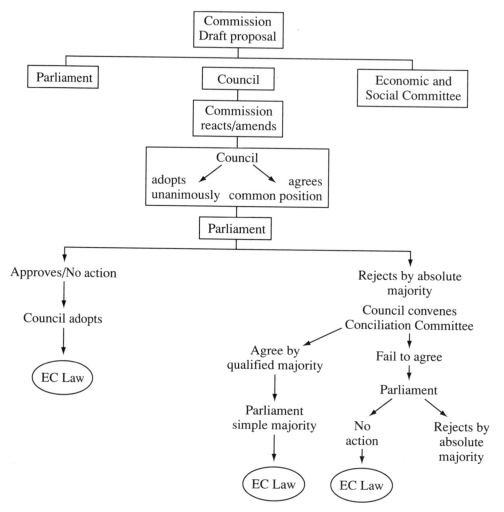

Figure 4.2 The Co-decision Procedure (*Source*: European Union, European Commission, 1994)

fields. The Committee may also issue opinions on its own initiative where it considers that specific regional interests are involved. The Committee held its first session on 9 and 10 March 1994.

The Economic and Social Committee

The Economic and Social Committee is based in Brussels. It is an advisory body of 189 members consisting of representatives of employers, trade unions and consumers. It must be formally consulted by the Commission on proposals relating to economic and social matters. Members of the Economic and Social Committee are appointed for four years from lists supplied by member states, and are drawn from the three groups mentioned above. Members are independent of individual governments. The Committee meets eight times a year. The Treaty consolidates the role of the Economic and Social Committee and its advisory function, by granting it the right to issue opinions on its own initiative.

The European Court of Justice

The European Court of Justice rules on the interpretation and application of Community laws and sits in Luxembourg. Judges are appointed for six years, renewable. The judges select their own president. For each case, the president appoints a *judge-rapporteur*, who takes the lead in deliberations. The staff of the Court is headed by the Registrar, who is appointed by the Court. The Court is also served by a number of advocates general. An advocate general makes a reasoned presentation of the case before the Court, usually giving a summary of the submissions of the parties, observations on matters raised in the oral hearings, and on the relevant Community status law and previous cases, and an opinion on the decision which the Court might take. His opinion is not binding. A Court of First Instance has been established by the Single European Act (Article 168a of the EEC Treaty) where rulings on matters pertaining to the internal market can be made, and where issues relevant to business, including competition policy infringements, can be brought. However, this new court, specializing in the processing of commercial cases, does not take cases brought by member states or the Commission.

Functions and power of the Court of Justice

The European Court rules on the application and interpretation of Community law. It gives final judgement on the interpretation of the Treaties. It also deals with infringement of the European Treaties by member states, and initiates preliminary rulings on questions referred to it by national courts. It also helps national courts in the process of interpreting EC legislation.

The European Court works in a similar way to the Appeal Courts of member states. The process of appealing to the Court on infractions of Community law is often complicated and can be very lengthy. Private individuals, firms, local authorities and others can appeal to the Court when they consider they have been unjustly served by Community legislation. There are no court costs involved, but appellants must pay their own lawyers' fees. The easiest first step, however, is to complain to the Commission by initiating a letter to any of the Commission's offices.

Judgments of the European Court are binding on member states. Even though there is no explicit provision in the Treaty which states that Community law ranks above national law, Community law has precedence over national law by implication, because it is a principle of the Treaty that the status of Community law cannot be called into question by member states.

INFLUENCING THE DECISION-MAKING PROCESS IN THE EUROPEAN UNION

Business people can play an active role in EU policy formation in partnership with government. Any firm, local authority, trade or professional association has the right to plead its case to the Community. To influence the decision-making process effectively, pressure must be exerted at the stage when drafts are being written, evidence gathered and opinions expressed.

Before legislation is proposed to the Council, the Commission will often discuss its ideas with national experts and professional and business organizations. It is during these first stages of the Community legislation process that it is important to ensure that business interests are properly represented. It is the Commission's absolute duty to canvass as many points of view as it can reasonably assimilate. As one Eurocrat has explained:

The Commission official is a very lonely official with a blank piece of paper in front of him, wondering what to put on it. Lobbying at this very early stage therefore offers the greatest opportunity to shape thinking and ultimately to shape policy. The drafter is usually in need of ideas and information and a lobbyist who is recognized as being trustworthy and a provider of good information can have an important impact at this stage.

(quoted in Morrison, 1995, p. 215).

Business managers need to be aware of this system and work with the Commission to ensure that *'fiches d'impact'* provide adequate assessments of the effect of new proposals on business (Department of Trade and Industry, 1992, p. 12).

In order to ensure that firms contribute their views at the proper time, the Department of Trade and Industry in the UK recommends the following key points for success in Brussels.

- *Get in early*
  Try to get your views in before the Commission has reached a decision and produced formal drafts for EC proposals. To do this, the first step is to obtain clear and up-to-date information on what is happening. Each year, the European Commission publishes a proposed legislative work programme, *Spreadhead*, which is a comprehensive database on current and prospective Single Market measures, gives a government contact point, and is regularly updated. It is accessible via personal computers, and through many Chambers of Commerce, Trade Associations and Public Libraries. You may also consult the European Information Service. This is a bulletin published 10 times a year by the International Union of Local Authorities. There is also the Annual Reports and monthly Bulletins of the Community, Agence Europe and the *European Report*, which are published in Brussels. MEPs also will be up to date on the work of their committees and can be consulted. Once you are satisfied you have the information you need, you will need to make your views known as early as possible in the decision-making process. Business, given the scarcity of resources, should limit itself to those issues which are of greatest importance to it and which it is most likely to influence.
  The best way to influence the European Commission is through its staff, the Commission services. The Council is influenced via government. The European Parliament is influenced by lobbying appropriate MEPs. The Economic and Social Committee and the Committee of the Regions are advisory bodies which, like the Parliament, are consulted on Commission proposals, and are increasingly important sites for lobbying.
- *Work with others*
  Working with others is usually more effective than acting alone. Keep in touch with your own trade or professional association. The staff of these organizations know exactly what legislation is planned and the stage it has reached, and can put you in contact with other members who might have the same concerns. Even firms that compete with one another should coordinate their efforts when trying to influence Brussels.
- *Think European*
  Your lobbying should reflect a clear understanding of the Single Market programme and Community interests, so that specific or general business interests are presented that are consistent with 'European' interests and developments. A focus on partnership with government is increasingly being recognized as crucial to meet the challenge of internal growth, competitiveness and employment in the new Europe.

A checklist of key contacts you (or your trade association) will need to make would be useful. The list should contain the following:

- the official in the government department who deals with the subject
- your trade association
- the relevant European-level trade association and the trade associations in other member states
- the Commission official primarily responsible
- the commissioner responsible and the member of his or her private office ('Cabinet') who deals with the subjects
- the appropriate official in the UK Permanent Representation
- your member of the European Parliament
- the European Parliament Committee responsible and its UK members
- the MEP who is the *rapporteur* for the proposal, (Department of Trade and Industry, 1994a, p. 41).

- *Be prepared*
  Collect as much information and evidence as you can in preparing your report to support your views.
- *Get involved*
  It is very important to remain linked to the Brussels network so that you will be able to react quickly to events affecting your business as and when they arise. A single trip to Brussels is unlikely to do the trick. You need to establish long-term contacts in Brussels and keep in touch with European MPs there.

(adapted from Department of Trade and Industry, 1992.)

Influencing the Community decision-making process: the US experience

Collective action by US business in Europe is one of the most effective collective action networks. According to Henry Jacek, the lobbying techniques of US firms work best on issues surrounding European policy harmonization for at least five reasons (Jacek, 1995, pp. 197–207):

1. US firms have the ability to organize themselves into a well-integrated, cohesive position. They find it natural to present themselves as the enthusiastic proponents of a pan-European approach to policy problems.
2. US firms never put all their eggs in one basket. For them, the only safe strategy is a multitrack strategy. At the European level, this means cultivating all the institutional complexity of the EU. This includes the Commission, the European Parliament and the Council of Ministers.
3. US lobbyists present policy harmonization as an exercise in technical standards-setting. The issues involved are presented as merely technical ones, and not political. By apparently depoliticizing policy issues, the US lobbyist aims to reduce national emotions and political symbolism and to remove the issue from public attention.
4. US firms quickly learned the utility of having their interests represented by Europeans, or

Americans with a substantial European education. US firms not only try to look European in their representation, they also restructure their operations so that these look European.
5. US business interests provide useful information, systematic facts and legal help, the latter for drafting purposes. Americans recognize that the directorates general are understaffed. Most EU directives and regulations begin as the work of a single official and thus needs help in drafting. US lobbyists are only too happy to provide that help in the form of credible outside information (Hunter, 1989, p. 43).

The European telecommunications industry provides an excellent example of how US firms can use arguments about technical harmonization to increase their policy influence. The European Telecommunications Standards Institute (ETSI) is the major policy maker on telecommunications standards in Europe. However, ETSI depends on the European Committee for standardization (CEN), and the European Committee for Electrotechnical Standardization (CENELEC) for standards of terminal equipment. Since the telecommunications standards produced by these various bodies affect the ability of telecommunications equipment, having European standards harmonized with US standards is crucial for US manufacturers. In order to achieve this end, US firms use US standards bodies. The US manufacturers have been able to get the American National Standards Institute (ANSI) a voice in CEN and CENELEC. Particularly important is the ability of US organizations to comment on drafts of European standards. They also leverage their influence still further by having membership in national standards associations which are the 18 members of CENELEC and CEN.

US firms are also successful at the national level, in some cases in mobilizing an EU member state as its ardent defender due to their economic power and the independent political infrastructure of US firms.

US business interests in Europe are also represented by the American Chambers of Commerce headed by the United States Council for International Business (USICG). The USICG communicates information to US business through its EC update and its newsletter summarizing economic developments in the EU. The USICG purpose is to ensure that US business speaks with one voice to the European Commission on matters affecting operations in Europe. The European Council of American Chambers of Commerce (ECACC), founded in Paris since 1963 has now 15 national American chambers as members: Austria, Belgium, France, Germany, Greece, Hungary, Israel, Italy, The Netherlands, Portugal, Republic of Ireland, Spain, Switzerland, Turkey and the UK (Daniels and Schwartz, 1994).

Influencing the Community decision-making process: the Japanese experience

The Japanese prefer to lobby at the level of the nation-state capital before raising issues in Brussels. A representative of one Japanese trade association commented:

> My organization normally does not try to change EU legislation single-handedly. If a directive is created which could affect us, we can always ask the UK government to lobby on our behalf.
>
> (quoted in Morrison, 1995, p. 209).

Japanese corporations use grass roots lobbying in Europe. Grass roots lobbying refer to the channels which are outside the political framework, e.g. public relations efforts to promote Japanese companies and trade associations as 'good European citizens' within local communities (Morrison, 1995, p. 210). Japanese lobbying methods used in Europe are illustrated in the 1990 report entitled *Public Relations Strategy for the Japan Automobile Manufacturers' Association (JAMA) in Germany* as follows:

- **Public Relations Projects**   In order to establish and emphasize that JAMA is also concerned with German topics and linked to social and environmental subjects, (we) recommend that JAMA finance and support studies about subjects which altogether or in parts are related to the automobile industry in Germany. The results of these studies will be used for media and lobby work. Respective press releases/features could be placed with suitable newspapers and magazines.
- *Sponsorships*   There is no doubt that sponsoring has many advantages and encourages goodwill and understanding for a company. With regard to JAMA, the prime reason for sponsorship is to show a sense of social responsibility in Germany and close linkage to German ... (we) recommend sponsorship in the following spheres:
  - *Education*   JAMA will support students who study mechanical engineering, design, automotive technology or other subjects which are linked to the automotive industry.
  - *Cultural Events and Interests*   (We) propose supporting cultural events such as concerts, art exhibitions, etc. ... in Germany. ... An ideal constellation would be if a famous Japanese musician or orchestra were to tour Germany. A concert could be supported by JAMA for a selected audience. The concert should be recorded and copied on CDs. These would be used as incentives for further PR activities.
  - *Speaking Platforms*   (We) will ... identify possibilities for background talks, round table discussions, expert workshops, etc. at which JAMA representatives will be given opportunities to talk about suitable automotive issues ...

In addition to cultural events and speaking platforms, large amounts of Japanese funding are given to scholarly research (Morrison, 1995, p. 212). The Kobe Institute at St Catherine's College, Oxford, and the Asia section of the Royal Institute of International Affairs at Chatham House regularly receive Japanese funding. In Belgium, the Europe–Japan Economic Research Centre at Louvain is under the joint patronage of the European Commission, the Japanese Mission and the EU and Japan External Trade Organization (JETRO).

The Japanese have also established consulates and trade offices throughout the EU. The Japanese External Trade Organization for example has 76 offices worldwide of which 11 are in the EU.

Finally, the Japanese lobby Europe as 15 separate markets, despite the Single Market programme and regardless of efforts by the Commission to create a perception of the EU as a single entity. The reason for this is, simply, that nationalism is still healthy and localization by Japanese companies continues to be profitable (Morrison, 1995, p. 220).

REVIEW QUESTIONS

1. Which of the changes introduced by the Treaty of European Union into the Community decision-making process are most significant in respect of business in Europe?
2. To what extent, if at all, has democratization of the decision-making process in the Community since the Treaty on European Union presented opportunities or threats (or both) for doing business in Europe?
3. It is frequently argued that 'The European Court of Justice poses a direct challenge to the

sovereignty of member states'. Do you agree? Illustrate your answer with relevant cases recently dealt with by the European Court of Justice.

4. As a business person wishing to expand your business in Europe, which approach (European, American, or Japanese) do you think is more likely to be effective in influencing the decision-making process in the Community to your benefit?

EXERCISE 4.1: EU legislation and European business

Aim   This exercise provides students with the opportunity to examine and study a specific European legislation affecting a particular business sector.

Assignment   Students are asked to investigate a European legislation of interest to them and retrace it from its initial proposal to the European Commission, until it became a directive to be implemented by all member states.

Format   Students are expected to prepare a presentation to the class explaining the decision-making process through which this particular proposal went through, describing the debates that took Place at various stages, the lobbying by interested parties, and how the final agreement was reached.

Sources

European documentation

Bulletin of the European Union reports on the activities of the Commission and other institutions.

Official Journal of the European Communities contains full official texts of EU legislation in force, including debates of the European Parliament.

Reports of Cases before the Court of Justice contains the official record of cases before the European Court of Justice.

Commission of the European Community lists detailed proposals made to the Commission.

`http://europa.eu.int`   This is the European Commission's server on the WWW. It contains information on EU institutions, news and links to other sites.

FURTHER READING

Duff, A., Pinder, J. and Pryce, R., (eds), *Maastricht and Beyond, Building the European Union*, Routledge, New York, 1995.

European Commission, *Intergovernmental Conference 1996, Reflection Group. Commission Report*, European Commission, 1995.

McDonald, F. and Dearden. S. (eds), *European Economic Integration*, 2nd edition, Longman Group Limited, Harlow, Essex, 1995.

Nicoll, W. and Salmon, T., *Understanding the New European Community*, Harvester Wheatsheaf, Hemel Hempstead, Hertfordshire, 1994.

Noel, E., *Working Together. The Institutions of the European Community*, Office for Official Publications of the EC, Luxembourg, 1991.

EUROPEAN COMMUNITY POLICIES

Physical, technical and fiscal barriers were originally erected by states to protect national markets from external competition. Their removal consequently opens up those markets to much increased competition, and rigorous competition policy was therefore essential to the development of an efficient Single European Market. The Commission believed that a strong competition policy and social policy are necessary to ensure that the freedom for trade provided by the creation of an internal market is not constrained by anti-competitive practices, whether initiated by governments or by enterprises. Competition rules seek to prevent enterprises from distorting trade rules or abusing their power in the marketplace. EC competition law was thus designed to ensure that trade between member states takes place on the basis of free and fair competition, and that state barriers to trade between member states, when dismantled, are not replaced by private barriers which might fragment the Single Market. EC competition law affects any business large, or small, national or international. Firms may be heavily fined if they do not take proper and full account of the EC competition rules. The maximum fine is one per cent of the undertaking's turnover for the previous year, and this could relate to the total turnover of the whole group of companies for all their products, worldwide (Korah, 1994, p. vii). Heavy fines can also be imposed by the Commission for anything that is considered to deter trade across national boundaries, for example, actions of a dominant firm perceived to deter new entrants to the market from growing. Business managers should be wary that simple compliance with existing national competition law does not necessarily provide a defence against contravening EC law if that law has not been adequately transposed by national legislation.

A complete awareness and understanding of EC law by all managers is advisable to avoid a contravention, and thus additional, possibly heavy financial costs. The aim of this chapter is to provide students and managers with an introductory knowledge of European Community policies specifically related to business, and assess their implications for doing business in the 'new' Europe.

LEARNING OBJECTIVES

- To provide an overview of EC competition law, in particular Article 85 and Article 86
- To introduce the Community Merger Control Regulation and explain its implication for business
- To examine the difference between the 'Community Charter of Fundamental Social Rights

for Workers' introduced by the Single European Act, and the revised contemporary 'Agreement on Social Policy', established by the Treaty on European Union

EC COMPETITION LAW

Even a brief description of EC business law within the EU would far exceed the space available in this section. Attention will therefore be directed towards those aspects which are the most relevant from a practical business viewpoint. Articles 85 and 86 of the 1957 Treaty of Rome form the legal basis for the Commission's mandate over competition. Article 85 essentially bans cartels, price-fixing and other forms of collusion, placing them under the Commission's jurisdiction when they distort competition in the Common Market. Article 86 empowers the Commission to police mergers.

Article 85 (1)

Article 85 (1) prohibits collusion that restricts competition and threatens the unity of the Single Market. Even practices such as a supplier seeking to impose a minimum retail resale price on a distributor or retailer are considered to be price-fixing, because they restrict that retailer's ability to set his own policies and carry out his own trade. Companies should be careful about entering into joint sales-promotion agreements, exchanging information with competitors, or even any attempt at coordinating market activity through trade associations. Any agreement which seeks to inhibit what, how much and where a retailer may operate is a contravention of Article 85. If a company has separate agents in each member state, it should not therefore seek to restrict one from operating in another area.

To infringe Article 85 (1), three conditions must be satisfied. There must be:

1 some form of collusion between undertakings
2 which may affect trade between member states, and
3 which has the object or effect of restricting competition within the common market (Korah, 1994, p. 37).

Article 85 (1) states:

> The following shall be prohibited as incompatible with the common market: all agreements between undertakings, decision by associations of undertakings and concerted practices which may affect trade between Member States and which have as their object or effect the prevention, restriction or distortion of competition within the common market, and in particular those which:
>
> (a) directly or indirectly fix purchase or selling prices or any other trading conditions
> (b) limit or control production, markets, technical development, or investment
> (c) share markets or sources supply
> (d) apply dissimilar conditions to equivalent transactions with other trading parties, thereby placing them at a competitive disadvantage
> (e) make the conclusion of contracts subject to acceptance by the other parties of supplementary obligations, which, by their nature or according to commercial usage, have no connection with the subject of such contracts.

Undertaking covers any collection of resources to carry out economic activities. It embraces a company, partnership, sole trader or an association. Liberal professions are also treated as undertakings. A group of companies is treated as a single undertaking. However, joint ventures do not constitute a single undertaking because they are subject to control by more than one parent. The following case study illustrates how collusion between undertakings may affect trade between member states and restrict competition with the EU.

CASE STUDY 5.1: Consten and Grundig v. Commission

Grundig had agreed with Consten that Consten should be its exclusive dealer in France. It agreed to supply no one else in France, and Consten agreed not to handle competing brands, to promote Grundig products, to arrange for an after-sales service, to buy in minimum quantities, to order regularly in advance and to make sales forecasts. Incurring these costs would be worth while for Consten only if it could reap where it had sown. The investment was risky, in that the costs were sunk: the effort would be wasted unless it could be recovered through the sale of Grundig products at a time when an import licence was required to import them.

To encourage Consten's commitment to this expenditure, Grundig tried to confer absolute territorial protection on Consten, by isolating the French market. Its distributors in other member states and dealers in Germany were forbidden to export, as was Consten. Moreover, all Grundig machines of that period bore the mark GINT (Grundig International) as well as the Grundig mark. Consten was allowed to register GINT as a trade mark under French law, and so was able to sue for trade mark infringement anyone importing commercially or selling without its consent a machine bearing that mark.

When a third party, UNEF started to buy Grundig apparatus in Germany and sell it in France at lower prices, Consten sued it for trade mark infringement, and also for the French tort of unfair competition, on the ground that UNEF knew that sales by the German dealers were in breach of their contracts with Grundig and would undermine Consten's exclusive distributorship. Not only did the Court uphold the Commission's decision that the agreement infringed Article 85, it upheld its order that neither party should make it difficult for dealers and other buyers to obtain Grundig apparatus elsewhere. The court added: 'The contract between Grundig and Consten, on the one hand by preventing undertakings other than Consten from importing Grundig products into France, and on the other hand by prohibiting Consten from re-exporting those products to other countries of the Common Market, indisputably affects trade between member states'. The insulation of the French market from the lower-priced German market clearly affected trade between the countries, and infringed the basic principle of the free movement of goods, and the treatment of the whole Community as a Single Market

(quoted in Korah, 1994, pp. 49–50)

Exemptions from Article 85

The Commission has recognized the tension between the commercial desire to enter into cooperative agreements across the EC and Article 85, particularly for small- and medium-sized companies, and has therefore said that it is unlikely to invoke Article 85 where the turnover of the undertakings is less than 200 million ECUs, and the agreement involved covers less than five per cent of the market share, within the relevant geographical area (Brown, 1995, p. 53). It has further introduced a number of specific regulations which provide a degree of exemption from or clarification of Article 85 in certain areas. These are:

- exclusive distribution agreements (EEC/1983/83), which restrict the types of agreements, for example prohibiting companies from banning parallel imports
- exclusive purchasing agreements for beer and petrol (EEC/1984/83)
- motor vehicle servicing agreements (EEC/1985/125)
- research and development agreements (EEC/1985/418)
- air transport (EEC/1987/3976)
- certain franchising agreements (EEC/89/556) define the types of restrictions which may be imposed by a franchiser

Similar rules govern licensing agreements.

Article 86

In the European Union, there is a real concern that large firms may make it hard for smaller firms to compete. To protect small firms, and prevent large firms from abusing a dominant position, the Article asserts:

> Any abuse by one or more undertakings of a dominant position within the Common Market or in a substantial part of it shall be prohibited as incompatible with the Common Market in so far as it may affect trade between member states. Such abuse may, in particular, consist in:
>
> (a) directly or indirectly imposing unfair purchase or selling prices or other unfair trading conditions
> (b) limiting production, markets or technical development to the prejudice of consumers
> (c) applying dissimilar conditions to equivalent transactions with other trading parties, thereby placing them at a competitive disadvantage
> (d) making the consultation of contracts subject to acceptance by the other parties of supplementary obligations which, by their nature or according to commercial usage, have no connections with the subject of such contracts.
>
> (Treaty of Rome, Annexes 85 and 86)

The Commission defined the concept of a dominant position as follows. Undertakings are in a dominant position when they have the power to behave independently, which puts them in a position to act without taking into account their competitors, purchasers or suppliers. That is the position when, because of their share of the market, or their share of the market combined with availability of technical knowledge, raw materials or capital, they have the power to determine prices or to control production or distribution for a significant part of the products in question (Korah, 1994, pp. 68–69).

The primary concern of business managers with regard to competition policy is therefore to ensure compliance. It should be noted that an agreement does not have to be in the form of a contract: an informal, even verbal agreement can still be in contravention of Articles 85 and 86. Business managers must be alert also to competitors acting in contravention of the policies. Most investigations carried out by Directorate General 4 (DG 4) are as the result of a tip-off from competitors or an aggrieved consumer (Brown, 1995, p. 53).

EC Merger Control Regulation

Articles 85 and 86 made no specific provision for control by the Commission of concentrations or mergers within the Community. The Single Market opened up great opportunities for firms to engage in cross-border mergers. A merger mania swept Europe in the mid-1980s highlighting the need for a Community text on mergers and acquisitions. The value of takeovers tripled from 1985 to 1988 in the UK to 57 billion ECUs, and increased sevenfold in France to 26.5 billion ECUs (Coopers and Lybrand, 1989).

In 1989, the Merger Control Regulation was passed into European Community law. The EC adopted the European Merger Regulation which came into force on 21 September 1990. Under the Merger Control Regulation, any plans involving cross-frontier mergers of firms having a combined turnover amounting to at least 5000 million ECUs must be notified to the Commission for approval, or when the turnover in the EU is to be more than 250 million ECUs. However, if each of the firms concerned obtains two-thirds of its business within the EU in one and the same member state, the merger is not subject to EU control, but is to be regulated by the domestic authorities. In other words, not more than 66 per cent of the turnover of either partner is to be in any single member state. Infringement of the Regulation may lead to the imposition of heavy fines.

Although the European Commission is currently reviewing the Regulation, it is important at this stage to examine, with special regard to business, the operation of certain aspects of the Merger Control Regulation currently in operation particularly the 'one-stop-shop' approach. The 'one-stop-shop' only applies to mergers that can satisfy the Regulation's definition of a concentration with a community dimension (CCD). At present, community dimension is defined by reference to the aggregate turnovers of the parties involved. A concentration will have a community dimension when:

- the combined aggregate worldwide turnover of all the undertakings concerned exceeds 5 billion ECU; and
- the aggregate community-wide turnover of each of at least two of the undertakings involved exceeds 250 million ECU; unless
- each of the undertakings concerned derives more than two-thirds of their community-wide turnover within one and the same member state.

The concentration is vetted either by the Commission or by the authorities of the member state, but not by both. This makes it easier for businesses planning merger activity, because it clearly identifies whether they will have to deal with the Commission, or with national authorities. The Merger Control Regulation has important implications for business because it has, as part of its purpose, the avoidance of scrutiny of proposed mergers in the EU, and at the national level.

Article 2 of the Regulation empowers the Commission to block mergers where they create or threaten to strengthen a dominant position so that competition in the Common Market may be substantially impeded. In assessing whether a dominant position is created or strengthened. Article 2(1) requires the Commission to take into account:

(a) The need to preserve and develop effective competition within the Common Market in view of, among other things, the structure of all the markets concerned and the actual or potential competition from undertakings located either within or without the Community.

(b) The market position of the undertakings concerned and their economic and financial power, the opportunities available to suppliers and users, their access to supplies or markets, any legal or other barriers to entry, supply and demand trends for the relevant goods and services, the interest of the intermediate and ultimate consumers, and the development of technical and economic progress provided that it is to consumers' advantage and does not form an obstacle to competition.

The Commission list in its 1994 *Competition Report* the following relevant criteria:

- the extent to which the merger increases concentration of supply in a market

- the conditions of demand. Stagnant demand and low price elasticity might suggest oligopoly
- the extent of similarity between oligopolies in terms of financial resources, market shares, and cost conditions
- capacity utilization – oligopolistic industries characterized by high fixed costs and associated with elastic demand, infrequent order and/or a lack of transparency, and facing a situation of spare capacity, may engage in outbursts of competition, thereby undoing the prevailing stability
- the countervailing power of buyers
- the degree of market transparency
- the extent and scale of entry barriers

The Commission, however, does not have a fixed frame of weightings that would apply in all cases. This gives the Commission considerable discretion and flexibility when it examines such cases, and hinders business in its ability to assess how Brussels will deal with oligopolistic dominance cases (Davison and Fitzpatrick, 1996, p. 14).

Today, mergers with a Community dimension must be notified to the European Commission and suspended for at least three weeks. The Commission will examine the consequences of the merger, and decide within a month whether to initiate proceedings within four months, to declare it compatible with the Common Market, or to declare it incompatible and thus prohibited.

FROM THE COMMUNITY CHARTER OF FUNDAMENTAL RIGHTS FOR WORKERS TO THE AGREEMENT ON SOCIAL POLICY IN THE EUROPEAN UNION

The Single European Act was greeted as added a caring, social dimension to the purely entrepreneurial aspects of the Single Market. The main concern was that the competition could damage employment in some areas while favouring growth and welfare in general. Consequently, the Community Charter of Fundamental Social Rights for Workers was adopted at a meeting of the European Council in Strasbourg on 8 and 9 December 1989 by the heads of state or governments of the EC, with the exception of the UK (*European File*, 1990). In the European Union Treaty, however, the Agreement of Social Policy formed a separate protocol to the Maastricht agreement, because of the UK's inability at the time to accept its provisions. The agreements set out in the protocol apply therefore only to the other 14 member states. A comparative analysis of the original Community Social Charter and the contemporary Social Agreement is therefore essential to understand the UK's position.

The Community Charter of Fundamental Social Rights for the Workers, also known as the Social Charter

Much was said and written about the Community Charter of Fundamental Social Rights for Workers. Former British Prime Minister Margaret Thatcher was known on numerous occasions to have called it 'Socialism by the back door' (Mazey, 1989). For Jacques Delors, former president of the EC Commission, on the other hand, this social dialogue and collective bargaining were essential pillars of democracy. The aims of the original Community Charter of Fundamental Rights were:

1. To combat unemployment and reduce the inequality of its impact
2. To ensure growth and greater job opportunities, and to reject all forms of discrimination or exclusion
3. To promote improvements in living and working conditions
4. To increase the economic and social cohesion of member states

To achieve these aims the Social Charter of Fundamental Rights comprised a set of rights:

1. *Freedom of movement* According to the Social Charter, each citizen of the European Union should have the right to freedom of movement throughout the territory of the Union, subject to restrictions justified on the grounds of public policy, public security or public health. The right of freedom of movement enables any citizen to work in the EU country of his or her own choice, and to engage in any occupation or profession in the Community under the same terms as those applied to nationals of the host country, subject to the provision of Community law. This includes, for example, equal opportunities. Wages and social benefits applied in the host country must be granted to workers in another EC state. The right also ensures that social protection is extended to all citizens of the European Union in gainful employment in a country other than their country of origin, on terms identical to those enjoyed by workers of the host country.

2. *Employment and remuneration* A principal objective of the Social Charter is to ensure fair remuneration for all employment in the Union, which means establishing a 'decent' wage or 'fair' remuneration. The Charter states that all employment shall be 'fairly remunerated and that all employees should be able to earn 'equitable' wages which allows them a decent standard of living. The Commission regards the setting of such 'fair' wages to be up to the national governments and the prevailing national systems.

3. *Improvement of living and working conditions* This relates to the organization of work, with an emphasis on flexible working time arrangements and the establishment of a maximum duration of working hours per week, a weekly rest period and an annual paid leave. Working hours per week vary in member states from 39 hours to 48 hours. Statutory public holidays are similarly varied, and range from 6 to 14 days of public holidays and from 18 to 30 days of statutory leave.

    According to the Charter, all part-time and temporary workers should have the same status, occupational social security benefits and pensions rights as full-time workers. Part-time workers should also receive the same holiday, dismissal and seniority allowances as full-time employees. Finally no temporary contract should be renewed for more than 12 months and no period of temporary work should exceed a total of 36 months. Compensation should furthermore be paid for early termination of temporary contracts. Part-time workers should also have the same access to vocational training as full-time workers.

4. *Social protection* Every worker in the EU, according to the Social Charter, should have a right to adequate social protection and enjoy an adequate level of social security benefits. The unemployed should also receive sufficient subsistence benefits and appropriate social assistance.

5. *Freedom of association* This right provides every worker in the EU with the opportunity to belong freely to any professional or trade union organization of his or her choice. This

general right also includes the freedom to negotiate and conclude collective agreements and the right to resort to collective action, including the right to strike.

6. *Vocational training*   The Social Charter also declares that every European should have the opportunity to continue vocational training. Every European citizen should have the right to enrol for occupational training courses, including those in universities and technical colleges, on the same terms as those enjoyed by the nationals of member states, and in the country of which the course takes place.

7. *Equal treatment of men and women*   Equal opportunities must also be developed with regard to access to employment, remuneration, working conditions, social protection, education, vocational training and career development for men and women.

8. *Information, consultation and participation of workers*   This is to be implemented by all multinationals operating in the European Union. This was one of the most controversial areas of the Social Charter and is discussed later in this chapter.

9. *Health protection and safety at the workplace*   According to this right, every worker must enjoy satisfactory health and safety conditions in his or her working environment. This means that health and safety measures need to be significantly improved in some member states. Minimum standards of fire prevention, lighting and ventilation are being instituted, as well as stricter guidelines for the use of machinery and protective equipment. The technological dimension is particularly highlighted, in so far as it involves changes in employees' working conditions, the restructuring of the company arising from mergers, collective redundancy procedures and when policies of the parent company affect trans-frontier workers.

10. *Protection of children and adolescents*   The minimum age of employment must not be lower than the minimum school-leaving age and in any case, not lower than 15 years. The right also stipulates that young people who are in gainful employment must receive equitable remuneration in accordance with national practice. Night work is prohibited in the case of workers under 18 years of age.

11. *Elderly persons*   According to this right each member of the Community, in retirement should be entitled to receive a minimum income giving him or her a decent standard of living and suitable medical and social assistance.

12. *Disabled persons*   Measures should be taken to ensure the fullest integration of the disabled into working life through vocational training, professional re-insertion and re-adaptation and social integration by means of improving accessibility, mobility, means of transport and housing.

Problems and barriers of implementation

Four major problems were identified for implementing the Social Charter (Venturini, 1988).

The first major problem was that the full implementation of the Charter remained the responsibility of individual member states. It was their task to ensure that all resources, legislation or collective agreements are being used to implement fully the social measures mentioned above. It was therefore doubtful whether all members were pursuing the implementation of those rights fully. Article 189 of the Treaty clearly stipulates that although 'a directive shall be binding as to the result to be achieved, upon each member state to which it is addressed, the choice of form and method for achieving the desired results shall be the responsibility of national authority'.

The second problem with implementation was the lack of legal muscle of the EC and the difficulty of converging national laws to meet the requirements of the internal market. In other words, establishing one basic set of social rules which can be adapted to the entire Community was difficult to develop and sustain.

The third barrier was the lack of political support. Member states did not seem convinced that Community development of this kind was a vital element in their national interests. Hence the failure to provide Community institutions with adequate resources and the political authority to promote and proceed with the development process. In the UK, for example, it was argued that parts of the Social Charter went beyond what was acceptable to the British government, which still had memories of the strikes and disputes of the 1980s and was not keen to see them re-emerge (Goodhard, 1992). The Social Charter, it was further asserted, might help trade unions to regain an influential role in bargaining and worker participation, and might boost the unions by restoring an ideological climate favourable to unions.

Finally, the fourth major problem of implementing the Social Charter was the great diversity of social systems within the member states. There is a great disparity in the resources, standards of living and of the structures of social security schemes between one member state and another. The payment of unemployment benefits at the German level, for example, it was claimed would encourage people in Portugal never to work again.

The implementation of the Charter it was argued would furthermore impose costs for business. For example, in the UK, where nearly 4.5 million people work part-time, and where its legislation did not require equivalent treatment of part-timers and full-timers, the implementation of the Social Charter would create additional expense for employers.

The Commission, however, believed that if all firms are expected to implement the same directives, then no firm will be at a disadvantage. The problem here was that firms were beginning from different bases. German firms, for example, have a long history of worker participation and involvement, and are unlikely to be faced with the same transaction costs of implementing key directives.

EVALUATION OF THE SOCIAL POLICY PROGRAMME: WHAT HAS BEEN ACHIEVED SO FAR?

In the negotiations leading to the Treaty on European Union in 1991, there was strong support for the amplification of the social policy. The Commission felt that the social dimension of the internal market was being neglected, despite many proposals made by the Commission under its social action programme, which were not enacted by the Council. Member states were willing to go further with the Treaty on European Union, but the UK did not consider it necessary for the Community to be given responsibility for social matters, and continued to dissent. An agreement was finally reached among 11 member states, excluding the UK, changing the language and aims of the Social Charter, renaming it for the purpose Social Chapter and converting them into treaty terms. In the agreement, 11 member states stated their wish to continue along the path laid down in the 1989 Social Charter. The UK will not vote on matters of common social policy, and legislation adopted in this way will not be applicable in the UK. With the election of the Labour Government in May 1997 the position of the UK on this issue is highly likely to change in favour of the Social Chapter legislation.

The agreement of Social Policy introduced by the Union Treaty provides a new basis for social action at Union level. The objectives of the agreement signed are:

- the promotion of employment
- better living and working conditions
- proper social protection and the encouragement of social dialogue between management and labour

Although the Social Policy agreement is now governed by Title II of the Treaty on European Union and the Agreement enables 14 member states (all with the exception of the UK) to legislate at European level, the Commission has used the Agreement only when it is impossible to obtain the support of all 15 member states.

According to the new Social Policy Agreement, the Council will support the activities of the member states and may issue directives (adopted by a qualified majority) laying down minimum requirements for the improvement of the working environment, health and safety protection, working conditions, information and consultation of workers, equality between men and women on the labour market and in treatment at work, and occupational integration.

In other areas the Council must act unanimously. These areas include: social security, social protection, protection when a contract of employment is terminated, and representation and collective defence of the interests of workers and employers, including co-determination. Provisions on the right of association, the right to strike or the right to impose lockouts are excluded. The Council must also act unanimously in relation to conditions of employment for non-Community nationals legally residing in Community territory. The Council can also make financial contributions for the promotion of employment and job creation. The Commission's role is to listen to the view of the two sides, employers and employees, before it makes new recommendations (European Commission, 1994, pp. 20–22).

In addition the Agreement on Social Policy opens new possibilities for collective agreements between the Social partners. The White paper 'European Social Policy – a way forward for the Union', adopted on 27 July 1994, seeks to set out the main lines of social action at Union level for the coming years. These are: job creation, improving professional qualifications, flexibility in working time, fight against long-term unemployment, and the promotion of part-time work as one of the possible ways to improve the employment situation in the European Union. In terms of education and training, all member states recognize that one of the essential requirements of the competitiveness of the Union is further investment in education and training. All member states expressed their determination to improve the quality of their education and training systems, and agreed that national qualification systems should be developed along convergent (but not harmonized) lines at Union level to underpin the free movement of persons on a transparent and practical basis.

The White Paper on 'Growth, Competitiveness and Employment' sets out the following priorities:

1. To ensure that no young person can be unemployed under the age of 19. The Union will contribute to this objective with the Youth Start initiative.
2. To set progressive targets up to the year 2000 for the elimination of basic illiteracy, and lack of other basic skills, on the part of school-leavers.
3. To raise the status of initial vocational education and training.
4. To extend the scope and range of existing apprenticeship schemes, and/or other forms of linked work and training.
5. To improve the coordinated provision of guidance and placement services.
6. To examine ways of introducing tax incentives for firms and individuals to invest in their continuing training.

Since the objectives of free movement relates to building a European labour market, a European Employment Services (EURES) body has been set up, which provides information on transnational job and recruitment opportunities.

As far as the right to information, consultation and participation is concerned, an agreement to set up a Europe-wide 'information and reflection' Council was signed, for a fixed four-year term with the new central management of the Credit Lyonnais. Shop stewards from 10 different countries sit in this Council. The Council meets once a year with an agenda prepared by the management.

In the field of health and safety at work, where decisions are taken by qualified majority, the Commission tends to use the Treaty in preference to the Agreement. Thus far, the Agreement has been used only occasionally, for example, for a Directive on informing and consulting workers in Community-scale companies and groups of companies and a resolution on the outlook for social policy (Commission Report, 1995, Part Two, Chapter 1, Section 104, p. 48).

The most important revision of the agreement is the extension of qualified majority voting to cover the adoption of measures relating to working conditions, the consultation of workers, and the promotion of contractual relations between employers and employees at the European level (Gold, 1992). A revised draft of the 1990 directive on employee information and consultation – the Works Council Directive was adopted by the Council in September 1994. In its final version, the Directive provides a model for establishing a European Works Council where it is requested by employees or their representative, unless the interested parties prefer some other arrangement. The Council will have the right to meet central management once a year to be informed and consulted on the progress of the business, and can also request special meetings to discuss exceptional circumstances affecting employment, such as relocation, plan closures or mergers. While the Council may suggest ways to lessen the impact on employment, it cannot require management to change its decision. This new directive will affect an estimated 1500 companies – those having at least 1000 employees within the EU (EIU, 1995, p. 59).

The Labour Council also adopted in June 1994 another revised version of a 1991 draft directive on protection of young workers. It strictly regulates work carried out by adolescents aged 15–18 and bans virtually all work by younger children. The UK was given an extra four years to introduce some of the rules. Additionally, at their Essen Summit in December 1995, EU leaders approved guidelines for improving conditions on national labour markets – including greater flexibility on wages and working time, labour mobility and training, improved job placement services, measures to help reintegrate the long-term unemployed, and cutting non-wage costs such as social charges (EIU, 1995a, pp. 59–60). However, a deadlock still remains over the 1990 draft directive aimed at assuring part-time or temporary workers pay and conditions on a par with full-timers, and the directive on parental leave (pending since 1983) which would give both men and women the right to three months' unpaid leave at the birth or adoption of a child.

REVIEW QUESTIONS

1. What are the ultimate objectives of the EC competition law? Identify and describe them.
2. What are the arguments for and against the European Merger Control Regulation?
3. Can the view of the Social Charter, as 'Socialism by the back door' still be sustained in view of the changes introduced by the new Social Policy Agreement in the Treaty on European Union?
4. The European Parliament, a strong partisan of the Social Europe, called the Social Policy Agreement 'a balance to the Business in Europe'. Explain and evaluate this claim.

EXERCISE 5.1: Comparative study of the EU Social Policy and the social policies implemented in the UK, USA and Japan

Aim   The purpose of this project is to familiarize students with social policies adopted by countries within and outside the European Union.

Assignment   The class is divided into three groups: UK, the USA and Japan. Each group is asked to research and investigate the various social policies adopted by their assigned countries.

Format   Students are expected to present their findings to the class, highlighting in their discussion the similarities and differences of the social policies implemented in their assigned country with the EU Social Policy Agreement, and their implications for business in Europe.

Sources

For general information related to the EU Social Policy, students are encouraged to consult the following documentation published by the Commission of the European Communities:

- *Journal of European Social Policy*
- *Journal of European Public Policy*
- *Social Europe Magazine*
- *Women of Europe Supplements*

FURTHER READING

Brown, R., *Managing in the Single European Market*, Butterworth, Oxford, 1995.

Commission of the EC, Intergovernmental Conference, 1996, *European Commission Report*, Luxembourg, 1995.

European Commission, European Union, Luxembourg, 1994.

European File, Community Charter of Fundamental Social Rights for Workers, Commission for the European Communities, European Documentation, May, 1990.

Korah, V., *An Introduction Guide to EC Competition Law and Practice*, 5th edition. Sweet & Maxwell, London, 1994.

Venturini, P., *The Social Charter. Potential Effects of the Internal Market*, ECSC, Brussels, 1988.

COUNTRY PROFILES OF THE 15 MEMBERS OF THE EUROPEAN UNION

To get an initial 'feel' for business in the European Union, a brief introductory portrait of each of the member states of the European Union is necessary. Each country profile contains the basic geographical, political and economic information needed to become familiar with each member state. A brief summary of the business culture and business etiquette prevailing in each country is also included.

AUSTRIA (Joined 1995)

Geographical location

Austria occupies a strategic position in the centre of Western Europe. It is bordered by Switzerland, Germany, the Czech Republic, Slovakia, Hungary, Slovenia, Italy and Liechtenstein. Two-thirds of the country is composed of mountainous alpine regions, with the Alps dominating the western and southern provinces.

Political background

Austria is a federal republic of nine provinces (*Länder*) – Burgenland, Karnten (Carinthia), Niederosterreich (Lower Austria), Oberosterreich (Upper Austria), Salzburg, Steiermark (Styria), Vorarlberg and Wien (Vienna). The president of Austria is the head of state. He is elected directly by the people, for a six-year term. The president appoints cabinet members, and convenes and discontinues parliamentary sessions.

The federal government is headed by the chancellor (prime minister) chosen by the president. The federal assembly is composed of two houses, the national council and the federal council. Legislative power rests with the federal assembly. The national council comprises 183 members, who are elected for four-year terms from the nine *Länder*. The federal council consists of 58 members, who are elected by the legislatures of the nine *Länder*. They serve four- to six-year terms.

Economic characteristics

Basic data:
- Population (000): 8040 (1995)
- Land area (sq km): 83 855

- Gross domestic product (billion US dollars): 196.5 (1994)
- Percentage growth of GDP (1977–1994): 307.4
- Annual inflation rate (% growth): 3.0 (1994)
- National currency: schilling
- Exchange rate against US dollar: 1.04 (October 1995)
- Unemployment: 4.5 per cent (1995)

(*Euromonitor*, European Marketing Data and Statistics, 1996)

Industry accounts for one-third of GDP. Most firms are small to medium size. The total number of industrial and trading firms is about 95 000 of which 95 per cent employ fewer than 50 people. The bulk of Austrian heavy industry is nationalized. However, the Austrian government is now considering privatizing the iron and steel, aluminium and petrochemicals concerns. Agriculture produces some three per cent of Austrian GDP, and tourism contributes 8.5 per cent (Department of Trade and Industry, 1994, *Austria Country Profile*, p. 11).

Inflation is among the lowest in the OECD area (OECD, 1992, p. 76). (The original member countries of the OECD are Austria, Belgium, Canada, Denmark, France, Germany, Greece, Iceland, Ireland, Italy, Luxembourg, the Netherlands, Norway, Portugal, Spain, Sweden, Switzerland, Turkey, the UK, the USA, Japan, Finland, Australia and New Zealand.) The effect of EU membership is estimated to have lowered consumer prices by three-quarters percentage point by the end of 1995 (European Commission, *European Economy 1996*, p. 106). Austria accession to the EU also increased its total public spending by a further two per cent of GDP in 1995 (European Commission, 1996, p. 107).

Austria has one of the lowest recorded unemployment rates in the EU, following Luxembourg. Over the last few years, however, unemployment has been on an upward trend mainly due to large inflows of foreign labour from Eastern Europe. Unemployment rate in 1992 was at 3.6 per cent, in 1993 at 4.2 per cent, 1994 at 4.4 per cent and 1995 4.5 per cent (European Commission, 1996, p. 27). Austria had a workforce of just over three million in 1992 of which some 275 000 were foreign workers, mainly in construction jobs (Department of Trade and Industry, 1994, p. 32).

Trade and business opportunities

Over two-thirds of Austrian trade is with the EU and Germany is the dominant trading partner. Forty per cent of Austrian exports go to Germany and 43 per cent of the country's imports come from there, followed by Switzerland, Italy and Great Britain (Department of Trade and Industry, 1994, p. 11). The opening of Eastern Europe is bringing new opportunities in consumer and investment goods as a gateway between West and East.

Business opportunities exist mainly in the areas of medical equipment, physical and electronic security equipment, and computer software. Many Austrian software houses are small and are ill-equipped to service their clients (Department of Trade and Industry 1994, p. 18). As far as consumer goods are concerned, there is a steady demand for quality clothing, including leisure wear. There are very few chains/stores and the market is dominated by small retail outlets. Other promising market sectors yet to be fully exploited are: confectionery, jewellery, and toys.

Business practices

The official language is German, but each region or village may have its own dialect. Minorities of Austrians also speak Slovene and Croat. English is a required subject in the educational system and is widely spoken in Austria, but business correspondence should be carried out in German. Austrians are a gracious and polite people. They use a lot of distinctive greetings. Any kind of request, be it for directions, for a room, for the time, or for an item in the store, should begin with *Bitte*, meaning please and, of course, should be followed with *Danke*, meaning thank you (Johnson and Moran, 1992, p. 1). Guests should stand when the host enters the room and remain standing until he suggests sitting down. A younger person should always rise when an older person enters the room. In addition, men should rise when a woman enters the room or when speaking to a woman who is already standing (Johnson and Moran, 1992, p. 2). Social rank in Austria is based on education and profession, and not on heredity. Each person is evaluated on the basis of efforts and accomplishments. Those in administrative positions in the government, members of Parliament, or university professors are considered of high social status.

Punctuality ranks high among priorities in making appointments with Austrians. Prompt handling of correspondence is greatly appreciated even if the answer is negative. Austrians expect face-to-face contact with their suppliers, but hard-sell strategies are not appreciated and business strategies should be designed with long-term goals in mind rather than immediate sales (Johnson and Moran, 1992, p. 2). As far as advertising and publicity are concerned, there is no national press. Each provincial capital has an independent newspaper. Broadcasting, both radio and TV is administered by a corporation set up by the state and owned by the federal and provincial governments. Business dress code is traditional and conservative.

About 88 per cent of the population is Roman Catholic, six per cent is Protestant and the remaining is either Jewish or without religious affiliation (Johnson and Moran, 1992, p. 5).

BELGIUM (Joined 1957)

Geography

Belgium is one of the smallest countries in Europe. It is situated on the North Sea coast of Western Europe. Belgium has about 64 km of coastline and land frontiers with the Netherlands to the north, France to the south-west and Germany and Luxembourg to the east. The land is largely flat and has excellent road and rail communications. Antwerp, is the third largest port in the world, and is the rival to Rotterdam as a gateway to the rest of Europe.

Political background

Belgium had been a constitutional monarchy since 1831. The present king is also the head of state. He has often been required to mediate and to propose governments. There is a 160-seat Chamber of Representatives, normally elected for four years and a 184-member senate.

Economic characteristics

Basic data:
- Population (000): 10 131 (1995)
- Land area (sq km): 30 520
- Gross domestic product (billion US dollars): 227.8 (1994)
- Percentage growth of GDP (1977–1994): 186.9

- Annual inflation rates (% growth): 2.4 (1994)
- National currency: Belgian franc
- Exchange Rate against US dollar: 1.04 (October 1995)
- Unemployment: 10.0 per cent (1994) (Eurostat, 1994)

(*Euromonitor*, European Marketing Data and Statistics, 1996)

Belgium has one of the highest standards of living in Europe. Inflation is the lowest in the Union at 1.5 per cent (European Commission, 1996, p. 77). Unemployment rate, however, rose in the whole year of 1995 from 10.0 per cent in 1994 to 10.2 per cent. Belgium is heavily dependent on international trade, 69 per cent of its total imports come from the European Union. German imports represent 21 per cent share of total imports, followed by the Netherlands, France and the UK.

Business practices

Belgian workers have the highest productivity average in Europe. They see themselves as more efficient, more reliable and producing higher quality goods than most other countries (Gibbs, 1990, p. 86). Belgian business relations are very formal. Casualness is often mistaken for rudeness (Johnson and Moran, 1992, p. 10). Business cards are essential in Belgium and should be printed in French or Dutch. The business dress code is formal but very stylish.

Belgium has three linguistic communities: Dutch, French and German. In Brussels the official languages are French and Dutch. All official Belgian publications, laws and government orders are printed in both Dutch and French.

Seventy-five per cent of the population are Roman Catholic with the remainder mostly Protestant. There is a sizeable Jewish community in Antwerp.

DENMARK (Joined 1973)

Geography

The kingdom of Denmark is one of the smallest countries in the EU. It is about 60 per cent the size of Scotland. The country consists of the peninsula of Jutland, which has a land border with Germany to the south, the larger islands of Zealand and Funen, and many smaller islands. It lies at the same latitudes as northern England and southern Scotland. Denmark is mainly flat and the capital city is Copenhagen.

Political background

Denmark is a small constitutional monarchy in which executive authority lies with a prime minister who answers to a 179-member unicameral Parliament, the *Folketing*. The *Folketing* in turn is elected through proportional representation on the basis of universal adult suffrage, for a term of four years. As in the UK, the monarch may, on the recommendation of the prime minister, dissolve the *Folketing* at any time and allow new elections. At present eight parties are represented: there has been a centre left four party coalition government since June 1993 consisting of the Social Democrats and the three small centre parties: the Centre Democrats, the Radicals and the Christian People's Party. Together the four parties have 90 *Folketing* members (71 of whom are Social Democrats).

Economic characteristics

Basic data:
- Population (000): 5216 (1995)
- Land area (sq km): 43 075
- Gross domestic product (billion US dollars): 146.0 (1994)
- Percentage growth (1977–1994): 214.1
- Annual inflation rate (% growth): 2.0 (1994)
- National currency: Danish kroner
- Exchange rate against US dollar: 5.55 (October 1995)
- Unemployment: 6.7 per cent (1994) (EU Commission, 1996)

(*Euromonitor*, European Marketing Data and Statistics, 1996)

Denmark is now a world leader in marine diesel and motor technology, as well as a leading supplier of cement, beer, hearing aids, thermostatic controls, merchant vessels, and industrial enzymes (Johnson and Moran, 1992, p. 20). Denmark's agricultural sector remains the backbone of the economy with thousands of mainly small farms producing pig meat products, dairy goods and cereals. Because Denmark is relatively small in size, Danish firms tend to concentrate on overseas markets, 80–90 per cent of manufacture output is sold overseas. Danish exports to EU countries account for 45 per cent. Manufactured goods lead the way, with food second and chemicals third. Great Britain is the largest purchaser of Danish agricultural produce, followed by Germany. Sweden is Denmark's biggest market for manufactured goods and its second largest market overall.

A sharp decrease in registered unemployment occurred in 1995, brought down to 6.7 per cent as a result of active labour market measures: leave schemes, early retirement schemes and special job training or education (European Commission, 1996, p. 80).

Business practices

The Danes are obsessed with punctuality, and are very formal in their business relations. They might insist on one more meeting just to ensure that everything is in order. Danes like to be comfortable with all the details of a deal (Johnson and Moran, 1992, p. 17). Danish firms tend to concentrate on high-quality products of high performance and reliability, whose price is not of first importance. The business dress code, however, is less formal than in other countries in the EU. Blazers, suits and sweatshirts are all acceptable modes of dress for the Danish business person (Gibbs, 1994, p. 100).

The Danish language is closely linked to Swedish, Norwegian, Icelandic and Faroese, but most Danes speak English well. The third most commonly spoken language is German. Most firms are willing to correspond in English and most trade literature in English will be acceptable.

FINLAND (Joined 1995)

Geography

Finland lies on the Baltic coast with its western border bridging Sweden and Norway. Its entire eastern flank meets the countries of the former Soviet Union. Finland was ideally placed to develop as an *entreport* for East–West trade in the 1970s and 1980s. Most of the territory is forested with the main habitation centres to the south.

Political background

Finland is largely an egalitarian society. Finland has a semi-executive president who exercises extensive political powers even though the main executive functions are vested in the prime minister. The president is elected by universal suffrage for a six-year term. He may appoint any prime minister and cabinet who can secure the approval of the 200-member *Eduskunta* (parliament). The *Eduskunta* is itself elected for a four-year term.

Economic characteristics

Basic data:

- Population (000): 5099 (1995)
- Land area (sq m) 337030
- Gross domestic product (billion US dollars): 98.0 (1994)
- Percentage of GDP growth (1977–1994): 201.6
- Annual inflation rate (% growth): 1.1 per cent (1994)
- Currency: markka
- Exchange rate against US Dollar: 4.31 (October 1995)
- Unemployment: 12.3 per cent (Eurostat, 1994)

(*Euromonitor*, European Marketing Data and Statistics, 1996)

Finland once boasted the most prosperous economic conditions of all the Nordic countries, but found itself at a crossroads in the early 1990s. The abrupt loss of business in the East at the beginning of the decade shook the country's self-image to its foundations, and the government was obliged to enforce a painful austerity programme.

Finland's major industry is forestry which supplies a large paper and timber products sector. There is also a developed sector, manufacturing glass and ceramics, household goods and other consumer items and an extremely important heavy goods industry producing ships, cement and steel products and machine tools. But unemployment remains very high. Western fashion, popular music and fast food are very popular with the younger generations.

Business practices

The Finnish term *sisu*, untranslatable into English, sums up the national character in a single word. This trait combines the odd mixture of violence and placidity inherent within the Finnish temperament, a balance of ardour, patience, industriousness, and the desire for power that has been evident throughout the country's history (Johnson and Moran, 1992, p. 46). Ninety-two per cent of the population speak Finnish, and the remaining minority speak Swedish.

FRANCE (Joined 1957)

Geography

France is the largest country in western Europe. It borders on six countries and has coastlines on the Mediterranean, Atlantic and the Channel. It lies at the heart of the continent. It meets Spain and Andorra in the south across the Pyrennes, Italy in the south, Switzerland and Germany to the east and Belgium and Luxembourg in the north. France has the largest land area in western Europe and there are wide differences in both soil and climate. The country enjoys diversified geography and climate conditions. The richest lands for cereals and dairy and beef farming are mostly to the north of the Loire and benefit from temperature climatic conditions. Below the Loire, the Atlantic sets a temperate effect on the regions of Poitou-Charentes and Aquitaine, both of which have a lot of good farmland, while, near the Mediterranean coast, the irrigated plain around the river Rhône to the north and south of Avignon provides excellent conditions for the cultivation of fruits and vegetables. France's wine-growing areas are scattered across most of the country, and the diversity of fine wines – from Alsace, Bordeau, Burgundy, Champagne, to the Loire and the Rhône valley, testify to the variety of grapes, climate and soil (Economist Intelligence Unit, 1995, *Country Profile: France*, p. 26).

Political background

The president of the Republic is elected by direct universal suffrage and the presidential mandate is for seven years. The president appoints the prime minister and chairs the weekly Council of Ministers meeting. Other ministers are appointed by the president on the proposal of the prime minister. The president may change prime minister at will. He also exercises certain powers independently, notably in the domain of security and defence (Economist Intelligence Unit, 1995, *Country Profile: France*, p. 6). The president is also responsible for the top judicial appointments which are made through the Council of Ministers. He chooses the nine members of the Higher Council of the Judiciary. The president also appoints three of the nine members of the important Constitutional Council and selects its president.

Economic characteristics

Basic data:
- Population (000): 958 027
- Land area (sq km): 543 965
- Gross domestic product (billion US dollars): 1 329.3 (1994)
- Percentage growth in GDP (1977–1994): 239.6
- Annual inflation rate (% growth): 1.7 per cent (1994)
- National currency: French franc
- Exchange rate against US dollar: 5.01 (October 1995)
- Unemployment: 11.5 per cent (1994)

(*Euromonitor*, European Marketing Data and Statistics, 1996)

France is the world's second largest food exporter and its agricultural sector is significantly larger, and more important than other members. The main strengths of France are in cereals, dairy products and alcoholic beverages. Tourism is also important, as well as technological services. This latter includes civil engineering contracts, engineering consultancy, nuclear reprocessing and management services. More than one-sixth of France's foreign trade is with Germany while more than a third of its total trade is with the rest of the European Union other than Germany (Economist Intelligence Unit, 1995, *Country Profile: France*, p. 39).

One of the major economic and social problems in France is the continuing high rate of unemployment. The unemployment rate in 1994 for men climbed to well over the 20 per cent mark, and for women 30 per cent (Economist Intelligence Unit, 1995, p. 18). Labour unions are highly politicized and adversarial. The most important are the pro-communist CGT, the socialist SFDT and the pluralist FO. However, only a fifth of the workforce is unionized, the lowest proportion in Europe (Mole, 1993, p. 16). French attempts to control inflation were not very successful at 2.5 per cent in 1992, but came down to 2 per cent in 1995 (European Commission, 1996, p. 92).

The banking system falls under the dual control of the Minister of the Economy, Finance and the Budget on the one hand, and the Governor of the Banque de France, the Central bank, on the other. The three leading commercial banks are the Banque Nationale de Paris, the Credit Lyonnais and the Societe General. Together they control 22 per cent of the branches in France. Other important banks are the Banque Parisbas and Banque Indo-suez which specialize in major business clients and international banking, the Credit Industriel et Commercial and the Credit Commercial de France (Thomson, 1994, p. 70).

Business practices

French business etiquette can be summarized as follows: formal courtesies, titles and correct dress. French business is conducted very formally and an initial interview is best requested in writing. The letter must conform to the best in business French. A poorly constructed letter will lose impact or be totally disregarded (Gibbs, 1994, p. 109), French business people are not tolerant when French is written badly. Even slight memos and notes are written in a mandarin style that in other countries is the preserve of senior civil servants. To write correctly is a sign of education and breeding.

Meetings are highly structured with an established format and a detailed agenda. For discussion, input from others is usually secured before a formal meeting takes place. Meetings are therefore less time consuming than in team-oriented cultures. The purpose is for briefing and coordination rather than a forum for debate or decision making (Mole, 1993, p. 21). As far as punctuality is concerned, about 15 minutes is the average accepted slippage. Humour is rarely used on formal occasions or meetings. Always shake hands when entering a meeting with all those present and those joining the meeting, and do the same on leaving. Meetings are conducted in French. Even if you have had initial contact outside France in a business setting or social contacts in spoken English, this will not be the case at the meeting (Gibbs, 1994, p. 110).

Professionalism is highly valued. New ideas and techniques are welcomed as long as they are well researched and logically argued and have a conceptual rigour. French people enjoy abstract thought, theory, formulas and a degree of logic and analysis which often seems impractical to pragmatic thinkers such as the British or the Dutch (Mole, 1993, p. 25). Formal wear and style are very important to the French. Men will almost always wear a suit and tie, and women smart, chic, classic clothes. Dark suits are appropriate for men.

Ninety per cent of the population is Roman Catholic, slightly over two per cent are Protestant, three per cent are Moslem and one per cent is Jewish.

GERMANY (Joined 1957)

Geography

The dramatic unification of Germany took place on 3 October 1990. Germany occupies a central position in western Europe. Its neighbours to the west are the Netherlands, Belgium, Luxembourg and France, to the south Switzerland and Austria, to the east the Czech Republic, Slovakia and Poland and to the north Denmark. It is bounded in the north by the Baltic Sea and the North sea.

Political background

Germany is a parliamentary democracy with powers divided among the legislative, executive and judicial branches. The federal constitution, called the Basic Law, is essentially the provisional constitution of former West Germany. The titular head of state is the federal president. The chief executive and head of government is the federal chancellor who selects a cabinet of ministers. The parliament is divided into an upper chamber, the *Bundersrat*, which represents the German states, and the lower chamber of popularly elected deputies, the *Bundestag*. Parliamentary elections are held every four years (Department of Trade and Industry, 1995).

Unified Germany is a federation. There are ten *Länder* (federal states) of West Germany now joined by five *Länder* from the east with a unified Berlin replacing West Berlin. The powers of the *Länder* cannot be reduced. Each of the *Länder* and Berlin has its own constitution, a democratically elected parliament, a government, administrative agencies and independent courts. However, the constitution is binding upon the *Länder* and the federal parliament is responsible for major legislation and policy. The *Länder* parliaments have prime responsibility for two major policy areas: education, and law and order. Administration of federal legislation is mainly the responsibility of the *Länder*, to allow greater consideration of local needs and issues and thus bring government closer to the people. In many cases, *Länder* powers are delegated further to local authorities.

Each *Länder* has between three and six votes in the *Bundersrat*, depending on the size of its population. *Bundesrat* members are appointed by the *Länder* governments for the duration of their service with their particular *Länder* government. The consent of the *Bundersrat* is required for around 50 per cent of legislation, notably the budget, and those laws affecting the *Länder*.

The lower house, or *Bundestag*, comprises a minimum of 656 deputies, while 16 additional members were elected in October 1994 as a consequence of the electoral process. The *Bundestag* has a speaker, or president, usually elected from among the largest parliamentary group. It has three main tasks: to act as the legislative body, to elect the federal chancellor and to control government activity. Any amendment to the Basic Law requires two-thirds majorities in both houses of parliament. Thus the opposition parties can prevent amendments to the constitution through their representations in either the *Bundestag* or the *Bundesrat* (Economist Intelligence Unit, 1995, p. 10). The federal president is head of state, including signing treaties and following procedure for appointing the chancellor, but the role is basically ceremonial. Presidential directives and orders require the counter-signature of the chancellor or relevant minister. The president is elected for a five-year term by the *Bundestag* and an equal number of delegates from *Länder* parliaments.

The federal constitutional court is a major policy-making institution in the German governmental system. Its central position derives from its role as a judicial law-making body created for the specific purpose of resolving constitutional disputes under the Basic Law.

Economic characteristics

Basic data:
- Population (000): 81 553 (1995)
- Land area (sq km): 356 840
- Gross domestic product: DM 3100 billion (1994) (DTI, 1955)
- National currency: Deutsche Mark
- Exchange rate against US dollar: 1.43 (October 1995)
- As of 1994, unemployment was at 8.2 per cent in West, 13.5 per cent in East (Department of Trade and Industry, 1995)

- Religion: Roman Catholic 35 per cent, Protestant 40 per cent

(Euromonitor, European Marketing Data and Statistics, 1996)

Germany is the third largest economy in the world after the USA and Japan. It is the second largest exporter and importer (after the USA) in the world. Slightly under half of German trade in 1993 was conducted with the EU compared with slightly over half in 1992 (Economist Intelligence Unit, 1995, p. 452). Within the European Union, France, Italy, the UK and the Netherlands are the major trading partners, with France leading the group.

Germany is strongest in capital goods, followed by automobiles and chemicals. Unemployment rate at the time of unification in 1990 and over the next two years was well below the European average despite a huge influx of immigrants and work-seekers from Eastern Germany. After unification, unemployment in Eastern Germany rose dramatically to 1.2 million or 14.5 per cent of the workforce in 1992 (Economist Intelligence Unit, 1995, p. 27).

Business practices

Germans are in general formal in their business dealings not only with foreigners but among themselves too. They are structural and rigid in their dealings. Germans are title-conscious. Proper etiquette often requires addressing individuals by their titles. It is also considered rude to sit with the soles of one's shoes visible to another. Germans will cross their legs at the knees rather than resting an ankle on the other knee. Handshaking is one of the most striking elements of a German business meeting. This occurs on every possible occasion, at the beginning and close of meetings and extends to everyone joining the meeting, and leaving midway through (Gibbs, 1994, p. 124). The man should wait until the lady stretches out her hand. Punctuality is essential. The dress code is also very formal. A conservative suit, well polished and necessarily dark shoes.

Germans are competitive and ambitious. They do not identify or sympathize with failure. They place a great deal of importance on individual success (Mole, 1993, p. 41). Maximizing profitability, however, is not always the German's first priority, as is the case with many other Europeans. Germans feel often that the firm has a responsibility to society and the environment (Johnson and Moran, 1992, p. 60). Many Germans have an excellent command of English, but the official business correspondence should be in German. When conducting business, out of courtesy it is important to show that you have at least a basic knowledge of German. The second language of most Germans is French. When negotiating a business deal with German managers, make sure you know all the technical aspects of your businesses.

GREECE (Joined 1981)

Geography

Greece has a total area about the same size at England. The Greek peninsula is bounded on the north by Albania, Yugoslavia and Bulgaria and on the east by Turkey. Major Greek islands are Crete, Euboea, Corfu and Rhodes. The close proximity with Turkey and the large number of Greek islands have caused occasional conflict between the two states, the most important of which has been the conflict over Cyrpus, placed in a status quo position following the Turkish military intervention in 1974. Much of Greece is mountainous, about three-quarters of the area, and a quarter of the land is cultivated.

Political background

Following the abolition of the monarchy in 1973, Greece has a republic with an executive president. The president is elected by popular mandate for a period of four years. He appoints his own cabinet and is answerable to a 300-member assembly (parliament) which is itself elected for a five-year term under a system of proportional representation.

Economic characteristics

Basic data:
- Population (000): 10 422
- Land area (sq km): 131 985
- Gross domestic product (billion US dollars): 81.3 (1994)
- Percentage growth (1977–1994): 210.2
- Annual inflation rate (% growth): 10.9 per cent (1994)
- National currency: drachma
- Exchange rate against US dollar: 161.70 (October 1995)
- Unemployment: 10.1 per cent (1994)
- Religion: Greek Orthodox

(*Euromonitor*, European Marketing Data and Statistics, 1996)

Agriculture is the mainstay of the economy employing a quarter of the population and producing up to a third of GDP. The European Union is Greece's most important trading partner. Greek supplies much of the world with olive oil, citrus fruits and wine. Tourism is also very important.

Business practice

The Greek are proud of their history and role as the first centre of European civilisation. This pride is reflected in their manner of doing business (Gibs, 1994, p. 136). The Greek mentality shows little preference for long-term industrial projects and is more suited for trade. Greece is a hard place to do business, built on notions of who you know, and on handouts (Gibbs, 1994, p. 136). Greeks shake hands as frequently as most Europeans, but unlike most Europeans the Greeks like to get to know the person with whom they are doing business, and they may spend some time in small talk, effectively summing you up (Gibbs, 1994, p. 138).

Greek business protocol is virtually non-existent (Johnson and Moran, 1992, p. 74). Business formalities such as professional titles, codes of behaviour, and business taboos are considered terribly boring (Johnson and Moran, 1992, p. 74). As far as punctuality is concerned the Greek will routinely arrive 30 minutes late for a meeting. There is seldom a formal agenda to most meetings and rarely are there formal minutes, other than the ones individual participants take (Mole, 1994, p. 127). Greeks also distrust written communication (Mole, 1994, p. 127). They are expressive people, raised voices, a variety of facial expressions and gestures are commonplace. A visitor to Greece who is unfamiliar with Greek culture may believe that a violent argument is underway when in fact two people are merely having a lively conversation (Johnson and Moran, 1992, p. 77). Government officials and business people speak French or English besides Greek. Formal dress is not always that important in Greece. Suits are reserved for purely formal meetings.

IRELAND (Joined 1973)

Geography

The Republic of Ireland comprises the greater part of an island off the west coast of Great Britain. The remaining northern part of the island forms part of the UK. Principal cities and towns are Dublin (the capital), Cork, Limerick, Waterford, Galway, Dundalk and Drogheda.

Political background

The Republic of Ireland is ruled by a president who is elected for a seven-year term by universal suffrage but most executive powers are exercised by a prime minister and cabinet appointed from among the national parliament.

The Irish parliament is divided into two houses. The upper house or senate of 60 members and a lower house or house of representatives of 166 members. Membership of the senate is partly by nomination, and partly by election from panels of candidates drawn from industry and education. Election to the house of representatives is from 41 constituencies for a term of five years.

Economic characteristics

Basic data:
- Population (000): 3577 (1994)
- Land area (sq km): 68 895
- Gross domestic product (billion US dollars): 52.1 (1994)
- Percentage growth of GDP (1977–1994): 448.4
- Annual inflation rate (Percentage growth): 2.3 per cent (1994)
- National currency: Irish pound
- Exchange rate against US dollar: 0.62 (October 1995)
- Unemployment: 17.8 per cent (1994)
- Religion: Roman Catholic 93 per cent, Church of Ireland 3 per cent, Presbyterian 0.4 per cent

(*Euromonitor*, European Marketing Data and Statistics, 1996)

The Irish economy is the least prosperous in the European Union. The Republic of Ireland has limited natural resources and historically has been a farming and food producing and exporting country. Meat and dairy products constitute the leading agricultural activity with some cereals on cultivated lands. Ireland is noted for its exports of livestock and bloodstock. However, in recent years the industrial base has become quite sophisticated. Ireland has become highly dependent upon foreign companies, especially in the high technology, pharmaceuticals, and instrument engineering fields. The government provides substantial investment incentives for foreign companies with very low tax rates.

Business practices

Ireland has an elaborate class system based on education, health and professional status (Mole, 1994, p. 131). Business etiquette and modes of address are similar to those in the UK but Irish manners are less reserved, and more tolerant of good humour. The Irish will also move quickly to using first names, even at the initial meeting.

The Republic of Ireland is the only English-speaking country that is predominantly Roman

Catholic with 93 per cent of the population. The church is the only thing that comes before obligations to the family, and the influence of Irish Catholicism is evident in all aspects of daily life and work. The Irish are very hard-working. Clothing is plain, simple and generally dark.

ITALY (Joined 1957)

Geography

Located in the centre of southern Europe, Italy is a long strip of land, seldom exceeding 200 km in width, which extends south-eastwards for some 1000 km into the Mediterranean. In the north, where it meets with France, Switzerland, Austria and Slovenia, the territory broadens out to include the industrial cities of Milan, Turin and Genoa. In the south it divides into two peninsulas, the lower of which almost connects with the island of Sicily. Italy has a north/south divide, demarcated just south of Rome. Milan in the industrialized North is the centre of business.

Political background

Italy has been a republic since 1946 when it abolished the monarchy and initiated the present system. It is a parliamentary democracy, with the government chosen not directly by the electorate, but requiring the support of the parliament that is the chamber of deputies and the senate. However, the balance of power between them is so finely calculated that legislation can be batted between them for years (Mole, 1993, p. 48). The president is elected by parliament for a seven-year term, but he has semi-executive functions. The 630-member chamber of deputies (lower house) is elected for five years by universal suffrage, as are all but seven of the 315-member senate.

Italy operates a system of proportional representation. Following a referendum on electoral reform in 1991, electors vote from a party list and may express a further preference for one candidate on that list. For electoral purposes, the country is divided into large electoral colleges and there is a bewildering abundance of candidates.

Economic characteristics

Basic data:
- Population (000): 957 248 (1995)
- Land area (sq km): 301 245
- Gross domestic product (billion US dollars): 1017.7 (1994)
- Percentage growth of GDP (1977–1994): 319.7
- Annual inflation rate (% growth): 4.0 per cent (1994)
- National currency: lira
- Exchange rate against US dollar: 1617.35 (October 1995)
- Unemployment: 12.0 per cent (1994)
- Religion: Roman Catholic 90 per cent

(*Euromonitor*, European Marketing Data and Statistics, 1996)

Italy is the world's fourth largest manufacturer of machine tools after Japan, Germany and Russia but ahead of the USA, Switzerland, the UK, and France. Italian designers and Italian design are among the most celebrated in the world. Italy has a well-diversified economy which includes a large and well-developed industrial sector producing sophisticated engineering, electronics, chemicals, steel products and above all food products. Italy exports mainly to the USA, East Asia, Latin America and Eastern Europe (37 per cent). Export to the EU in 1993 was only at 12 per cent (OECD, 1995, p. 23). The private sector economy, however, is proportionately the smallest in Europe. Italy has the largest number of shopkeepers in Europe (Randlesome, 1993, p. 154). Textile manufacturing is Italy's third-biggest business after engineering and construction. Textile sales account for almost 14 per cent of the value of Italian manufacturing and one-third of the entire textile turnover of the EU. Italy has about 840 000 textile workers. Italy is also Europe's leading exporter of clothing. The food industry in Italy is small scale and fragmented and wide open to foreign takeovers (Randlesome, 1993, p. 161).

After the depreciation of the lira, Italy enjoyed an export-led economic recovery earlier than other countries. However, its unemployment rates remain one of the highest in the European Union, reaching a peak of 12.2 per cent in January 1995 (European Commission, 1996, p. 99). Inflation increased in 1995 to 5.4 per cent as compared to 3.9 per cent the previous year (European Commission, 1996, p. 99).

In June 1994 as part of an overall package to revive the economy, the new government took direct action to stimulate labour demand, introducing the following measures:

- granting of tax breaks to firms that hire young people, unemployed or disadvantaged persons
- giving tax incentives to firms established by young entrepreneurs, unemployed and disadvantaged people. Over a three-year period, these firms would only pay a flat global tax, replacing a variety of taxes including the personal and local income taxes
- ending a temporary ban on local government recruitment

(OECD, 1995, p. 90)

Most banks in Italy are state-owned. Only two special credit institutions, IMI and Mediobanca have developed wide-ranging merchant-banking activities. The IMI specializes in acquisitions, and merchant-banking activity is performed by Mediobanca. Most major private groups, as well as a few foreign banks have shareholdings and a seat in the governing bodies of the bank, which thereby constitutes a clearing house and repository for all the interwoven shareholdings in key private enterprises (OECD, 1995, p. 77). Due to the relative lack of merchant-banking service and the narrowness of the market for corporate control, advisory services in mergers and acquisitions have been usually provided by business consultants, lawyers and fiscal experts.

Most economic opportunities are open to foreigners, as Italy's foreign investment laws are among the most liberal in Europe. Repatriation of capital and related earnings wihtout limit is guaranteed for 'productive' enterprises, that is those engaged in the production of goods and services requiring investment in capital equipment over an extended period (Johnson and Moran, 1992, p. 94).

Business practices

Italian business relationships are based on mutual dependence and a sense of mutual obligation most easily satisfied with members of the extended family (Mole, 1994, p. 58). Meetings are usually unstructured and informal. The purpose of meetings is to enable the decision takers to evaluate the mood of the others, to sense supporters and test the water, not usually to make decisions (Mole, 1994, p. 59). Decisions taken and agreed in formal meetings, minuted and scheduled for implementation may never happen.

Communication channels are complicated and informal contacts are vital. Formal presentations are not common in the Italian business environment and business etiquette is based on an easy formality. All correspondence should be in Italian. Professional titles are often used, but titles could mean relatively little in Italian companies, and very often the person who would normally have decision-making authority turns out to need approval. Italians have a high tolerance of inefficiency but low tolerance of arrogance or rudeness. Changing or cancelling appointments is unacceptable. The business dress is formal and conservative. Ninety per cent of Italians claim to be Roman Catholic, but few actually practise their religion, yet religion has always been a prime unifying factor in Italy. The Catholic Church still plays a significant social and political role (Johnson and Moran, 1992, p. 91).

LUXEMBOURG (Joined 1957)

Geography

The Duchy of Luxembourg is the smallest member of the EU. It is situated in north-western Europe, on the coalfields which extend from Lille in northern France through Belgium and into the Ruhr valley. Luxembourg is bordered by Germany to the east, Belgium to the north-west and France to the south.

Political background

Luxembourg is a constitutional monarchy. Executive powers are exercised by the grand duke and the council of government. The council consists of nine members: a prime minister and eight other ministers. The prime minister is the leader of the political party, or coalition of parties, possessing the most seats in parliament. The legislative power rests with the chamber of deputies, elected by the people of Luxembourg. In addition there is a second legislative body called the council of state. The grand duke appoints the representatives to this body. Legislative authority is vested in the unicameral chamber of deputies and in the cabinet. The chamber is elected by popular mandate for a term of five years. The Commission of the European Union has permanent offices in Luxembourg, and it is also home to the European Court of Justice.

Economic characteristics

Basic data:
- Population (000): 497 (1995)
- Land area (sq km): 585
- Gross domestic product (billion US dollars): 10.8 (1994)
- Percentage growth (US dollars) (1977–1994): 274.821
- Annual inflation rate (% growth): 2.2 per cent (1994)
- National currency: Luxembourg franc
- Exchange rate against US dollar: 29.39 (October 1995)
- Unemployment: 3.0 per cent (1994)
- Religion: mainly Roman Catholic 95 per cent
- Language: French, Letzeburgesch is the local French dialect, and German is also widely spoken as a first language, also Luxembourgish

(*Euromonitor*, European Marketing Data and Statistics, 1996)

Luxembourg is very highly industrialized for its size. Its major trading partners are Germany, Belgium and France. Steel industry remains the backbone of the Luxembourg economy. It is also flourishing as an international banking centre and is ranked as the third-largest banking centre in Europe (Johnson and Moran, 1992, p. 97), and is particularly strong in providing financial services and bond trading.

Business practices

The business environment in Luxembourg is very formal. A traditional social structure of titles and appropriately styled respect are still required. Addressing by surname is retained for much longer than is usually the case elsewhere in Europe (Gibbs, 1994, p. 171). Assertiveness, strong criticism and especially personal remarks are seen as aggressive and rude. (Mole, 1994, p. 139). Punctuality is very important, and the European practice of handshaking is much in evidence. Formal and conservative suits with shirts and ties are worn on most business occasions. The main languages spoken are French, German and Luxembourgish.

THE NETHERLANDS (Joined 1957)

Geography

The Netherlands is a small European territory occupying some 250 km of the North Sea coast, between Belgium in the south and Germany in the north and east. The country's strategic position on the Rhine, and close to Belgium, Luxembourg and Denmark ensure a prosperous role in foreign trade.

Political background

The kingdom of the Netherlands is a constitutional monarchy in which the monarch rules through a council of ministers. The bicameral parliament comprises a 150-member lower house (second chamber, or *Tweede Kamer*), whose members are elected by universal suffrage for a four-year term; and a 75-seat in the first chamber which is appointed by the various provincial legislatures for a term of four years. The Netherlands formally rules over the Antilles and Aruba, but in practice wide autonomy prevails.

Economic characteristics

Basic data:
- Population (000): 15 433 (1995)
- Land area (sq km): 41 160
- Gross domestic product (billion US dollars): 329.7 (1994)
- Percentage growth of GDP (1977–1994): 199.7
- Annual inflation rate (% growth): 2.8 per cent (1994)
- National currency: Netherlands guilde
- Exchange rate against US dollar: 1.60 (October 1995)
- Unemployment: 10.2 per cent (1994)
- Religion: Roman Catholic 38 per cent, Protestant 30 per cent

(*Euromonitor*, European Marketing Data and Statistics, 1996)

The Netherlands was one of the world's main seafaring nations during the sixteenth and seventeenth centuries and the hegemonic unit in the world prior to the ascendency of Britain, but is now mainly a manufacturing nation. The Dutch economy is based on private enterprise, and the government has little direct ownership (Johnson and Moran, 1992, p. 102). The Dutch have the most open economy in Europe. Petroleum products are of the utmost importance. There is also a large number of coast and international vessels providing cargo services, and an important ship servicing and repair industry around Rotterdam. The Dutch are one of the world's leading exporters of natural gas. Other leading export sectors are plastics and chemicals, agricultural products and electronics equipments. Main export crops include greenhouse vegetables, wheat, horticultural goods and vegetables. Industry is reasonably well developed with engineering, vehicle manufacture, electrical and electronics, chemicals, aerospace and petrochemicals all of international importance. Half of Europe's truck fleet is owned by the Dutch (Mole, 1994, p. 69). Major imports are machinery, transport equipment and raw materials. Banking, insurance and publishing are also key industries with extensive international alliances and investment (Johnson and Moran, 1992, p. 104). The most important trading partners are Germany and Belgium followed by France and the UK. The Netherlands has one of the highest rates of unemployment in Europe.

Business practices

Dutch business people are more worldly, well-travelled and probably more cosmopolitan than most of their foreign partners (Johnson and Moran, 1992, p. 99). Dutch business ethics are strict. Punctuality, straightforwardness and lack of pretension illustrate best Dutch business practices (Gibbs, 1994, p. 178). The Dutch place a high value on punctuality and have a compulsion to make productive use of every minute (Mole, 1994, p. 78). Speeches and formal presentations are frequently tinged with good humour. Greetings are formal, and the handshake is an all pervasive custom. Meetings are regular and frequent. They are primarily for decision making after thorough discussion.

The Dutch are less fashion-conscious than the Germans, Italians or Spanish (Johnson and Moran, 1992, p. 100). Men's suits are far less body tailored than they are in other European countries and are reserved for outside meetings and special occasions (Mole, 1994, p. 77). Business dress code in the Netherlands is generally informal. In some companies, this may mean open-necked shirts and sweaters and brown shoes, sometimes may be even down to jeans and t-shirts.

The official language is Dutch, but English, French and German are widely spoken and understood.

PORTUGAL (Joined 1986)

Geography

Portugal occupies about half of the Atlantic coast of the Iberian peninsula, and more than three-quarters of the west-facing section, with Spain its only immediate neighbour. The country is broadly rectangular in shape and extends only a maximum of 200 km inland. The Azores and Madeira also belong to Portugal. The terrain of the mainland country is largely mountainous inland, but there are innumerable fertile valleys. There is no north-south divide. Algarve is the main tourist centre while Lisbon and Oporto are the main business centres.

Political background

The republic of Portugal has an executive president who is elected by universal suffrage for a renewable term of five years. The president appoints the prime minister. Legislative authority is vested in the unicameral assembly of the republic, whose 230 members are elected by universal suffrage for up to four years at a time.

Economic characteristics

Basic data:

- Population (000): 9912 (1995)
- Land area (sq km): 91 630
- Gross domestic product (billion US dollars): 71.7 (1994)
- Percentage growth in GDP (1974–1994): 338.6
- Annual inflation rate (% growth): 4.9 per cent (1994)
- National currency: Portuguese escudo
- Exchange rate against US dollar: 150.13 (October 1995)
- Unemployment: 6.5 per cent (1994)
- Religion: mainly Roman Catholic

(*Euromonitor*, European Marketing Data and Statistics, 1996)

There is a sizeable cement industry in Portugal. Agriculture, however, remains the backbone of the economy with citrus fruits, olives, wines and vegetables predominating. Cork is grown for export and the country has an important fishery industry. Spain is the main trading partner in the European Union. Tourism is the third main source of revenue.

Current unemployment levels are low in comparison with other EU countries.

Business practices

Several elements discourage foreign investment in Portugal, the main one being the government bureaucracy, which must be patiently tolerated and which often turns away potential investors. Other disincentives include the inadequacy of the telecommunications and transportation systems within the country, and the lack of qualified management and poor organization across many industries (Johnson and Moran, 1992, p. 115).

Punctuality is another obstacle to successful business meetings. Sometimes waiting up to two hours is not unusual (Gibbs, 1994, p. 191). There is a wide usage of the title Doctor in Portugal. You need to recognise that this title does not have the implications which pertain to it in other countries, it only acknowledges the receipt of a first degree, but it is still polite to use it where appropriate (Gibbs, 1994, p. 191). Business relations are informal, with an informal code of dress.

SPAIN (Joined 1986)

Geography

Spain occupies the greater part of the Iberian peninsula, and commands coastal orientations in all four directions: eastward into the Mediterranean, south and west into the Atlantic, and north into the Bay of Biscay. Its only neighbours are Portugal, which it surrounds on both its land borders, and France across the Pyrenees. The territory of Spain also includes the

Balearic islands, the Canary islands off the Atlantic coast of Morocco and the Moroccan enclaves of Ceuta and Melilla.

Madrid is the geographical, political, and cultural centre of the nation. There are six distinct regions in Spain, Castile, in the centre of the country encompasses Madrid, and is the most densely populated. Castilian is spoken there. Catalonia is in the eastern part of the country and includes Barcelona. All of Spain tends to be insulated from the rest of Europe by the Pyrenees (Johnson and Moran, 1992, p. 120).

Spain is a predominantly urban country. Two-thirds of the population live in towns of over 20 000 people while there are 56 municipalities of over 100 000 inhabitants (Economist Intelligence Unit, 1995, p. 18). The immigrant population is relatively small with 283 000 immigrants legally resident in Spain, or 0.7 per cent of the total population.

Political background

Spain is a constitutional monarchy in which the king plays a relatively modest political role, although he is active in trade promotion. The Spanish parliament, or *Cortes*, is bicameral. The more important body is the lower house (Congress of Deputies) but to ensure effective government the constitution allows it less power over the executive than in most other west European countries. The 350-seat lower house is elected by a system of proportional representation through multi-member constituencies while the upper chamber (the Senate), which has powers of amendment has 208 directly elected members and a further 48 members designated by the regions. Elections must be held at least once every four years. The king has the power to dissolve the parliament on the advice of the prime minister or after a constructive vote of no confidence in the government in the *Cortes*. The prime minister is elected by the *Cortes*.

Economic characteristics

Basic data:
- Population (000): 39 170 (1995)
- Land area (sq km): 504 880
- Gross domestic product (billion US dollars): 482.8 (1994)
- Percentage growth in GDP (1977–1994): 299.8
- Annual inflation rate (% growth): 4.7 per cent (1994)
- National currency: peseta
- Exchange rate against US dollar: 123.70 (October 1995)
- Unemployment: 23.3 per cent (1994)
- Religion: Mainly Roman Catholic
- Languages: Spanish (Castilian, Catalan, Gallician), Basque

(*Euromonitor*, European Marketing Data and Statistics, 1996)

Spain is Europe's third-largest wine producer and the world's largest olive oil producer. Tourism is a key element of the Spanish economy and makes a crucial contribution to the balance of payments. Spain also has highest consumption of fish per head in the EU: an average 43 kg per person per year and the largest fishing fleet, of about 20 000 boats (Economist Intelligence Unit, 1995, p. 29).

Spain has a highly profitable retail banking sector which is dominated by BBV, Argentaria, Banco Popular and BCH. State participation in the sector is limited to a remaining 50 per cent holding in Argentaria (Economist Intelligence Unit, 1995, p. 24). There are two major banking mergers in Spain: Banco de Vizcaya and Banco de Bilbao, and Banco Central and Banco Hispanoamericano. Recently, a network of powerful regionally based savings banks have been expanding aggressively. The deposits of the two largest, the Barcelona-based La Caixa and Caja de Madrid, are similar to those of the top six banks.

The vehicle manufacturing industry is by far Spain's leading exporter, accounting for 23 per cent of total exports in 1993 (Economist Intelligence Unit, 1995, p. 31). This reflects Spain's position as the third-largest car producer in Europe and the fifth largest in the world. Seventy per cent of all cars produced in Spain are exported. The automotive industry is one of the few major sectors in which Spain registers a trade surplus. Others include fresh fruit and vegetables and the shoe and ceramic industries. Farming is still very important with a wide variety of crops grown in the lowland areas. Fruits, nuts, olives, tomatoes and peppers are chief export products. The fishing industry is very strong, while tourism is a major foreign exchange earner. The EU accounted for 68.7 per cent of Spanish exports in 1994 and 60.9 per cent of its imports (Economist Intelligence Unit, 1996, p. 31). France represents the main export destination of Spanish goods and in 1993, Spain overtook Germany as the main source of imports.

There was a sharp rise in unemployment particularly in industry and construction which rose by 41.3 per cent in the two-year period 1992–1993 to reach 22.7 per cent of the labour force – the highest level in the EU. (Economist Intelligence Unit, 1995, p. 15). The unemployment rate has fallen relatively moderately but has remained clearly above 20 per cent in 1995 (European Commission, 1996, p. 90). The downward trend in inflation is supported by moderate wage increases, a stable currency, a slowdown in import price growth and the anti-inflationary stance of the Bank of Spain (European Commission, 1996, p. 90).

Business practices

Class distinction is alive and well in Spain and the monarchy holds the highest place of honour of all. Spain is not a meetings culture (Mole, 1993, p. 89). Spanish business people like to be independent and make decisions on their own. The purpose of meetings is to communicate instructions. The idea that a meeting can be used to decide on an action plan, allocate responsibilities and coordinate implementation is a novelty. Communication is predominantly oral and face-to-face (Mole, 1993, p. 91) and there is a marked absence of correspondence and memos and staff noticeboards. Spanish business is very informal. Familiarity is a basic fact of Spanish life. However, family names and titles are used to address people until one becomes better acquainted. The business dress code on the other hand is generally very formal. Dark suits with navy or grey ties are preferred (Johnson and Moran, 1992, p. 118). It is, however, common to take off jackets and even loosen your tie. Manners are based on an easy and relaxed informality. Demonstrating superiority or intelligence or ability is not highly valued (Mole, 1994, p. 94). Spaniards have a great sense of personal pride and honour. Technical ability, professionalism, competence does not concern a Spaniard as much as pride in personal qualities.

Catholicism is embraced by 98 per cent of the population.

SWEDEN (Joined 1995)

Geography

Sweden is roughly the same size as Spain. It occupies the eastern and southern section of the Scandinavian peninsula which runs south-west from the Article Circle to meet with Denmark across the narrow sea channel which gives access to the Baltic from the North Sea. About half of the country is covered by forest, and there are almost 100 000 lakes. The main cities are Stockholm, the capital and commercial and political centre of Sweden, while Gothenburg is the country's largest port, and the home of a number of important Swedish industries and companies.

Political background

The kingdom of Sweden is a constitutional monarchy in which the king appoints the prime minister on the basis of parliamentary advice. Legislative authority is vested in a unicameral 394-seat *Oarlkiament* which is elected by universal suffrage for a term of only three years. Swedish society is based on the exercise of local autonomy by county councils and municipalities. There are 23 county councils and about 2809 municipalities. The tasks of the local government sector fall into two distinct categories: those within the general power granted to municipalities and those based on special legislation. Municipalities and county councils conduct their own affairs. Under the general power granted to local governments, they devote themselves to tasks in such areas as cultural affairs, leisure activities, streets and roads, parks, communications, water and sewage and electricity generation.

Economic characteristics

Basic data:
- Population (000): 8816 (1995)
- Land area (sq km): 449 790
- Gross domestic product (billion US dollars): 205.4 (1994)
- Percentage growth in GDP (1977–1994): 149.8
- Annual inflation rate (% growth): 2.2 per cent (1994)
- National currency: Swedish kronor
- Exchange rate against US dollar: 7.03 (October 1995)
- Religion: Evangelical Lutheran Church 95 per cent

(*Euromonitor*, European Marketing Data and Statistics, 1996)

The Swedish economy, although nominally among the most affluent in northern Europe has high taxation levels enough to depress real living standards. The service sector is growing at the expense of the manufacturing sector. Engineering, the largest sector accounts for more than 45 per cent of industrial production and about 50 per cent of Swedish exports (Department of Trade and Industry, *Country Profile: Sweden*, 1993, p. 15). Swedish firms own 10 per cent of all paper production within the EU (Department of Trade and Industry, *Country Profile: Sweden*, 1993, p. 17). A relatively small number of companies account for the production of foodstuffs. There is a state monopoly on sales of wine and spirits. State-owned companies dominate the production, importation and sale of alcoholic beverages. Fifty per cent of Swedish exports go to the European Union. Germany is by far Sweden's largest export market, receiving 15 per cent of total exports. The UK is Sweden's second largest export market. As far as imports are concerned, Germany is the largest supplier, Britain is Sweden's second largest trading partner (Department of Trade and Industry, *Country Profile: Sweden*, 1993, p. 19).

The central bank is the Bank of Sweden (Riksbanken) and it is the oldest central bank in the world. It is operated under the supervision of the Parliament. The chairman of its board of governors is appointed by the government, and the bank liaises with the government to coordinate economic policy. Its functions are the same as those of other central banks: to issue notes, administer the foreign exchange reserves and the country's gold and to act as the bank of the state and of the other banks. Sweden has three groups of deposit banks: commercial, savings and cooperative banks. There are also 20 international banks established since 1986. Besides the banks, there are approximately 100 authorized finance companies, many of them owned by banks whose main lines of business are leasing, factoring, inventory financing and consumer financing (Department of Trade and Industry, *Country Profile: Sweden*, 1993, p. 63).

Unemployment is very high in Sweden. It has risen especially since 1991. In March 1993 official unemployment was 7.5 per cent compared to 4.4 per cent in January 1992 (Department of Trade and Industry, *Country Profile: Sweden*, 1993, p. 19).

Business practices

Swedes are very competitive. Similar to the Japanese, they reserve their best competitive weapons for their foreign rivals (Johnson and Moran, 1992, p. 125). Swedes have a taste for teamwork. Good manners are valued and the display of open emotion is rare. Doing business in Sweden requires the typical restraints of northern European culture. Handshaking is a standard practice. Correspondence and trade literature may be written in English, but all instructional material or labels are required to be in Swedish. The business dress code is slightly more conservative and formal than styles in western Europe. A dark business suit is generally acceptable.

Ninety-five per cent of Swedes are nominally Evangelical Lutherans. Church attendance, however, is low and the church's impact on Swedish political and cultural life is minimal (Johnson and Moran, 1992, p. 126).

THE UNITED KINGDOM (Joined 1972)

Geography

The UK consists of England, Scotland, Wales and Northern Ireland. The first three constitute Great Britain. The United Kingdom lies off the coast of western continental Europe between the Atlantic Ocean and the North Sea. It comprises mainly two distinct land masses – the larger incorporating England, Scotland and the Principality of Wales, and the smaller consisting of Northern Ireland, actually the north-western part of the island of Ireland and an area of intense political dispute particularly since 1960.

Political background

The UK is a constitutional and hereditary monarchy even though it has no written constitution. Although the monarch is head of state, all effective authority resides with the elected lower chamber of parliament, the House of Commons, which is supplemented in an advisory capacity by a House of Lords (upper house). The monarch retains the power to call and dissolve parliament, although this is almost invariably done at the request of the prime minister. The monarch must also give formal assent to legislation. The UK has no written constitution as such. It exists as a body of statutes and common law, which is based on judicial decision and precedent, and convention.

The parliament is divided into two houses: the House of Lords and the House of Commons. The former consists of a mixture of hereditary peers, and life peers who are nominated by the main political parties as working members or who receive a peerage as an honour. The main purpose of the House of Lords is to revise laws suggested by the House of Commons. The House of Commons is democratically elected and passes laws which are then checked, debated and subject to revision by the Lords. The House of Lords is also the highest Court of Appeal for England, Wales and Northern Ireland in both civil and criminal cases. The House of Commons consists of 651 members elected by the majoritarian system. The country is divided into 651 constituencies, each of which returns one member of the House of Commons. The candidate who polls the highest number of votes in each constituency is elected (EIU, *Country Profile: United Kingdom*, 1995, p. 8).

Economic characteristics

Basic data:

- Population (000): 58 276 (1995)
- Land area (sq km) 244 755
- Gross domestic product (billion US dollars): 1022.8 (1994)
- Percentage growth in GDP (1977–1994): 320.3
- Annual inflation rate (% growth): 2.5 per cent (1994)
- National currency: pound sterling
- Exchange rate against US dollar: 0.63 (October 1995)
- Unemployment: 9.9 per cent (1994)
- Religion: Protestant

(*Euromonitor*, European Marketing Data and Statistics, 1996)

The service sector is today the strongest area of the economy with the country specializing in banking and insurance activities for the worldwide market. The UK is a major financial centre, ranking third in the world after New York and Tokyo. Most activity takes place in the City of London which has the greatest concentration of banks and the largest insurance market in the world. Foreign banks are also strongly represented in the UK. The Big Four London clearing banks are National Westminster, Barclays, Midland and Lloyds. These banks carry out most of the commercial banking in England and Wales. In Scotland there are three clearing banks: The Bank of Scotland, The Clydesdale Bank and the Royal Bank of Scotland. Building societies have begun to compete with the clearing banks by providing current and deposit account facilities.

The Bank of England, a public sector body since 1946 is central to the financial system. Its banking department functions as banker to government and to banks in general. The bank's role includes implementing monetary policy through influencing interest rates in the bill market, using direct controls and restricting bank credit. It regulates the issues of notes and coins, manages the issue of government stock, and intervenes for the government in the foreign-exchange market. The central bank also exercises general supervision over the banking system and acts as lender of last resort to banks (Stone, 1995, p. 134).

Unemployment has recently fallen from its recent high of close to 3 million in 1993 to below 2.5 million in 1995, which is more than 2 per cent below the EU average (European Commission, 1996, p. 119). The government welcomes foreign investment. It does not discriminate between different types of investment but particularly favours investment in the high-technology industries. The government, however, offers little in the way of incentives to encourage foreign investment. Aid to foreign investors is available but only on a limited budget (EIU, *Country Report: United Kingdom*, 1995, p. 25). Foreign interests tend to be concentrated in the medium and high research-intensive sectors, with proportionately high representation in chemicals, mechanical engineering, electrical and electronic engineering, motor vehicles, instruments and office machinery. In some sectors (notably computers, consumer electrical and electronic goods, cars and North Sea oil) foreign producers are dominant (Stone, 1995, p. 126).

Trade with the UK's EU partners between 1993–1994 (excluding the three new EU member states) accounted for well over 50 per cent of both exports and imports in value terms. Germany remains the second largest single export market after the USA. Germany is also the largest source of UK imports. (EIU, *Country Report: United Kingdom*, 1995, p. 29). Manufacturing is the second most important area in UK. It encompasses a wide range of products including both consumer and heavy industrial goods, aerospace and information technology.

Business practices

British business relations are quite rigid, with a high sense of power hierarchies. However, first names are used immediately among colleagues of all ranks and both sexes and is increasingly common among all business contacts. Visitors should not be too casual or relaxed. Feet should always be kept off the furniture and legs should not be conspicuously crossed. Men should keep their jackets closed. Loud voices are rude. Shouting across open spaces is improper (Moran, 1992, p. 68). Humour is accepted but only if it is natural. The handshake is a customary form of introduction but people who meet regularly do not shake hands. Backslapping or any other form of physical display is considered improper.

Meetings are the most important and time consuming management tool in the UK. Only the least important decisions or instructions are not formulated, discussed, approved, ratified, communicated, or implemented at a meeting (Mole, 1993, p. 104). A meeting without a concrete result of some sort is deemed a failure. Meetings are informal in style and begin and end with a social conversation. Participants are expected to make a contribution, if only questions and not necessarily in their specialist area. Opinions are encouraged and listened to. Punctuality is important.

The British style of dress is more conservative than in many areas of the world. A dark suit is essential – black, dark blue or grey, plain or striped shirts and polished black shoes should be worn for all business and social engagements. The primary religion in the UK is Protestant with approximately 27 million people belonging to the Church of England. About nine per cent of the population is Roman Catholic and there are substantial Islamic communities made up of unassimilated immigrants from India, Pakistan and other foreign colonies (Johnson and Moran, 1992, p. 70).

Finally, it is worth noting that Norway was to have joined the European Community in 1972, along with the UK, Denmark and Ireland. However, following a national referendum, Norway withdrew its application in September 1972.

BUSINESS OPERATIONS IN THE NEW EUROPE

Two people were walking through a part of the Black Forest where it was rumoured a very dangerous lion lurked. They took a break and were sitting in the sun when one of them changed from his hiking boots to jogging shoes. The other one smiled and asked:

'You don't think you can run away from the lion with those jogging shoes?'
'No', he replied. 'I just need to be faster than you'.

Companies that wait will be those who lose. 'It is not necessary to be first, but what is needed is to be faster than the others' (Guianluigi, 1991).

The creation of a Single Market of 350 million consumers constitutes a major challenge for companies. Every company with operations or sales in more than one European country has to consider the implications of the Single Market for its business activities, while in the modern world, even small domestic firms with no foreign operations are subject to the increasing impact of the internationalization of business. Community firms may find their current business threatened by the changes in customs and supply practices or changes in technical regulations. Their own national and European markets could be threatened by the arrival of new competitors, not only from within the Community but also from foreign firms. US and Japanese multinational firms, attracted by the harmonized market, are now rushing to expand across the Community. These giant multinationals are realizing the importance of securing a presence in Europe in order to maintain their international competitive advantage against their global rivals. Business opportunities and threats within the EU are thus equally affected by aspects of the increasingly global political economy and the position of the EU within it. John Owens, then deputy director general of the Confederation of British Industry, warned in January 1989 that nearly 10 000 UK companies were sleepwalking towards 1992, and that many of them would go out of business in the 1990s unless they started preparing now for the complete abolition of trade barriers within the European Community (Walker, 1989).

The central objective of Part Two is to trace the impact of the Single Market on European, US and Japanese firms and examine their strategic responses to the challenges created by the 'new' European business environment. On the basis of this evaluation, some guidance will then be offered about how to compete and manage successfully in the 'new Europe'. Chapter Six describes business reaction to the creation of the Single European Market and examines the various strategies being implemented in the 'new' European business environment. Chapter Seven provides guidance on how to compete successfully in the 'new' Europe. The existence of a multicultural diversity in the European Union poses many challenges for business. The traditional marketing concept needs to be adapted to meet the needs of demanding European customers. This 'renewed' marketing thinking is introduced in Chapter Eight. The divergence of culture across Europe is another difficulty facing firms operating in the EU. Failure to address this issue can be very costly. Chapter Nine examines the impact of cultural diversity on doing business in the EU and provides various frameworks for analysing and managing the European cultural environment.

COMPETITIVE STRATEGIES FOR EUROPE

Tugul Atamer and Gerry Johnson conducted a survey of five major industries in Europe (breweries, retailing, book publishing, retail banking and the automobile industry) to see what strategies companies were developing in order to deal with the new competitive situation in Europe. Nineteen researchers of eight nationalities were involved in this research. Managers from 90 companies in seven member states were interviewed. The overall message and conclusion from the study was that managers cannot expect to maintain strategic success in Europe by a reliance on the 'proven strategic formulae of the past'. Europe is developing in ways that challenge managers to understand and cope with the nature of this complexity, and to review their management systems to cope with it (Calori and Lawrence, 1991, p. 229). The aim of this chapter is to provide managers and business students with an overview of business reaction to the creation of the Single European Market and to introduce the various competitive strategies adopted by multinational firms in their European operations.

LEARNING OBJECTIVES

- To explain what is meant by business strategy
- To examine European competitive strategies formulated and implemented by US, Japanese and European firms in the Single European Market
- To provide a wide range of case examples illustrating experiences of firms operating in the 'new' European business environment

THE NATURE AND FUNCTION OF BUSINESS STRATEGY

Before examining some of the most successful strategies developed in order to survive the increased competition and challenges created by the Single Market in Europe, it is important to understand what business strategy is all about.

There is a lack of consensus over what strategy is. A variety of definitions and conceptions exists in the literature of management. For some, strategy is the effective adaptation by the firm to its environment. It refers to the process of finding the perfect match, or fit between the internal capabilities of the firm, and the opportunities and threat in its external environment. Strategy, in this view is a set of plans, decisions and actions for achieving a firm's successful adaption to its environment. Others, refer to strategy as simply a process of finding the best way to meet the firm's goals and objectives and designing effective administrative plans and implementation decisions. Strategy is also often referred to as an internal perspective emphasizing the firm's way of doing things, particularly with regard to people and processes.

Despite these different approaches, 'what distinguishes strategy from all other kinds of business planning is – in a word, competitive advantage. Without competitors there would be no need for strategy, for the sole purpose of strategic planning is to enable the company to gain, as efficient as possible, a sustainable edge over its competitors' (Ohmae, 1983, p. 36).

Examples of factors contributing to a firm's competitive advantage include:

- ownership of patents, brands, know-how or other intellectual property
- superior product offer, novel product design features, high-quality output and/or excellent customer care facilities
- economies of scale, efficient organization and/or the possession of modern machinery, equipment or premises
- effective distribution systems, ability to service niche markets, an attractive corporate image, good public relations and customer loyalty the firm's brands
- abilities to alter the firm's organization structure quickly and to introduce new models at short notice
- easy access to financial capital or high levels of financial reserves
- well-qualified and highly motivated employees
- ownership of raw materials or other input suppliers and of distribution outlets
- superior R&D facilities
- access to low-cost labour

(Bennett, 1996a, p. 335)

Accordingly the job of the strategist is to 'to achieve superior performance, relative to competition, in the key factors for success of the business' (Ohmae, 1983, p. 91). Some common critical success factors include: fast and reliable delivery, product quality and customer care, the ease with which a product can be modified, has appealing features, fulfils a clear need and has multiple uses, the rate of expansion of the market and whether it is concentrated in accessible areas, brand images and the location of products in their life cycles. (Bennett, 1996a, p. 336).

In the construction of any business strategy three main players must be taken into account. These are the corporation itself, the customer and the competition, which have become commonly known as Ohmae's strategic three Cs (Ohmae, 1983, pp. 91–162).

1. *Corporate-based strategies* These are the functional aims to maximize the company's strengths relative to the competition. The role of functional strategy, according to Ohmae, is to design and deliver a cost-effective function, which is done in three ways. The first method is to reduce costs much more effectively than the competition. The second method is simply to exercise selectivity in terms of orders accepted, products offered or functions to be performed. The third method is to reduce functional cost and to share a certain key function among the corporation's other business or even with other companies.
2. *Customer-base strategies* Since the corporation cannot reach out to all its customers with equal effectiveness, it will have to segment the market and identify one or more subsets of customers within the total market, concentrating its efforts upon meeting their needs. Segmentation can be done either by product objectives (different ways customers use the products), or by the corporation's own circumstances, such as the corporation's ability to sell and the constraints limiting its resources.
3. *Competitor-based strategies* Competitor-based strategies can be constructed by looking at

possible sources of differentiation in functions ranging from purchasing, design, and engineering to sales and servicing (Ohmae, 1983, p. 126). Firms can also create competitive advantage by 'perceiving or discovering new and better ways to compete in an industry and bringing them to market, which is ultimately an act of innovation' (Porter, 1990. p. 45). Some competitor-based strategies include the power of an image, exploiting functional strength, capitalizing on profit and cost structure differences.

Figure 6.1 illustrates the way in which a firm could achieve a competitive advantage over its competitors using the strategic triangle.

FIRMS' STRATEGIC REACTION TO THE CREATION OF A SINGLE EUROPEAN MARKET

The removal of trade barriers and the new framework for competition introduced by the creation of the Single European Market has pushed many European, US and Japanese firms to formulate new strategies for sustaining their competitive advantage in European markets. The most popular competitive strategies developed so far can be grouped into three categories, using the Ohmae strategic triangle as illustrated in Fig. 6.1.

1. *Customer-based strategies* These include local production through mergers and acquisitions, 'globalization', market integration and product differentiation.
2. *Corporate-based, or functional strategies* These include consolidation and downsizing, restructuring, subcontracting and outsourcing.
3. *Competitor-based strategies or strategies for optimizing functional performance* These include product quality, product innovation and cross-border link-up with EU partners commonly known as strategic alliances.

The best way to gain an insight into how these strategies were developed and implemented is through case studies, and comments made by a distinguished group of business leaders giving their views and ideas on how to compete successfully in Europe. Despite its very prescriptive approach, the next section could be used as a springboard by business managers towards the articulation of their own competitive strategy for Europe.

Figure 6.1   The strategic triangle

Customer-based strategies

Local production

Despite the removal of trade barriers, Europe still comprises a myriad of countries with different cultures, languages, histories, customs, tastes and preferences, not to mention levels of wealth. Business firms cannot reach out to all these customers with equal effectiveness. In addition to segmenting the European market and identifying one or more subsets of customers within the total market and concentrating their efforts on meeting their needs, US and Japanese firms had to relocate their production facilities into Europe to sustain their competitive edge. Their invasion of the European car industry illustrates this strategy well.

CASE STUDY 6.1: Localization strategy in the car industry

Nissan's penetration into the European market began as early as 1959. The company concentrated first on the northern European countries by exporting to Finland. It did not enter western Europe until the late 1960s, where it began to move location production due to increasing restriction from the EC. In 1983, Nissan acquired a 35 per cent equity stake in Motor Iberica, SA, the largest commercial vehicle manufacturer in Spain. It started to manufacture these vehicles under its own brand and gradually increased its shareholdings to 68 per cent by 1989.

In 1986 Nissan founded Nissan Motor Manufacturing UK, Ltd, to make passenger cars in the UK. The factory in Sunderland, in north-east England was completed in 1986 and started producing an upper medium-sized car called the Bluebird. The UK-made Bluebird began to be exported to EU member countries in late 1988 after reaching 70 per cent local content.

In the autumn of 1988 Nissan formulated a plan to strengthen its competitive position until 1992. The main goals to be achieved were:

1. To raise Nissan's market share in the European car market to 4.5 per cent by 1992 and increasing car production in the UK to 200 000 and truck production in Spain to 100 000.
2. To improve Nissan's brand image by reinforcing the quality of its sales and service organizations in Europe.
3. To further decentralize Nissan's responsibility for European operations, including product design, production, marketing and sales.

(Lynch, 1993, p. 232)

Toyota too moved towards local production in Europe and established production plants both in the former West Germany and in the UK. **Honda** moved the production of its Mazda into the UK, its Suzuki into Spain and its Subaru into France.

Ford the world's second-largest vehicle manufacturer, with an output of nearly six million vehicles in 1993 (about 12 per cent of global industry total) controlled 21.8 per cent of the UK market accounting for more than one in five cars sold. Ford reported growth to 22.3 per cent in its UK share in 1994, and 11.8 per cent of new car registrations in western Europe. Ford employs around 500 000 people, directly and indirectly, in the region (European Motor Business, 1st Quarter, 1995, p. 68). Ford was also the third-biggest supplier in Germany and Italy in 1993, accounting for just under 10 per cent of new car sales in each market. In France, it controls 8.1 per cent of the market and in Spain 14.4 per cent of new registrations. In Portugal, Ford has established a joint venture with

Volkswagen which began in 1995. The vehicle is being made by a jointly owned company Auto Europe Ltd.

Local production through acquisition, however, has its problems. Many manufacturers in Europe have been burned by an acquisition that turned out to be strategically or financially unwise, for example Ford and Jaguar, GM and SAAB, VW and Spain's SEAT, Fiat and Alfa Romeo. Meshing separate engineering operations and product lines – especially across national boundaries – is difficult and often results in the weaker partner being consumed by the stronger one (Taylor, 1994).

In their recent BMW and Rover deal, **BMW** has vowed not to integrate the two companies. Helmut Panke, formerly BMW's chief strategist and head of its North American operations claimed: 'You don't want to lose the creative independence in either organization or the feeling that each is responsible for what it does'. BMW has developed a novel strategy for Rover. It wants to use Rover's popular-priced cars to open new markets – particularly in developing nations – for BMW's high-priced cars. It also gets to sell Rover's much sought four-wheel drive vehicles, and it hopes to use Rover's historical but dormant brands such as MG and Austin-Healey, on new limited-production sports cars.

The 'glocal' or global – local approach to the Single Market
Ralph Cooper, president of Coca-Cola's European Community Group summarizes this new approach as follows:

> In Coca-Cola we're seeing a dichotomy taking place in business today. Some of the customers of the Coca-Cola system in Europe, such as large international companies, are becoming more European. Many of them want one programme for Europe. On the other hand, the consumer is becoming more local, in our view. We are advertising Coca-Cola in Barcelona today in two languages – Spanish and Catalan. It is a recent phenomenon and we see it taking place in Scotland, the French regions, the German *Länder* ... People are becoming more culturally attuned their localities and marketers have to recognize it and be prepared to deal with it. To deal with new Single Market.

Ralph Cooper explains further 'Coca-Cola is trying to combine a European concept" with local implementation'. Cooper runs the European Community Group from Atlanta, Georgia, with a staff of five plus the functional heads of finance, external affairs, marketing, etc. But the actual operations are in Europe, where the company has a European Operating Board that meet with him in Europe once a quarter, and sometimes more often, to discuss strategies, aims, review operations, and share experiences. As Cooper puts it, (the company) is:

> much more integrated than ever, but the marketing is still very local, underneath an umbrella strategy. Let me give you an example. In supply, I have a person who is head of supply for Europe. Why is that? Because we looked at our infrastructure. Take a simple case like cans. If we let each country manage its own can business exclusively, somebody somewhere is going to run out of cans because all of a sudden the weather is very hot in Germany, or in France, and the business takes off and that operation runs out of cans. In the past we would have lost those sales because we were operating inside that country. Now we have a European supply group whose job it is to make sure that we always have an ample supply of finished products – whether it is coming from franchised bottlers or from company-owned canning facilities or wherever.

(Bloom, *et al.* 1994, pp. 50–51).

To balance the need for 'insiderism', or a local market presence with economies of scale, Coca-Cola started to build a few pan-European alliances for bottling and distribution infrastructure, while still relying on local or regional networks and maintaining close-to-the-field multi-local marketing and account service representatives (Coca-Cola Annual Reports, 1990–1991; Friedman, 1992). According to Coca-Cola's president Donald Keough:

> the key growth in Europe is better selling right there, where the cola meets the customer. That means closer relationships with retailers, bolder merchandising, cheaper prices and faster delivery.
>
> (quoted in Sellers, 1990)

The board game 'Trivial Pursuit' provides another illustrative example of the 'glocal' approach to doing business in Europe, where the questions were adapted to match the needs of each targeted segment and each culturally different market. For example, in Spain, both Spanish and Catalan versions of the game were available. Such an approach assisted the company to quickly exploit national events and celebrations: thus, in France, a French revolution edition was ready to coincide with the 200th anniversary (Brown and McDonald, 1994, p. 289). The following case illustrates how Nestlé had to develop a strategy to address the problem of localization in Italy where a strong coffee-consumption culture is one which has been highly receptive to the concept of Nescafé instant coffee.

CASE STUDY 6.2: Nescafé: glocal strategy

Nestlé is the world's leading producer of instant coffee. It is also the major buyer of raw coffee. The concept of instant coffee was born in the 1930s when stocks far exceeded demand. Over-production and excess stocks of raw coffee led to the search for an optimum method by which coffee could be preserved in concentrated and soluble form while retaining its flavour.

Nescafé's launch in 1938 just before the Second World War, resulted in rapid diffusion. Nescafé was adopted by all the armed forces involved in the conflict because of its ease and convenience of use. Consumption of instant coffee quickly spread throughout the world. By 1988 the world drank more than 170 million cups of Nescafé a day. The advertising budget to promote Nescafé worldwide amounted to 350 million Swiss francs annually, and its market share of total coffee consumption ranged from between 10 per cent and 30 per cent in its various markets throughout the world.

Instant coffee was introduced into Italy in 1962. It has been in the Italian market for over 30 years yet it had never quite succeeded. Because the Italian market possesses a very specific and deep-rooted coffee culture, Nestlé's main objective when it first launched Nescafé was to have the product, although soluble, perceived as 'real' coffee. Every effort was made to affirm the goodness and quality of the product, comparing it directly to other Italian coffees. However, between 1979 to 1983 the message did not convince consumers in terms of product quality or goodness. Nescafé decided to change its advertising to present testimonials by real people. The message aimed to show that Nescafé was a coffee suited to and made for any one who wants something more out of life. But the advertising once again did not improve the image. Nescafé was still an unattractive product to those who wanted gratification and a recharge from their coffee and sales decreased very slowly.

Nescafé then discovered a niche market in those aged 55 and above. Here, whose consumption of Nescafé was biased towards use by older people who were more sensitive to the effects of caffeine. Nescafé was preferred for its less aggressive image and for its ease of preparation during moments of relaxation. Also Nescafé was considered useful in Italian families' emergency provisions, especially when on holiday.

(adapted from Costabile and Ostillio with Valdani, 1994)

Market integration and product differentiation

So the job in the Single Market will be to do both – integrate and differentiate at the same time.
(president Vittorelli, Pirelli vice-president quoted in Bloom, 1994, p. 53)

It can be done, I picture it in my mind like the human body: it is a unity, yet at the same time it has all these different parts able to move in different directions doing different things. As an ensemble they form the individual, who is unique.
(Papalexopoulos of Titan Cement, quoted in Bloom, 1494, p. 53)

To succeed in the Single Market, companies are having to integrate diversity. Many companies are recognizing this by building the integration of diversity into their operating structures. What results is a European form of the 'glocal' strategy and organization, mixing global and local approaches. BP was structured in a spirit of integration. As Robert Horton explains:

When I took over I inherited an organization that was designed to have 12 businesses in 70 countries. But when you looked at it, we really had three businesses and three regions: America, Europe and the Far East. Once you make that sort of intellectual breakthrough, you can do all sorts of things. We saw that we didn't have to have separate brands in the United States, Europe, and Japan, so we re-branded the whole thing. We now run the corporation worldwide from London, but the refining and marketing company for Europe is sited in Brussels, so we run the UK from Brussels. ... of course the savings are enormous. Instead of having 12 head offices, 12 research centres, 12 sales forces, you have one of each. And instead of having 12 strategies, you have one. I do believe that you should segment your markets, but by product. You should not segment markets simply by geography.
(Bloom, 1994, p. 52)

Corporate-based strategies

Some of the most cost-effective strategies recently developed to survive increased competition in the Single European Market are the following.

Consolidation and downsizing

One of several ways of reducing functional costs and remain economically competitive is achieved through consolidation and downsizing or rationalization. This is illustrated, for example, by Renault's recent re-structuring and rationalization plan for its European production operations which was aimed at reducing the number of factories, increasing plant integration and consolidating production volume into larger plants to achieve greater scale economies. Major changes were included in the rationalization process such as the phasing out of the Billancourt assembly plant in France and the transfer of operations to other facilities in France and Spain. The plant at Valladolid in Spain was also closed, with operations transferred to two other Spanish assembly plants.

This trend towards rationalization is not restricted to firms or sectors in immediate trouble. European multinationals such as ICI, Unilever, Nestlé, Cadbury Schweppes to name but a few, have recently gone through similar changes aimed at reducing costs and improving efficiency through the closing of inefficient plants, the reduction of manpower levels, and the consolidation of production into fewer, larger facilities (Sparrow and Hiltrop, 1994, p. 101)

US firms operating in Europe have also begun to reconsider their European strategy in terms of organization and operations in order obtain an optimal balance. They are now increasingly rationalizing their production and logistics operations, centralizing their common functions such as finance, R&D and marketing, while decentralizing their decision-making responsibility from corporate headquarters to product-line managers with cross-border responsibilities, and to local sales and service offices. For example, in order to manage local customer differences, Levi's European operations are organized on a country-by-country basis, with each unit fully empowered to take responsibility for customer financing, sales and distribution in their own markets. Levi's European headquarters coordinates pan-European production, merchandising and advertising to capitalize on economies of scale. Additionally, Levi-Strauss has a worldwide information system that is used to control production and inventory levels to take advantage of flexible, cost-effective production alternatives.

The growing trend towards downsizing is best illustrated by European auto-makers. Peugeot cut five per cent of its jobs in 1944 and another four per cent in 1995. Renault started downsizing early in 1989 and its payroll at the end of 1995 was 140 000, 17 per cent less than five years ago. It plans to continue shedding about 2000 jobs a year. Volkswagen which lost $1 billion in 1995, started late and may not have cut deeply enough. After trimming its payroll at six German plants by 12 000 to 102 000 it negotiated to put all its employees on a four-day week.

Restructuring

Restructuring mostly involves gaining clarity and transparency *vis-à-vis* the financial performance and strategic position of an individual business and decentralization or the setting-up of business units, portfolio analysis and portfolio planning processes (Doz, 1991, p. 304). The process is clearly illustrated in the case below.

CASE STUDY 6.3: Restructuring Pilkington

Until recently, Pilkington's European production system was typical of a multi-domestic configuration in which most of the factories supplied their national market. For example, British factories tended to supply Great Britain, German factories did the same for Germany, Austria for Austria and Switzerland for Switzerland, and so on ... Then the company decided to adopt pan-European organization along business lines in the flat and safety glass operations.

The new matrix organization adopted by Pilkington for its European operations has been effective since 1 April, 1993 and has three objectives. First, to establish an organization which aims at achieving strong product leadership throughout Europe, second, to optimize the group's resource allocation and improve efficiency, and finally, to develop international management structures that conform to local laws and practices.

The new structure comprises four business lines: automotive original equipment, automotive glass replacement, building products, and special glasses, each line having its own executive manager. The building products line is itself divided into two regions: northern Europe (Great Britain, Finland, Sweden, Norway, Poland, France and Spain) and central Europe (Germany, Austria, Switzerland, Benelux and Italy). The whole is coordinated by a chief executive for Europe who has every business line manager and country manager under his responsibility. The country managers are in charge of institutional communication, public relations, and legal matters concerning accounting and personnel relations. There is no subordination relationship between business line managers and country managers. Middle managers report to one or the other as required.

Setting up this new structure has not been easy and took about 18 months to become fully operational. Business line managers had to be selected carefully: some are British, others

German or Finnish. Today, each is responsible for all the industrial subsidiaries in their entire geographical area and they can adopt the production configuration of their choice in order to improve efficiency significantly. Each subsidiary unit becomes specialized in a certain number of products and supplies the whole European territory. Thus the new matrix structure fosters the rationalization of Pilkington's entire European production system and strongly encourages the adoption of a European strategy and management system.

(Adapted from Calori and de Woot, 1994, pp. 223–224)

Restructuring can also be achieved through national consolidations. National banks, and frequently the state encourage the merger of weaker companies into stronger ones and the creation of national groups in the hope that they will become large enough to stand a chance in international competition. In France, Germany, Italy and the UK such a policy of consolidation into national champions has been at work in a wide range of industries, including heavy industrial equipment, computers, aircraft and space systems, chemicals, electrical machinery, robotics, and others.

Mergers and acquisitions can also be adopted in the restructuring process. However, joint ventures and alliances, because of their 'softer' approach, as Doz (1991) argues, are more likely to bring the same rationalization and re-structuration benefits as mergers are expected to provide. (The problems commonly associated with mergers and acquisitions were identified earlier under local production.) Partnerships provide a relatively low-cost opportunity to learn about the value of the partner's skills and resources before having to make a major resource commitment. The process of collaboration itself allows this assessment of skills and resources (Doz, 1991, p. 309). Partnerships allow participants to identify potential merger opportunities better and may solve the problem of unnecessary assets accompanying mergers and provide opportunities to leverage the partners' competencies better. Nestlé and General Mills, for example, set up a joint venture only for their breakfast cereals in Europe, remaining independent in all other areas. Finally partnerships usually involve less risk of tying up resources in unnecessary assets than do acquisitions.

Subcontracting
The reliance on subcontracting for the supply of goods and services is gradually being adopted by many European firms. Marks and Spencer, for example, contract out all their production to specialized firms. The company's philosophy is to concentrate on 'core' activities – those in which the management have expertise – and to leave 'peripheral' activities to others.

Outsourcing
The recession and slow growth of the early 1990s have led many companies in Europe to focus on core activities and consequently devolve many other functions to external specialists. In 1994, the EU outsourcing market was worth some ECU 1.7 billion, a figure that is expected to rise to ECU 3.5 billion over the next decade (Turner, 1996, p. 19). Cost and technological flexibility are the most frequently cited reasons why out sourcing has emerged particularly in corporate telecommunications in Europe. The rapidity of technological change and the costs of updating the network place a large financial burden on firms. Given these large capital costs many firms are deciding to devolve network upgrading to a carrier who can share such costs among a large number of users.

Competitor-based strategies

Product quality

To remain competitive in the European Single Markets, low-cost leadership alone is not sufficient any more. Quality improvement is becoming increasingly essential even necessary for economic success in Europe. One way of achieving quality is through the implementation of ISO 9000 standards. ISO 9000 was originally designed to meet the need for product quality assurances in purchasing agreements. It refers to the voluntary registration and certification of a manufacturer's quality system. A company requests a certifying body to conduct a registration assessment for certification every four years, and this is becoming an important competitive tool in the Single European Market (Caetora, 1993).

Quality can also be achieved through the introduction of intensive training to stimulate creativity and problem solving in the labour force. In the European car industry, workers duties now go beyond purely assembly work to include quality, maintenance and materials management. BMW allocates £50 million from its annual budget on training, equivalent to the annual budget of a small university (Carter, 1996, p. 32).

CASE STUDY 6.4: Quality at Rover

At Rover, the total quality management objective requires the involvement of all employees in delivering customer quality. As of 1994, for 85 per cent of employees, empowerment has been achieved.

Rover at first introduced a 'job for life' clause in its employment policy. which take responsibility for people's employment until they wish to voluntarily leave. This, however, did not mean the same job, nor even necessarily a job within Rover. It simply meant that the company took responsibility for the employability, that is, skill level of its people. The new deal does not of itself increase involvement or learning, but it provides a clearly understood framework within which people could improve their processes without worrying about putting themselves out of work.

Quality circles or 'discussion groups' were then gradually introduced to encourage employees' involvement in improving the quality of their services. In 1992 Land Rover won the Perkins Award for the highest level of voluntary teamwork through this scheme. As a means of introducing training on problem solving, communication and teamwork, they are highly recommended because they are voluntary. Quality circles are also much less threatening to the status quo and the trade unions as the agendas usually focus on the working environment and grow towards quality, waste elimination and finally continuous improvement.

Personal development files were then developed. This was one of the first products of Rover Learning Business and was aimed at all associates. Personal development files (PDF) were later supported by the development review. The PDF is the individual's property: it contains his certificates and qualifications – internal and external – and performance appraisals (staff). The file also includes an agenda for a meeting with the manager aimed at agreeing areas for learning and improvement which the associate wished to pursue. It was not a performance appraisal but much more a 'what would you like to do' exchange.

To back up the personal development file, a company training fund was created to encourage employees to attend courses outside working hours at local FE colleges. Any subject is acceptable, providing the manager gives his approval. The objective was to re-introduce the people to learning paths which they want, as discrete from company courses that are compulsory.

(Adapted from Stephenson, 1994)

Product innovation and diversification

Innovation is here defined broadly to include both improvements in technology and better methods or ways of doing things. It can be manifested in product changes, process changes, new approaches to marketing, new forms of distribution, and new conceptions of scope (Porter, 1990, p. 45). Product innovation and diversification has been central to the car industry in Europe. In response to the market demand for small cars in Europe, Chrysler created a mini van especially for Europe, which can seat only six passengers compared to the seven or eight seats in US markets. Five new models were introduced at the Paris show in 1994. General Motors is also considering the development of a tiny city car, and Ford a mini car for Europe. Mercedes-Benz, by 1997 will begin building a stubby, high-roofed, four-passenger vehicle codenamed the A car. Also planned is an even smaller Mercedes: a two-seat micro-compact about eight feet long – less than half the length of an S320 sedan. When BMW purchased Rover cars in January 1994 for £800 million, BMW wanted to gain an immediate 'access' to the established front-wheel drive know-how and to the off-road and city-car markets associated with the Range Rover and Mini (*Director*, January 1996).

Cross-border link-up and strategic alliances

According to a recent survey conducted by Peat Marwick, 87 per cent of US firms in the survey formed strategic alliances with EU companies (Saghafi *et al.*, 1995). Given the increasing rise and development of strategic alliances in European business a separate chapter is allocated entirely for their study in Part Three.

CASE STUDY 6.5: SEAT strategy for penetrating the European market

SEAT was founded in 1950 by the Spanish government with the Instituto Nacional de Industria as the major shareholder. The idea was to create a national industry and a fleet of Spanish automobiles and to save foreign currency. SEAT operated as an independent company, manufacturing Fiat's low-cost, fuel-saving vehicles under licence until 1978. The Italian company provided the Spaniards with technology, but did not take part in management.

The first SEAT car came out of the Barcelona factory in May 1953. However, following the oil crisis of 1973, SEAT although producing fuel-savings cars, started losing money. SEAT's competitiveness declined as the result of a number of factors: rigid structure, problems with service and quality, a deteriorating image, and above all the fact that the market was opening up and more brands were becoming available.

In 1980 SEAT's affiliation with Fiat ended and SEAT was left alone. It had no technology of its own, no plans for developing products of its own, an excessive production capacity, too many employees and a weak financial structure. The company was furthermore heavily in debt. Export markets had dried up because the company no longer had access to Fiat's distribution network and it had no corporate image abroad. Prospective customers were unfamiliar with, and uninterested in, its products. SEAT had no sales network and was unfamiliar with the way the export market operated with its distribution channels and with the structure of European markets. Its exports went to a limited number of countries: Egypt, Chile, Greece and Cyprus. The image of Spanish/Italian cars in Europe was not very competitive. SEAT did not have a brand image known outside of Spain and the European consumers had little inclination to purchase Spanish-made cars.

To survive and hopefully compete more successfully in the Single Market SEAT designed the following strategic plan for its operation in Europe:

1. Guarantee the survival of SEAT company without breaking completely with Fiat technology through: cooperation agreements with Fiat, reduction of personnel, and restructuring of the sales network.
2. Develop a SEAT technology through the introduction of SEAT models, and developing a SEAT foreign network.
3. Cooperate with multinational groups, such as the recent agreement with Volkswagen.

The initial strategic plan consisted of four main programmes for action:

1. *Industrial rationalization programme*   This involved cuts in costs and improvement of productivity. Manpower was reduced by almost 25 per cent between 1981–84 while production increased from 209 000 cars in 1981 to 279 000 in 1984, an increase of 33 per cent.
2. *Quality*   SEAT also introduced its first total quality programmes.
3. *Innovation and product diversification*   The SEAT new product development programme began by introducing new versions of existing SEAT products: models 131, 127 Ritmo and Panda, and renovated Fura and Ronda models, followed by the introduction of the new Ibiza (1984) and Malaga (1985) models.
4. *Technological cooperation*   In 1981, collaboration agreements were signed with specialized firms such as Guigiarto, Karmann and Porsche. In September 1982 a technological-transfer agreement was signed with Volkswagen enabling SEAT to produce 120 000 Volkswagens per year, 50 000 of which were VW Polos to be exported through the VW European network. In September 1982 an Industrial Cooperation, Licensing and Technical Assistance Agreement was signed between SEAT and Volkswagen which allowed SEAT to produce the Volkswagen models Polo/Classic and Passat/Santana variant.
5. *Joint ventures*   The collaboration arrangements between VW and SEAT took on a new meaning when VW decided to buy into SEAT. Under the new agreement, 51 per cent of shares were sold to VW on 31 December 1985. In exchange VW undertook to meet the goals set in SEAT's 1981 strategic plan. The association would provide the advantages of economies of scale in terms of both investments and costs. SEAT and VW/Audi product ranges would complement one another. SEAT would benefit from VW technology and VW would be able to profit from the SEAT facilities in Spain, and from a second distribution channel in Europe. SEAT secured its production levels, and VW was able to take advantage of both the potential Spanish market and lower production costs, because of the labour factor.
6. *New image*   SEAT was virtually unknown in Europe which meant that the company had to promote its image before introducing its cars on the European market. The new strategy was based on the idea of ECONOSPORT which stressed the following features: individualism: range, accessories, personalized features; economy: quality, reliability, low maintenance costs, value for money; sportiness: design/aesthetics, performance, and driving pleasure.
7. *After sales service*   SEAT established a high quality after sales service network able to quickly solve customer problems and provide a service that was commensurate with the

brand image the company wanted to promote. Special care was taken in selecting and training dealers

(Adapted from Montana and Trell, 1994, pp. 43–63)

REVIEW QUESTIONS

1. 'The existence of corporate strategy is but one of numerous variables affecting a firm's success or failure'. Discuss.
2. What is meant by the 'Strategic 3 Cs'. How useful are they in competitive analysis?
3. Briefly summarize and evaluate the various strategies formulated by US, Japanese and European firms for competing in Europe.
4. What are the lessons to be learned from all the case studies presented in this chapter. What would you suggest are the best recommendations for competing in Europe?
5. 'Managers cannot expect to maintain strategic success in the Single European Market by a reliance on the proven strategic formulae of the past. The European Union is developing in ways which challenge managers to understand and cope with the nature of this complexity, and to revise their management systems to cope with it.' Discuss.

EXERCISE 6.1: Competing in the Single Market

Aim   The aim of this project is to stimulate students' awareness of the different strategies adopted by multinational firms to compete in the Single European Market.

Assignment   The class is divided into three groups. Each group is asked to select either a European, a US or a Japanese multinational firm operating in the Single European Market. Based on the literature available, students within each group are asked to fully investigate the specific strategy adopted by the firm for its operation in Europe.

Format   Presentation to the class should include:

- An introduction to the multinational firm and its international operations in world markets.
- Description of the company's competitive strategy for the Single European Market.
- Reasons why that particular strategy was chosen for Europe and how it was implemented.
- Evaluation of any lessons to be learned.

Sources

Company Annual Reports often include company specific statistics relating to market share, performance, product sales, business strategy, etc.

AMADEUS is a CD-ROM database providing four years' summary accounts and company details for 125 000 European companies. It covers the 15 countries in the European Union plus Norway and Switzerland. It can be searched by company name, industry, geographic area and financial performance

European Company Directories such as *Europe's Medium Sized Companies Directory*, *D and B Europe*, *Kompass France and Deutschland*, *Who Owns Whom Europe*, *FT European Handbook*, *Thomas Register Europe*

International Company Directors The following directories provide basic data and complement the international coverage of *Datastream* and the European coverage of *AMADEUS*

- *International Directory of Company Histories*
- *Principal International Businesses*
- *World's Major Companies Directory*
- *Standard and Poors Register* (US companies)
- *Million Directory* (US companies)
- *Moody's International Manual*
- *Macmillan Directory of Multinationals*
- *Who Owns Whom* US edition
- *FT Handbooks* - Asia Pacific, America, etc.
- *Small Business Sourcebook* (US companies)

Journals and magazine articles on companies
- *Management Today*
- *Investors Chronicle*
- *Business Week*
- *Financial Times Business pages*

Electronic databases CD-ROM
- ABI/Inform (International)
- Helecon (European)

These databases can be searched by company name to identify company specific journal and magazine articles. ABI/Inform has a good company index to select articles from.

EBSCO Masterfile is an Internet service providing the full text of selected business and economics journal articles. The URL is:
`[http://www.niss.ac.uk/ebsco/m/ebmf.html]`

COLIS database includes a list of management case studies held at Cranfield and Harvard business schools. It can be accessed free of charge via the Internet at:
`[telnet://colis@ecch.babson.edu Log in as colis]`

FURTHER READING

Bennett, R., *International Business*, Pitman, London, 1996.

Brown, L. and McDonald, M., *Competitive Marketing Strategy for Europe,* Macmillan, Basingstoke, 1994.

Ohmae, K., *The Mind of the Strategist*, Penguin, Harmondsworth, 1983.

Porter, M., *Competitive Strategy: Techniques for analyzing industries and competitors*, Free Press, New York, 1980.

Porter, M., *The Competitive Advantage of Nations*, Macmillan, Basingstoke, 1990.

SEVEN
STRATEGIC PLANNING FOR THE SINGLE EUROPEAN MARKET

Although there is no one single strategic plan that can be universally valid for doing business in the Single European environment, there is a general framework that can operate as a basis for the development of a specific strategic plan. This chapter aims to offer guidance to business managers and to students in formulating strategic plans for the Single European Market.

LEARNING OBJECTIVES

- To introduce the various stages involved in the formulation of a strategic plan for the Single European Market
- To learn how to conduct a Single European Market audit
- To develop an understanding of the various methods of entry available for Europe, and highlight the advantages and disadvantages of each method
- To identify and formulate competitive strategies for Europe

FORMULATING A STRATEGIC PLAN FOR THE SINGLE EUROPEAN MARKET

Figure 7.1 provides a comprehensive model for constructing a strategic plan for the Single European Market. Readers are invited to use this model to delete, modify, reject, or use as a springboard towards the design of their own preferred model.

Stage one: Defining corporate mission/corporate objectives

The first step in formulating a strategic plan for Europe is to determine the overall goal of the company. This could be maximizing profit, gaining control of a market, or production of pan-European products. In other words, deciding what the company hopes to achieve from its European operations and what its objectives in Europe are in terms of profitability, marketing, production, finance, technology, personnel and industrial relations.

Stage two: Evaluation of current position

This must be done in relation to the identified overall company objectives. It involves analysis of the European environment, and internal resources analysis.

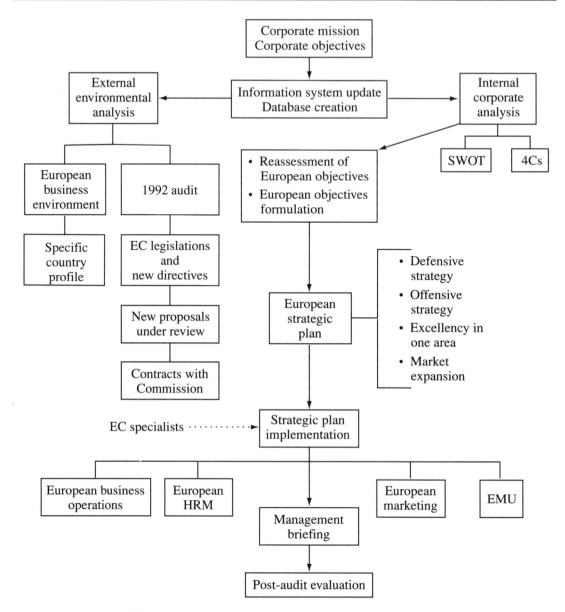

Figure 7.1 Strategic plan for the Single European Market

European environmental analysis

Database creation and information systems Designing a strategic plan for the Single European Market requires comprehensive and up-to-date information on what is happening in the Single Market. With increased European competition, business firms must have the relevant information necessary for the conduct of their business. A company must first determine how much information it will require and assess its information system. It might consider the benefit of using commercially available information services, such as electronic

data interchange, electronic mail and access to databases. It must decide w
information system is capable of meeting the growth in demand from the
market, and whether it is sufficiently flexible to cope with these new dem⌐
important in evaluating the present system to check new suppliers of hardware
and their products, and to evaluate public telecommunications, services and tariffs,
them with what is available from privately managed network providers. The comp⌐
stage should also ensure that someone is responsible for monitoring the changes in E
telecommunications regulations.

Analysis of the European business environment The main issue here is to find out what
changes, threats or opportunities the Single Market has brought, and how they might affect
the business. As mentioned in Chapter Five, heavy fines are being imposed for negligent
infringements of Community legislation, and business managers thus should become aware of
the latest Community legislation and its precise relation to the business they are involved in.
This process requires the development of a 'Single Market Readiness Audit' (Gibbs, 1990).
This includes obtaining clear and up-to-date information on what is happening. A company
needs to know whether there are any current trade barriers affecting its business that are due
to be dismantled by Community actions, or on which it would like to seek action. Events are
moving and changing all the time in Brussels, and this action might need to be repeated
several times in order to keep up with the latest developments. It is also important to keep up
to date with new proposals being drafted in the Commission or debated in the Parliament to
determine whether there is a need to try to influence legislation to protect the company's
interests. A good source of information is the *Official Journal of the European Communities*,
or you could consider exploiting the Euronet DIANE (Direct Access to Information in
Europe). This is an information retrieval system which is fast, efficient and relatively
inexpensive. Its databases store all kinds of information on almost all subjects that businesses
will be required to research. They are constantly updated so that the most complete data is
always available (Perry, 1994, p. 254).

If there is any piece of legislation that a company wishes to influence, the first thing that
needs to be done is to decide whether to approach Brussels directly or indirectly, by working
with others in the same trade (see Chapter Five: Influencing the Community decision-making
process). Some companies have established offices in Brussels specifically for this purpose.
Hitachi, for example, opened a representative office in Brussels to enable it to stay abreast of
the EU Commissions 1992 activities. The office was staffed by two Japanese employees whose
main responsibilities were to study the Commissions' rulings, prepare political and economic
reports on Europe and gather information on how best to do business in the new EU (Egan
and McKiernan, 1993, p. 210).

Stage 3: European environmental analysis

Once the Single Market Readiness Audit is completed, a general assessment of the European
business environment is needed. Questions such as: Is there a European opportunity? What is
the size of that opportunity? Who are our competitors in that market? Who are their major
competitors, suppliers and customers and where are they located?

There is no single or universal formula for analysing the European business environment.
European environmental analysis is in principle similar to global environmental analysis.
Economic and political situations vary widely across Europe. Technology is also constantly
and rapidly developing. In addition, people in Europe have different cultures, and hold
different values, beliefs and attitudes which need to be understood and brought into planning.

There is no simple procedure for dealing with this. The company will take some months of research before resolving this issue.

The easiest and quickest way to conduct a European environmental analysis is to watch where the firm's competitors are going and follow them, on the assumption that they know what they are doing and that by following them abroad you will receive the same benefits they might get by locating in Europe (Garland, 1991, p. 41). Another way is to purchase individual country profiles of EU member states and review them. The surveys, although general, might provide a base to start from. Banks are particularly active in providing information on countries and markets in the EU. The task then, is to shortlist the countries reviewed to two or three, and develop more detailed individual country profiles through specific market research. The services of international market research agencies may be used at this stage. They may have offices in the member states concerned or a local agency that employs its own local staff to do the research. Information on competition in member states is usually available from individual company annual reports. Extel Financial Service provides financial data on European companies, while McCarthy has newspaper and magazine cuttings containing recent information about companies and markets. Alternatively, the company could consider hiring consultants who are experts in that particular field and ask them to conduct a comprehensive country analysis. It is often better to use local consultants because of their deeper understanding of the local environment and better access to relevant local data.

Selecting a site in Europe In any decision about whether, or where to go into Europe, all the influencing factors must be balanced. The countries of the Mediterranean offer the best weather and the cheapest labour costs. Northern countries have better telecommunications and infrastructure, but higher labour costs. It is also possible to hire a high-profile consultancy often found under the group umbrella of a major accounting firm to select the appropriate site for your business. An example of such a consultancy is Plant Location International, a Brussels-based arm of Price-Waterhouse which does 40 to 50 location studies a year. Its services include general location studies, site research and analysis, relocation and consolidation studies, distribution centre organization, assistance in negotiations and access to its Euro-Site Public Database.

An executive from Apple Computer, a company with several manufacturing sites in Europe, recently said at a seminar on corporate relocation that he evaluates an area's regional development authority before looking at the area itself. Are they pro-business? Do they have a coherent development strategy? Are they selective in the companies they take? Are they consumer-oriented or bureaucratic? Companies such as Apple love people who can clear away the red tape (Harper, 1993, p. 19). The following case describes clearly how NCR developed and implemented its own 1992 audit.

CASE STUDY 7.1: Implementing a 1992 audit at NCR

NCR a leading provider of information technology systems and services established its first European sales agency in England in 1985. By 1989 NCR had a presence in all of the European countries and employed 1300 people in the region. The company had four development and production facilities in Europe, each functionally linked to central company divisions for financial systems, general purposes systems, and personal computers.

NCR took the view that 1992 would result in a restructuring of the industry through more mergers, acquisitions, joint ventures, and partnerships. But the company preferred growth from within which meant improving products and service. In response to the Single Market. NCR management initiated a four-phase project called: 'Project 1992'.

Phase I   For the introductory phase, NCR retained a European consulting firm to carry out a broad investigation of the issues associated with the integration of the EU market by 1992. It asked the consultants to analyse the effect of the Single Market programme not only on the IT industry, but also on a half-dozen target industries that were heavy users of NCR products. NCR also wanted to know how the overall business infrastructure would change in such areas as standards, taxation and company law. Consultants worked on Phase 1 for about five months out of offices in Brussels, the UK, Paris and other locations, completing their work in October 1988.

Phase II   During Phase II issues were assigned to NCR experts with the task of providing preliminary recommendations on how NCR should position itself relative to each issue. Company executives commissioned the development of a set of scenarios for the Europe of the 1990s. Phase II covered manufacturing, law, marketing, distribution, services, software consulting, hardware maintenance, finance and treasury, telecommunications, standards and issues related to suppliers.

Phase III   The third phase began in the autumn of 1989 with the implementation and monitoring of the experts' issues, and recommendations. A 1992 executive board was established to ensure that the issue owners' recommendations were evaluated.

Phase IV   During this phase, and as a result of the 1992 audit, the company formed 1992 partnerships with leading companies in the targeted industries.

(Adapted from Egan and McKiernan, 1993, pp. 185–193)

Stage 4: Internal corporate analysis

The ability of a company to expand into Europe or to protect its domestic market depends to a great extent on its competitive advantage. Peter Drucker has identified eight performance areas critical to the long-term success of a company, which can be useful for any internal corporate analysis (Drucker 1974)

- market standing
- innovation
- productivity
- physical and financial resources
- profitability
- management performance and development
- workers' performance and attitude
- public responsibility

Michael Porter, of the Harvard Business School, also identified major forces in a competitive advantage analysis, each of which threatens an organization's ventures into a new market. According to Porter, it is the company strategist's job to analyse these forces and to propose a programme for influencing or defending against them. These five forces are:

1. the threat of new entrants
2. the threat of substitute products or services
3. the bargaining power of suppliers
4. the bargaining power of buyers
5. rivalry among existing competitors

Analysis of these five factors can contribute to an evaluation of the company's strengths and weaknesses. As Porter explains:

> the strengths of these five forces vary from industry to industry and would determine the long-term industry profitability, because they shape the prices that firms can charge, the cost they have to bear, and the investment required to compete in the industry. The threat of new entrants limits the overall profit potential in the industry, because new entrants bring new capacity and seek market share, pushing down margins. Powerful buyers or suppliers bargain away the profits for themselves. Fierce competitive rivalry erodes profits by requiring higher costs of competing, or by passing on profits to customers in the form of lower prices. The presence of close substitute products limits the price competitors can charge without inducing substitution and eroding industry volumes.
>
> (Porter, 1990, p. 35)

To assist students and business managers in their construction of a comprehensive and detailed strategic analysis based on Porter's five forces, the following questions have been developed by *Gore et al.* as a useful guideline:

- Threat of new entrants
  - Is the customer base, present and potential, sufficient to support new entrants?
  - How heavy is the capital investment requirement in the industry, and is finance available?
  - Is there a strong brand image to overcome?
  - How costly would access to distribution channels be?
  - What operating cost advantage might existing competitors hold (experienced staff, patent protection, etc.)?
  - Is there governmental/legislative protection for existing players?
  - How vigorously will existing operators be expected to react against entry attempts?
- Threat of substitute products
  - Do customers perceive other products/services to perform the same function as ours?
  - Do substitutes offer higher value for money?
  - Do substitutes offer higher profits?
- The bargaining power of suppliers
  - Is there a concentration of suppliers?
  - Are the costs of switching from one supplier to another high?
  - Is a supplier likely to integrate forward if it does not obtain the price, profits and performance it seeks from us?
  - What is or would be the extent of any countervailing power we might be able to employ?
- The bargaining power of buyers
  - Is there a concentration of buyers?
  - Is product/service information easily available?
  - Do customers have bargaining 'will and skill'?
  - Is there a threat of backward integration if customers do not obtain satisfactory supplies and prices?
- Rivalry among existing competitors

- How intense is rivalry now and what is it likely to be in the future?
- Are market rivals seeking dominance?
- Is the market mature and subject to 'shake out' activity?
- Do high fixed costs provoke users to maintain capacity?

(Gore et at., 1992, pp. 172–173)

Finally, in analysing competition in the Single Market, it is important to look briefly at the features of principal potential competitors and their characteristics and to analyse their impact on the Single Market as well as their overall effect on global competition from North America, the Pacific Rim and Japan (Dudley, 1990, pp. 62–84). North America multinationals existed in Europe long before the Single Market was established. Together with the US state government, they played a major role after 1945, in the European post-war reconstruction efforts. The Single European Market offers them great opportunities for expansion due to the harmonization of products and freedom of movement for goods across borders. Acquisitions have so far been the method adopted by most US multinational firms for entering the Single Market because of their interest in a quick return on their investment and their fear of a 'Fortress Europe' developing. Competition is also emerging from Pacific Rim countries, such as Korea, Taiwan, Singapore, Hong Kong, Indonesia, Thailand and Malaysia, offering cheap labour and technology while Japan is becoming the second-largest economic force in the world. Japanese companies are currently under pressure to source outside Japan. The Single Market provides them with many opportunities for components and service suppliers but these suppliers will have to meet the Japanese total quality and services standards to survive. Global competition and the European Union is discussed in more detail in Chapter Eleven.

Stage 5: Formulating strategies

At this stage a company needs to reassess its objectives on a pan-European basis, reformulate its objectives and redefine its Single Market objectives, in order to decide what it should do *vis-à-vis* the changes introduced by the Single Market. In choosing a strategy for Europe the company has four alternative choices: it can adopt a defensive or offensive strategy, aim to achieve excellence in one area or expand into the Single Market and benefit from economies scale.

Defensive strategies

A defensive strategy is 'a concerted and unified set of missions targeted on competitors to make it expensive and difficult for them to establish a foothold in the domestic home market (Dudley, 1990, p. 127). To do this, it is important to research competitors and their products to find out, for example, what competitive advantage they will bring to the market in terms of cost, uniqueness, broad market capacities or narrow niches; to review their marketing promotion to find out, for example, whether their existing promotional message is sustainable against competition laws; and to investigate their customers' behaviour and response to their activities.

There are three main aspects to defensive strategies. The first is to find a strong position behind which to defend the home market, and to force up a competitor's cost of entry (Lynch, 1990, p. 256). The company needs to be clear about what precisely it is defending, its position in the market, its customers and distribution networks. It is important to decide whether the company's intention is to defend everything it owns, especially in the case of larger companies with a portfolio of many products, or whether some small businesses must be disposed of because, although viable now, they will no longer be able to survive. Philips NV of the

Netherlands, for example, decided in 1989 to sell its defence companies in France, Belgium, Holland, Switzerland and Germany when it realized that these interests were no longer defensive at reasonable cost due to growing concentration in an increasingly competitive industry and the steep cost escalation in developing new defence systems (Lynch, 1990, pp. 258–259).

The second aspect of a defensive strategy is the decision to deny those segments and customers to competitors upon which their market entry strategy will depend for success. The company here needs to look after its customers and not allow new entrants to become established.

Finally, the third aspect is to attack competitors' weaknesses in terms of service, product range, and so on. New entrants are usually vulnerable in the early stages. This is the time to hit back before they gain a foothold. The company here might reinforce its domestic market by matching its advantages to foreign company needs through collaboration with local firms to increase domestic competitive position (Dudley, 1990, p. 127).

A market leader can also defend dominance with preemptive strategies, but this requires investment in innovative strategies to maintain longer term leadership or dominance and ensure market profitability. Dominant firms need to identify early enough threats from outside the industry in the form of large companies making an entry, threats posed by technology widening the boundaries of competition, government regulations and policies that allow restructuring of the industry and widening of competition, and threats from niche competitors who suddenly change to an aggressive growth strategy (Brown and McDonald, 1994, p. 331).

Brown and McDonald suggest the following recommendations for successful defensive strategies (Brown and McDonald, 1994, p. 333):

- be prepared to cannibalize your own business
- preempt, block or match strong competitive moves
- attempt to prevent any battles that will be damaging
- adopt legal actions or industry sanctions to block illegal offensives
- use rumour to advantage

There are, however, many problems with defensive strategies. The most important one is lack of market analysis. Many plans include voluminous market data, but little real interpretation or strategy. Lack of market analysis may also occur because of unreliable data or gaps in important information. The second problem is over-estimating the impact of marketing effort. Marketers have a positive and opportunistic attitude to business. This can lead them in part to unrealistic expectations of the effect of marketing efforts. The third problem is under-estimating the capabilities of competitors, especially small ones. This usually occurs because of limited strategic information on competitors, owing to gaps in competitive intelligence. The importance of competitors and likely reactions to particular strategies need to be assessed. Other problems include lack of analysis of the cost effects between products and markets, failure to match required resources to support the strategy, insufficient and superficial financial analysis, or reliance on computer-based models. 'Competitive marketing is a human endeavour that requires judgement, a sixth sense, a mentality and a "feel" for what makes sense in the market place in which we operate.' (Brown and McDonald, 1994, p. 339).

Offensive strategies
These involve attacking competitors in their own market. There are four main possibilities for attack developed from military strategy: head-on attack, flanking manoeuvres, occupying new territory or guerrilla warfare.

A head-on strategy is when the firm decides to attack its main competitor's market leader in another country head-on. It is a very expensive strategy process, often needing resources for a sustained campaign to be successful. It can take a long time, perhaps several years for branded goods, or more than six years for capital goods. Sony, Hitachi and Toshiba have all taken the European TV industry head-on, but for European companies this strategy might be too costly and risky to undertake. Attacking the leader directly involves finding a weakness in the leader's strength and then launching the attack. Launch the attack in as concentrated a form as possible. Resources have to be committed to sustain the attack, and to defend also against market leader retaliation.

Flanking manoeuvres consist of moving into an uncontested market segment, and differentiation. Timing and surprise are valuable advantages to obtain some lead time for market penetration. The flanker operates in the mainstream market with a clearly differentiated and alternative position from the dominant companies or the market leader. To enjoy continued success, the flanker must maintain the position of the differentiated alternative. The best strategy for taking on the leader is through flanking with innovation that redefines the market in favour of the flanker. Apple is a good example of this in the personal computer markets (Brown and McDonald, 1994, p. 332). Argos' flanking strategy is illustrated below.

CASE STUDY 7.2: Argos' flanking strategy

Argos is currently the UK's leading retailer of keep-fit equipment, small electrical appliances, sofa beds and telephones. It was launched in 1973 selling a wide range of goods at low prices. By 1993, it had over 300 stores and a turnover in excess of £1 billion. Argos has managed to race ahead with catalogue showrooms. while others have fallen at the first post, even in the USA, where catalogue showrooms are considered 'well past their sell by date'. For example, Sears, the US leader in catalogue business, announced the closure of its catalogue operation in early 1993. What is the main key factor in Argos' success?

Argos adopted a flanking or niche offensive strategy, specializing in a market segment that can be defended against large competitors. Argos' strategy is based on cost leadership, and one clue to Argos' success in achieving cost leadership is the sophisticated computer systems used to track day-to-day sales at every store. Introduced 16 years ago, well ahead of most other retailers, the IB mainframe, based at the retailer's headquarters in Milton Keynes, recently doubled in capacity. Each night it assesses the day's takings and is able to order accurately for each store. Argos also claims that 96 per cent of goods requested will be in stock. The Milton Keynes store manager comments: 'Customers won't tolerate the fact that we are out of stock, and rightly so. That's the best reason to have the most up-to-date computer systems'.

(*Source*: Brown and McDonald, 1994, pp. 209–212)

Flanking manoeuvres can also refer to an attack on a specific part of the leaders' franchise that is relatively undefended, or currently holds little interest to the major multinational firms. This is also known as a 'loose-brick' approach, by which an entrant exploits the weak strategic position of a European business or business sector. For example, the weak point of the European car industry in the UK, namely with problems of quality, manpower and manufacturing, has allowed the Japanese market to penetrate the UK by exploiting this weakness and gap in the market (Hamel and Prahaland, 1985, pp. 139–148). The 'loose-brick' approach requires investment for some years before gaining a foothold and then to keep it and prevent others from getting in. Great attention and care has to be given to pricing, performance and service.

Occupying new territory requires the creation of a totally new sector or 'niche' market, choosing a small area that the leaders are simply not interested in or geared to handle. Prices play a major role here. A company will need to operate at a premium price, and launch on a modest scale in specialized outlets where the targeted group is located. Innovation is the key to success in this strategy, while improving existing products would lead nowhere.

The guerrilla approach refers to when a company decides to produce one-off machinery designs or limited-run fashion products, launched to take advantage of a gap left by market leaders. Guerrilla tactics need reliable. up-to-date information, and the ability to respond to market opportunities quickly, regardless of location. The company should also be prepared to withdraw rather than to stand and fight if a large company moves in. For this strategy to be successful in the Single Market, the removal of trade barriers is not enough. The infrastructure is not yet in place for many companies to move fast enough to fully exploit opportunities across the Community.

The strategy of achieving excellency in one area may be adopted as an alternative strategy. This concept concentrates on achieving total quality in one particular area of the business (Dudley, 1990, p. 128–129) as illustrated in the following case.

CASE STUDY 7.3: 'A paperless trading' relying on 'peopleless administration': The case of Bruno Passot

In the early 1980s, Bruno Passot, a French family business with a small market share in the distribution of office supplies, sought a differentiation strategy that would allow it to offer a superior customer service. Central to this strategy was the development of a set of tele-purchasing applications through which customers could electronically view catalogue and product images, send purchase orders, as well as receive acknowledgement receipts, delivery notices, and invoices. These applications are based on videotex and electronic data information (EDI) technology.

The office-supplies industry in France is highly fragmented. Distributors are of different sizes and degrees of specialization. The total number of distributors in France in 1992 was about 5000. Approximately 25 per cent of the French office-supplies distribution market is held by the four main companies: Guilbert, Gaspard, Saci, and Bruno Passot. The remaining 75 per cent of this FF11 billion market is divided among numerous small players. The size of the European Community office-supplies market is FF185 billion. The two main players are Germany and Great Britain who have a share of FF35 billion and FF15 billion respectively. The 1993 Euro market will also allow some large US, German and British firms to enter the French market.

Bruno Passot introduced the concept of tele-purchasing. The vision came from Jean Philippe Passot, deputy general manager and then head of IT, who thought that the company should offer a service and not just a product. Because of tele-purchasing's potential for reducing the costs of acquiring, storing and managing office products, Bruno Passot saw it as a means to win the loyalty of existing customers. Customer benefits from having Bruno Passot as a single supplier resulted from eliminating warehousing and inventory management, getting lower prices due to larger order quantities, and reducing negotiation time and effort since they have only one supplier to deal with.

The introduction of the tele-purchasing applications at Bruno Passot simplified the supply procedure and the related administrative work. This freed up to 25 people to do more sales and customer visits. Tele-purchasing also enabled the company to predict more accurately customer needs and, consequently, to have a better idea of what goods to order from the wholesalers and when it should be done. Qualitative benefits were also achieved. The tele-purchasing applications also helped Bruno Passot to improve its personnel productivity. For example, salespeople no longer made field visits simply to take orders but to promote new products and sell more. Tele-purchasing also enabled the company to differentiate itself from its competition, by first establishing Bruno Passot as an innovative user of new technologies and then by sustaining this advantage over time through the continuous enhancement of these applications. The tele-purchasing service has also helped Bruno Passo to attract new customers, as well as create and maintain client loyalty. A 'Just-in-time' purchasing system was also achieved. Because of its strong knowledge of the nature and quantity of products its customers order, Bruno Passot needs to send electronic orders for replenishment purposes to its suppliers only once a week. In some rare cases, when a customer requests an exceptional quantity of products, for example, Bruno Passot places an urgent order immediately with its supplier without waiting for the regular weekend consolidation.

Action plan for the Single Market at Bruno Passot

Barriers for entry to foreign competitors
Aware of the potential 1993 entry of competitors, the company merged with another distributor, broadened the company's product portfolio, and developed a multilingual version of the tele-purchasing application system. Aware also that some US companies have already established themselves in England as well as some British and German firms having expanded their operations in Europe, and in response to the threat of possible market entry, Bruno Passot merged in 1992 with SACI, another distributor of office supplies with a similar market share. The objective here was to raise the entry barriers to foreign competitors through the formation of a strategic alliance for sharing tele-purchasing. Fiducial, the new, larger group, aims at increasing profitability margins by benefiting from economies of scale, thus strengthening bargaining power *vis-à-vis* wholesales and customers.

Expansion into Europe
Bruno Passot intends to expand its business scale beyond France through multilingual tele-purchasing. To do this, it developed multilingual English and Spanish versions, in addition to the French version of its tele-purchasing applications.

Acquire some national companies and integrate them through IT
Among management plans to implement the geographical coverage expansion are acquiring, or joint venturing with some national companies, as well as setting up some distribution centres near potential new European customers.

(Adapted from Jelassi and Figon, 1994, pp. 337–352)

Stage 6: Methods of entry

At this stage, firms are faced with the decision about which mode of entry to employ in order to secure a competitive position in the Single Market. While the effects of 1992 and the creation of the Single European Market are likely to vary from firm to firm, a simple prescription for a future method of expansion into Europe is impossible. Various international business operations can be adopted. Nor are there any methods of entry specific to the European market. Companies can use any of the various methods of international business operations available to assist them in their European operations. Each method has its own strengths, weaknesses, benefits and limitations. The choice depends upon the nature of the business, company goals and objectives, environmental conditions, company products and competition abroad.

Exporting

Exporting is the oldest form of entry into international markets, where a firm may decide to maintain its production facilities at home and export its products to foreign countries. There are two types of exporting: direct and indirect.

In *direct* exporting, export tasks are carried out directly by the company itself. Direct exporting functions include market research, study of potential international markets, international insurance, shipping and preparing export documentation, financing, pricing and accounting. All these tasks are initially handled by local employees as the orders come through. However, if the export business expands the company may then decide to set up a separate international division to handle the increased volume of export business.

Direct exporting requires relatively little capital, personnel and resources. Direct exporting also provides the company with the opportunity to test foreign markets for its product without committing too much of its resources in doing so. It allows the company to sell its product overseas without transferring some of its capital into foreign markets, or exposing its personnel to the problems of operating in foreign environments. Direct exporting requires expertise in handling the technical aspects of export trading, in preparing export documents, in dealing with customers, and in safety and security codes, as well as in local import restrictions.

Indirect exporting is when the firm is not engaged in international business operations in a full sense, but delegates this function to outsiders. These can be either agents or export firms. Export agents can either be independent intermediaries or export merchants, who may buy the product outright with the intention of reselling in foreign markets, or sell the company's products on a commission basis. The use of agents in exporting goes back at least a few hundred years, when both buyers and sellers would appoint representatives residing in each other's countries to carry out business on their behalf (Dudley, 1990, p. 171). Agents are useful in dealing with government contracts. They can also be useful for their knowledge of the local market, culture and business ethics. Agents may also have established relationships with major customers in the foreign market or the host government, otherwise unavailable to a new exporter.

Using an agent carries some risks too. Most agents are concerned with earning commission, and may adopt selling methods that do not reflect the company's image. Additionally, few agents act solely for one firm. They usually have other products to sell, and cannot devote all their time to a particular company's products. Therefore, and in most cases, they favour acquiring established and profitable brands, and are often reluctant to spend their time on new and untried products.

Using exporting firms is another alternative to using foreign agents. Exporting firms can be foreign freight forwarders, export management companies or international trading companies. A foreign freight forwarder company specializes in the export and import of goods across national borders. Once a foreign sale has been made, the freight forwarder acts on behalf of the export in recommending the best routing and means of transportation based on space availability, speed and cost. The forwarder also secures such space and storage, reviews the Letter of Credit, obtains export licences and prepares the necessary shipping documents. The main advantage of using foreign forwarders is that they can provide advice on packaging and labelling, purchasing of transport insurance and repacking shipments damaged en route, and are usually up to date with the latest shipping regulations (Daniels and Radebaugh, 1992, p. 529).

Export management companies act to some extent as the export departments of many manufacturers. They provide advice on overseas markets and help in marketing the company's product more efficiently, effectively and at lower cost. Export management companies operate on a contractual basis, usually for two to five years, and provide exclusive representation overseas. They are particularly suitable for small companies contemplating exporting their products, because they can provide instant knowledge of the foreign market. They are also cheaper to use because their costs are spread over the sales of several manufacturers' lines, which provides for economies of scale in shipping and marketing to foreign markets (Brash, 1978, pp. 59–72).

Foreign production or direct investment
This simply means 100 per cent ownership by the firm of its overseas operations. There are various ways in which a company may establish its production facilities in another country while retaining total ownership. This can be achieved by acquiring foreign production facilities or by establishing a complete manufacturing system or assembly plants through direct investment by the firm in a host country.

The advantage of wholly owned subsidiaries to the parent company is that the parent company will have total control of operations, decision making and control of profits, management and production decisions. Wholly owned subsidiaries also help the firm to maintain greater security over its technological assets and know-how.

The major constraints of having wholly owned foreign subsidiaries are the capital requirements and the shortage of management personnel with necessary international experience. The host government and its nationals may have some degree of anti-foreign sentiment, or might be resentful about foreign domination of its economy. The company might therefore risk expropriation.

International licensing
International licensing is the process in which one firm – the licensor – provides certain resources, for example technology, brand-name use, the right to use certain patents, copyrights or trade marks, to another firm – the licensee – in exchange for a fee or a royalty or any other form of payment according to a schedule agreed upon by the two parties. International licensing can be negotiated for intellectual properties such as patents, know-how, trade marks, copyrights, brand names and technical production.

There are a number of internal and external circumstances where international licensing seems appropriate. Some of these are, for example:

1. When the cost of entry into a foreign market is too expensive due to high rates of duty, import quotas, prohibitions or technical barriers, and the firm lacks the capital, managerial resources or knowledge of foreign markets but wants to earn additional profits with minimal commitment.
2. When a firm needs to test its product in a foreign market before deciding on foreign direct investment.
3. When the host country is politically unstable and the risk of nationalization or

expropriation is high. International licensing provides some protection against political risk, it also protects the firm's intellectual property in some countries where they ignore trade marks and patent rights, at the risk of patent litigation.

4. When the licensor wishes to exploit a secondary market for its technology, but where the smaller market does not justify large investment.

International licensing is often used as a first step towards entering a new market and to gain knowledge of the foreign environment before the firm establishes foreign plants and service facilities. It also provides a relatively quick, low-cost, low-risk means of penetrating new markets. It allows new firms to test foreign markets for their product, and to become associated with locally established firms. International licensing provides the firm with additional revenues in the form of fees or royalties in return for information or assistance that the company can provide at very little cost to itself. Finally, international licensing does not require heavy investment in the production and marketing facilities required in the foreign environment.

Although international licensing may seem the easiest, cheapest and quickest way to enter a foreign market, there are several disadvantages and risks involved in international licensing agreements.

First, the licensor's profit is limited to receiving royalties, and it cannot share in the licensee's profits. Second, the licensor might create its own competitor in the foreign market. Since the licence is usually limited to a certain period of time, and may not be renewed, after the expiry date of the licence, foreign manufacturers may still be able to produce the product using the licensor's technology acquired over the previous years. Third, the international licence is usually drawn under the local laws of the host nation, and thus comes under its local jurisdiction. The licensor may also lose control over the quality of its products, due to the possible difficulties of controlling and ensuring the maintenance of quality and service standards for foreign licenses. The use or misuse of the international licence might damage the corporate reputation and image. Fourth, the licensor may face difficulties in receiving the royalties under the agreement, especially in countries where there are strict foreign exchange controls or other restrictions on royalty payments, such as withholding tax on royalty payments to non-resident licensors (Beamish *et al.*, 1991, pp. 61–65 and Stitt and Baker, 1985).

Techniques for minimizing the pitfalls of international licensing and increasing its potential advantages (taken from Stitt and Baker, 1985)

- Capability, reliability and trust are absolutely crucial in selection of the licensee.
- A draft agreement with the licensee must be carefully put together. The licence agreement should make explicit reference to the product, a description of the two parties to the agreements, their reasons for entering into the agreement, and their respective roles.
- The duration of the agreement, and any necessary provision for its automatic extension or review, should be clearly specified.
- Details regarding the royalties, methods of payments and the percentage rate of the royalty must be explicitly defined.
- Control and monitoring. Minimum performance requirements must be specified. Penalties for lack of diligence, rights of inspection and number of visits permitted per year, together with inspection of the licensee's accounts, should be determined.
- Agreement on arbitration methods, in case of infringement of the licence agreement and the type of appeals permitted, and details of specific reasons for termination by licensor or licensee must be determined.
- Requirements for the training of technical personnel must be set out.

International franchising

International franchising has become the fastest growing form of international licensing in recent years. In an international franchising agreement, the franchiser provides the franchisee with its trade mark and the necessary material to run the business. This may include equipment, products, product ingredients, managerial advice and often a standardized operating procedure (Opack, 1977, pp. 102–105; Hayashi, 1989, pp. 22–25; Harrigan, 1983). Franchised operations usually have a specific set of procedures and methods and a set of quality guidelines set up by the franchiser, as well as the layout of physical facilities that the franchisee must use to produce and market the product. The franchisee is also expected to provide the capital needed to run the franchise. International franchises vary from service industries and restaurants, fast food, soft drinks, home and auto maintenance, automotive services, motels and hotels to car rentals. Examples of successful international franchises include the Holiday Inn, Baskin Robbins, Kentucky Fried Chicken, McDonald's, Hertz and Avis. Not all franchises are American. Some European franchises have also acquired an international reputation, such as Pronuptia. the French bridal-wear company, Benetton, the Italian retailer, and The Body Shop, the famous British cosmetics retailer.

The advantages of international franchising are similar to those of international licensing. In addition, it provides for the expansion of brand-name recognition and requires low capital investment.

The major disadvantages of franchising are the restrictions in marketing and at the start, slight adjustments or adaptation to the standardized product or service. Difficulty is often faced when changes to ingredients need to be introduced to suit local tastes and preferences, or operating adjustments are made to suit local culture. But this is not an impossible task to overcome. Many successful international franchises have shown more flexibility in adapting their product to local needs and tastes than expected.

International joint ventures

International joint ventures are business partnerships jointly owned by two or more firms from different countries, foreign multinational firms and local governments, or foreign multinational firms and local business people. In an international joint venture each party contributes capital, assets or equity ownership, but not necessarily on a 50/50 basis. Some countries limit the amount of ownership allowed to foreign firms to 40 per cent.

Peter Killing identifies four basic purposes for establishing international joint ventures. The first is to strengthen the firm's existing business, the second is to take existing products in new markets, the third is to obtain products which can be sold in the firm's existing markets, and the fourth is to diversify into new business (Killing, 1982, pp. 72–89).

Establishing international joint ventures can have many advantages. These include, for example, the opportunity for a firm to share its risks, to learn about a partner's skills and proprietary processes, and to gain access to new distribution channels (Lei and Slocum, 1991, pp. 44–62). Joint ventures are also less exposed to the danger of expropriation.

Unlike wholly owned foreign subsidiaries, international joint ventures also enable the firm to utilize the specialized skills of local partners, together with their knowledge of local markets, culture and government contacts. They provide wider access to the local partner's distribution system, particularly when the company lacks the capital and personnel capabilities itself to expand overseas (Habib and Burnett, 1989, pp. 7–20). A further advantage of using international joint ventures is that they are less expensive. One party may provide the technology and management skills needed, and the other might raise the capital (Beamish *et al.*, 1991, pp. 74–89; Killing, 1982, pp. 120–127).

Firms considering entering a joint venture should make sure that this is the best option available to them. International joint ventures are difficult to maintain. A company should determine clearly its objectives and its partners' objectives before forming the venture. What type of partnership, in terms of management role – dominant role, degree of independence of operations, or share management – needs to be established (Beamish *et al.*, 1991, pp. 66–71). International joint ventures carry risks and problems as well. Successful operations could become a target for nationalization or expropriation by the host government although this is rare for joint ventures. The transfer of management skills to the other partner might create a local competitor in the foreign market by providing greater access to information and technological know-how. Different parties might also have different objectives for the joint venture. A local partner might be more interested in long-term profit. There could also be a wide difference in management styles, corporate cultures and missions between the two partners.

International management contract

An international management contract is an agreement by which a business firm provides managerial assistance to another firm by training its personnel to assume managerial position in return for a fee for providing such assistance. These arrangements are usually for a short period of time, and are usually preferred by small firms that lack sufficient capital. International management contracts require less capital investment than any other international business operation. No political risk is involved either, since the company simply receives a fee for providing the expertise needed. International management contracts are often operated in combination with turnkey operations.

Turnkey operations

Under this type of agreement, a business firm agrees to construct an entire manufacturing plant or production facility, equip it and prepare it for operation in a foreign country, and then turns it over to the local owners when it is ready for operation. When a turnkey operation is used in combination with a management contract the multinational has to provide training and instruction for local personnel. Turnkey operations include the whole process of establishing an operation, from design and construction through to operation. Examples of turnkey projects include road construction,. factories, refineries, airports, dams and automobile plants. Turnkey projects are very popular in Eastern Europe.

Counter-trade

There are six aspects of a counter-trade agreement that international business managers must be aware of. Counter-trade is a process that links imports with exports. One of the advantages of counter-trade is that it helps to overcome foreign exchange shortages. The company can make purchases from abroad and pay for them out of future exports, or in exchange for other nationally produced products. Counter-trade also helps to overcome distortions caused by inappropriate exchange rates. It also serves as a forward sales agreement which may be valued both by exporters and importers, and provides greater access to closed markets and controlled economies. The disadvantage of counter-trade is mainly that such an operation needs particular skills and should be left to counter-trade experts. For example, many products might not measure up to world standards.

Barter and counter-trade have been significant tools of trade throughout the 1980s, mostly because firms confronted by saturated traditional markets were propelled into searching for new markets, which were mostly debt-burdened (Huszagh and Huszagh, 1986, pp. 7–19).

There are three features that distinguish counter-trade from barter. First, barter is an exchange of goods and services without money, as opposed to counter-trade, which includes

partial or full compensation in money. Second, a barter agreement normally requires only one contract, while counter-trade transactions require a minimum of two contracts – one representing the initial sales agreement between the supplier and foreign customer, and the other representing details of the supplier's commitment to purchase goods from either the foreign customer or a designated industry. Third, barter in general has a short-time frame of one year, while counter-trade transactions may extend over several years.
(This section is taken from El Kahal, 1992, pp. 123–130.)

Stage 7: Marketing for europe, and **Stage 8: European human resources management** are discussed separately and consecutively in Chapters Nine and Ten.

Finally strategies for Europe are only one piece in a global puzzle. Operating in Europe cannot be wholly abstracted from global competition but must be coordinated with activities in other areas, into a coherent global strategy. Most industries today face an increasingly international competitive environment. Geographical niche strategies, where firms set out to dominate a country, or even a region such as Europe, are increasingly becoming more difficult due to the globalization of markets (Solvell and Zander, 1991, p. 354). This is discussed in detail in Chapter 11.

REVIEW QUESTIONS

1. Analyse the competitive position of a firm or a product known to you in Europe. What strategic alternatives would you propose? Identify the steps that need to be taken and how they should be implemented.
2. European firms may find their current business threatened by the changes introduced by the Treaty on European Union. Their own national and European markets could be threatened by the arrival of new competitors, not only from within the community but also from foreign firms. What are the various strategies that firms can adopt to survive the increasingly intense competition created by the Single European Market?
3. Identify and evaluate the various stages that are necessary for the construction of a strategic plan for the Single European Market.

CASE STUDY 7.4: the EU pharmaceutical industry

The EU pharmaceutical industry will produce the largest pharmaceutical market in the world. In 1992 it accounted for ECU 63.5 billion, some $77.6 billion, which represents about one-third of the world market (Eykmans, 1995, p. 36).

Barriers to the distribution of pharmaceuticals

These were tackled in a directive introduced in 1992, establishing new rules to prevent counterfeit and potentially harmful products from reaching the market. The directive also introduced a licensing system for pharmaceutical wholesalers that enables them to operate anywhere in the EU once they have received a licence to operate in one member state. Another directive adopted in 1992 attempted to clamp down on misleading advertising. It prohibits the advertising of prescription-only medicines and the distribution of free samples to the general public.

Labelling, distribution and advertising

In March 1992, the Commission adopted rules to standardize labelling and harmonize the requirements for patient information. These rules spell out the information that must be included on the products' packaging and in the new compulsory patient leaflet. This information must be provided in clear and understandable terms and in the official languages of the member states where it is marketed.

The first sign, however, that a common pharmaceutical market was finally taking shape came in March 1994, in the form of a comprehensive Commission policy document, laying out the Community's industrial policy for the pharmaceutical industry. This document promised measures that will 'ensure a quick access to the entire Community market, will create a more favourable environment for R&D and therapeutic innovation, and will facilitate access to third country markets for European companies'. The first measure consisted of establishment of the European Medicines Evaluation Agency (EMEA).

The EMEA'S mission is to coordinate and oversee two new authorization procedures designed to provide easier and quicker access to an EU-wide market. The two new procedures are:

- A centralized procedure (compulsory for biotechnology products and veterinary medicines used as performance enhancers, optional for certain other innovative medicinal products) leading to authorization valid throughout the member states.
- A decentralized procedure based on the principle of mutual recognition and allowing authorization from one member state to be extended to some or all of the others.

(Eyckmans, 1995)

Until December 1994 each nation of the EU could decide itself what products came into its market. From l995, the European Commission, facilitated by the European Medicines Evaluation Agency, has had the power to decide on applications for pan-EU market licences.

The pre-1995 EU procedures

Up until December 1994, there were three procedures: a national procedure for each individual member state with no restrictions on when the next application went to another member state; the multi-state procedure based on the principle enshrined in the Treaty of Rome of mutual recognition, and a concertation procedure based on concerted effort by the member states' licensing authorities.

At the ECU level, Directive 75/319 EEC set in place a market approval system whereby when a product was allowed into one member state's market the company could apply through the European Committee for Proprietary Medicinal Products (CPMP) for market licences in initially five but, subsequently, (by amendments in Directive 83/570/EEC) to two other member states. This was called the multi-state procedure. The other countries' licensing authorities would then have 120 days in which to consider the application and come to their decision. Appeals and disputes would be facilitated by the CPMP. However, the CPMP's final opinion on whether or not the product should be granted a market licence in other countries was not binding: at best other countries had to 'take the CPMP's opinion into consideration'. Thus, member states had sovereign power over what drugs came into their market. The number of products using this procedure represented fewer than four per cent of the products licensed by national authorities in the EU (Earl-Slater, 1996, p. 18).

So until December 1994 there may have been three procedures but there was really only one route: national licences. Under both the multi-state or concertation procedure the CPMP could only give opinions on the applications.

The new pan-European licensing system that came into effect in January 1995 in the EU is the European Medicine Evaluation Agency system. The system has two main parts: the European Medicines Evaluation Agency and the European Commission's decision. The EMEA located in London shall be responsible for coordinating the existing scientific resources put at its disposal by the competent (sic) authorities of member states for the evaluation and supervision of medicinal products (Article 49, Chapter 1, Title IV, Council Regulation EEC No. 2309/93 of 22 July 1993).

The EMEA will coordinate the scientific expertise across member states. It will operate two routes: mutual recognition and centralized. In one sense these two routes are approximately a reworked version of the pre-1995 CMPM, for the EMEA gives opinions on market applications. As in the pre-1995 system, limits apply in the processing of applications. It is not yet clear how or if they can be enforced. The new system, however, differs from the pre-1995 system on three fundamental points. First, the routes will become compulsory by 1998. Second, the European Commission will decide on whether or not an application through the routes gets a product licence. It is not just a matter of licensing to get on the EU market that is involved. The European Commission, assisted by the EMEA, is to make binding decisions in so far as 'An authorization to place on the (EU) market a medicinal product coming with the scope of this Regulation shall not be granted, varied, suspended, withdrawn or revoked except on the grounds set out in this Regulation; (Article 68, Chapter 1, Title V, Council Regulation EEC 2309/93 of 22 July 1993). Furthermore, 'Some products may be authorized only for use in hospitals or for prescription by some specialists' (para3, Article 13, Chapter 1, Title II, Council Regulation EEC 2309/93 of 22 July 1993). The new system therefore relates to the regulation of entry, and exit from the defined market: the relevant jurisdiction of the market in this case is the EU market. The third difference between the pre- and post-1995 routes is that the product licence, if granted by the Commission, will cover all member states i.e. it will be a pan-EU product licence.

Thus, three routes to product licences are effectively in operation in the EU since January 1995. These are: single national procedures for products that only want to be licensed on that one single member market, the route of mutual recognition and the centralized route.

Starting from 1995, pharmaceutical managers have to deal with a single decision-making body, the European Medicines Evaluation Agency. Under this centralized regulatory body, the pharmaceutical firm can use a two-tier system as follows: a centralized procedure, leading to a single authorization for the whole of the European Community, reserved for certain medicinal products and mandatory for those derived from biotechnology. A decentralized procedure, designed for most medicinal products, based on mutual recognition of national marketing authorizations (with disputes settled by binding Community arbitration). ('On the Outlines of an Industrial policy for the Pharmaceutical sector in the European Community', 1994, p. 12).

Impact on pharmaceutical business

A survey of 36 multinational pharmaceutical firms, from the USA, Switzerland, UK, Germany, France and Denmark as major competitors in the first tier of the EU pharmaceutical market was conducted in 1993 (Chaudry, *et al.*, 1994). Each firm had sales greater than ECU150 million. The purpose of the research was to examine what would be the expected perceptions of pharmaceutical managers concerning the effect of regulatory and competitive changes in the EU environment on specific business practices of the pharmaceutical industry.

According to the survey results some pharmaceutical managers saw parallel (trade) imports as an unavoidable fact of life in the EU, and expected it to continue in the ECU marketplace. Price would not change. Managers did not believe that governments had sufficient power to bring about price convergence. The majority of the participants in fact expect pharmaceutical prices to remain the same, that is, at different regulated price levels in the EU marketplace, and that the concept of one Pan-European selling price in an integrated marketplace is elusive. In responding to the questions about expenditure on research and development, all of the pharmaceutical managers discerned innovation as the mission objective of their industry, regardless of whether the EU regional trade bloc would develop in the future. However, as far as rationalization of manufacturing facilities are concerned, the results indicated that the majority of managers were planning to rationalize their production facilities as a result of market integration, and most perceived this, in general, as an opportunity for the pharmaceutical industry. The majority of the participating pharmaceutical managers expected future consolidation in the industry through mergers and acquisitions, referring mostly to small and medium-sized companies realigning themselves to prepare for the EU marketplace. Managers felt very strongly about increased mergers and acquisitions at the national level, but did not perceive the EU market integration as the catalyst for industry consolidation among the large multinational pharmaceutical firms. Horizontal mergers, however, such as the one between Smithkline and Beecham Bristor-Myers and Squibb, and the recent bid by Hoffman-Laroche to purchase Syntex are examples of trends in the industry to form strategic alliances. Such a consolidation of this industry should enable firms to achieve several opportunities. These include strategic alliances to hedge against North American and Japanese competition and government deregulation, economies of scale in manufacturing facilities and research and development, greater market access through the combination of each firm's sales personnel or territories or both, and a chance for small pharmaceutical firms to align with larger companies to survive in a changing competitive environment (Chaudhry *et al.*, 1994, p. 445).

EXERCISE 7.1: Questions for discussion

1. To what extent has the removal of trade barriers in the Single European Market influenced the competitiveness of the European pharmaceutical industry?
2. How effective do you think European legislation has been in ensuring that the European pharmaceutical industry does not lag behind its foreign competitors?
3. What do you expect the international pharmaceutical industry to look like ten years from now?

EXERCISE 7.2: Taking your business into Europe

As a consultant working for Price Waterhouse in Brussels, you have been approached by a small firm wishing to expand its operations in Europe. Conduct an EU audit (similar to the one above related to the pharmaceutical industry) and write a report to the director general briefing him on the state of the industry in Europe, the latest Community legislation related to that particular line of business, and any new proposals being debated in the Community institutions that might affect the future operations of this business.

EXERCISE 7.3: Designing and implementing a single European strategic plan

Aim   The purpose of this project is to give students an opportunity to apply the theories and material covered so far regarding European business operations and strategies to a realistic situation. The project involves substantial outside work. Students should be given at least two to three weeks to prepare for it.

Assignment   Choose a UK-based company wishing to expand its operations/sales/services into Europe. Devise a strategic plan for breaking into the European market, and include your own recommendations for its implementation in the European country of your choice.

Format   Presentation to the class should take the form of a Single Market strategic plan, supported by a group project.

Sources

Euronet: DIANE (Direct Access to Information in Europe)

Barclays Banks: Country profiles

Price Waterhouse: Information guide

OECD country reports, statistics of foreign trade, and economic surveys

Euromonitor country report and statistics

European Marketing Data

Economist Intelligence Unit reports

Export Today

Euromoney

ECU Official publications
- *Eurostat*
- *External Trade Bulletin*
- *Official Journal of the European Communities*

Current periodicals and journals
- International/European Marketing Data
- *Euromonitor* with its bi-monthly *Market Research Europe*, and its annual *International/European Marketing Data and Statistics*
- Economist Intelligence Unit with its monthly *Marketing in Europe*
- *Export Today*
- *Euromoney*
- *Financial Times*
- *The European*
- *Journal of European Business*
- *Journal of Marketing in Europe*

Commission publications
- The *Command Paper on Developments in the ECU* is a six-monthly publication which includes a regular update on single market developments
- The official *EU Journal* publishes full texts of newly adopted community measures and is available at any European Documentation Centre
- *Euro Info*: A monthly bulletin providing information on Community initiatives

FURTHER READING

Beamish, P.W., Killing, J.P., Lecraw, D.J. and Croockell, H. (eds), *International Management: Text and Cases*, Irwin, Homewood Il, 1991.

Bennett, R., *Prospects for Business in the European Union*, Croner Publications, London, 1994.

Egan, C., McKiernan. P., *Inside Fortress Europe. Strategies for the Single Market*, Addison-Wesley, London, 1993.

Jolly, A. (ed.), *CBI European Business Handbook*, (Kogan Page, London, 1996.

Rugman, A., and Hodgetts, R., *International Business. A Strategic Management Approach*, McGraw-Hill, New York, 1995.

EIGHT

MARKETING IN THE NEW EUROPEAN ENVIRONMENT

Despite the removal of the trade barriers and the creation of a Single European Market, Europe still consists of countries with different languages, cultures, histories and customs, not to mention different tastes and preferences and levels of wealth. Marketing in the 'new' Europe might still mean dealing with different consumer tastes, different production processes and marketing approaches despite the efforts in Brussels to create a homogeneous market through increased harmonization and common legislation. Although marketing principles have been recently internationalized due to the growth of multinational firms operating throughout the world, entering the European single market can still involve dealing with a variety of different environments, different consumer tastes, different production processes, marketing approaches and national legislations.

LEARNING OBJECTIVES

- To clearly understand the differences between 'pan-European' marketing strategy and 'globalization of markets'
- To introduce the European marketing mix concept
- To provide guidance on how to formulate a marketing strategy for the Single European Market

MARKETING PRINCIPLES AND PRACTICE

Marketing principles are held to be universally applicable to all types of commodities, from consumer packaged goods, consumer durable and industrial goods, to professional services, such as insurance and medical services, legal consultancy and accountancy. Even non-profit organizations, such as museums, hospitals, police, colleges and leisure centres are now turning to marketing ideas for delivery of their services.

Marketing ideas were first adopted in Japan around 1650 by a member of the Mitsui family when he opened his first store in Tokyo based on policies such as 'to be a buyer for his customers, to design the right products for them, and to develop sources for their production; the principles of your money back and no question asked; and the idea of offering a large assortment of products to his customers rather than focusing on a craft, a product category, or a process' (Drucker, 1974, p. 62).

In the west, marketing appeared in the middle of the 19th century, when Cyrus H.

McCormick first made the distinction between marketing as hard selling and advertising, and marketing as 'the unique and central function of the business enterprise'. He invented the basic tools of modern marketing, including market research and market analysis, pricing policies, parts and service supply to the customer, and instalment credit (Drucker, 1974, p. 62).

Marketing as a discipline was further developed in 1905 when W.E. Kreusi taught the first course, 'The Marketing of Products', at the University of Pennsylvania, and in 1910 when R. Butler offered a course in 'Marketing Methods' at the University of Wisconsin. Marketing departments did not appear within firms until the early 20th century, and marketing did not crystallize as a business philosophy until the mid-1950s (Kotler, 1984, p. 20).

E. Jerome McCarthy was the first to develop the four factor classification, which has come to be known as the famous Four Ps of the marketing mix: Product, Price, Place and Promotion (Kotler, 1984, p. 42).

- *Product* This includes a study of the product features, packaging, branding and servicing policies and style
- *Price* This refers to the money that customers have to pay for the product, such as a wholesale price or retail price, allowance and credit terms
- *Place* This stands for various activities the firm undertakes to make the product accessible and available to consumers. This includes, for example, choosing retailers, wholesalers, physical distribution firms and intermediaries
- *Promotion* This is simply the effort of the firm to persuade customers to buy the product, and includes activities such as advertising, sales promotions and publicity

Marketing principles in the mid-1990s

Due to the recession of the late 1980s and early 1990s many marketing departments came under severe pressure and careful scrutiny. The large budgets traditionally afforded to marketing departments were criticized and marketers accused of being a drain on company resources. These accusations were fuelled by a lack of innovation and product development with a few new successful products carving out a successful position in the highly competitive recessionary markets (Welford and Prescot, 1996, p. 265). In response, several organizations have been forced to rethink the principles on which their marketing operations are based. They came under new pressure to redefine what marketing means in an environment dominated by retailer power, multiple inter- and intra-firms relationships, shorter product life cycles and aggressive competition. This has led to the establishment of a new paradigm for future marketing development based on:

1. *Knowledge-based marketing* Which stresses the importance of market review and analysis, company review and analysis and environmental scanning. With a vast armoury of knowledge marketers are better prepared to integrate the customer into the product development process (ensuring products are developed for specific customer needs and strategies), to identify niches which the company can own, and develop an effective infrastructure of suppliers, intermediaries and partners to enhance learning and technological knowledge
2. *Experience-based marketing* Which focuses on interaction, creativity and connectivity – working with customers and suppliers to develop products and services which are tailor made to individual needs. The development of feedback loops to process changing needs is also stressed
3. *Focus on processes and not on functions* Instead of emphasizing on marketing functions

such as advertising, sales and promotion, firms are developing systems based on brand development, innovation and delivery system improvement. New marketing departments are likely to be process and task based rather than functionally organized

(McKenna, 1991, quoted in Welford and Prescot, 1995, p. 265)

The implications of these new trends towards marketing approaches in Europe are:

1. The replacement of mass marketing with pan-European marketing strategy
2. A greater emphasis on differential marketing: 'think global, act (local) European'

These are discussed in further detail in the following section.

PAN-EUROPEAN MARKETING STRATEGY VERSUS GLOBAL MARKETING STRATEGY

There is at present a continuing debate over the issue of whether consumer tastes and behaviours are converging on a pan-European basis. Increases in international communication, urbanization, disposable income, education, English language ability, similar product ownership patterns, and a continuing surge in travel, are all presented as reasons for convergence in consumer behaviour in Europe (Murray and Fahy, 1994, p. 192).

McDonald's restaurants' marketing mix across Europe clearly illustrates their marketing success.

CASE STUDY 8.1: McDonald's marketing mix across Europe

In 1992, McDonald's had a worldwide turnover of $7133 million and was the world's largest restaurant chain. The company served over 22 million customers every day from 12 000 restaurants, one-third of which were owned directly, the other two-thirds being franchised.

McDonald's opened their first outlets in Europe in the late 1970s. Ray Krok, McDonald's founder, was convinced that his vision of a consistent quality, value-for-money menu worldwide appeal to increasingly global tastes.

While the menu range is partially standardized, McDonald's recognized that customers' tastes have developed differently on a national basis across Europe and has adapted their menu range to suit national tastes. In Norway, for example, McDonald's customers are served with MacLaks, a form of salmon sandwich well known in Norway. In Austria, McDonald's offers a wide salad range and vegetarian burgers. In Paris, the menu includes salads, chicken and decaffeinated coffee (Lynch, 1993).

In early 1993 McDonald's European communications director, Martin Campiche, was quoted as saying that for the company the Single Market in Europe was largely meaningless. McDonald's in Europe selects its local franchise holders in each country and uses local suppliers. Advertising and promotions are also handled on a national basis. As a result there is little cross-border trade and, in this sense, lowering tariff barriers and removing customs controls would make little difference to the company's activities. The company hardly traded across borders (Buckley, 1993, p. 8).

It is, however, unrealistic to expect the 320 million consumers in the EU to be 'suddenly transformed into 320 million Euro-clones drinking Euro-beer, eating Euro-wurst and watching Euro-soaps on Euro-satellite television (Guianluigi, 1991, p. 24). Deep-seated differences in culture, language and consumer preferences continue to exist in Europe despite the creation of a Single Market. It is, however, still possible to adopt a pan-European strategy. Some of the approaches developed so far are the following.

Euro-Clusters

VanderMerwe and L'Huiller forecast the emergence of six clusters of 'Euro-consumers' based on geographic proximity as well as cultural, demographic and economic factors. According to their research developed in Geneva, the Euro-market is reasonably homogeneous in those six major 'clusters' having similar demographic and economic characteristics that cut across cultural and national boundaries. They suggest that even small companies can compete effectively in the new Europe by accurately targeting the needs of narrow multi-country segments. These geographical clusters are: the UK and Ireland; France and Switzerland; Spain and Portugal; North Italy and Austria; South Italy and Greece; West Germany, Luxembourg, the Netherlands and Denmark. Managers working in those markets should be able to reach larger cross-cultural Euro-consumers' groups without marketing separately. The clusters indicate important changes in market configuration, but within each there are segments that share life-style and specific psychographic needs (Kossoff, 1988, pp. 43–44; VanderMerwe and L'Huillier, 1989, pp. 34–40).

Distinctive social groups

Another basis for a general pan-European strategy is to distinguish between four distinct segments, or social groups, across the Community with similar interests, tastes and attitudes. Three distinct segments, or social groups have been identified by a study conducted by Eurisko, an Italian research company. First, the young people who have unified tastes, across Europe in music, sports and cultural activities. IKEA, for example, a Swedish furniture company focuses in its marketing strategy in Europe upon relatively young consumers across Europe, with a common marketing strategy of reasonably priced, self-assembly products, retailed in combination with showroom-warehouses across the continent. IKEA is as attractive to young urban couples with mid-range but rising incomes in the UK or Hungary as it is in Sweden.

Second, the trend-setters and social climbers, who are the wealthier and more educated Europeans. This group tends to value independence, refuse consumer stereotypes, and appreciate exclusive products. Third, Europe's business people, who are a rich target audience of six million. They are on average about 40 years old, regularly travel abroad and have a taste for luxury goods; they are almost exclusively male (quoted in Guianluigi, 1991, p. 24).

The fourth group, old people, is increasingly becoming an important segment to consider. Demographic trends in Europe signal an important medium-term growth in the older age groups. European teenagers and pre-teenagers are predicted to decline in numbers by approximately nine per cent during the 1990s, from their current 25 per cent of the population. In contrast, those of 60 and more years of age, who already account for 20 per cent of the EU population, are set to increase further. By the year 2000 it is estimated that 34 per cent of Europe's population will be over 60 years of age, compared with 20 per cent in the USA and 36 per cent in Japan (World Bank, 1987–88). This 'greying of Europe' will bring special market demands on competing firms as an increasingly large, demanding and longer lived group of consumers makes itself heard in the marketplace (Murray and Fahy, 1994,

p. 184). This trend is causing shifts particularly in the pharmaceutical, tourism, and leisure industries.

Declining household size

Finally the changing size and nature of the household in Europe, with more women going out to work, might need further consideration. European consumers spend the single largest percentage of their disposable income on food and soft drinks. Murray and Fahy argue that, in the market for food, declining household size, combined with the increased number of working parents and the rise of what consumer researchers term 'latch-key kids' has fuelled the rise of prepared frozen and chilled meals in small serving sizes for preparation with microwave technology. Changes to accommodate these trends have already led to radical alterations in product policy, manufacturing methods, and packaging design in consumer food companies (Murray and Fahy, 1994, p. 185). The market for cookers has also been changed by the needs of small households, whose members often eat alone and value convenience highly. Smaller households might also have implications for expenditure per head on children in areas such as toys and clothing.

Globalization of markets

Debates about the globalization of market were sparked off by Theodore Levitt who argued strongly that while

> "...the multinational corporation operates in a number of countries, and adjusts its products and practices in each at high relative costs...(companies should) know that success in a world of homogenized demand requires a search for sales opportunities in similar segment across the globe in order to achieve the economies of scale necessary to compete. Such a segment in one country is seldom unique – it has close cousins everywhere precisely because technology has homogenized the globe.
>
> (Levitt, 1983, pp. 92–94)

Inexpensive air travel and new technologies, Levitt asserts, have led consumers the world over increasingly to think and shop alike (Levitt, 1983). Ohmae agrees with Levitt, but he takes the argument even further. He argues that the globalization of finance and information has made national geographical boundary lines on maps disappear and has given rise to what he calls a 'borderless world' (Ohmae, 1990). As the world is becoming more homogeneous, Ohmae argues, further distinctions among national markets are fading. On a political map, the boundaries between countries are as clear as ever. However, on a competitive map showing the real flows of financial and industrial activity, those boundaries have largely disappeared. What has eaten them away is the persistent ever speedier flow of information, which has made old geographic barriers become irrelevant (Ohmae, 1991). Ohmae argues further that (since) 'Information has made us all global citizens. Customers needs have globalized and we must globalize to meet them' (Ohmae, 1985). Consequently we have become global citizens, with global needs. And since global needs will lead to global products 'so must the companies that want to sell us things' become global. For Ohmae then, the pressure towards globalization is driven not so much by diversification or competition as by the needs and preferences of customers. Their needs have become globalized, and the fixed costs of meeting them have soared. This is why, he asserts, we must globalize. In his analysis of the 'borderless world', Ohmae identified a new group of consumers that is emerging in a

Triad composed of the USA, Japan and western Europe. Marketers, he proposes, should treat the Triad as a single market with the same spending habits (Ohmae, 1985).

Kashani (1992) summarizes the globalization thesis by arguing that markets increasingly reflect:

- the disappearance of national market boundaries
- declining numbers of competitors and increasing size of survivors
- competition between essentially the same set of 'world-class' companies in each national market
- interdependence between local marketing strategies as what is done in one market increasingly affects what happens in another
- growing similarity among segments of customers worldwide as divergence in lifestyle, tastes and behaviour narrows is the scenario for the future

Globalization and standardization are, however, not synonymous. Companies may adopt global strategies that contain varying degrees of adaptation to local conditions, thus the new term: glocal, or glocalization (for further details see Chapter six). Cadbury, for example, believes that across Europe there is no single taste, and has followed a fragmented branding approach, retaining the brand names on various companies it has acquired such as Poulain in France and Hueso in Spain (Simpson, 1993).

EUROPEAN MARKETING STRATEGIC MIX

Given that previous fragmentation of the European market, arising from the existence of national regulations and non-tariff barriers has in the past discouraged companies from operating in more than one country, the removal of trade barriers, physical, technical and fiscal, between the 15 member states might lead some companies to consider a pan-European marketing approach to exploit market economies (Guianluigi, 1991, p. 23–33).

The first step in Euro-marketing is to identify the changes in the 'new' European business environment created by the Single Market and then to decide on the appropriate European marketing mix.

Product policy in Europe

There are two general classes of products marketed either domestically or in Europe. First, industrial products which are goods sold to manufacturing firms, businesses and governments. These include durable goods, such as steel, hardware, machinery and electronic components. Second, consumer products, which are goods sold to the public who may have different needs and tastes. Consumer goods include items such as clothing, luxury goods, food products, appliances and automobiles. It is difficult to establish firm rules for product policy in Europe. Much depends on the nature and location of the markets in which a company is seeking to operate. A choice has to be made between promoting a national champion or to go for a European branding.

Pricing for European markets

It is not possible to make any firm general rules as to what constitutes a good pricing policy independently of information on the location and characteristics of the markets being examined. The removal of trade barriers in the EU has increased competition in some markets and put downward pressures on them to lower their prices. But some other markets have not been affected either due to cultural differences, or to their consumers resistance to buy products where they have little knowledge of the characteristics of the companies that supply them (Harris and McDonald, 1994, pp. 66–67). Only in a few cases it is likely that a pan-European pricing policy can be adopted (Harris and McDonald, 1994, p. 67). Ohmae argues in his book, *The Borderless World*, that the concept of pricing in the 20th century has become obsolete, and has shifted from costs to value. In a borderless world, Ohmae writes, profit is no longer the major criterion, and does not mean 'building pyramids of cash flow by focusing on the discovery of new places to invest. Nor does it mean tracking down your competitors and preemptively undercutting them in their own home country … instead it means delivering value to customers' (Ohmae, 1990, p. 31). Pricing policy therefore is not always the main ingredient for success as illustrated by the following case study.

CASE STUDY 8.2:   The impact of pricing on Euro-consumers: the case of Benetton

A survey was conducted in the UK during the 1992 financial year, to evaluate and assess the impact of pricing on purchasing decisions of Euro-consumers, especially during the 'special' sale period.

The survey was conducted in a store in two phases, covering both a sale and a non-sale period. During the sale period 54 per cent of purchases regarded quality as their prime objective, with only 44 per cent naming quality as number one during the non-sale period. During normal trading 83 per cent of respondents stated that they would pay more for an item at Benetton even if they could purchase an equivalent item from the competition at a lower price. This was supported by 76 per cent of respondents approached during the sale period.

Seventy-one per cent did not list price as the most important factor when shopping at Benetton. Only three per cent regarded a cheaper price as the most important factor in making this decision, as compared to two per cent during normal trading. New customers entering the shop during the sale period did not seem to frequent the store solely looking for a bargain; price came quite low on their list of priorities.

According to the survey conducted, the sale period, while attracting new customers, did not succeed in its objective of off-loading deep-mark-down stock from previous seasons. The survey results indicated that for Benetton products, premium prices are deemed acceptable by the consumer. It proved that the consumer will not easily accept a competing brand as a substitute for the brand just because it is cheaper.

The survey confirmed further to Benetton that it is getting across the consumers: the brand is associated with colour, strong quality appeal and is associated with style and fashion. Premium prices for this combination were deemed acceptable by the consumers.

Table 8.1   Key influences on the purchasing decision

	Sale period (%)	Non-sale period (%)
Price	2.5	1.9
Quality	54.4	44.2
Style and fashion	32.9	29.6
Colour	6.3	17.3

Continued

Table 8.1 *Continued*

	Sale period (%)	Non-sale period (%)
Convenience	–	–
Service	3.8	9.6

(Adapted from Schmidt, R., Vignali, C., and Davies, B., Benetton: Risk and Reward in Franchise Distribution, in Harris, P. and McDonald, F., *European Business and Marketing Strategic Issues*, Paul Chapman Publishing Ltd, 1994, p. 95).

In contrast to the Benetton example, Theodore Levitt (1983a) in his powerful essay 'The globalization of markets' argues that well-managed companies have moved from an emphasis on customized items to offering globally standardized products that are advanced, functional, reliable and low priced. National differences in product preferences, he goes on to say, have been steadily declining as markets have become global. Consumer needs, interests and desires are also becoming increasingly homogeneous. Different cultural preferences, national tastes and standards, Levitt asserts further, are 'vestige of the past'. Consumers all over the world are now more willing to sacrifice preference in product features, functions, design and the like for high quality at low prices (Levitt, 1983, pp. 92–102). The reality of marketing in the modern world is probably that both tendencies, that is towards homogenization of products on the one hand, and towards diversity and distinctive product features on the other, are simultaneous aspects of globalization, not the least because markets, and consumer preferences, are stratified still, for example, across class, gender, age and other important social dimensions and this point will be discussed further in the chapter.

Promotion and distribution policies in Europe

In the absence of standardized promotion policies in Europe, it is very important to keep up-to-date with Commission regulations and standards, and there is still different advertising legislation in different member states to take into account.

Another important consideration is EC competition rules (discussed earlier in Chapter Five). Companies that 'place' their products in the European marketplace are faced with EC competition rules, for example, regarding their distribution channels. Agreements between undertakings that prevent, restrict or distort competition are in principle not tolerated according to Article 85. Companies should check whether or not their distribution policy in Europe is in conflict with EC law, in particular the clauses under Article 85 prohibiting parallel imports, granting absolute territorial protection or arranging market sharing, export bans and resale price maintenance schemes.

CASE STUDY 8.3: European-wide advertising and sale promotion: the case of GB-INNO-BM

GB-INNO-BM operates supermarkets in Belgium, one of which is close to the border of the Grand Duchy of Luxembourg. The company distributed advertising leaflets in Luxembourg and Belgium which included information about price reductions available for a limited time and about reduced prices as compared to the previous price. This publicity was in accordance with the Belgian Trade Practices Act (Article 4) but was not in accordance with a Grand-Ducal regulation which stated that offers for sale at reduced prices may neither indicate the duration of the offer nor refer to previous prices. In that case (*GB-INNO-BM* v. *Confederation du Commerce Luxembourgeois*, C-362/88) the Court ruled that 'under Articles 30 and 36 of the EEC Treaty an advertising campaign lawfully conducted in another member state cannot be made subject to national legislation prohibiting the inclusion, in advertisements relating to a special purchase offer, of a statement showing the duration of the offer or the previous price'.

(Source: Hilderbrand, Lawyers and Marketers,
European Business Journal, Vol. 2, Pt 6, 1994 pp. 45–54)

The GB-INNO-BM case shows that the rule of Article 30 regarding obstacles to the marketing of goods also applies to advertising and sales promotion practices. The judgment of the Court, however, should not be interpreted as saying that member states may never prohibit the distribution of certain information. If information appears to be misleading the so-called framework directive on misleading advertising 84/450 (OJ L 250/17, 1984) is applicable. The directive fixes a minimum level of harmonization for the member states and expressly provides that member states may introduce or maintain more stringent rules against misleading advertising (Hildebrand, 1994, p. 53).

This simply means that the substantive rules for misleading advertising are still regulated by national provisions. In the case of GB-INNO-BM, for example, the Court states clearly that "The marketing of imported goods may be prohibited if the conditions on which they are sold constitute an infringement of the marketing usages considered proper and fair in the member state of importation' (*Dansk Supermarket* v. *Imerco* 58/80, 1981, ECR 181). Marketers in Europe should therefore check carefully those provisions when developing a European advertising campaign.

A set of guidelines has been prepared by the European Federation of Sales Promotion in Brussels. The main objective of the Code of Practice is to eliminate practices prejudicial to the reputation of sales promotion, as, for example, the advertising of an offer price as compared to a standard price relating to goods on sale in only one store out of many where the goods are available. Provisions of the European Code of Practice are: (a) any promotional activity should not conflict with public interest in such areas as public order or material, or moral damage; (b) promotional products should be suitable for the target audience; (c) the privacy of the beneficiary, in particular, minors should be protected; (d) advertising for the promotion should not be misleading or deceptive and should be accurate in relation to quality, value usage and availability. The code is meant to supplement the law of member states which takes precedence. The policy of the Commission is to maintain the concept of subsidiarity leaving legislation to member states where it is appropriate to do so. Kellogg's advertising in Europe is illustrative of these conditions. In the Netherlands Kellogg's commercials must delete any references to iron and vitamins. In Austria, children as actors must be removed, and in France they are not allowed to endorse products on TV. In Germany Kellogg's had to change its message that Kellogg's make the best cornflakes because of German rules against making competitive claims.

Although Community directives clearly stipulate that member states must give access to goods accepted for sale in other countries, opinions about what is tasteful still vary immensely from one Community member to another. Physical taste changes too, as well as the precise use to which a product is put. Other problems that may be encountered in marketing in Europe are linguistic and cultural problems as illustrated below.

CASE STUDY 8.4:   Problems faced when conveying a message in European languages

- *Pepsi Cola*   'Come alive with Pepsi'
  When technically translated in German the message conveyed the idea of coming alive from the grave.

- *Parker Pens*   'Avoid embarrassment, use Parker Pen'
  The message meant to be transmitted was that a Parker Pen is a truly reliable fountain pen and could be worn in a shirt pocket without concern for embarrassing ink stains. But when technically translated into Spanish the same word for embarrassment is also often used to indicate pregnancy.

- *Egypt Air 'Misair'*   when pronounced in France sounds like *'misére'*, or misery.

- *General Motors*   low-cost truck 'Fierra'. When technically translated into Spanish the word means 'ugly old women'.

- *Rolls-Royce 'Silver Mist'*
  Rolls-Royce's model the 'Silver Mist' is literally translatable into 'excrement' in German.

- *Colgate Palmolive 'Cue'*   toothpaste was not only offensive in the French market but also obscene, since 'Cue' is a pornographic word in French meaning *'derriére'*, or bottom.

- *Schweppes* tonic water when translated into Italian idiomatically refers to the bathroom.

Diversity of culture, taste and language all prevent the effectiveness of a pan-European marketing and advertising strategy and execution. The advertising industry in Europe should recognize the broad differences in executional styles. In Germany, for example, the style should be rational, descriptive, informative, while in the UK it must be more subtle, understated, ironic and humorous. In France, by contrast, it should be innovative, modern and attention-getting (Morgan, 1995, p. 33).

MARKETING PLAN FOR THE SINGLE EUROPEAN MARKET

Many of the facets of an international marketing plan can be employed at the level of pan-European marketing strategy. There are six major stages in constructing a marketing plan for the Single European Market as illustrated in Fig. 8.1.

Stage 1: Country profile

Environmental scanning
This involves the collection of information about the environment of various countries necessary for the construction of country profiles. Various methods of environmental

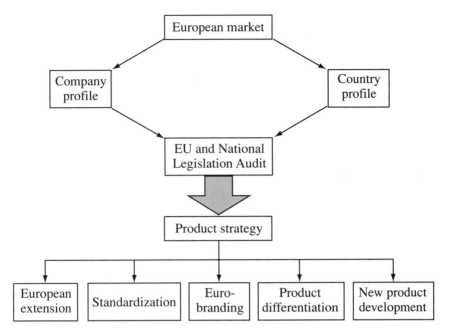

Figure 8.1   Marketing plan for the Single European Market

analysis can be used. If the firm has a local subsidiary in any country under consideration, and if the purpose of the analysis is to assist in the planning for further expansion or diversification into new industries, a two-tier analysis is usually carried out (Khambata and Ajami, 1992, pp. 187–188). At the first tier the local subsidiary collects all the relevant local data and passes them, along with its own assessment of the situation and future prospects, to the home headquarters office. This will then examine the information received and the recommendations of the subsidiary, and makes its own assessment. If the firm has no subsidiary already established and the country considered is totally unknown the firm has three alternatives. First, it might consider hiring consultants who are experts in that particular field and ask them to conduct a comprehensive country analysis. It is often better to use local consultants in such cases because of their deeper understanding of the local environment and better access to relevant local data. Second, it might purchase reports already prepared by commercial firms such as Ernst & Ernst International Business Services; Barclays Bank: *Country Profiles*; Price Waterhouse: *Information Guide*, or the Department of Trade and Industry (DTI): *Country Profiles*. Third, it might subscribe to a newspaper clipping service.

Information collected in this way may be exhaustive, complex and too general. Business executives thus need to identify the relevant data, classify them and construct a concise country profile specifically related to the firm's objectives and particular needs. Various approaches have so far been developed for this purpose. The most popular model for environmental analysis is the PEST analysis: political and legal; economic, social and cultural; and technological analysis. It is important to note that, although these elements are classified separately and studied in detail within their own structures, many of them are interdependent. The PEST analysis therefore, to be complete should also show the interaction and relationship between the various elements.

Market research: consumers profile

An assessment of common features across countries of the EU is not sufficient. The challenge for a company marketing on a pan-European basis is to identify common strands of attitudes and behaviour. These can then be mobilized within communication and distribution strategies for a large group which transcends national boundaries. Within this context, the traditional concepts of segmentation theory apply (Morgan, 1994, p.152). In assessing, or identifying major differences between member states either the cluster groups or the social groups segmentation discussed above can be adopted.

Stage 2: Company profile

This stage consists of conducting a SWOT analysis (strengths, weaknesses, opportunities and threats) to determine the firm's ability to market its product in Europe. These SWOT analysis findings can then be grouped into a TOWS matrix. This matrix was developed by Weihrich, and is proposed as a conceptual framework for a systematic analysis that facilitates matching the external threats and opportunities with the internal weaknesses and strengths of the firm (Weihrich, 1982, pp.59). The analysis starts with the external environment by listing the external threats (T) which are of immediate importance to the firm, followed by a list of the opportunities (O). These threats and opportunities are usually related to economic, social, political and demographic factors, products and services, technology, markets and competition. The firm's internal environment is then assessed for its strengths (S) and weaknesses (W). These factors are found in management and organization, operations, finance, marketing and in other areas. A combination of these SWOT factors often requires distinct strategic choices as illustrated in Fig. 8.2.

Stage 3: EC and national legislation audit

This consists of identifying the laws, technical standards, and commercial practices acceptable in each member state, in addition to the EC competition law and directives regarding the harmonization of advertising and promotion before building the European marketing policy.

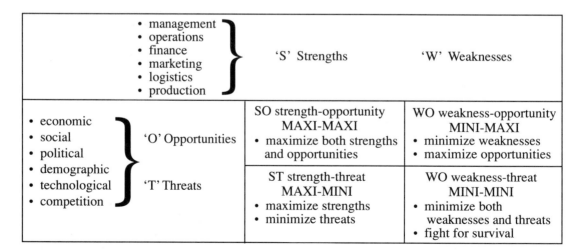

Figure 8.2 TOWS matrix (adapted from Weihrich, 1982)

Stage 4: Product profile

In considering which products to market in Europe, a firm must decide whether it wants to sell the same product as it is across Europe or whether it should adapt the product to suit local culture and appeal to local tastes and social trends. There are five main strategies from which to choose for targeting European markets: European extension, standardization, Euro-branding, product differentiation or adaptation, and new product development.

European extension

This occurs when a firm decides simply to sell exactly the same products in European markets as in domestic markets. The underlying assumption here is that domestic and European market needs for the product are the same, and that the product would fulfil the same needs or serve the same functions abroad, as it does at home. Such a strategy is applicable to scientific and medical instruments, laboratory equipment and heavy machinery, for example.

Standardization

This occurs when a company decides to produce one product and sell it in the same way everywhere in Europe with the same specification and characteristics. Consumer products adopting such a strategy include, for example, the French Cartier watches, Chanel perfumes, Estee Lauder cosmetics, the German Mont Blanc pens and so on. The basic argument for adopting a global strategy as discussed earlier is that national and regional differences are steadily declining due to the new technology, improved communications and transport, and that customers' needs and interest as a result are becoming increasingly homogeneous worldwide. Customers around Europe, it is argued, now have now one thing in common: an overwhelming desire for dependable, worldwide modernity in all things, at aggressively low prices which can only be achieved through product standardization (Levitt, 1983, pp. 92–102).

Standardizing production in Europe can be economically efficient when a product has only one production source, standardizing it will gain the economies of scale brought by long production runs (Terpestra and Sarathy, 1991, p. 253). Research and development expenses normally needed to accommodate and adapt the product to each foreign market can also be redirected towards improving the product itself and towards innovation. A standardized production policy can also maintain strong control over design, technology and quality thus achieving a worldwide reputation and maintaining the global image of the product (Ohmae, 1990, p. 25).

Euro-branding

This occurs when a company decides to establish a European brand identification for its products, even when it cannot standardize them. Benetton's strategy of dyeing the garment instead of dyeing the yarn – a process which could be completed in two hours for each batch – helped the company to respond quickly to differences in customers' demand, while maintaining its brand.

The main advantage of Euro-branding is that production and quality can be better controlled because of standardized production methods and product design. Another advantage of Euro-branding is that it increases profits by being capable of quickly responding to changes in consumers trends, tastes and unexpected environmental changes. The main disadvantage, on the other hand, is the cost involved in producing various products for various markets, and the possibility of the loss of home national image as a result of constantly introducing product variations to suit local markets' needs and tastes, with the risk of ending up with a completely new line of product.

There is also a number of constraints that severely restrict a firm's ability to standardize its products and to adopt a Euro-brand. Some of these restrictions arise from a relative lack of product pricing or promotional regulation across Europe. The question of subsidiarity which allows national government regulations on product packaging and labelling, marketing and distribution across Europe is another major constraint on business. Advertising regulations too can severely restrict the use of standard media campaigns. For example, under the EC legislation of harmonizing advertising, it is proposed that cigarette print and poster advertisements should be restricted to the presentation of the cigarette packaging, while information about tar and nicotine content, with health warnings, must take up between 10 and 20 per cent of the advertisement space. Such restrictions can prevent foreign companies from using their familiar company images, such as the Marlboro man and the Virginia Slims women (Terpestra and Sarathy, 1991, p. 268).

Product differentiation

Product differentiation is when a company realizes the need to introduce some modifications to its product in various foreign markets due to different lifestyles, tastes, religion, habits, language or other cultural elements, legal requirements, physical difference and different infrastructure. With the boundary lines on maps increasingly fading, as argued by Ohmae, the underlying clusters of value and preference are becoming increasingly more visible, thus making it easier for global firms to design their product accordingly. With the assistance of new technology, firms are now more capable of adapting their products to specific local needs and tastes quickly and cheaply. But some firms have decided to achieve this differentiation simply by purchasing new brands through acquiring existing firms, or entering joint ventures and alliances (see Chapter Six, for more detail).

New product development

With the increased globalization of markets, consumers now have a wider access to products from all over the world. They are increasingly becoming more sophisticated in their product demands and needs. Firms are now competing for quality, product innovation and service more than for price.

Stage 5: Implementation

Pan-European sourcing is a growing phenomenon. Firms in Europe need to put in place systems that allow them to service the diverse needs of their customers in highly geographically dispersed areas. Customers in Europe are more demanding in terms of delivery times. Companies should take advantage of the harmonization of transport regulations and investigate the possibility of contracting out distribution and logistics requirements on a Europe-wide basis.

REVIEW QUESTIONS

1. What are the major marketing benefits offered by the creation of a Single Market in Europe?
2. Identify and discuss the key problems associated with marketing in the Single European Market. How might these be resolved?
3. Choose a product sold in four different member states and determine how far marketing the product has been influenced by moves towards a Single European Market.

Does the company concerned follow the same promotional strategy in Europe as at home?
4. To what extent, if at all, does the creation of the Single European Market contribute to the homogeneity of the market?

EXERCISE 8.1: Designing a marketing strategy for Europe

Aim This exercise is intended to develop students' skills in formulating a European marketing strategy, to help them consider some of the cultural and national issues that affect a European advertising campaign, and to develop their creative skills in using various media and designing their own advertisements and promotion campaign.

Assignment Choose a particular local product that appeals to you and devise a marketing plan for entering a particular European market, or the whole region.

Format: Students should work in small groups for this assignment. Each group should develop its own European marketing plan, including an advertisement and promotional campaign, to present to the class.

Student are strongly encouraged to include in their presentation any slogans, drawings, models, music or voice-overs, or even to get some experience in developing their own commercial on video, if possible.

Sources

Europe in Figures which is published by the Statistical Office of the EU EUROSTAT

Euromonitor publications: *The European Compendium of Marketing Information*

European Marketing Data and Statistics

The *Overseas Trade Statistics of the UK* (OTS) published monthly by HMSO gives a detailed breakdown of the UK's imports and exports by product and principal countries of origin and destination. Studying them can give the exporter a real indication of the main west European markets for products

The Statistics of Foreign Trade published by the Organization for Economic Co-Operation and Development (OECD) give details of trade between EOCD member countries (which include all Community countries) broken down by product and trading partner

The Economist Intelligence Unit with its monthly *Marketing in Europe* covers three product groups: food, drink and tobacco; clothing, furniture and leisure goods; and domestic appliances, household and chemist goods

EURONET DIANE (Direct Access to Information in Europe). This information retrieval system is fast efficient and relatively inexpensive. Its databases and databanks store all kinds of information on almost all subjects that businesses will be required to research. They are constantly updated so that the most complete data is always available.

FURTHER READING

Harris, P. and McDonald, F., *European Business and Marketing Strategic Issues*, Paul Chapman Publishing, London, 1994.

Kashani, K., *Managing Global Marketing*, PWS Kent, Boston MA, 1995.

Levitt, T., The globalization of markets, *Harvard Business Review*, Vol. 61, May–June, 1983, pp. 92–102.

Morgan, S., *Marketing Management. A European Perspective*, Addison-Wesley, 1995.

Nugent, N. and O'Donnell, R., *The European Business Environment*, Macmillan, London, 1994.

Ohmae, K., *The Borderless World. Power and Strategy in the Interlinked Economy*, Collins, 1991.

MANAGING IN THE EUROPEAN UNION

When a Frenchman receives a letter and he is not in agreement, he does not respond. And that sends the message 'I do not agree'. On the other hand, when a German writes a letter to you and you do not respond, you are sending the signal 'I agree'. These are the things you have to know!

(André Leysen quoted in Bloom *et al.*, 1994, p. 40)

How can European diversity be put more productively to work? While it is undoubtedly true that the priority for most companies is to investigate the Single Market implications for sales and marketing, and for products or services, human resource implications are equally important and need to be considered seriously. The notion of European management is still a relatively recent phenomenon. Business managers need to be made more aware of cultural backgrounds and how they influence business practices and management styles in the European Union. The aim of this chapter is to consider whether a common approach to European management is emerging in the EU, different from the US or Japanese approach.

LEARNING OBJECTIVES

- To examine the various approaches to European management
- To introduce a basic framework for analyzing cultural differences in Europe
- To provide guidance on how to manage more effectively in the Single European Market

APPROACHES TO EUROPEAN MANAGEMENT

There are still competing arguments for and against the emergence or utility of the concept of European management or even its existence. Three approaches to the notion of European management have been developed so far. The first approach attempts to define and describe the features that distinguish management in Europe as opposed to management in the USA or Japan. The second approach provides a detailed description of national styles and examines them alongside each other on a competitive basis. In the third approach, the socio-economic, political and cultural dimensions of European management is closely examined.

First approach: Definition and description of European management

A study was initiated in 1992 by Lyon Graduate School of Business, under the auspices of the European Round Table of Industrialists. Chairmen, chief executive officers, vice-presidents, directors and human resource managers of 35 international companies based in 14 European countries participated in the study. The result of the survey showed that the culture and history of Europe have deeply influenced (European) management philosophy, standards and practices. Although there is not one management style in Europe as yet, the north is different to the south, and within those categories there are more distinctions. Yet common European characteristics seem to overcome these differences the moment we compare them to the USA or Japan (Bloom, Calori and de Woot, 1994). The similarity in viewpoints, attitudes and approaches in European business is remarkable. But diversity still exists – and probably always will. People are Italian, French, British, Swedish and so on, but at the same time they are Italian Europeans, French Europeans, British Europeans ... and managers are becoming Euro-managers – considering the entire European economic area as their domestic market and using it as their base to compete in the world market (Bloom *et al.*, 1994, p. 19).

Basic characteristics of the European management model

Diversity Europeans understand diversity, respect it and like it. Their history and trading needs have taught them how to deal with it, and most importantly how to integrate diversity without stifling it to the extent needed to achieve flexibility and enhance their company's ability to ride the waves of change.

Social responsibility European companies see themselves as an integral part of society. This means that although they consider profits to be one of the main goals of the company, these are not its *raison d'être*. Most European companies act in a socially responsible way, mainly due to strict legislation and regulation.

Long-term thinking Most European companies opt for long-term thinking on strategic decisions and investments. In European firms negotiation takes place not only with 'external stakeholders', but also inside the firm – with a mixture of top-down and bottom-up communication between different levels of management and employees, and between headquarters and business units.

Orientation towards people Europeans believe that people are to be served by progress – not the reverse. Companies therefore reflect this in the quality of life offered to their workers, their tolerance of individual differences, and the way they manage human resources.

Combined shared characteristics, perceptions and beliefs of European managers
- an almost cynical realism schooled by history
- a belief that individuals should be at the centre of life
- a sense of social responsibility
- a mistrust of authority
- a feeling that all people have weaknesses and sometimes one has to muddle through life
- a desire for security and continuity
- a belief that maximum profit is not the primary aim of business

(Adapted from Bloom *et al.*, 1994, p. 37)

Second approach: Comparative description of national styles

Management philosophies and business practices in Europe are stretched between three poles: the Anglo-Saxon management model to the west, the German model to the east, and the Latin model to the south, based in the Mediterranean countries (Calori and de Woot, 1994, p. 28). Calori and de Woot summarize the characteristics of each model as follows:

1. Anglo-Saxon management
- a short term orientation
- a shareholder orientation
- an orientation towards trading and finance
- a higher turnover of managers
- a greater liberalism towards foreigners
- more freedom for top management *vis-à-vis* the workers and the government
- more direct and pragmatic relationships between people
- more viable remuneration

2. The Latin model
- more state intervention
- more protectionism
- more hierarchy in the firm
- more intuitive management, management by 'chaos'
- more family businesses, especially in Italy
- more reliance on an elite (especially in France)

3. The German model
- strong links between banks and industry
- the system of co-determination with workers' representatives present on the board
- the loyalty of managers (and employees in general) who spend their career in a single firm, which then gives priority to in-house training
- the collective orientation of the workforce, which includes dedication to the company, team spirit and a sense of discipline
- the long-term orientation which appears in planning, in the seriousness and stability of suppliers – client relationship and in the priority of industrial goals over short-term financial objectives
- the reliability and stability of shareholders, influenced by a strong involvement of banks in industry

(Adapted from Calori and de Woot, 1994, pp. 22–29)

A recent European cross-cultural study was undertaken by Professor Kakabadse at Cranfield School of Management in which executives from Austria, Finland, France, Germany, Ireland, Spain, Sweden and the UK participated. Four types of culture at top-management level were finally identified by the research, after six years.

The first type of management culture is **consensus** and is typical of Swedish and Finnish top managers. Consensus is mainly characterized by team spirit, effective communication, attention to organizational detail, open dialogue, and consensual decision making.

The second type is **'towards a common goal'**. This management culture is predominant with Germany and Austria. Its main characteristics are: valuing functional expertise, authority-based leadership style, clear roles of responsibility, discipline oriented, identity with systems and controls.

'**Management from a distance**' is the third management culture identified by the study and is characteristic of the French with its strategic/conceptual thinkers, lack of discipline, pursuit of personal agendas, ineffective communication and ambiguity.

Finally, '**leading from the front**' adopted mainly by the British, Spanish and Irish. Such a management culture is characterized by charisma, reliance on individual's leadership ability, rules and procedures hinder performance, self-motivation and dominance (Myers, *et al.*, 1995).

The results of the study thus indicate that distinct cultural differences in management do appear in Europe and that there is no general European management style at a senior level. A common European management style is therefore unlikely to become reality in the short term. Consequently to 'act European' is at present, an unrealistic expectation (Myers *et al.*, 1995, p. 11).

Third approach: The socio-economic argument

According to the socio-economic argument the emergence of a European style of management is related to contemporary trends towards the convergence of values in European societies, especially northern European, in terms of:

- a decreasing importance of religion as a source of moral obligation
- a fairly stable attitude towards a democratic political system
- an increasing democratization of norms and values
- quality of life is becoming a new religion in European countries (Dijck, 1990)

Consequently, Child (1981) argues that differences in national culture – although an important determinant of national management practice – are clearly eroding over time as international recognition of best practice, management education and the growing influence of multinationals create an international management culture. Managing in Europe, however, is much more complex than that. It is difficult to prescribe an ideal approach to managing in the Single European Market. Attention must be given to the working conditions, different employment laws and the Social Charter, cultural differences, training, language and new skills needed for Europe.

EFFECTIVE MANAGEMENT IN THE SINGLE EUROPEAN MARKET

Pinder, identifies clearly the major issues to be addressed by the personnel manager in relation to the Single European Market (Pinder, 1990, pp. 76–95). First, the changing needs of the company must be taken into consideration. Companies in the Single Market, he argues, will undergo fundamental structural and cultural changes as a result of wider and more intense competition, whether they are seeking to improve their market position or pooling their resources through joint ventures, mergers or acquisitions. They will either need to 'buy' in the talents of new managers with the cross-cultural skills necessary to create a competitive advantage, or to develop such skills within their existing cadre of managers.

The second major concern relates to the attitudes of the present managers themselves. The Single Market creates a very competitive employment market. Those companies who cannot or do not offer a pan-European career structure to their talented employees will be likely to lose them to rivals with more attractive European career structures. The third concern is the attitudes of those who will become the managers of the future.

The Single Market introduces a new role for the personnel manager, which is different from performing the traditional function of human resource management at the domestic level. In addition to the normal functions and duties, the European personnel manager must keep up to date with the timing and content of Community legislation related to social policy and employment, for this will be crucial to his or her role. Some of the changes might affect the company's personnel policies directly and require specific measures. Personnel managers need to know, for example, about the extent to which mutual recognition of qualifications is achieved for certain positions; or what EC initiatives or funding areas are available to organize and assist the company's language and cultural training programmes. Other issues include equal opportunity for women, the harmonization of childcare and maternity leave standards, vocational training for women, pension entitlements, health and safety measures at the workplace, part-time and temporary contractual rights, employee involvement in decision making, and information for, and consultation with, employees.

A decision must also be made about whether to redeploy or relocate part of the company's operation in order to be closer to the new market, to reduce employment costs, or to tap new sources of labour. A feasibility study needs to be conducted, reviewing the cost of relocation, the cost to the company of the loss of key staff, availability of labour, local workforce skills, employment standards and norms of the country where relocation is to take place.

The personnel manager also needs to identify the demand for foreign nationals, and then decide how and where to advertise in Europe, how to organize recruitment campaigns and how to determine the levels of pay and conditions that will be attractive to foreign candidates.

Sony solved these problems simply by localizing its management in Europe. Sony management used local managerial talent as much as possible in its European operations, whereas most Japanese companies assigned Japanese to their important foreign subsidiaries. For example, the general manager of its European television division was a German, and head of Sony Europa was Swiss. English is the common language for Sony in Europe, and most of its European workers speak some English and the Japanese executives stationed there learned the language (Egan and McKiernan, 1993, p. 218)

CASE STUDY 9.1: Who is the Euro-executive?

A London-based headhunter published a survey entitled: 'The Search for the Euro-Executive', in which the following description is offered (Pinder, 1990, p. 78):

> ...he or she – is a rare, exotic beast. Fluent in at least one other community language, of greater importance is the exposure to a diversity of cultures stemming both from family background – he or she is likely to have a mixed education, a multicultural marriage and parents of different nationalities – and working experience. In terms of career, the Euro-executive will have graduated from an internationally oriented business school, have gained line management experience in a foreign culture company, and have obtained experience, through various career moves, of different skills, roles and environments.

The survey even extends to a commentary on clothes, job pressures and lifestyle.

> Readily adaptable to living and working in different European capitals, the Euro-manager is likely to be unobtrusively but expensively dressed, to enjoy eating well, and above all to have the ability of assimilating rapidly the subtleties and values of different cultures. He or she must be capable of absorbing the pressures of a stressful lifestyle, which will involve extensive travel and disruption to social life. The European business manager should have the following characteristics:

- adaptable and cosmopolitan
- an understanding of change processes, and the ability to cope with a rapidly changing environment
- the ability to operate across cultural boundaries
- the ability to cope with demanding lifestyle, with frequent travel, relocation and disruption of family life

There are other additional attributes, such as general technical and managerial competence, that would also be expected of professional staff operating in a non-international environment.

(*Sources:* Pinder, M., *Personnel Management for the Single European Market*, Pitman, London, 1990, pp. 78–79; Vineall, T., What is European Management? How can it be developed?, *Personnel Management*, October 1981)

There is also a need to decide on effective lines of communication and control between managers operating in different countries. Decisions have to be made about whether the company should adopt a decentralized or a centralized approach, and which mobility policy is most appropriate for the company.

Other difficulties include different employment legislation across Europe related to: recruitment and selection in Europe, the formalization of educational certification and levels of pay. Although the Treaty of European Union emphasizes the right to fair and equitable pay for workers in the EU, establishing fair and equitable pay levels will be especially difficult given the diversity in current average wages within Europe, and large differences in the compensation expectation of individual workers in various EU countries. People in Belgium, France, Greece, Portugal and Spain seem to prefer equally based pay policies that reward group-level effort and efficiency. By contrast, Danish, German, Irish and British employees appear to prefer equitable pay policies that reward individual levels of performance (Sparrow and Hiltrop, 1994).

Human resources managers must also consider different values and morals when creating pay packages to meet the needs and expectations of people for fair pay beyond their own national borders. For example, the relative importance of cash and non-monetary rewards, such as company cars, holidays and office space varies across countries, and affects the motivating potential of reward systems. One compensation and benefits manager told Schneider (1988) that for the Germans, a big Mercedes was not enough; a chauffeur was also needed (because of status concerns). In Sweden, by contrast, monetary rewards were viewed as less motivating than providing vacation villages, in part as a result of the taxation system and inflation (Schneider, 1993).

Other variations in employment policies in Europe include health and safety, the working environment and hours of work, forms of employment contract and so on. The case of Renault and Volvo illustrates clearly the risks involved and the failure of effective human resources management in Europe. At the beginning of 1991 Renault and Volvo started to organize the international mobility of technical staff and managers between the two companies in order to stimulate 'cross-fertilization'. The objective was 'reasonable': 100 Swedish managers coming to France and 100 French 'cadres' moving to Sweden for the next three years. Two and a half years later only 20 manager swaps were achieved. The main reasons behind the disappointing implementation were: language problems, family pressures, and different social security and pension systems (Calori and de Woot, 1994, p. 1991). ICL, on the other hand, was more successful in its European approach by establishing a 'Europe 1992 Group' based at Putney in London. The group has some staff based in Brussels and Luxembourg who produce a regular 'Letter from Brussels' giving updated information on the progress of the Single Market legislation at the European Commission. This group reports directly to the European Strategy Board, and carries out the bulk of research work. The group also produces 'Europe sans Frontiers' which circulates to staff to create an awareness and interest in general European affairs. ICL has also established an ICL Euro-Graduate Programme (Pinder, 1990, pp. 217–259).

Cross-cultural awareness is another problem that a human resources manager needs to develop. The Swiss, Dutch and Belgians have the highest level of intercultural understanding. By contrast, the French, British and North Americans are judged as having the lowest level of intercultural understanding. Awareness of cultural differences does not necessarily mean that organizations can easily overcome their effects. However, knowledge at least provides a chance to avoid some of the problems that result from cultural blindness. Ignorance of cultural differences could end with fatal consequences, as dramatized so vividly in the story of the monkey and the fish.

> Once upon a time there was a great flood, and involved in the flood were two creatures, a monkey and a fish. The monkey, being agile and experienced, was lucky enough to scramble upon a tree and escape the raging waters. As he looked down from his safe perch, he saw a poor fish struggling against the swift current. With the very best of intentions, he reached and lifted the fish from the water. The result was inevitable.

> (Adams, 1969, pp. 22–24)

Ignorance of cultural difference could end in disastrous business blunders and several have been reported, as a result of such ignorance (Ricks, 1983). Many books have been written about business cultures and etiquette in member states in an attempt to identify cultural differences and various ways of conducting business meetings and negotiations or, the way reports are presented and projects carried out. The general assumption here is that being able to identify cultural differences provides a basis for modifying one's own behaviour and provides a chance to avoid some of the problems that result from cultural blindness in international business. Moran suggest that 'mastering the broad cultural context of your adopted country, or your new market, will be vital to success' (Johnson and Moran, 1992, preface). According to him, although the biggest barriers will be economic or political, the real obstacles will be the deep cultural differences – some inborn, some learned at mother's knee. Accidentally offensive behaviour of a potential foreign partner can raise false alarms, sow mistrust, and quickly kill off alliances that might otherwise have flourished (Moran, 1992, p. xi).

FRAMEWORK FOR ANALYSING CULTURAL DIFFERENCES

There is no best method of cultural analysis that is appropriate for the Single European Market. One popular approach is to break down the broad area of the socio-cultural environment into its various elements and to study each element in detail (Fig. 9.1). The main elements of culture that can have an impact upon business in Europe are: language and communication, education, attitudes and moral values, and to a lesser extent religion.

Language

There are almost as many different national languages in Europe as the number of member states: Danish, Greek, Portuguese, Dutch, Spanish, Italian, French, German, English, Swedish, Finnish, Irish. In addition to this, in some countries, several languages exist at the same time. Belgium, for example, has three national languages: Flemish in the north, and

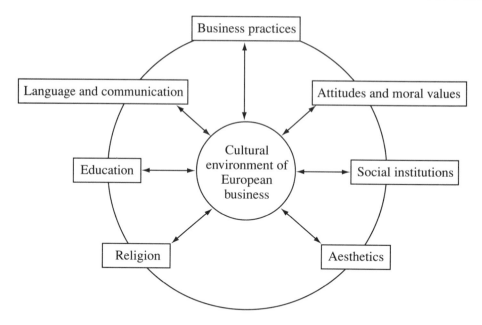

Figure 9.1 Cultural environment of European business (adapted from El Kahal, 1994, p. 33)

French and German in the south. Luxembourg also has three: Luxembourgish, German and French. Although 42 per cent of the EU member states can take part in a conversation in English, 58 per cent cannot.

Furthermore, the issue of language has been complicated by recent extensive immigration, and the influx of 'temporary' so-called guest-workers in many of the member states of the EU. The implications of this are many, and can affect all aspects of doing business in Europe.

There was an early attempt by Dr Lazarus Ludwig Zamenhof to develop an international language. Esperanto, by combining many languages to form words that are easy to understand and remember, and where grammar, punctuation and spelling are simple enough to learn in about an hour (Asheghian and Ebrahimi, 1990, p. 263). Esperanto is still now spoken in some parts of Europe but has not yet become a true language, and indeed, its spread and usefulness has declined noticeably.

Education

There are many different educational systems across Europe. Some place great emphasis on pure academic training, such as in the UK for example where until recently, education has traditionally been operated independently from business. The situation is rapidly changing today with the introduction of National Vocational Qualifications (NVQs) which aim to offer a uniform system of training and awards; and Training and Enterprise Councils, and Youth Training (YT) centres which replaced the Youth Training Scheme in May 1990. In France, the *Grandes écoles* provide education specially geared to technical, administrative and business needs in the civil service, and state and private industry, while the Italian education system is divided into four categories: academic, technical, teacher training, and state vocational training schools. In Germany the so called Dual System or *Berufsschulen* operates. The Dual System consists of job-related courses at polytechnics and universities, and management development training in companies (Sparrow and Hiltrop, 1994, p. 64). The individual states run the vocational schools, but the *Industrie-und Hadelskammern* (Chamber of Industry and Commerce) or the *Handwerkerkammern* (Craft Chambers) are responsible for inspecting approved training firms on a regular basis as well as for monitoring the training content.

The main focus within the Commission is increasingly oriented towards vocational training for Europe. For example, the FORCE action programme, started in January 1991 had the following objectives:

1. to develop transnational training projects with extensive exchange of information, experience and people, to improve Europe-wide skills necessary for tackling the challenges posed by the Single Market programme
2. to assist in designing training systems which respond to market needs by better identifying skills gaps and forecasting skills requirements
3. to encourage more innovation in training management
4. to provide information on the best continuing training available
5. to persuade organizations of the importance of training

(quoted in Welford and Prescott, 1996, p. 323)

Attitudes and moral values

Social institutions, beliefs and values refer to the ways in which people in different cultures relate to each other. Elements of social organization include gender, age, family and kinship, class structure and social hierarchy, values and beliefs. Some of these, which are particularly relevant to the conduct of business in Europe are attitudes towards work and achievement, business ethics and practices themselves.

Religion

Religious beliefs shape many kinds of individual behaviour, whether economic, political, legal or social. Understanding the dominant religion of a particular country, therefore, can provide business managers with a better insight into people's behaviour and cultural attitudes. Although religion might be an important source of frustration and misunderstanding, poor productivity and a drastic reduction in the sales of products, or even cause the ultimate failure of a business in international markets at particular times; in Europe, religious factors do not, in general, seem to affect business except as far as political risk is concerned when clashes occur with ethnic minorities, or when the labour force comes from different ethnic origins. Christianity is predominant in most member states in the EU, followed by Judaism, with Islam in a minority spreading mostly in France, Germany, Britain, Austria, and Eastern Europe, but of increasing significance throughout Europe.

Two major branches of Christianity are of importance in Europe, Catholicism and Protestantism. In Catholicism, money-making is considered socially degrading, and morally and religiously dangerous (Terpestra, 1985, p. 54). In recent years, however, Catholicism has adopted itself to capitalism much more than in the past. The Vatican itself may now be seen as a 'business' as well as the centre of the religious hierarchy of Catholicism. Protestantism, on the other hand, considers money-making not only acceptable but even respectable (Weber, 1952). Despite the claim that 'Capitalism' in Protestantism has become synonymous with Christianity' (Griffiths, 1982), it is still the first duty of Protestant Christians to glorify God in all they do. Glorifying God by working hard may lead to wealth accumulation as a by-product.

Islam means 'submission to God'. Islam is not simply a religion but also a way of life promoting equality and brotherhood of every Moslem, of whatever race or colour. The political influence of Islam cannot be underestimated, particularly in the face of recent events in Eastern Europe. Friday noon worship services, which all adult Moslems are required to attend, are often used by *'Ulamas'* or religious leaders to speak about contemporary problems facing Islam and the Moslem world. The political content of these sermons can provide useful indications to business managers about what issues are high on the domestic, political and economic agenda of the Moslem minority living in a particular country of Europe.

The five pillars of Islam are: the belief that there is only one God, and Mohammed is his prophet; prayer five times a day; fasting during the month of Ramadan; pilgrimage to Mecca once in a lifetime; and Zakat which is alms-giving or the sharing of wealth. It is an annual tax of 2.5 per cent collected from all individuals and used for charity. The consumption of alcoholic drinks is also forbidden in Islam as well as eating pork meat. Some companies have responded to this by producing all-beef hot dogs, non-alcoholic beer, wine and even champagne.

For a detailed examination of the multicultural diversity existing in Europe, refer to the Country Profiles in the Appendix, pp. 67–90.

The second approach to cultural analysis is using Hofstede's four dimensions of national culture (Hofstede, 1980). Hofstede conducted a survey with 116 000 employees of IBM in 48 different countries. The survey consisted of responses by individual employees to work-related value questionnaires. Two chronologically different questionnaire surveys were conducted during the period of 1967–73. His conclusions were that while some core business values such as productivity and individual abilities remained the same across countries, nationality does affect many cultural assumptions and business practices. These different responses, Hofstede concluded, can be explained to a large extent by four key factors: Power distance, Masculinity, Individualism, and Uncertainty avoidance.

1. *Power distance* This dimension indicates the extent to which a society accepts and expects that power in institutions and organizations is distributed unequally. Power distance is associated with centralization of authority and the extent of autocratic leadership. In cultures with high power distance, for example, bosses have much more power and privileges than their subordinates, and subordinates consider superiors as a different kind of person. Examples of such cultures are Portugal, Greece, France, and Belgium. Low power distance countries are Denmark, Norway and the UK where employees expect superiors to be accessible and bypass their bosses frequently in order to get their work done.
2. *Masculinity–Femininity* This dimension refers to the 'male' values such as assertiveness, the acquisition of money and goods, and not caring for others. Feminine societies promote relationships, cooperation and compromise, and a focus on life qualities rather than outcomes. Masculine society promotes competition, performance outcomes, reward-based systems, assertiveness and decisiveness. In feminine societies, emphasis is placed on the quality of work life and well-being of workers rather than profit. Feminine societies also encourage women at work, and a progressive attitude towards equality in work between men and women. According to Hofstede, Scandinavian countries are the most feminine, Austria is highly masculine.
3. *Individualism* This dimension describes individuals who expect to take care only of themselves and their immediate families and their relatives, and be more loyal to them in exchange. In addition, members of individualistic societies place an important emphasis on

self-respect. Individualism is highest in Anglo-Saxon countries, Italy, Belgium and France. It is much lower in Spain, Greece, and Portugal. Hofstede (1995) argues that individualism is positively correlated with economic performance and national wealth, which possibly suggests that the low scores of Greece and Portugal on individualism.

4. *Uncertainty avoidance*   This dimension is associated with the desire to control the future, and to avoid ambiguous or unstructured situations. It is associated with dogmatism, authoritarianism, traditionalism and superstition. Most Latin-European countries fall into this uncertainty avoidance group, while Scandinavian and Anglo-Saxon countries are typically countries with weak uncertainty avoidance. Hofstede also argues that uncertainty avoidance is linked with Roman Catholicism, with nations dominated by the Catholic ethos (Hofstede, 1995).

The following illustration is based on Hofstede's work, and describes the national attributes of various members of the EU.

Austria
- low power distance
- high uncertainty avoidance
- masculine
- average individualism

Belgium
- low risk tolerance
- high uncertainty avoidance
- moderate in masculinity
- high power distance

Denmark
- above average in risk tolerance
- feminine
- weak uncertainty avoidance
- low power distance

Finland
- average to low power distance
- average uncertainty avoidance
- feminine
- high individualism

France
- high uncertainty avoidance
- relatively low masculinity
- high power distance
- high individualism

Germany
- low risk tolerance
- high masculinity
- low power distance
- high individualism

Greece
- high power distance
- high uncertainty avoidance
- masculine
- low individualism

Ireland
- average to low power distance
- low uncertainty avoidance
- masculine
- high individualism

Italy
- low risk tolerance
- high uncertainty avoidance
- moderate power distance
- high individualism

Netherlands
- high risk tolerance
- high individualism
- average power distance
- feminine

Portugal
- high power distance
- high uncertainty avoidance
- feminine
- low individualism

Spain
- high power distance
- high uncertainty avoidance
- feminine
- low individualism

Sweden
- average to low power distance
- low uncertainty avoidance
- feminine
- high individualism

United Kingdom
- low power distance
- low uncertainty avoidance
- high individualism
- high masculinity

The danger here is that of falling into stereotyping which could be very misleading as vividly illustrated in a letter to the *International Herald Tribune*, which collected the following characteristics mentioned in a wide variety of publications:

- French: rude, chauvinistic, even greedy (*The Economist*)
- Germans: warlike, folkloric, relentlessly efficient, humourless, (*International Management*)
- Spanish: dramatic, jealous, lazy (*International Management*)
- Italians: *La dolce vita* minus all that Angst (*The Economist*)
- Belgians: formal, *petit bourgeois*, materialistic (*International Management*)
- Dutch: stingy, philistines (*International Management*)
- Austrians: devious, snobby, xenophobic (unidentified)
- Scots: drunken, feckless depressives (*The Economist*)
- Irish: amiable, ignorant (*International Management*)
- Swedes: naive, cautious, weak-willed (*Communication World*)
- Greeks: slow, loquacious, impulsive, irrational, chaotic (*La vie en grece*)

(quoted in Sparrow and Hiltrop, 1994, p. 80)

While it is important to note that despite the removal of trade barriers and the creation of a Single European market, Europe still consists of countries with different languages, cultures, histories and customs, not to mention different tastes and preferences and levels of wealth. To prevent serious misunderstanding between different cultural groups, and cultural conflict between employees, the human resources manager should organize cultural-sensitivity training for the expatriates before their departure to European destinations. Cultural-sensitivity training is crucial to the success of expatriates in handling their European assignments effectively, and in acquiring the ability to interact with people who may have different lifestyles, habits and viewpoints, without falling into stereotyping.

There are many cross-cultural training programmes conducted by professionals who understand cross-cultural education and challenges. There are three stages in developing cultural sensitivity:

- *Stage 1:* Cultural awareness of self-awareness   At this stage, the trainee is exposed to a critical analysis of the role of culture in everyday life. Understanding oneself is critical to understanding others. Emphasis is on making individuals aware of their own cultural habits and objectives, and thereby of cultural difference (Guy and Mattock, 1991).
- *Stage 2:* Simulation exercises and role playing   The purpose here is to expose candidates to various situations they are likely to face in a foreign culture, such as different management styles and practices in the country assigned, labour productivity and motivation, and to teach them how to function within it. In these sessions, participants are asked to act out the situations, with instructors reacting as local employees would.
- *Stage 3:* Field trips to the country of assignment   This involves sending candidates to the country of assignment to meet the people they will be working with, and to have a first contact with the foreign environment to reduce the initial cultural shock.

Cultural difference is quite significant between European member states, and is likely to remain so, despite Brussels' efforts to create a homogeneous market through increased harmonization and common legislation. However, when compared with American culture, oriental culture, or Middle Eastern culture one can clearly distinguish some shared common values, business practices and business etiquette in the European Union. Europeans do not necessarily want you to imitate them. Skilful interaction is a sensitive process of eliminating your offensive gestures while adopting just the right degree of your counterpart's behaviour.

Common European business etiquette

Meetings
- a firm hand shake on meeting and parting is common across Europe
- use last names in public or at formal meetings, and professional titles when appropriate
- punctuality ranks high among priorities
- prompt handling of correspondence is greatly appreciated
- humour is rarely used on formal occasions or meetings
- western and northern Europeans, in general, are formal in their business dealings
- casualness is often mistaken for rudeness
- slapping on the back is not tolerated
- feet on the table, or sitting on the desk or table are not acceptable

Presentations
- a high value is placed on reports being comprehensive, clear, well structured, well written and well presented
- circulation of reports for individual study before meetings is appreciated
- support your presentations by instructive visuals, photographs, drawings, diagrams, copies of key documents, catalogues and even samples of products

Dress code
- first impressions are very important
- Europeans take pride in their appearance
- wear conservative clothing for business meetings: suits blue, grey or black, jackets and ties are essential

Business entertaining
- working lunch and working breakfast are becoming more widespread, but they are still innovations
- avoid talking about your family or personal matters, or personal income in a business lunch, or dinner
- common topics for conversation in business entertaining: food, history, international affairs, culture, arts
- most business entertainment is not conducted at home
- office parties are rare and usually confined to celebrating transfer and promotion, and Christmas

Leisure
- weekends and vacation days, sport, cultural activities and family are very important
- most leisure activities are family-oriented
- most Europeans take all their holiday entitlements, and they do not keep in touch with the office when they are away or expect to be called
- a high sense of personal privacy keeps business life on quite a separate level

Negotiation
- aggressive, hard-sell techniques are not appreciated
- arguments should be avoided

- loud voices are considered vulgar
- do not interrupt another person's conversation
- avoid strong criticism, or personal remarks

REVIEW QUESTIONS

1. Compare and contrast the various approaches to the concept of European management. Which approach, in your view contributes best to our understanding of European management?
2. In what way does the Single European Market change the traditional role of personnel managers and their functions?
3. Which method would you consider most appropriate for analysing multicultural diversity in Europe and why?
4. What are the problems and advantages associated with the existence of a multicultural diversity in Europe?
5. How can managers be prepared to deal with their 'European assignments'? List the potential problems they might face and make a list of what can be done to prepare them for their 'new' European assignment.

EXERCISE 9.1: Cross-cultural sensitivity – managing cultural diversity in the EU

Aim   The purpose of this exercise is to familiarize students with the various ways of doing business in the European community, taking into consideration the cultural diversity of each member state.

Assignment   As part of its 'Single Market Awareness Programme' the Department of Trade and Industry is recruiting business graduates to contribute to its research programme on 'Doing business in . . .' Choose any member of the European Union of interest, study the various elements of its culture and outline the major cultural problems that the company might face and suggest steps that might be taken to overcome these problems.

Sources

For references on cultural diversity in Europe, consult the following:

Burton, K., *Business culture in Spain*, Butterworth-Heineman, 1994.

Gordon, C., *The Business Culture in France*, Butterworth-Heineman, 1996.

Johnson, M. and Moran, R.T., *Moran's Cultural Guide to Doing Business in Europe*, 2nd edition, Butterworth-Heinemann, 1992.

Mole, J., *Mind your Manners: Managing business cultures in Europe*, Nicholas Brealey Publishing, 1995.

Randlesome, C., *Business Cultures in Europe*, Heineman, 1990.

Randlesome, C., *The Business Culture in Germany*, Butterworth-Heineman, 1994.

Reuvid, J., *Doing Business with Germany*, Kogan Page, 1997.

Villanueva, P. and Bennett, R., (eds), *Doing Business with Spain*, Kogan Page, 1996.

Students can also contact the Cultural Attache of various Embassies for further information. Guides and booklets are usually published and available for prospective business investors.

FURTHER READING

Bloom, H., Calori, R. and de Woot, P., *European Management. A New Style for Global Market*, Kogan Page, London, 1994.

Hofstede, G., *Culture's Consequences: International Differences in Work-Related Values*, Sage, Beverly Hills, CA, 1980.

Jackson, T. (ed.), *Cross-Cultural Management*, Butterworth-Heineman, Oxford, 1995.

Sparrow, P. and Hiltrop, J.M., *European Human Resource Management in Transition*, Prentice Hall, London, 1994.

Terpestra, V. and David, K., *The Cultural Environment of International Business*, 3rd edition, Southweston Publications, Cincinnati, Ohio, 1991.

THREE

CONTEMPORARY ISSUES IN EUROPEAN BUSINESS

In the modern globalized world the content of what can be seen as relevant to European business has hugely widened. Understanding the dynamic and challenging process of change and competition brought about by the Treaty of European Union is no longer limited to the internal operations of business within the Single European Market of geographical Europe. Companies and their managers are expected to cope with the dynamic changes in their national business environment in Europe, as well as the challenges imposed by the openness of their market to world competition particularly from US firms which are already based in Europe, and Japanese firms which are pouring funds into Europe in an effort to establish a predominant base within the EU. European firms are also continuously under pressure to change and innovate if they want to survive world competition. 'Firms which are skilful at innovation – the successful exploitation of new ideas – will secure competitive advantage in a rapidly changing world market, those which are not will be overtaken' (HMSO, 1993). It is therefore important for business managers to be aware of global trends towards change, and how these might affect their business operations in Europe. Part Three introduces some of these contemporary global issues and trends. Chapter Ten examines the globalization of markets and assesses its implication for the globalization of competition in Europe. EU directives towards an increased liberalization and deregulation within the Single European market have caused firms to rethink their strategic operations in Europe. Cross-border alliances and acquisition strategies are becoming crucial for surviving the increased competition created by the Single Market. Chapter Eleven examines the rise and development of strategic alliances in the European Union and provides guidance on how to manage them efficiently . The creation of a Single Market in Europe not only increased competition and economic growth but also brought with it consequences for the environment. European consumers are demanding broader environmental and social responsibilities from business. Chapter Twelve considers the contemporary growth of public environmental awareness and examines the pressures now being placed on firms operating in the European Union. Another major contemporary issue affecting business in the 'new' Europe is the opening up of central and eastern European markets. Chapter Thirteen reviews the current changes in central and eastern Europe, and assesses their implications for European business. Finally, Chapter Fourteen provides a comparative analysis of the role of women in business in western, central and eastern Europe.

THE GLOBALIZATION OF COMPETITION IN EUROPE

Labels such as the global village, global marketplace, global factory, borderless world, and seamless markets have become buzzwords of the 1990s. The aim of this chapter is to provide a conceptual and practical understanding and appreciation of the contemporary phenomenon of 'globalization' of business, and its implications for European business.

LEARNING OBJECTIVES

- To provide an overview of the theoretical approaches to the 'globalization' of business in general
- To examine the causes of the globalization of business in general and their implications for business in Europe
- To explain the meaning of 'global triads', and evaluate their impact upon European business operations

THEORETICAL APPROACHES TO THE 'GLOBALIZATION' OF BUSINESS

The starting point for understanding globalization is the distinction between 'international' and 'global'. There is a great deal of conceptual ambiguity concerning the distinction between these two terms. Both are often used interchangeably although they are not synonymous.

'Internationalization' refers simply to the increasing geographical spread of economic activities and interaction across national boundaries. The 'globalization' of economic activity is qualitatively different. Globalization is a more advanced and complex form of internationalization which implies a degree of structural integration between internationally dispersed economic activities. Here, the global political economy can be said to set the conditions within which individual units such as firms, banks, national governments or regional institutions such as the EU, NAFTA or APEC construct their policies. Within this setting, the traditional distinction between domestic political economies, and the international environment is considered to be increasingly irrelevant.

For Michael Porter (1990) the distinction becomes clear when we compare multi-domestic industry with global industry. A multi-domestic industry is one that is present in many countries, but in which competition occurs on a country-by-country basis. The competitive advantage of multi-domestic industry is largely specific to each country, and the 'international' aspect of the industry is here referred to in geographical terms. Multi-domestic or 'international' industry is thus seen as an aggregate of various domestic industries, relatively independent of each other.

In contrast, a global industry is one in which a firm's competitive position in any one country is significantly influenced by its position in other countries (Hoult and Porter, 1982, pp. 98–108). Consequently, the 'international' industry is not merely a collection of independent domestic industries, but a series of linked domestic industries in which the rivals compete against each other on a truly worldwide basis. In a 'global' industry, a firm must in some way integrate its activities on a worldwide basis to capture and benefit from the linkages among countries.

Some illustrations of how global activities are integrated on a worldwide basis are useful here. Take Mazda's newest sports car, the MX-5 Miata. It was designed in California, and financed from Tokyo and New York. Its prototype was created in Worthing, England, and it was assembled in Michigan and Mexico using advanced electronic components invented in New Jersey but fabricated in Japan. The new Boeing airliner is designed in Washington state and Japan and assembled in Seattle, with tail cones from Canada, special tail sections from China and Italy, and engines from the UK.

For Theodore Levitt the distinction between 'international' and 'global' can be established by comparing multinational and global corporations. The multinational corporation operates in a number of countries, and adjusts its products and practices in each – a high relative costs. The global corporation, on the other hand, operates with resolute constance – at low relative cost – as if the entire world (or major regions of it) were a single entity; it sells the same things in the same way everywhere (Levitt, 1983a). Inexpensive air travel and new technologies, Levitt asserts, have led consumers the world over to increasingly think and shop alike (Levitt, 1983b).

Globalization as a process which extends the internationalization of business is explained well by the global shift theory developed by P. Dicken. Dicken's overall argument is that globalization of economic activity is primarily the manifestation of the internationalization of capital as organized through business enterprises, of which the most important is the transnational corporation (Dicken, 1992). Globalization for Dicken depends on three major factors:

1. The existence of appropriate technology to overcome geographical distances for standardization and the possibility of fragmenting the production process.
2. The role of states in regulating and controlling international business.
3. The pursuit of global profit.

Consequently, the process of globalization cannot be explained only in terms of the internationalization of capital. The process is also heavily influenced by politics and state power. Although in his view, the balance of power has shifted towards multinational firms, Dicken argues that the extent to which multinational firms can expand across political boundaries and impose their own corporate strategies and implement them globally is strongly influenced by, and dependent upon, national governments' support (Dicken, 1992).

Against this, Cyrus Freidheim, vice chairman of the consulting firm Booz Allen and Hamilton has a provocative perspective upon the global firm. According to Freidheim, the conventional model of the global firm is flawed. Most so-called global companies are still perceived as having a home base (Freidheim, 1993). Freidheim argues that there are various constraints that hinder companies' efforts to become truly global. For instance when capital is limited, firms tend to protect their home market at the expense of developing untapped markets overseas. Second, antitrust laws limit the ability of global firms to expand through takeovers. Most important of all in his view is the problem of nationalism. No country likes foreigners controlling its industry. This view sharply contrasts with Ohmae's 'faded' nationalism.

Ohmae agrees with Levitt, but takes the argument even further. He argues that the globalization of finance and information has made national geographical boundary lines on maps disappear and given rise to what he calls a 'borderless world' (Ohmae, 1990). As the world is becoming more homogeneous, Ohmae argues, further distinctions among national markets are fading. On a political map, the boundaries between countries are as clear as ever. However, on a competitive map, a map showing the real flows of financial and industrial activity, those boundaries have largely disappeared. What has eaten them away is the persistent and ever speedier flow of information, which has made old geographic barriers become irrelevant (Ohmae, 1991b). Consequently, in Ohmae's view, we have become global citizens, with global needs. And since global needs will lead to global products 'so must the companies that want to sell us things' become global (Ohmae, 1991). For Ohmae then, the pressure towards globalization is driven not so much by diversification or competition as by the needs and preferences of customers. Their needs have become globalized, and the fixed costs of meeting them have soared. This is why, he asserts, we must globalize (Ohmae, 1991).

In this analysis of the borderless world, Ohmae identified a new group of consumers that is emerging in a triad composed of the USA, Japan, and western Europe. Marketers, he proposes, should treat the triad as a single market with the same spending habits (Ohmae, 1985). In this increasingly interlinked economy, three clear regional blocs are evident: north America, the European Community and east and south east Asia (focused on Japan).

Seventy-seven per cent of total world exports are generated by the triad, while 62 per cent of world manufacturing output is produced within it. These three regions are the 'mega-markets' of today's global economy and they are carefully analysed in detail in Dicken (1992).

The triad is characterized by a unique blend of cooperation and competition among US, European and Japanese counterpart multinationals. Ohmae favours a pragmatic alternative to competition: cross-national alliances which immunize their members to protectionism and state action and make for complementary global economies of scale (Ohmae, 1985). The countries of the triad, according to Ohmae, are in effect the engine of the world economy. As they grow the tend to pull the rest of the world along with them; conversely, if they enter recession they drag the rest of the world into recession. The USA, for example, is the EU's biggest supplier and customer. In 1990 US exports to the EC reached £100 billion and sales from US subsidiaries in the EC amounted to $400 billion (Perry, 1994, p. 214).

Another reason for the importance of the triad is that most of the large multinational companies have their base in the USA, Japan or Europe. The USA is well placed to benefit from growth in the EU as it already has a strong presence in many of the markets of the EU. Its presence is felt not only in exports, but in the large number of US subsidiaries which operate in the European Union. Many of these subsidiaries are market leaders and could well benefit from the removal of trade barriers within the EU. Some US companies are forming joint-ventures with European companies in order to ensure continued access to the European market.

The creation of the Single European Market has pushed many Japanese companies to develop new strategies regarding their production, investment, marketing and exporting into the new European business environment. Japanese presence in the EU is rapidly expanding in some sectors, in particular in cars, and consumer and business electronic equipment. Japan in providing direct foreign investment in the EU increases the importance of relations with them as a way around necessary protection of European-owned companies. This is connected to the so-called 'screwdriver plant' problem (McDonald and Dearden, 1995). Member states of the

EU face growing penetration of their markets from Japanese multinationals. Some claim that Japanese companies simply assemble products within the EU from kits exported from Japan, thereby escaping the protectionary measures implemented by the EU. The creation of the SEM seems to have increased the activities of Japanese firms in setting up production plants within the EU. Some member states regard this foreign direct investment (FDI) as a welcome contribution to boosting productivity and the quality of products. Others regard it as as threat to the future of existing European-based companies.

Japanese investment into the EU is greatly influenced by a desire to overcome trade barriers (Heitger and Stehn, 1991). Countries in the EU have attitude differences towards Japanese FDI into the EU. The UK and Netherlands are keen to maximize the flow of FDI from USA and Japan. They see this as an effective and quick method of losing productivity, acquiring high-technology products and processes and more effective management systems (McDonald and Dearden, 1995, p. 317). Other member states, in particular France, regard such FDI with some apprehension. They are concerned about the possibility of US and Japanese domination of high-technology industries, and about the effects of such FDI on existing European industry, notably the car industry. Given that many of the most effective and technologically advanced companies are US or Japanese owned, McDonald and Dearden argue, it would seem to make little sense to place strong restrictions on these companies, whether they are exporting or operating subsidiaries in the EU. One of the main benefits of creating the SEM is the increase in competition. Undoubtedly some European companies would suffer from increased US, Japanese or newly industrialized countries competition, but this would also be true of increased competition from other member states. For a company operating within the EU it would not matter whether the increased competition came from a Japanese or a German source. The increase in competition might be painful for the company but beneficial for the consumer (McDonald and Dearden, 1995).

FDI is one way US and Japanese companies gain access to the EU market but it is not the only way. Alternative and sometimes easier methods include: exporting, franchising, licensing agreements, and more recently strategic alliances which are discussed more fully in the next chapter.

CAUSES OF GLOBALIZATION

Globalization is driven by various powerful elements such as market factors, environmental factors, competitive factors, economic factors, and political factors.

- **Economy of scale of production**   Due to the advancements in technology that outpaced the growth of the world economy.
- **Technology**   This is one of the most important contributory factors underlying the internationalization and globalization of economic activity. It has long been understood that technological change, through its impact on the economics of production and on the flow of information is a principal factor determining the structure of industry on a national scale. This has now become true on a global scale. Long-term technological trends and recent advances are reconfiguring the location, ownership, and management of various types of productive activity among countries and regions. The increasing ease with which technical and market knowledge, capital, physical artefacts, and managerial control can be extended around the globe has made possible the integration of economic activity in many widely separated locations. In doing so, technological advance has facilitated the rapid growth of the multinational corporation with subsidiaries in many countries but business

strategies still largely determined by headquarters in a single nation (Brookes and Gulle, 1987, pp. 1–15. See also Dickens, P., Chapter 4).

- **Homogeneity of consumer needs**   Product needs become more homogenized in different countries as knowledge and industrialization is diffused. According to Levitt (1983) the world's needs and desires have been irrevocably homogenized. 'They are all expecting the same things: goods of the best quality and reliability at the lowest price'. Levitt explains this further through the Model T:' If a company forces costs and prices down and pushes quality and reliability up – while maintaining reasonable concern for suitability – customers will prefer its world-standardized products' (Levitt, 1983).

- **Globalization of business practices**   Growing similarities in business practices and marketing systems (chain stores) in different countries have also been a facilitating factor in homogenizing needs.

- **International communication and information technology**   Communication has become easier, faster and cheaper.

- **Globalization of markets**   The ability to coordinate activities in different countries has also been facilitated by growing similarities among countries in marketing systems, business practices, and infrastructure.

- **Transport**   Another driver of globalization has been a sharp reduction in the real costs of transportation. This has occurred through innovations in transportation technology including increasingly large bulk carriers, container ships, and larger more efficient aircraft.

- **Regional integration**   Regional economic pacts have emerged to facilitate trade and investment. To take advantage of these, and avoid tariffs, multinationals have formed partnerships from the three major trading blocs – USA, Europe and Japan – which have resulted in what Ohmae calls global triads, 'the future shape of global competition'. (Ohmae, 1985). Over the past decade, the triad has accounted for an extremely large percentage of both FDI and world trade. More than 80 per cent of foreign direct investment made annually occurs among triad members: the USA, European Union and Japan (Rugman, 1995, Chapter 3). Triad countries make billions of dollars of investments in one another. In 1992, total US FDI (Foreign Direct Investment) was $0.5 billion in the EC and $2.6 billion in Japan (US Department of Commerce, *Survey of Currency Business*, July 1993).

THE USA AND JAPAN'S RELATIONS WITH THE EUROPEAN UNION

US foreign direct investment is greater in the EU than in any other area of the world. The EU is also a favourite target for the Japanese, who have invested more in this area than in the Pacific Rim. Economic relations between the EU, the USA and Japan, however, have not been particularly good.

The USA and the European Union

The USA adopted a benign attitude towards the EEC in the 1950s and 1960s. The demise of the Bretton Woods system and the relative decline of the dollar, in the early 1970s, combined with the rise of the Deutschmark and the increasing industrial power of the EEC led to a change in US attitudes towards the Community (McDonald and Dearden, 1995, p. 307). The prime disputes were over the Community Agriculture Policy (CAP), the World steel industry dispute in the 1970s, 1980s, and mainly the US Omnibus Trade Act of 1988, Provision 301: 'the US government (was required) to identify countries using unfair trading practices, and such countries must take action to stop these practices. If they do not the US government unilaterally (should) impose trade restrictions against them'. The European Community perceived this as evidence of the growth of protectionism in the USA and maintained that such trading conflicts should be resolved by GATT.

But in the 1980s and early 1990s, after the collapse of the Soviet Union and the completion of German reunification in 1989–90, there was a precise and determined effort by the EU Commission and the Bush administration to coordinate policy on world trade, aid to developing states and eastern Europe. Delors was able to calm US fears that the Single Market programme would result in a 'Fortress Europe' with US products excluded. During the 1989 visit to Washington, Delors said: 'The completion of the internal market will increase the purchasing power of the EC, providing vast opportunities to our partners worldwide, and firstly to the United States' (quoted in Perry, 1994, p. 214). To this, Carla Hills, responded that the 'US administration strongly supported the 1992 programme and believed that its open and non-discriminatory implementation would benefit both the EC and its major trading partners, including the USA' (Perry, 1994, p. 214).

In 1993 EC–USA trading relations were clouded by disagreement on several issues, and aggravated by the new Clinton administration. Some of these issues included disputes over steel. Perry recounts these events as follows. The Americans claimed in 1980 that EC steel, bolstered by unfair state subsidies was being dumped in the USA, and thus imposed countervailing duties. The EC steel exporters then faced the imposition of quotas in 1982 and 1984. The EC retaliated by imposing its own anti-dumping duties on US steel exports to Europe. But, eventually a compromise was reached by which the EC was able to export a reduced amount of steel to the USA (Perry, 1994, p. 216). Another contentious issue was the 1991 civil aircraft production dispute between the EC and the USA (Perry, 1994, p. 216–217). US aircraft producers, especially Boeing, the leader of the civil aircraft industry, expressed outrage in 1991 at the allegedly unfair subsidies enjoyed by the European Airbus project. Boeing's fastest rising challenger Airbus is a four-nation consortium of French, German, Spanish and British companies which Boeing claimed in June 1991 had already received up to $26 billion in direct subsidies plus billions more through indirect military subsidies and privileged access to Community research programmes. The chief US trade negotiator, Carla Hills demanded that government aid for Airbus be limited to 25 per cent of its product development costs, and that such aid be provided by loans repayable within 15 years at a real rate of interest. The European position was that they would provide a 45 per cent limit on launch aid but only if the USA disclosed the true level of support (through tax relief and government orders) enjoyed by US aircraft producers. To Europeans, the US attitude seemed hypocritical, and a response to Airbus's success in 1990 in capturing 36 per cent of the jetliner orders won by the three largest producers, compared to Boeing's 48 per cent share and Douglas's 16 per cent share – the first time that Airbus had pushed Boeing below 50 per cent of the market in any one year. Eventually, in April 1992, the two sides reached a compromise whereby government support for Airbus was capped at between 30 and 35 per cent of development costs, but the quarrel was not so easily forgotten. When the US company, United Airlines agreed to lease 50 of Airbus's A 320 aeroplanes in July 1992, Carla Hills promised an immediate investigation of the deal in case Airbus was offering an artificially low price. In February 1993 the Clinton administration appeared to be threatening to renege on the April 1992 accord. The EC response was to stress that Airbus was not responsible for depressed conditions in the US aircraft industry. Aircraft manufacture worldwide was experiencing a crisis as a result of a global recession and the reduction in defence spending arising from the end of the Cold War. The Clinton administration made a proposal for a government prohibition on the award of contracts by federal agencies to companies in some or all EC states. EC companies were already effectively barred from defence and public health contracts, owing to rules under a Buy American Act. The US action was in retaliation against the EC's own public procurement policies which favoured Community companies (Perry, 1994, p. 217).

Japan and the European Union

The relationship between Japan and the European Union has almost always been somewhat difficult. In the immediate post-Second World War period, Japanese interaction with Europe was minimal. Japan became a member of GATT in August 1955. In the 1960s Japan traded with Europe mostly in light industry exports such as textiles, cutlery, sewing machines and so on. But in the early 1970s European–Japanese economic relations began to change. In 1973, the Community experienced a major enlargement with the accession of Great Britain, Denmark and Ireland, just two years after devaluation of the US dollar and the Nixon administration's imposition of a 10 per cent import surcharge, on certain imports, along with US pressures on Japan to restrain its exports to the USA. By 1974, the first oil shock had led to recession and a sharp drop in Japanese consumer demand. The Community's export to Japan fell drastically. As the US market seemed temporarily saturated, Japan focused on Europe which still held significant market opportunities and rich consumer markets. Between 1969 and 1975 Europe–Japanese trade grew from US $2 billion with a US $200 million European deficit to a US $8.7 billion with a US $3.2 billion European deficit (McIntyre, 1994, p. 66). Japan invested in all the EC countries some US $3 billion during the period 1951–1977. Most of these investments were in the UK, Germany, Ireland, Portugal and Spain where the Japanese found willing joint-venture partners. In the late 1970s, and early 1980s, Japan targeted Europe for its car industry, and in 1979 managed to sell over 630 000 Japanese vehicles in Europe compared to 1.5 million in the USA. In response, the French government immediately reinstated its three per cent import limit on cars from Japan. Italy had a Treaty quota of 20 000 vehicles from Japan per year. Germany informally set the bar at below 10 per cent of the market and the UK did likewise. Japan car manufacturers began to search for joint ventures with European partners. The EC Commission in November 1980 tried to preempt separate policies by individual member states by issuing the following policy:

1. Japanese VERs on cars and electronics should be as uniform as possible throughout the Community
2. A stronger yen truly reflective of the strength of the Japanese economy was required
3. A great opening of the Japanese market though the removal of NTBs was essential
4. Equal treatment of US and EC demands by Japan should be pursued

(*Financial Times*, 11 November, 1980)

The so-called 'screwdriver plant' regulation or anti-circumvention of anti-dumping duties laws was passed in June 1987 by the EC. Under the provisions of this regulation when a product is subject to an EC dumping finding, duties are then also assessed on the product assembled in the EC by corporate entities which are related to the foreign manufacturer, if the EC assembly plant was started or substantially augmented after the dumping investigation began. Sixty per cent of the parts used in the assembly must come from the foreign country subject to the dumping findings. If the content from third countries is increased to 40 per cent, then anti-dumping duties are not applied. This policy led Japanese firms to open chip plants in Europe to satisfy the EC requirement and avoid rules aimed at screwdriver assembly plants. A

Toshiba spokesman stated that 'our basic position is that we want full production in the EC by 1992' (*Wall Street Journal*, 3 February, 1989, p. A12).

In the 1990s, the Community became increasingly anxious about the level of Japanese penetration of the EC economies and, as a direct corollary about the unfair obstacles which EC firms seeking entry into Japan had to contend with, (McIntyre, 1994, p. 58). Madame Edith Cresson, then French prime minister, and former minister of trade and industry (1983–86) is quoted as making the following pronouncement:

> Japan is an adversary who does not respect the rules of the game and whose overwhelming desire is to conquer the world...Japanese investments are not like others. They destroy jobs. Those who can't see that must be blind...We hear all too often that we must open up our markets, which really means first to the Japanese. In the name of what must we abandon France?
>
> (*The Economist*, 1991, p. 52)

Perry (1994) distinguishes three major factors which have created strains in European–Japanese relations:

1. The imbalance of trade, with Community exports to Japan equivalent to representing only one-third of Japanese sales to the Community.
2. The concentration of Japanese exports in the most sensitive sectors of the European market – cars, motor-cycles, machine tools, and domestic electrical goods.
3. The innumerable obstacles faced by European firms wishing to export to Japan. Japanese customs duties are on average no higher than those in the Community but the real problem is the manipulation by Japanese authorities of technical barriers to trade as a device to keep out imports. For example, it takes nine days for imports to clear Japanese customs because goods must be inspected and then given at least eight safety and certification tests required by Japanese ministries.

The British, along with other Europeans feel as exasperated as the Americans. Negotiating with the Japanese is like shooting at a changing target. As soon as you shoot one restriction down, another is put in its place', commented an official at the Department of Trade and Industry in the UK (Perry, 1994, p. 220).

European countries do not all have the same attitudes when it comes to dealing with the Japanese challenge. Some seek to attract Japanese foreign investment in the Community while, at the same time, many EU government and business leaders favour restrictions on trade-related foreign investment. The liberal free trade-oriented political centre in the EU considers that Japan represents a possible model for European economic growth and industrial renewal. Japanese exports, on this view, can be a positive stimulus to make European industries more competitive, while Japanese investment may create needed jobs and push the technological frontier forward. The nationalist right and the more left-oriented parties, on the other hand, are wary of Japanese exports and industrial practices. Their reasons may vary but their analysis does not. Japanese exports, they argue pose a real threat to their existing European domestic industrial order. The question that now arises concerns the implications of these developments for European businesses, and whether firms in Europe should view this as a threat or an opportunity?

IMPLICATIONS OF THE GLOBALIZATION OF MARKETS FOR EUROPEAN BUSINESS

European businesses need not necessarily fear and avoid Japanese or US 'entanglements'. The real problem they face is how to select carefully from alliance prospects with either US or

Japanese partners, and then how to jointly manage them to mutually satisfactory benefit. This is discussed more fully in the next chapter.

The economic impact of Japanese investment with respect to the EU includes the following:

- Japanese manufacturing investment is moving beyond the 'screwdriver' stage to full-fledged production in the EC, with the possible introduction of Japanese production methods and new organizational forms to EC locations.
- The build-up of networks of Japanese firms is likely to raise local content levels, a key concern for European policy-makers. European suppliers might suffer, however, if Japanese production networks remain closed to them, that is, if Japanese manufacturers extend preferential treatment to the Euro-affiliates of their Japanese suppliers. Conversely, European suppliers could become strengthened if Japanese networks are opened to include them.
- The introduction of new production methods and organizational forms in the EC might be to the benefit of the EC economy if it improves upon the prevailing performance of domestic industry, particularly where EC firms are relatively strong *vis-à-vis* Japanese rivals.
- In industries in which EC countries have strong locational advantages, and in which EC firms are weak relative to Japanese competitors, the transfers of Japanese practices to the host country may enable Japanese firms to establish strong footholds in EC industries, to the possible long-term detriment of EC firms.
- Distortions could occur in European factor markets if *keiretsu* members extend preferential treatment to one another; challenges to European competition policy may also arise in the face of a large-scale build-up of *keiretsu* groupings (Gittleman and Graham, 1994, p. 155).

Lessons European firms should learn from the Japanese success in Europe
- a long-term perspective
- drive for market share
- market and customer research
- exploiting strategic windows
- product and market adaptation
- aggressive marketing tactics
- employee planning involvement
- top management dedication

(Egan and McKiernan, 1993, p. 126)

Business Week International (1993) described the Japanese 'Battle for Europe' as follows:

(The Japanese) have systematically forged alliances with companies short of cash and hungry for technology. When local production was required, they launched investments in plants, sometimes from scratch. And most recently they have been buying big chunks in companies outright, from clothing makers such as Laura Ashley and Hugo Boss to Germany's construction gear maker Hanomag. They have also worked at becoming good 'corporate citizens' funding soccer teams, university chairs, museums and art galleries across Europe.

A major implication of globalization for European business firms is thus the increasingly important role of coalitions, or strategic alliances, linking firms in the same industry based in different countries. Strategic alliances are a major consequence of globalization and of the need for an integrated worldwide strategy, and will be the subject of the next chapter.

A second implication of the contemporary globalization of business is the changing relationship between states and firms, which has led to an increased blurring of the relationship between public and private, and between governments and multinationals. At the end of the Second World War, free trade was promoted as the best remedy for international, and particularly European economic recovery and reconstruction. Tariff barriers to international trade were gradually abolished, allowing the free flow of goods to flourish in the 1950s and 1960s. International trade grew rapidly, achieving fast economic growth. During the 1970s and early 1980s, however, the situation changed drastically. With the rise of inflation, increased unemployment and world recession, high demands for government protectionism were made in industries for both agricultural and manufactured products. Government intervention in international trade and regulations in the form of quota restrictions and exchange controls, import rationing, and export restraints increased considerably. By the mid-1980s, and as a result of extensive stagflation, there was a general disappointment and disillusion with government efficiency in regulating international trade, reinforced further by the events in Eastern and Central Europe at the close of the 1980s. New trends towards privatization and deregulation are at present calling for the retreat of the state from the market throughout the world and demanding that government take a 'back seat' in guiding the national economy (Ohmae, 1990). Instead of the passive role of governments mostly favoured in the early 1980s, the early 1990s witnessed a change of attitude towards the role of governments in international trade.

In his influential book *The Competitive Advantage of Nations*, Michael Porter insisted that although the role of governments in international trade was partial, it was nevertheless influential in improving the national environment and in pushing and challenging its industry to advance (Porter, 1990, Chapter 12). For Porter, the government's main objective should be to enhance national competitive advantage. Its role in international trade should be to create an environment in which firms can upgrade competitive advantages in established industries by introducing more sophisticated technology and methods and by penetrating more advanced segments of the market. National government policies, according to Porter, should be initiated to improve competitiveness rather than to 'help' industry by means of protective measures. Industry needs competition to succeed internationally and the national government's role should be to open markets by dismantling trade barriers. Some of the most effective policies to be adopted to achieve national competitiveness are devaluation, deregulation, privatization, relaxation of product and environmental standards, promotion of inter-firm collaboration and cooperation of various types, encouragement of mergers, tax reforms, regional development, negotiation of voluntary restraint or orderly marketing arrangements, improving the general education system, and expansion of government investment in research, and government programmes to find new enterprises. In other words, the role of the government according to Porter is to become a 'facilitator, signaller and prodder' (Porter, 1990).

However, in the 1990s and due to the internationalization of information and communication, production and finance, the old view that the government's role is to preserve national sovereignty, and protect and represent the national interests of its people against foreign domination and foreign competition is no longer seen as appropriate.

As a result of the increased globalization of the world, we are, according to Ohmae, moving towards a 'borderless world' where people have greater access to global information, and consumers have become more informed about the availability of goods and services from around the world. Government intervention in this interlinked economy, as he calls it, becomes an obstacle. In the light of the ending of the Cold War between the superpowers and the liberalization of eastern and central Europe, national security is becoming more of a myth. The government's role, Ohmae argues, should be to ensure that people have access to the best and cheapest goods and services from anywhere in the world, and not to protect certain industries of certain clusters of people. To do this, government's role today must now concentrate on providing a first-class infrastructure for business by improving national education, providing wider access to information, and in making the national environment a more attractive location for global companies to do business, invest and pay tax (Ohmae, 1991a).

Peter Dicken, in contrast argues that 'not only are states still significant actors in their own right in the world economy but also they have the capacity to encourage or to inhibit global integration' (Dicken, 1992). Despite the increasing globalization of the world, Dicken argues that the state remains a most significant force in shaping the world economy. It has significantly played an extremely important role in the process of industrialization in all countries. Indeed it would be quite difficult to see how global firms could have achieved the economic and export performance they have without the crucial input of government policies. It could be argued in fact, that all governments intervene to varying degrees in the operation of the market, and therefore help to shape different parts of the global economic map. Nation states, explains Dicken, operate within a world system of differential power relationships. Expressed in the simplest terms, if the central goal of business organizations is to achieve maximum, or at least satisfactory profits, one of the central goals of nation states is to maximize the material welfare of their societies. In an increasingly integrated and interdependent global economy, nations are forced to compete with one another in a struggle to attain such goals. States compete to enhance their international trading position and to capture as large a share as possible of the gain from trade. They compete to attract productive investment to build up their national production base, which, in turn, enhances their international competitive position (Dicken, 1992). The competitive basis of nation states is derived from a complex set of sources. The international competitiveness of national economies is built on the competitiveness of the firms which operate within, and export from, national boundaries. To a large extent, it is thus an expression of the dynamism of domestic firms, their capacity to invest and to innovate both as a consequence of their own R&D, and of successful appropriation of technologies developed elsewhere (Chesnais, 1986, pp. 85–129).

National governments play an important role in shaping the global economic map, and indeed in encouraging or inhibiting the global ambitions and strategies of business firms. National boundaries create significant differentials on the global economic surface. Political spaces are among the most important ways in which location-specific factors are packaged. Political boundaries create discontinuities of varying magnitudes in the flows of economic activities and governments can modify or even help to create or destroy comparative advantage. Take the example of newly industrialized markets which are virtually without exception less-developed states. These are market economies in which the state performs a highly interventionist role, although the precise role of the state varies greatly from one newly industrialized country (NIC) to another. In some cases, state ownership of production is very substantial, in others it is insignificant. In some cases, the major policy emphasis is upon attracting foreign direct investment, in others such investment is tightly regulated and the policy emphasis is upon nurturing domestic firms (Useful surveys of government policies in the NICS are provided by OECD 1988 survey which deals with the four leading Asia NICs plus Brazil and Mexico.)

This concept of an 'interlinked' world economy, or the growing global interdependence of states and firms in the 1990s has been explored further by Stopford *et al.* (1992). Their aim was to show how global changes in finance, technology, knowledge and politics often impel governments to seek the help and cooperation of managers of multinational firms. The conclusion of their study is that the rivalry between states and firms to secure a place in world markets in the 1990s is becoming fiercer. Instead of competing for power as a means to wealth, they argue that states nowadays are competing more for wealth as means to power – power to maintain internal order and social cohesion rather than power to conduct foreign conquest or defend themselves against foreign attack. Consequently, instead of negotiating between themselves, states are now negotiating with foreign firms to acquire the basic means to create wealth within their territory. Global competition has also affected the operations of firms. They are now facing increasing difficulties in seeking new sources of competition and in establishing themselves in world markets. Realizing their need for government support and help to maintain their capacity to compete in global markets and to obtain states' cooperation and alliances, they are now having to change their traditional exploitative and colonial attitudes towards ownership and control and act more like 'statesmen'.

According to the theory of triangular diplomacy, governments in the 1990s, as a result of the increasing global competition and globalization of business, no longer merely negotiate among themselves but are increasingly pushed to negotiate with foreign firms. Multinational firms too are increasingly having to act in a statesman-like way in seeking corporate alliances to enhance their combined capacities to compete with others for world market shares. These negotiations are nowadays carried out on a triangular basis. This interaction between firms and states is conducted in three dimensions, as shown in Fig. 10.1.

National boundaries no longer define the rules. International negotiations and action are now carried out on a triangular basis, where traditional players in the embassies and foreign ministries are increasingly being joined by members of other governments' ministries and by executives of firms, both local and multinational.

In order to substantiate their thesis, Stopford *et al.* show how global structural changes in finance, technology, knowledge and politics have affected the ways in which governments and managers of multinational firms interact. Six general propositions are made:

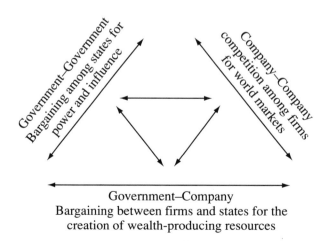

Figure 10.1   Triangular diplomacy (adapted from Stoppford and Strange, 1991)

1. States are now competing more for the means to create wealth within their territory than for power over more territory. They now compete more for wealth as a means to power rather than for power as a means to wealth.
2. The basis of competition is shifting to emphasize product quality, not just costs. Attractive sites for new investment are increasingly those supplying skilled workers and efficient infrastructures.
3. Small, poor countries are facing increased barriers to entry in industrial sectors most subject to global forces of competition.
4. States no longer negotiate only among themselves. They now must negotiate with foreign firms. This has recently become the norm, where as previously it was exceptional.
5. The increased number of possible policy options for governments and firms complicates further the problems for both of managing multiple agendas.
6. All of these shifts have increased the volatility of change and divergence of outcomes.

(Stopford *et al.*, 1992)

REVIEW QUESTIONS

1. The 'globlization of business is a trend that is causing sleepless nights for many business managers'. Explain and evaluate this proposition.
2. List and explain the main factors behind the increasing globalization of business.
3. Should the EU adopt tough measures to prevent further Japanese penetration of its home market?
4. In his recent book *The Borderless World*, Ohmae argues that in the interlinked economy of today's world, governments should stand back and let the people vote with their pocket book. Explain and evaluate this proposition. To what extent, if at all does this proposition apply to the European Union?

EXERCISE 10.1: Globalization and business in Europe

Aim: The aim of this exercise is to familiarize students with various globalization strategies adopted by multinationals and their implications for business in Europe.

Assignment: 'The triad is characterized by a unique blend of cooperation and competition among US, European and Japanese counterpart multinationals'. Compare and contrast the various global strategies adopted by multinationals in the triad, and assess their implications for business in Europe.

Format: Students are divided into three groups. Each group is allocated one region of the triad: Europe, the USA, and Japan. In their presentation to the class students are expected to:

- provide an exposition of the globalization strategies of US, European and Japanese multinationals of their choice
- describe their strategic implementation in Europe
- assess the implications (if any) for European business

Sources

Students are encouraged to research this project using the various sources of information provided in previous chapters. They should be, by now, familiar with most databases and capable of being more selective in their research.

FURTHER READING

Dicken, P., *Global Shift. Industrial Change in a Turbulent World*, 2nd edition, Paul Chapman, London, 1992.

Levitt, T., *The Marketing Imagination*, The Free Press, New York, 1983.

Mason, D.T. and Turay, A.M., *Japan, NAFTA and Europe. Trilateral Cooperation or Confrontation?* St Martin's Press, New York, 1994.

Ohmae, K., *The Borderless World. Power and Strategy in the Interlinked Economy*, Collins, 1991.

Perry, K., *Business and the European Community*, Butterworth-Heinemann, Oxford, 1994.

Porter, M., *The Competitive Advantage of Nations*, Macmillan, London, 1990.

Stopford, J., Strange, S. and Henley, J., *Rival States, Rival Firms. Competition for World Market Shares*, Cambridge University Press, Cambridge, 1991.

MANAGING STRATEGIC ALLIANCES IN EUROPE

The Single Market directives, deregulation, liberalization and privatization, the opening up of the eastern bloc have made Europe the focus of global acquisitions and alliances, with roughly half of global linkages involving a European company as acquiror of alliance partner (Bleeke and Ernst, 1993, p. 111). Over the last 10 years or so, and especially since the creation of the Single European Market, Europe has witnessed a tremendous surge in the number and types of strategic alliances. To date many large European companies have competed primarily within their home markets. The future of these companies hinges on their ability to collaborate with foreign partners in order to improve skills, increase scale, or gain access to new markets. For these companies developing appropriate cross-border alliance and acquisition strategies is crucial. These European companies are just beginning to learn what states have long known: 'in a complex, uncertain world filled with dangerous opponents, it is best not to go it alone' (Ohmae, 1991). Two linked questions seem central here. First will multinational cooperation become the common practice in Europe in the foreseeable future, and second what are the implications of this trend for European business.

Alliances and acquisitions in Europe take a different approach, due to deregulation, opening of borders and expanded presence of new competitors. Consequently, managers trying to fashion cross-border strategies for Europe face unique challenges. The purpose of this chapter is to clarify the conceptual, theoretical and practical dimensions involved in understanding and managing strategic alliances in Europe.

LEARNING OBJECTIVES

- To examine the reasons behind the contemporary explosive growth in the formation of international strategic alliances
- To explain and illustrate how such forms of cooperation are taking place
- To provide guidance on how to manage European strategic alliances more efficiently

THE RISE AND GROWTH OF STRATEGIC ALLIANCES

In the last decade, strategic alliances have grown by more than 25 per cent annually. Several developments in the global political economy have contributed to such a growth. Some of these, for example, are the globalization of production, finance, and information technology; economic integration, increased regionalization of markets and deregulation; technological innovation and shorter product life cycles; global competition and cultural evolution (i.e. the homogenization of tastes) through the mass media and other forces (refer to Chapter Ten for details). Companies all over the world are now having to develop relationships with peers abroad, to team up with partners to ameliorate resource shortages, to gain time – even if only to remain abreast of important external developments, and perhaps to influence them. Strategic alliances have also become an important means for firms of all sizes to develop a practical approach to increasing the possibilities of implementing their international strategies.

Alliances, however, are not simply tools of convenience for achieving international competitive advantage. They have become critical instruments for serving customers in a global environment. Very few companies are able to offer high levels of value to all their customers, all the time, all by themselves. They need partners and they need alliances. Glaxo, the British pharmaceutical company, for example, did not want to establish a full business system in each country where it did business. Given its costly commitment to topflight R&D, it did not see how it could – or why it should – build an extensive sales and service network to cover all the hospitals in Japan and the USA. So it decided to link with first-class partners in Japan, swap its best drugs with them, and focus its own resources on generating greater sales from its established network in Europe (Ohmae, 1991). That kind of value creation and delivery is what alliances make possible.

IBM, one of the most powerful multinational corporations in the world, after experiencing a significant decline in performance and suspecting a serious loss of competitive advantage, decided in 1991 upon a radical restructuring of its operations from that of an integrated worldwide firm with a strong single culture to that of a federation of 14 potentially competitive companies (Faulkner, 1991). It recently teamed up with Microsoft to exploit the latter's growing expertise in software for desktop computers. AT&T signed twin accords with the European leaders in information technology, Olivetti and Philips. By combining corporate expertise, AT&T hopes to grab a foothold first in Europe and them around the world. Philips partnership with AT&T will strengthen its hold on the North American market and will give it access to AT&T's technology in light and electronic components.

Multinationals are increasingly recognizing that joining forces can lead to large-scale economies, technology and resource pooling, improved access to foreign markets and avoidance of national regulations (Perlmutter and Heenan, 1991). Ohmae argues further that the increasing convergence of consumer needs and preferences in world markets is another factor why alliances are becoming a necessity. Whatever their nationality, consumers needs have increasingly become globalized (Ohmae, 1991). They all have access to the same source of information, and have similar needs and expectations, namely product quality, value, and innovation.

There are three further major trends in the global political economy which will influence the necessity for increased evolution of strategic alliances in the next two decades. These are the emergence of regional trading blocs, the evolution of new markets, and the dispersion of technological advances (Culpan, 1993).

CHARACTERISTICS OF STRATEGIC ALLIANCES

A strategic alliance is a collection of separate companies linked through collaborative agreements. However, not all the companies in a group have to be linked directly to all the others. Strategic alliances, also known as alliance networks often grow out of the need to gain scale economies or market share. Most alliance networks are built piece by piece and don't spring into existence fully formed. There are many forms of strategic alliances: minority equity alliances, international joint ventures, various forms of licensing agreements, international subcontracting sometimes known as contractual collaboration, contracts relating to supplies and technology exchange, and consortium strategic alliances.

- **Minority equity alliances**   These are voluntary relationships between two firms in which one company purchases a substantial, but less than 50 per cent portion of the other firm to undertake joint activities (Killing, 1992, pp. 57–75). The global auto industry contains many examples of this type of alliance. Ford, for example, owns 25 per cent of Mazda. Under this alliance, the two firms co-design and produce several brands of automobiles, but do not market the cars collaboratively.
- **International joint ventures**   These have been the most common form of strategic alliance for many years. An international joint venture involves the establishment of a new legal, corporate entity in which equity is shared by both partners. International joint ventures provide joint, but not necessarily equal, degrees of ownership and control.
- **International licensing arrangements**   Licensing arrangements have become more prominent worldwide both in manufacturing and in service and franchise industries. These represent the least sophisticated form of strategic alliance because the companies involved do not take an equity position in one another.
- **Cross-licensing agreements**   These are often found in industries in which R&D and other fixed costs are exorbitant, but where aggressive competition is needed to maintain industry-wide discipline and innovation. The pharmaceutical and chemical industries are replete with cross-licensing agreements between global firms.
- **International subcontracting, also known as contractual collaboration**   These are non-equity formal agreements between two or more firms. They include technical training agreements, buy-backs, licences and franchises, and management service agreements. Ciba-Geigy and Eli Lilly, for example, cross-license pharmaceuticals in different markets. Other examples include GM which buys cars and components from South Korea's Daewoo, and Germany's Siemens which buys computers from Fujitsu.
- **Consortium strategic alliances**   This type of strategic alliance can be found in research consortium programmes among several parties, each having too small a resource base to carry out all of the research on its own. Examples are with smaller rather than very large pharmaceutical firms, cooperation in the automotive industry among the slightly lesser players, for example Volvo, Renault, Mitsubishi, or with the electronics and chemical industries. EUREKA in Europe is a consortium formed by a number of European countries to bring together scientists and engineers to engage in research projects. Airbus Industry is another example of a consortium backed by four governments in Europe to produce commercial aircraft.

CASE STUDY 11.1: Airbus industrie

Airbus industrie is a strategic alliance of four major European aerospace companies. It was set up in 1969 to design, build, sell, and maintain airliners of over 100 seats. Its partners are: Aerospatiale from France, Deutsche Aerospace, a Daimler Benz subsidiary from Germany, British Aerospace from Britain and Construcciones Aeronautics from Spain. The structure of the alliance is a French one a *'Groupement d'interêt Economique'*. It has the advantage of being a formal legal entity, but one which allows companies to come together to collaborate for a range of common purposes while allowing them to remain wholly independent for the remainder of their activities. In 1992 Airbus Industrie turnover was US $7.5 billion. It had sold 1000 aircraft by 1993.

Within the GIE structure, formal control rests with a General Meeting of Members in which each of the partners has voting rights proportionate to its investment in the alliance. The day-to-day decision making is dealt with by an executive board of seven members. It prepares the ground for the strategic decisions to be taken by the supervisory board, makes key decisions in pursuit of the strategy agreed by the supervisory board, and provides oversight of the management of the consortium's programmes. Airbus managers run the consortium's programmes and supervise the work of the partner companies. In this context each partner's position is akin to that of a subcontractor having to produce work to an Airbus specification.

(Source: Lei and Slocum Jr., 1991, pp. 44–62)

Joel Bleeke and David Ernest categorize strategic alliances into six types based on their probable outcomes:

- collisions between competitors
- alliances of the weak
- disguised sales
- bootstrap alliances
- evolution to a sale
- alliances of complementary equals

To these alliances arbitrage, or 'sleeping with the enemy' can be added (Bleeke and Ernst, 1995, pp. 97–105).

Professor Rosabeth Moss Kanter classifies cooperative arrangements between companies along a continuum from weak and distant to strong and close. At one extreme are mutual service consortia, where similar companies in similar industries pool their resources to gain a benefit too expensive to acquire alone, for example, access to an advanced technology. At mid-range, in joint ventures, companies pursue an opportunity that needs a capability from each of them – the technology of one and the market access of the other, for example. The joint venture might operate independently, or it might link the partners' operations. The strongest and closest collaborations are value-chain partnerships, such as supplier-customer relationships. Companies in different industries with different but comlementary skills link their capabilities to create value for ultimate users. Commitments in those relationships tend to be high, the partners tend to develop joint activities in many functions, operations often overlap, and the relationship thus creates substantial change within each partner's organization (Moss Kanter, 1994, pp. 96–108).

MANAGEMENT OF EUROPEAN STRATEGIC ALLIANCES

Prior to the selection of an alliance, the prospective partners need to have a strong motivation to implement the alliance. As Roland Bertodo of the Rover Group commented: 'Strategic alliances are not tools of convenience. They are ... critical instruments in fulfilling corporate strategic objectives' (interview with Roland Bertodo, cited in Faulkner, 1995).

Consideration needs to be given to the principal motivations for establishing strategic alliances. In addition to those factors of the global political and economic environment mentioned earlier, internal factors have also played a major role in the creation of strategic alliances. These include resource dependency, financial risk and fast market entry. A strong motivation for creating a strategic alliance stems from internal needs for specific resources, or skills, or from competence inadequacy or imbalance. Each partner seeks a different resource or skill compensation from the other. Other needs include local knowledge, marketing skills and access to distribution channels, and strong brand names as illustrated by the following examples.

CASE STUDY 11.2: alliances in the car industry in Europe

Ford Mazda

Alliances provide opportunity for companies to acquire complex background knowledge that cannot be learned from manuals or from observation at a distance. Ford's 13-year alliance with Mazda illustrates this substyle but important transfer. Mazda teaches Ford about lean manufacturing and engineering, while Ford teaches Mazda about design, finance, and international marketing.

Honda/Piaggio

In Italy, Honda's alliance with an Italian manufacturer Piaggio, Europe's largest maker of motorcycles (*Financial Times*, 19 January 1993), was to set up working groups to explore product development opportunities for the European market, particularly in small and mid-sized motorcycles. Another objective of the alliance was that the two companies should develop standardized parts for their European models through cooperation in design, manufacture and procurement.

Honda/Rover

Rover, a well-known British-based car group had different motivations. In the mid-1970s Rover was seriously foundering, but it was rescued by the British government in the late 1970s in the hope of turning around the company's performance. One possibility was collaboration with major Japanese car manufacturers: Nissan or Honda. Honda felt insecure in this area, and although it knew European tastes differed from those in the USA, it did not trust its understanding of those differences. Furthermore, Honda did not believe it had time to develop its own European arm from scratch. The development costs of new European models would be too great at that stage of Honda's development, and the time scale too long to be acceptable (Faulkner, 1995, p. 149). But Rover had access to an acceptable UK and European network of component suppliers and subcontractors. It had ample spare capacity in its factories, and could manufacture as many cars for Honda as the Japanese could manage to sell. Rover also had an understanding of European tastes (Faulkner, 1995, p. 593).

Rover, on the other hand, then still operating as British Leyland Motor Corporation also felt it had specific weaknesses. On the product side, it needed something to offer in the lower-to-medium market segment – but did not have the resources, including finance and time, to tackle this product portfolio. On the operation side it lacked knowledge let along mastery of the Japanese-initiated modern methods of 'lean production', including total quality control, just-in time, and robotification of the manufacturing process – fields in which Honda had much management know-how.

In short there were mutual gains from the alliance between Honda and Rover. A collaborative agreement was finally signed between the two companies in December 1979. By 1993, the alliance turned an operating profit of £50 million. But the following year, British Aerospace, the dominant shareholder in the Rover Group announced the sale of its 80 per cent stake in the latter to BMW, the German car maker which was one of Honda's most potent rivals in the European market. The Honda–Rover alliance almost broke-up, but due to the remaining material benefits and costs of full separation that confronted the partners, an agreement was reached in May 1994, concerned mainly with the continuation of current collaboration (Burton, 1995).

BMW/Rover

BMW's motivation differs slightly from Honda, BMW's interest in Rover is to use Rover's now popular-priced cars to open new markets for BMW high-priced cars. Through the alliance, BMW also gets to sell Rover's much sought after four-wheel drive vehicles. BMW also hopes to use Rover's historical brands – MG and Austin-Healey on a new limited production of sports cars.

One way of characterizing strategic alliance motivations according to Lorange and Ross (1995), is by looking at the strategic positions of each prospective partner's position in terms of two dimensions. One dimension concerns the strategic importance of the particular business within which the strategic alliance is being contemplated, and how it fits the overall portfolio of a particular partner. The issue then is whether this business (with its prospective strategic alliance) is part of the core activities of this prospective partner, or can be seen as somewhat more peripheral. The second dimension regards the firm's relative position in the business it is in, that is whether it is a leader or more of a follower. As a leader it would typically have the larger market share, leading technology, or superior quality. It would approach a strategic alliance differently than if it has a small share and is attempting to catch up.

Focusing on these two strategic positioning dimensions, four generic motives for strategic alliances emerge. When the strategy of the strategic alliance is core within the parent firm's overall portfolio, and the firm enjoys a relative leadership in this business, the typical motive for entering into strategic alliances is defensive. The two major rationales for strategic alliances stem from this access to markets and/or technology and securing resources. Defensive strategies may also be needed to secure the sourcing of raw materials and/or inexpensive products. This rationale has been a factor for many multinational firms in developing countries. Also many leading Japanese firms have entered into strategic alliances in south-east Asia for this reason.

When the business still falls within the core area of a firm's portfolio, but the firm is more of a follower in the business segment, the primary motive for strategic alliances is often to catch up. It might be highly critical for a firm to strengthen its competitive position in order to make it viable, and a strategic alliance may be the only realistic option, other than outright sale. When the business plays a relatively peripheral role in the overall portfolio, but where the firm is a leader, the main rationale is to remain. Here one might decide to form a strategic alliance to get the maximum efficiency out of the firm's position. To preserve a firm's continued presence in a given country the firm may have to give up full ownership and seek a local partner.

Finally, if the firm is more of a follower in the business area and if the particular business plays a relatively peripheral role in the parent's portfolio, the main motive for cooperative strategies is to restructure the business. The goal might also be to restructure the business with an eye toward creating some strength and value which might enable the parent company eventually to unload this business (Lorange and Ross, 1995).

Having established the nature and the conditions leading to strategic alliances, it is important now to examine how strategic alliances are actually established, why so many of them fail, and what are the conditions for their success.

ESTABLISHING SUCCESSFUL STRATEGIC ALLIANCES

Partner selection

Selecting the appropriate partner is a vital decision that will have considerable influence on the effectiveness of the alliance. Faulkner (1995 p. 64) identifies four key criteria for a successful selection. These are: complementary assets, the existence of synergies between the companies, approximate balance in size and strength and compatible cultures.

- **Complementary assets** If a company needs market access, for example, it must not only find a partner that can supply the necessary access, but that partner must also require something in return, i.e. technology or product, if an alliance is to follow. Firms tend to seek a partner whom they perceive to have complementary assets for which synergies can be realized. The goals between the two partners may be different, but should be complementary. In the example of Hitachi and Fiat, their strategic alliance has allowed partners of similar position to achieve global scale in the hydraulic excavator business with much less risk and expense than would have been possible for either with a go-it-alone strategy. Hitachi was an attractive partner for Fiat-Allis because it was strong in hydraulic excavators, but lacked the full product line necessary to control European distribution of earth-moving equipment. The fact that Hitachi was not, like Komatsu or Caterpillar, a dominant competitor in the global market for construction equipment made for a more even balance of power. By allying with Hitachi, Fiat significantly strengthened both its technological skills and its position in a global business.
- **Compatible business and management cultures** Most failed alliances cite incompatibility as a key reason for their failure. This does not mean, however, that business and management cultures between the alliances must be similar, as long as culture is explicitly on the agenda and partners recognize the need to become more attuned to each other's cultural reactions to situations. A sensitive attitude to cultural differences is necessary if the alliance is to succeed.
- **Commitment and trust** An alliance to be successful should operate in a spirit of trust, cooperation and integrity. An atmosphere of mutual distrust and domination by one partner may jeopardize the stability of the alliance.
- Finally **termination** A formula for termination should be built into the initial agreement as reassurance for both parties. If the alliance is to be successful, in addition to the clearly defined goals, the limits of the alliance should also be recognized.

(Lorange and Ross, 1995)

The major possible pitfalls of strategic alliances can be summarized as follows:

- future conflicts due to the differing agenda of the partners
- inadequate partner rapport leading to misunderstandings
- fear during technology transfer that a future competitor is being created
- business cultural incompatibility
- lack of commitment by the partners as personnel are seconded for two years then rotated
- A change in the strategic condition and objectives of the partners, which is not reflected in the arrangement of the alliance

(Faulkner, 1995)

MODEL FOR PLANNING SUCCESSFUL STRATEGIC ALLIANCES FOR EUROPE

The following model is provided to offer guidance in the planning and implementation of strategic alliances in the European Union.

Stage 1: External and internal analysis

The first stage in the planning process consists of an external and internal analysis of the forces leading to the need for the formation of the strategic alliance. The external analysis should include reference to the major factors leading to the increased globalization of markets, technological advancement, global competition and so on, while the internal analysis should include the motives of the firm such as resource pooling, risk sharing, market entry and so on.

Stage 2: Decision-making

The second stage is to decide on the type of alliance to be set up, its nature, general objectives, and long- and short-term targets. Managers considering an alliance must have a clear, strategic understanding of their company's current capabilities and the capabilities it will need in the future. It is important to assess the current core competencies the firm possesses, and the perceived potential profit opportunities from the proposed alliance. Porter (1980) recommends the following sequence:

1. Analyze the industrial environment for opportunities
2. Assess the internal capacity available to take advantage of these opportunities
3. Identify, evaluate and select the appropriate strategies
4. Implement the chosen strategy

Stage 3: Strategic choice

Once it is decided on what type of strategic alliance is most suitable for the company, a decision needs to be made as to which strategy for cooperation to adopt. There are various strategies to choose from:

- *Market development and expansion* Cooperating firms try to develop and expand the present market to benefit mutually from such progress.
- *Research and development partnership* Many multinational firms (especially high technology) are formed to engage in joint product development.

- *International production sharing* This strategy refers to the manufacturing parts of a product in more than one country to achieve maximum economic effect with minimum investment.

Stage 4:   Forms of agreements

Once objectives and strategies are clearly defined, the form of cooperative agreement to be concluded must be decided upon. This could be either a minority equity alliance, international joint venture, contractual collaboration, international licensing, international sub-contracting, or a consortium alliance, as discussed earlier in this chapter.

Stage 5:   Expected outcome

It is very important to clarify from the start the expected outcomes for the proposed strategic alliance. These could range from benefits in sales, profits, economies of scale, gaining new know-how, reduction of host country trade restrictions and so on.

Stage 6:   Partner selection

Managers must consider a wide range of possible partners, and identify the nature and strength of each partner's potential competitive advantages. The size and strength of the partner is important to consider. Size mismatch could cause problems. The larger partner may impose more bureaucracy on the smaller one, and the smaller partner may become over-dependent (Moss Kanter, 1994).

Stage 7:   Alliance management

Managing the human aspects of the alliance is crucial to the success of any strategic alliance. This should include:

- An assessment of the cultural compatibility between the partners. Managers must scrutinize the values, commitment and capabilities of prospective partners. Complex business and management cultural differences distinguish firms, not only in the same country, but even in the same city and the same industry.
- Identification and evaluation of the attitudes and business practices to be adopted between the partners such as differences in authority, reporting and decision-making styles, who gets involved in the decision-making process and how quickly decisions are made, how much reporting and documentation are expected, what authority comes with a position, and which functions work together.

(Badaracco, 1991, Chapter 6)

OBSTACLES TO SUCCESSFUL STRATEGIC ALLIANCES IN EUROPE

Many strategic alliances fail in the early stages of their formation. A major obstacle for successful strategic alliance is the management of human resources within a multicultural and multinational settings. Attention must be given to recruiting and selecting the right people to be involved in the strategic alliance, the transferability of key people within the alliance, managerial reassignment, managerial competencies and skills requirements, management loyalty, and career and benefits planning (Lorange and Ross, 1995, Chapter 5).

A second challenge to successful strategic alliance is the fact that a partner must give up some autonomy over its own strategic resources. A third challenge is avoiding politics in the working of the strategic alliance. The role of various stakeholders should be laid out, calling for a codification of tasks and mutual expectations. A fourth challenge is unequal gains. Some partners may gain more than the others. Such unequal benefits may hamper the partnership especially when the expectations differ and stakes are high. A fifth challenge is the possibility of cultural clash. Individual and separate cultures may clash with others, especially within corporations encompassing distinctly differing cultures (Culpan, 1993). The sixth obstacle is a partner's alliance with competitors. A partner may establish cooperative linkages with competing firms and this situation may hamper the present alliance. As a result, an expectation of continuing cooperation with the partner in a series of projects or ventures may result in disappointment. Finally there is a learning challenge, the challenge in developing and/or increasing one's willingness to learn from the partner. Learning among partners must be even to enable partners to help each other to bring about overall organizational competence. The strategic alliance should be seen as a laboratory, or a positive experiment, with active involvement from people in the organization.

CASE STUDY 11.3: Competing through strategic alliances in Europe – The cereal market

In 1992 Kellogg dominated the European breakfast cereals market. It had a market share in excess of 50 per cent in all the main EC countries (Salier, 1991, p. 12). Kellogg had over 30 brands in Europe. All Kellogg's products were well supported by extensive TV advertising and by strong franchises with European grocery outlets: no European supermarket chain could really afford to be without Kellogg's products.

Weetabix is a private company. It had sales largely confined to the UK. Cereal Partners is the 50/50 company formed by Nestlé (Switzerland) and General Mills (USA) to attack the European breakfast cereal market. It bought the traditional UK product Shredded Wheat in 1990 from another company. Nestlé had great marketing experience and resources, and was interested in acquiring either Kellogg or Quaker in the USA. In 1989 it formed a global strategic alliance with General Mills. The latter had the technology and spare production capacity for initial production in Europe. It had also some US brands such as Golden Grahams and Cheerios which it had been exporting to Europe on a limited scale. Given the complementary resources of the two partners, they came together in 1989. Cereal Partners were hoping to obtain 20 per cent of market share in Europe by year 2000 and Nestlé manufacturer's name will appear on all products outside North America and Canada.

In Europe, the first task in 1990 was to acquire Shredded Wheat and simply introduce the brand name Nestlé as the manufacturer in the top left-hand corner. Cereal Partners then launched a series of new products. In May 1991 Golden Grahams were launched by Cereal Partners. It was a unique product with heavy TV advertising support. Kellogg reacted by relaunching its Golden Crackles products, and made sure its product was shelved in store right alongside its rival. In 1992, CP launched its second product Lucky Charms, a new product to Europe with crisply mallow pieces. Kellogg reformulated Ricicles to include similar mallow pieces. In May 1992 CP brought Clusters, with crunchy nuggets of almonds, pecans and walnut crisp wholewheat flakes; Kelloggs responded with Golden Oatmeal Crisp.

In 1993 CP changed the formulation of Cheerios to four different kinds of cereal rings to make it difficult to manufacture by Kellogg.

(Sources: Knowlton, 1991 and Lynch, 1993)

REVIEW QUESTIONS

1. Explain why strategic alliances have become such a widespread global phenomenon? Illustrate with real-life examples.
2. Commenting on their strategic alliance with Honda, Roland Bertodo, chairman of Rover Group said 'We have a shared bed, but we dream separate dreams'. Explain what Bertodo meant by this, and using examples from other strategic alliances, discuss how this kind of problem might be resolved.
3. 'Increasingly, to be globally competitive, multinational corporations must be globally cooperative' (Perlmutter and Heenan, 1991). Explain and evaluate this proposition in relation to the increased competition opened up by the Single European Market.

EXERCISE 11.1:   Strategic alliances in Europe

Aim   This project intends to develop students' analytical approach in assessing strategic alliances. The aim is to stimulate their awareness of the problems faced by establishing and managing strategic alliances in the European Union.

Assignment   Students are asked to investigate various strategic alliances in Europe, research fully their cases and present their findings to the class.

Format   Students should consider the following points when preparing for their class presentation:

- overview of the aims and objectives of the strategic alliance examined
- how was it established, why and where
- the European business environment and its impact upon the alliance considered
- an evaluation of the advantages gained, and analysis of the difficulties experienced as a result of implementing such an alliance
- evaluation and recommendations

FURTHER READING

Badaracco, J., *The Knowledge Link: How Firms Compete through Strategic Alliances*, Harvard Business School Publications, 1991.

Contractor, F., and Lorange, P., (eds), *Cooperative Strategies in International Business*, Lexington Books, New York, 1992.

Faulkner, D., *International Strategic Alliances. Cooperating to Compete*, McGraw-Hill, New York, 1995.

Lorange, P. and Ross, J., *Strategic Alliances: Formation, Implementation and Evolution*, Blackwell, Oxford, 1995.

Porter, M., *Competitive Strategic: Techniques for Analyzing Industries and Competitors*, Free Press, New York, 1980.

TWELVE

THE GREENING OF EUROPEAN BUSINESS

The 1990s will be the decade of the environment

(president, Petroleum Marketers Association)

There has been a noticeable increase of interest in environmental issues since the 1970s. Public interest in global environment issues such as global warming, deforestation, disposal of toxic wastes, and acid rain has reached a high level of concern in the 1990s. At the same time public awareness of the impact of business on the environment has also increased sharply in the last few years. Scientific evidence has confirmed the reality of global problems such as ozone depletion and the greenhouse effect. Government and public awareness and concern has grown in response to such serious industrial accidents with global environmental consequences as the Chernobyl nuclear accident, the Exxon Valdez oil spill, or the Bhopal Union Carbide factory chemical explosion.

This public and governmental interest, sustained and widespread, has altered the setting within which business operates. Pressure groups and non-governmental organizations are increasingly exposing the worst environmental practices of industry, and are pushing businesses to be more proactive in respect of them. The environmental movement has emerged as a powerful social, moral and political force with wide-ranging economic and organizational implications. In Europe, for example, membership of environmental pressure groups in the UK alone in 1990 stands at more than five million (Burke, 1989).

Over the past few years an increasingly restrictive legislative framework for environmental issue has emerged in Europe. This framework has imposed a whole range of restrictions on companies from investments in compliance measures to financial strategies that minimize environmental taxes. Variations in regulation from one member state to the next have sometimes prevented firms from carrying out uniform pan-European operations. Companies are also facing a growing and sophisticated environmental awareness among consumers, particularly in Germany and Denmark. Northern European consumers too favour products with environmentally friendly packaging. Pressure has also been exerted by increasingly environmentally aware shareholders, employees, insurance companies and ethical investment funds. The CBI fully aware of the potential of the green investment market in Europe has warned its members that 'the environment means business', and that companies failing to take the green revolution seriously risk being put out of business permanently (CBI, 1991).

The creation of the Single European Market, by accelerating economic growth has also brought with it consequences for the environment. In the early 1980s damage to buildings from acid rain deposition in the EU was estimated in the range of 450 million to 2.7 billion

ECUs per annum. In the late 1980s, damage to the forests from acid deposition was around 300 million ECUs a year, while loss of agricultural production from the same cause was valued at 1 billion ECUs. Recently, the Organization for Economic Cooperation and Development (OECD) has estimated that pollution of the environment cost the former Federal Republic of Germany DM 200 billion per annum (Commission of the EC, 1992).

The explicit commitment of the EU to sustainable development can no longer be questioned. The Commission recently introduced a penalty for member states that fail to take the necessary measures to comply with EU legislation on the environment. Article 171 stipulates that 'If the member state concerned fails to take the necessary measures...within the time limit laid down by the Commission, the latter may bring the case before the Court of Justice. In so doing it shall specify the amount of the lump sum or penalty payment...If the court of Justice finds that the member state concerned has not complied with its judgement it may impose a lump sum or penalty payment on it'.

It is therefore important for businesses to acquire a better and more reliable understanding of the EU policies regarding the environment. Managers must also be aware, and need to anticipate and prepare for the changing regulatory framework which may, at a stroke, make a particular process or product illegal or commercially unviable.

LEARNING OBJECTIVES

- To understand the need for environmental management in Europe
- To examine the Community policies regarding the environment
- To provide guidance for managers on how to manage their environment more effectively in Europe and remain competitive

THE NEED FOR ENVIRONMENTAL MANAGEMENT IN EUROPE

Following major and minor environmental disasters, which have highlighted the consequences of failing to have proper environmental management codes and procedures, we are now beginning to see businesses:
- recognizing environmental issues as important elements in product design, manufacturing, packaging and transportation, to the extent that this is now central to the continued existence of some enterprise
- using excellence in environmental management as a means of promoting their product, the company, and their presence in the community
- raising the status and importance of the environment to board level
- reporting to the public on environmental performance and having their environmental impact and performance independently verified

At the international level, this impact of environmental concerns has significantly changed the context of business and management with developments such as:

- supranational groupings, including the European Union, have introduced much more stringent environmental directives, laws and regulations, and standards of quality, for example, those of the International Standards Office
- the 1992 Rio Summit, at which world state leaders gave their active support to promoting environmental good practice by business

- the formation of federations of business associations, for example, the International Network of Environmental Management (INEM) and the initiatives of the International Chamber of Commerce (ICC) to promote and develop good practice in environmental management
- workers' associations and trade unions taking an active interest in ensuring that more exacting health and safety regulations are adhered to
- continuing and successful efforts of pressure groups to monitor the conduct of businesses and government regarding environmental issues
- the beginnings of a profession, with the formation of Institutes of Environmental Managers (Winter, 1995), and the formation of the Business Council for Sustainable Development (BSCD)
- the introduction of eco-labelling. The growth of green consumerism has challenged companies to demonstrate that their products and processes are environmentally friendly while providing a major marketing opportunity for new 'green' products

It would be useful at this point to reflect on some statistics which illustrate the impact of environmental degradation on our lives.

- Human beings have injected some 50 000 synthetic chemicals into our natural environment
- current rates of destruction will eliminate the worlds remaining tropical forests by the year 2000
- A single company car driven 1000 miles a month can pump six tons of carbon dioxide (the main gas contributing to global warming) into the atmosphere every year
- In 1993 700 000 people suffered from skin cancer in the USA and some 2000 of them died from it (Pollack, 1995).

All these problems are partly caused by the organizations for which we work. The only way to ensure that environmental problems will not become progressively worse is to reduce and ultimately halt the processes that cause them.

Although there may be individuals and groups who for various reasons are willing to continue with the 'do nothing' or 'business-as-usual' approaches to current global environmental problems, they are a minority, and the urgent need to provide solutions is widely accepted. Some of the motives which have driven companies to behave in an environmentally responsible way even without government intervention are:

- Management morale: managers increasingly want to have an environmental record they can be proud of, while some also feel it improves the quality of management too.
- Staff morale: in many companies, the pressure to adopt sound environmental policies came initially from the workforce.
- Consumer tastes: shoppers have become more interested in the environmental pedigree of the products they buy.
- Desire for good publicity: companies began to see value in a reputation for good environmental citizenship.
- Fear of incurring the costs of environmental damage, which have risen dramatically as regulations have tightened and also become increasingly unpredictable.
- Savings: companies found that reductions in their use of raw materials and energy, and in the amount of toxic waste they produced could yield savings, partly because of the rising costs of waste disposal (Cairncross, 1995).

THE EUROPEAN UNION AND THE ENVIRONMENT

The European Commission considers the environment as 'a key element in the achievement of the internal market; the adoption of high environmental standards at Community level and their uniform application will strengthen the process of convergence and cohesion and remove the fears for many countries against products of other member states, allegedly produced under lax environmental conditions (Commission of the EC, 1993, p. 9). In 1985 the European Commission proposed to the heads of states and government that, as a basis of Community environmental policy, 'protection of the environment' was to be treated as an integral part of economic and social policies both overall (at macroeconomic level) and by individual sector (agricultural policy, industrial policy, energy policy, etc.); and that 'the point must be made that an active policy for the protection and improvement of the environment can help economic growth and job creation' (Bulletin of the European Communities, 1985, p. 101). This led to the provision within the Single European Act of 1987, that 'Environmental protection requirements shall be a component of the Community's other policies' (European Treaty, pre-Maastricht, Second para, Article 130r). This provision was further amended by the Maastricht Treaty and came into force on 1 January 1993 and now reads: 'Environmental protection requirements must be integrated into the definition and implementation of other Community policies' (Third para, Article 130r Treaty Establishing the European Community as amended by the Treaty on European Union).

The questions that arise from this are how environmental proposals become directives, and how these directives are then implemented in the European Union, and how they affect management in Europe.

EU environmental legislation process

Under the present EU Treaty, it is the Commission that has a monopoly over formal proposals for regulation made to the Council. The European Parliament, the Council or private pressure groups are certainly able to make suggestions for drafting environmental directives or regulations, but the Commission is not bound by such requests. It determines according to its own responsibility, if and what kind of proposal it will submit to the Council. The EU 'environmental action programme' contains a number of actions which are to be elaborated during the lifetime of the programme (Kramer, 1996).

Stage 1 The decision to start work on a specific directive is taken by the members of the Commission in charge of the environment and the director-general for the environment. The decision is largely influenced by the availability of staff, available data on the subject, pressure from outside, activities in member states, technical assistance and so on. Once the decision is taken, the first draft of a text is prepared by the technical units. Usually, the first draft of a directive is preceded by a general discussion paper which outlines the problem, the strategy to follow, available data and so on. Consultation with outside bodies follows as well as discussions with experts and lobbyists. Consultation with member states follows accompanied by background documents which explain the approach chosen, indicate the options and raise other matters that might be of interest. Multilateral discussions between the Commission's administrations and the member states are then arranged. These meetings take place in Brussels by invitation of the Commission that chairs them. The invitation is addressed to the permanent representation of member states within the European Community and asks them to designate 'experts' to attend the meeting. In theory, experts are chosen based on their experience, and should not represent the member state. However, in practice, the majority of all those who attend are government officials, and the 'independent expert' element has been lost almost completely.

Parallel to the meeting with government experts, discussions with organizations from trade and industry and environmental organizations take place. At the end of the consultation process a draft text is prepared which the environmental administration takes back into the Commission. The text is sent to all interested departments and also to the legal service with the request for approval. The approved text then becomes an official Commission proposal for a directive. This proposal is published in the *Official Journal of the European Communities*. The text is drafted in the nine working languages.

Stage 2 The proposal is then transmitted to the Council which passes the text to the European Parliament and the Economic and Social Committee (ECOSOC) for their opinion. The draft report is discussed in the Environmental Committee of the Parliament. The Committee then reports to the Parliament's plenary session where amendments to the proposal are made. The amendments suggested by the Parliament and their final resolution are published in the *Official Journal of the European Communities*. Kramer summarizes the European Parliament's attitude to environmental proposals made by the Commission so far as follows (Kramer, 1996, p. 304):

1. On general questions of the environment or on horizontal legislation, the European Parliament constantly urges the Commission and the Council to go further in their proposals and to better protect the environment.
2. Proposals which are of a more technical nature are only exceptionally challenged as to the approach chosen by the Commission. Normally, the approach is accepted. The amendments suggested by the Parliament concern the need for more and better, protection of the environment.
3. The European Parliament constantly pleads for more progressive and efficient environmental legislation at Community level. Also, it seeks more transparency of environmental measures, better access to information, and greater participation of environmental organizations in the decision-making process.
4. The European Parliament is also gradually managing to introduce environmental considerations into amendments to proposals for legislation in agricultural and regional matters, the internal market and other policies. In Parliament, the 'greening' of regulation – the integration of environmental considerations into other policies – is more advanced than within the Commission or the Council. This affects the very important role played by the Environmental Committee within the European Parliament; indeed in terms of the number of its members as well as the number of its resolutions and so on transmitted to the Parliament's plenary, The Environmental Committee is one of the biggest most active and most influential committees of the European Parliament.

In the ECOSOC, the Commission's proposal is first discussed. The approved report and the draft opinion are submitted to the Environmental section and finally to the ECOSOC plenary session which votes only on the opinion.

Stage 3 The Commission's proposal for a directive is first examined at the Council by a working group composed of civil servants from the member states. The proposal goes to an environment working group in Council to prepare the decision by the Council of Ministers. The working group can start examining the Commission's proposal without waiting for the opinion from the European Parliament and ECOSOC. The working group is chaired by a representative from the member state that has the presidency in Council. A report is then sent to COREPER (The Committee of Permanent Representatives) accompanied by remarks, or declarations by national delegations, reservations and suggested compromise solutions, and prepares the Agenda for the Council meeting.

At present, the Environmental Council meets four to six times a year, in other words two or three times under each presidency which rotates every six months. Council proceedings are confidential. An environmental proposal may only be adopted by the Council when Parliament and ECOSOC have given their opinion. If Parliament opinion is not yet ready, The Council simply approves the proposal and waits for Parliament's opinion. The Council needs to consult Parliament for a second time only when, and if, the Council changes the legal basis of an environmental proposal (Co-decision procedure is explained in Chapter Four).

EU environmental policy

Environmental protection found no place in the Treaty of Rome. With the upsurge of interest in environmental protection since the late 1960s, and 1970s, the European Community acquired an increasing momentum in its environmental policy. Prior to 1970, the only serious policy measures that could be defined as concerned with environmental protection covered the hazards of radiation, particularly for workers in industry and the public, and the notification of new chemicals, which was related to the safety requirements. However, with the increased concern with environmental protection, the Community in 1970 first began to control noise and exhaust emissions from vehicles. In 1973 it passed its first directive concerned with the control of dangerous substances. Two years later in 1975, it passed the first directive concerned with the control of ambient environmental standards in a directive controlling the quality of surface drinking waters. The recession of the mid-1970s, however, weakened the priority given to environmental protection. It was not until 1984 when the first directive on the control of large stationary sources of pollution was passed, followed in 1988 by the large combustion plant directive that imposed emissions targets for countries for sulphur dioxide and the nitrogen oxides. In 1990 further directives on the control of genetically modified organisms, the establishment of a European Environment Agency and public access to environmental information were passed.

EU environment action programmes

The first action programme

This was submitted to the Council in March 1972. In October 1972 heads of state and government of the European Community proposed the first action programme which was adopted in 1973 (first action programme, 22 November 1973).

The first objectives identified in 1972 were:

- to prevent, reduce, and as far as possible, eliminate pollution and nuisance
- to maintain a satisfactory ecological balance and protect the biosphere
- to avoid damage to the ecological balance
- to ensure that more account is taken of environmental aspects in town planning and land use
- to work for those ends with non-members of the European Union

The second action programme (22 November 1973–82)

The main emphasis of the programme's measures shifted away from remedial action in response to specific sources of pollution and specific industrial processes towards preventative action. Prevention rather than cure was adopted as a fundamental element of the policy.

The third action programme (17 May 1983–87)
Greater emphasis to the prevention rather than cure principle.

The fourth action programme (19 October 1987–92)
This programme was adopted at the same time as the Single Market programme, and represented a clear linkage of the economic and environmental policies taking place within the EU. The fourth environmental action programme highlighted the problems of lack of enforcement of the environmental legislation. The Commissions view was that there was clearly little point in preparing new legislation if existing legislation had not been applied. The Commission made recommendations to ensure that member states became more assiduous in their implementation of directives. The Single European Act put environmental policy on a legally firm foundation for the first time. Under Article 100 which allows for qualified majority voting for that legislation appertaining to the completion of the internal market, the Commission is instructed to take a high level of environmental protection as a base for all its proposals. The Single Act clearly stated a number of objectives for environmental policy:

- to preserve, protect and improve the quality of human life
- to contribute towards human health
- to ensure a rational use of natural resources

Action was to be taken by the application of three principles

1. prevention is better than cure
2. damage should be rectified at its source
3. the polluter should pay to clean up any damage (Article 130r SEA)

The fifth action programme (1992–2000)
The fifth environmental action programme was adopted by the European Union in March 1992. Article 2 of the Treaty on European Union set a new agenda for the European Union's Policy on the Environment: 'The Community shall have as its task…to promote… sustainable and non-inflationary growth respecting the environment'. Agreement was finally reached that there should be a more enlightened and systematic approach to environmental management. A great emphasis was given to the question of research and monitoring of environmental problems. A greater emphasis was also placed on member states to use economic instruments such as taxes, charges, and tradable permits, to protect the environment. For the next 10 years, this programme it was agreed will be aimed at meeting the following targets:

- reducing emissions of nitrous oxide by 30 per cent by year 2000
- reducing emissions of sulphur dioxide by 35 per cent by 2000
- reducing emissions of dioxins by 90 per cent by 2005
- reducing emissions of cadmium, and lead by 70 per cent
- phasing out of noise pollution in excess of 65 dB(A) and banning of public noise levels in excess of 85 dB(A)
- stabilization of current levels of waste generation

(Brown, 1995, p. 96)

Thus, the fifth environmental action programme was basically a statement of general principles and policy on environmental questions:

> Within the Community, the long-term success of the more important initiatives such as the internal market and economic and monetary union will be dependent upon the sustainability of the policies pursued in the fields of industry, energy, transport, agriculture and regional development, but each of these policies, whether viewed separately or as it interfaces with others, is dependent on the carrying capacity of the environment.
>
> (Commission of the EC, 1992, Vol. II, p. 3)

The fifth environmental action programme furthermore established a European Union Financial Instrument for the Environment (LIFE) to complement the legislative and the market-based approaches to environmental protection. LIFE was introduced in early 1992. The objective of LIFE, was not to establish a separate European Union environmental fund, but to be a way of ensuring that financial support from the different sources was coordinated in a rational way to achieve maximum impact. Five major priorities were identified:

- promotion of sustainable development, including new clean technologies, management of waste and improving the urban environment
- protection of natural habitats and nature
- administrative structures and services for the environment
- education and training awareness
- technical assistance outside the territory of the EU

(Barnes and Barnes, 1995, p. 304)

Environmental provision under Article 130r

Under this article, the Commission is directed to ensure that the integration of environmental concerns into other fields of Community policy occurs and that Community environment policy, in addition to protecting the environment, contributes towards the maintenance of human health and the conservation of natural resources, and that member states are not prevented from introducing more stringent measures than those agreed at EC level. The Maastricht Treaty amended Article 130r by adding a precautionary principle to the foundation stones of EC environment policy, and including the promotion of regional or global cooperation in the objectives of that policy.

Article 130r(2) sets out the principles on which European environment policy is based. These are:

- preserving, protecting and improving the quality of the environment
- protecting human health
- prudent and rational utilization of natural resources
- promoting measures at international level to deal with regional or worldwide environmental problems

Action by the community relating to the environment shall be:

- based on the principles that preventative action should be taken
- that environmental damage should as a priority be rectified at source
- and that the polluter should pay

In preparing its action relating to the environment, the article further directs the Community to take account of available scientific and technical data, environmental conditions in the various regions of the Community, the potential benefits and costs of action or of lack of action, the economic and social development of the Community as a whole and the balanced development of its regions. The Community is also expected to take action relating to the environment to the extent to which the objectives mentioned above, can be attained better at Community level than at the level of the individual member states. Member states are expected under the provision to finance and implement the other measures. **Article 130s** provides the Council, acting unanimously on a proposal from the Commission and after consulting the European Parliament and the Economic and Social Committee, with the power to decide what action is to be taken by the Community. And finally, **Article 130t** directs the Community not to prevent any member state from maintaining or introducing more stringent protective measures compatible with the Treaty.

IMPLEMENTING THE EU ENVIRONMENTAL POLICY

Several problems of implementation have been identified. The first is the difficulty of interpretation. The Community environmental policy is written in vague terms. Questions arise about the balance to be struck between the demands of environmental protection and measures for the liberalization of trade. The application of higher environmental standards is possible as long as it does not create an open or disguised barrier to intra-EU trade. If any member state wishes to apply higher environmental standards, there is a fear for companies within that state that their competitiveness will be undermined. There is therefore pressure within individual states to ensure that standards are applied equally across the EU. Low standards within a member state are a way of maintaining an unfair advantage over states where standards are higher. If the low standards are achieved by ignoring the damage to the environment then product prices could be lower, thus giving companies an unfair advantage in the Single Market. If a member state has lower standards then the cost of environmental damage does not have to be taken into account. High standards in a member state also can act as a non-tariff to the movement of goods. This is, as Barnes and Barnes argue, not the most effective environmental policy to pursue, as it may lead to a lowering and not a raising of standards (Barnes and Barnes, 1995, p. 298).

The second problem faced is the existence of varying motives. Environmental protection measures are frequently seen as contradictory rather than complementary. According to the Treaty: 'The Treaty on European Union does not prevent any member states from maintaining or introducing more stringent measures compatible with the EC Treaty in order to pursue the objectives of protection of the environment' (Council of the European Union, 1992). During the 1980s environmental policy became an area in which rival conceptions of European integration and competing national priorities came to be played out. Germany, the Netherlands and Denmark have been anxious since the early 1980s to legislate for high environmental standards and they have been keen to see the Community take the initiative in pushing through more stringent pollution control measures. The UK has often resisted these measures, partly on grounds of cost and partly on the grounds that it disputed their scientific basis.

The third problem is the public sentiment differences in the different member states such as the difference in political priority to be given to environmental policy over competing political goals, difference over the priority to be given to different forms of environment policy, differences of national understanding of policy problems, differences of economic capacity and different traditions of thinking about economic development and government intervention (Weale and Williams, 1995, p. 151).

Furthermore the application of the principles of subsidiarity to environmental policy has introduced a new uncertainty. It is seen by some member states as a curb on EU action, while in other states it is seen as the means by which higher environmental standards may be maintained. This principle states that: 'The Community shall take action relating to the environment to the extent to which the objectives referred to in Paragraph 1 can be attained better at Community level than the level of the individual member states' (Article 130r).

Another problem of effectiveness of implementation is the ability of the member states to 'ignore' the legislation on the basis that the environmental policy was not part of the Treaty of Rome. The Single European Act and the Treaty on European Union have given environmental policy a firmer legal basis, but the problem of how to ensure effective application of the legislation remains (Barnes and Barnes, 1995, p. 305).

Finally, lack of commitment among the member states to carry out the policy, might be another barrier towards effective implementation. Most environmental legislation has been adopted in the form of directives. These are binding as to the ends which are to be achieved, but leave the national authorities the choice of form and methods. As a result if a member state lacks commitment to a particular issue, its effective implementation will be uncertain. A firmer action by the Court of Justice is needed since all EU members are joined by the Treaty, and under the Treaty, EU legislation takes precedence over national legislation and member states acknowledge that rulings of the European Court of Justice on the implementation of legislation have precedence over their national rulings.

Having established the need for environmental management, and provided an overview of EU environmental policies, it is useful now to examine environmental policies and key strategies either adopted or available, for business to face the environmental challenge in Europe.

ENVIRONMENTAL STRATEGIES FOR MANAGING THE ENVIRONMENT IN THE SINGLE EUROPEAN MARKET

Doing business is an increasingly environmental sensitive world poses new challenges for managers. 'Help the environment and hurt your business, or irreparably harm your business while protecting the earth' (Walley and Whitehead, 1994), is often the general claim. Some of the challenges faced by business include anticipating demand for new environment-friendly products, designing safer, healthier and less polluting products and packages, developing less polluting manufacturing facilities which can minimize hazardous wastes, managing technological risks, conserving non-renewable natural resources, protecting the environment, and safeguarding worker and public health. Given the complexity of the problems being addressed, it is not surprising that there is at present no one approach that satisfies all needs.

Some of the key strategies available to companies to manage their natural environment more efficiently are the following:

1. Environmental review and environmental audit
2. Environmental impact assessment and life-cycle assessment
3. Total quality environmental management
4. Eco-auditing/Eco-labelling

Environmental review and environmental audit

The growth of green consumerism in the late 1980s, and early 1990s encouraged companies to call in environmental auditors in order to establish how green their company was.

Environmental audits are undertaken in order to provide a detailed review of the company's present position. Audits should be applied to support an organization's policies and should form an important aspect of an overall environmental management system. Environmental reviews and audits are usually carried out by teams which include lawyers, management consultants, engineers, scientists and environmental generalists drawn from industry, government and consultancy companies. Environmental audit, as defined by the International Chamber of Commerce (ICC), is a management tool comprising a systematic, documented, periodic and objective evaluation of how well environmental organization, management and equipment are performing with the aim of helping to safeguard the environment by: (1) facilitating management and control of environmental practices; and (ii) assessing compliance with company policies, which includes meeting regulatory requirements.

The key objectives of an environmental audit are:

- to provide management with information in order to help them make informed decisions relating to improved environmental action
- to determine the extent to which environmental management systems in a company are performing according to their documented procedures and aims
- To verify compliance with local, national, European, and international environmental and health and safety legislation and to verify compliance with a company's own stated corporate policy
- to develop and promulgate internal procedures needed to achieve the organization's environmental objectives and targets
- to minimize human exposure to risks from the environment and ensure adequate health and safety provision
- to identify and assess company risk resulting from environmental failure
- to assess the impact on the local environment of a particular plant or process by means of air, water and soil sampling; and
- to advise a company on environmental improvements it could make, and on improvements needed in the definition and/or operation of its environmental management system

Rob Gray (1994) has identified the following major elements to an environmental audit or review. These are:

- identify the most important of the organization's environmental interactions
- assess the degree of environmental impact
- learn about how to deal with and reduce or improve the organization's impact
- identify a priority list of interactions to be dealt with (this will develop, in part, from the first two and in part in response to actual and potential changes in law and in society's attitudes)
- establish standards and policies
- identify responsibilities
- train staff
- change practices and put policies into action
- develop environmental information systems
- monitor performance and performance appraisal
- assess performance against standards
- reappraise this list, starting from the top, on a systematic and continuing basis

The basic principles to remember when embarking on auditing, according to Welford and Gouldson (1993) are:

1. Clear and explicit objectives need to be formulated before the commencement of an environmental audit. In addition, there needs to be a clearly defined benchmark in terms of environmental legislation, standards and the best practice of other companies, in order that the audit results can be assessed and compared.
2. The audit team needs to be proficient and expert, with appropriate knowledge of the issues under consideration and an appropriate environmental understanding with respect to scientific, technical, legislative and management issues. All audit members need to be able to demonstrate their particular expertise.
3. Auditors need to be independent and to work in a confidential manner, while due professional care should be exercised at all times.
4. Firms specializing in environmental auditing and individual consultants, should be able to demonstrate their own adherence to general principles of environmental improvement.
5. The on-site audit should be planned, managed and supervised so as to ensure minimum disbenefit to the company, and appropriate security and safety to the individual auditor.
6. Environmental audits should include the proper study of management systems in operation, and an assessment of the liability of internal environmental controls. Tests should be devised so as to ensure the effectiveness of management structures.
7. Sufficient reliable evidence should be gathered through inquiry, observation and tests to ensure that the audit findings are objective.
8. Audit reports should be clear, concise and confidential. They should ensure full and formal communication of audit findings and recommendation.
9. Auditors should ensure that strategies for the implementation of the recommendations of the audit are practicable and possible, and that they are likely to contribute to the implementation of corrections.
10. Auditors should clearly indicate to companies the consequences of not correcting deficiencies, particularly where they may result in litigation being taken against the firm. If this is not done then auditors should accept their own negligence.

Finally, it is important to note that an environmental audit is not a one-off activity. It needs to be seen as an ongoing programme, a commitment towards continuous improvement.

There are a number of benefits to firms in having an environmental audit undertaken. Some of these advantages include the following: assurance that legislation is being adhered to and the consequent prevention of fines and litigation; an improved public image; a reduction in costs; an improvement in environmental awareness at all levels of the firm; and an improvement in overall quality.

The disbenefits of environmental auditing include first the initial costs of the audit, cost of compliance with it and the temporary disruption of plant operations. Management should ensure that recommendations of the environmental auditors are adhered to otherwise an audit report could be incriminating in a court case or insurance claim. The need to establish a contingency budget to cover expenditure which may be required in response to auditor's recommendations is another problem with environmental auditing. There is also the widespread natural reluctance on the part of management and workers to see outsiders entering the organization and assessing their own performance, which would need to be dealt with before the auditing process.

Environmental impact assessment or life-cycle assessment

Environmental impact assessment was introduced into EC law by a directive (Directive 85/337, JO L 175 dated 5.7.85). Life-cycle assessment (LCA) seeks to highlight those areas in the environmental profile of a product upon which producers should focus their attention in order to minimize their environmental impact through redesign. Life-cycle assessment, is also known as cradle-to-grave assessment. It attempts to provide information on all facets of a product's environmental performance, focusing in particular on environmental impact.

The main objectives of life-cycle assessment are: (a) to identify the main areas of environmental impact in order to enable further more detailed study; (b) to quantify energy and material inputs and emissions within these areas; (c) to assess the environmental impact of inputs and emissions at all stages; and (d) to establish the options for improving any stage of the life-cycle of the product (Welford, 1994).

There are four stages involved in life-cycle assessment.

1. **Inventory analysis,** which is the process of gathering information relating to the material and energy inputs into a product and its production and any emissions associated with this. Resources used and emissions generated should be measured per unit of output produced.

2. **Impact analysis,** which involves establishing the environmental impact of each of the areas documented under the inventory analysis.

3. **Impact assessment,** which needs to be established both quantitatively and qualitatively. Quantitative impact assessment develops a list of the amounts of emissions and some measurement of their impact.

4. **Improvement analysis,** this is the final stage of life-cycle assessment where the environmental profile of the product is altered through redesign of the product and the methods of its manufacture. Improvement analysis assesses the technically and economically feasible options available at all stages of the product's life, which can be utilized to improve the overall environmental impact of the good.

The major benefit of life-cycle assessment is that it provides a systematic and objective collation of quantitative data on company products. It facilitates a greater understanding of the issues involved and assists the company to change the attitudes and behaviour of those concerned with producing the goods. It also provides a systematic framework through which the constituents of the product and their environmental impacts, which are selected for study, can be analysed. The Volkswagen Audi Group has adopted a life-cycle environmental management system.

Total quality environmental management (TQEM)

While the total quality management approach in general aims for zero defects, that is, preventing any defects occurring in the first place, total quality environmental management (TQEM) is based on the central concept of continuous improvement. The focus to TQEM is on shifting environmental goals from compliance to customer satisfaction. The central assumption is that environmental damage is a quality defect, and should be treated like any other quality characteristics. TQEM is a long-term process. The goal is zero defects and zero pollution. That goal may never be reached but the aim is always to move ever closer to it on a continuous basis (Welford, 1995). British Telecommunications (BT) is a good example of how the UK's largest company, and its principal supplier of telecommunications services, is currently improving its performance in line with total quality environmental standards. (Taylor and Welford, 1995).

Eco-auditing/Eco-labelling

Eco-labelling remains a voluntary code, but is likely to become the predominant indicator of environmental friendliness.

Eco-management and audit scheme (EMAS)

Council Regulation 1836/93/EEC allowing voluntary participation by companies in the industrial sector in the EU eco-management and audit scheme (EMAS), was adopted by the Council on 28 June, 1993, and made applicable from 13 April, 1995 (*Official Journal* L168, 10 July, 1993). The eco-management and audit scheme aims to promote the use of environmental management systems and auditing as a tool for systematic and periodic evaluation of the environmental performance of certain industrial activities. A further objective is to provide information on environmental performance to the public. Companies registering under the scheme will commit themselves to establish, develop, implement, maintain and update as necessary, an internal environmental management system which will be beyond minimum regulatory requirements. Company participation in the scheme is intended to be voluntary but the scheme will be subject to review after five years. Companies registered under the scheme will be obliged to:

- adopt a company environmental policy, including a commitment to legal compliance and to continuous improvement of environmental performance
- conduct an environmental review to assess the environmental impact and environmental performance of activities
- introduce, in the light of that review, an environmental program and an environmental management system, including operating and record-keeping procedures that require monitoring and corrective action in case of non-compliance with the policy, procedures and management system
- carry out periodic environmental audits
- prepare an environmental statement of the audit results for the public domain that includes: a description of the site; an assessment of significant environmental issues raised; summaries of pollutant discharges, waste generation, noise and raw material consumption; a description of the company's internal environmental policy, site procedures and site management systems; and an evaluation of the performance of that system
- have the statement validated by an independent, accredited verifier

The management system covers policy, organization and personnel, operational control, and documentations.

Registrations can be withdrawn for improper application of the regulation such as failure to submit a verified statement and the registration fee.

Ecological labelling

This was adopted by the Council on 23 March, 1992, and entered into force on 23 March, 1992 (Official Journal L 99, 11 April, 1992). This regulation sets up a voluntary award scheme for so-called 'clean' products. For many years the EU has taken the view that mass consumption products are a potential cause of serious environmental degradation. In response to this, the eco-label award scheme was established. This scheme is designed to inform consumers about the quality of a product as well as the behaviour of that product in the environment. The scheme ensures that uniformly high levels of environmental performance are achieved by products bearing the eco-label. A Committee of member states, chaired by a Commission representative gives the final approval to the criteria before its publication in the *Official*

Journal. It is given only to those products that meet the general and specific criteria established in each product category. The scheme is voluntary, but it is hoped that it will provide incentives for the creation of more products which not only prevent waste, but also reduce pollution and nuisances such as odour or noise. Application by manufacturers is done through their national eco-labelling board.

The aim of the eco-labelling regulation is to create a market instrument to promote products with a cleaner technology, and industry welcomes the objective of harmonization which is built into the legislation (EU Environment Guide, The EU Committee, 1996).

BARRIERS TO ENVIRONMENTAL MANAGEMENT

Although the need for global cooperation in order to combat global environmental problems has been recognized, the implementation of measures to alleviate the effects of global environmental disruption is remarkably complex. The great economic gap between rich and poor nations adds to the difficulties of resolving environmental problems at the international level, exemplified starkly in the increasing evidence of international trade in toxic waste, in which the often hazardous waste products from advanced economies is exported into the territories of developing states.

A major concern at the international level is that measures aimed at preserving the environment will impose too high a cost on those least responsible and least able to pay. The challenge will be to define and present the issues in such a way that the nations involved will see it as in their own best interests – economic, social, political and environmental – to introduce measures to prevent further damage to the environment and ameliorate existing problems (Kemp, 1994). The argument that tough environmental policies are compatible with the commercial interests of business, and that strong environmental regulation may improve national competitiveness, was put most persuasively by Michael Porter in his 1991 essay on 'America's Green Strategies' published in *Scientific America*. In this essay, Porter's thesis is that inadequate environmental regulation in the USA was losing the country a wonderful opportunity to break into markets abroad. Other countries, notably Japan were stealing competitive advantage by imposing more stringent environmental regulations (Porter, 1991).

'Properly constructed regulatory standards', Porter argued, 'will encourage companies to re-engineer their technology. The result in many cases is a process that not only pollutes less but lowers costs or improves quality' (Porter, 1991). Environmental regulations may create markets for a company's products, but they could also drive some companies out of an existing market, often by increasing the capital requirements. Regulations can also be used to protect companies from foreign competition, or to give them a lead over their rivals. In these cases, it can be seen that the adoption of environmentally aware strategies might be based upon evaluations of competitiveness rather than a commitment to the principle of environmental safety itself.

Environmental policies, however, cost countries a large and increasing amount of money. To alleviate the costs involved in implementing tough environmental policies, particularly in developing countries, some of the extra costs are provided through international agreements. The Montreal Protocol, for example, includes a fund for such payments. The Global Environment Facility also pays developing countries some of the extra costs of policies to slow global warming. Environmental taxes could also raise government revenues. In 1994, for example, Denmark made this principle one of the keystones of a big tax-reform programme. The government aimed to cut income tax over a period of five years, and to meet the cost partly by introducing a broad range of 'green' taxes. In Britain, excise duties have been adjusted so that the price of leaded petrol has risen increasingly, relative to the price of unleaded (Cairncross, 1995).

Finally, the last alternative is that of 'bullying'. This may simply take the form of international disapproval. Nobody likes to be seen as a pariah. Britain eventually agreed to reduce sulphur dioxide output and to stop dumping sewage sludge in the North Sea, principally because of the political costs of being dubbed 'the dirty old man of Europe' (Cairncross, 1995).

IMPLEMENTING COMPANY ENVIRONMENT POLICIES

There is no ideal or complete model of corporate environmental policy that all companies should strive to adopt. The environmental impact of different companies varies greatly. Companies engaged in primary production, for example, have very different impacts from those in manufacturing or service sectors. The size of a company also alters its impact on the environment, and its capability to manage those impacts. Nevertheless, all companies, need to develop their own corporate environmental policies.

There are six main criteria for designing a company's environmental policy:

1. the policy should be comprehensive
2. goals should be easily measurable
3. the policy should be easily communicated
4. the policy should be implemented
5. the policy should be the result of a process
6. the policy must be led

(Burke and Hill, 1994)

CASE STUDY 12:1 The Green Book at the Body Shop

The Body Shop was founded in March 1976 by Anita Roddick. Her aim was to utilize raw ingredients such as plants, herbs and roots in products which should be acceptable to consumers. The Body Shop's principal activities are to formulate, manufacture and retail products which are primarily associated with cleansing, polishing and protecting the skin and hair. The Body Shop's full range contains nearly 400 products. The organization trades in over 40 countries and employees around 6000 people, either directly or in franchises.

Environmental strategies are at the centre of the company's approach to business. The environment policy of The Body Shop is written up in what the company describes as the 'Green Book'. It states: 'The Body Shop challenges the notion that any company can be environmentally friendly. This is just not possible. All business involves some environmental damage. The best we can do is clear up our own mess while searching hard for ways to reduce our impact on the environment' (The Body Shop International, 1993).

In formulating its life-cycle assessment, the company states that they:

- are committed to using renewable resources and conserving non-renewable ones
- strive to obtain raw materials from communities who want to use trade to protect their culture and who practise traditional systems of sustainable land use
- only use product ingredients that have not been tested on animals in the past five years and suppliers must provide reassurance on this

- natural ingredients from renewable resources are favoured by the research and development department where new product formulations are tested
- where ingredients and packaging come from non-renewable resources, for example, from synthetic chemicals, we make sure we minimize quantities and maximize biodegradability (for ingredients) and recyclability (for packaging) (The Body Shop, 1992)

Life-cycle assessment at The Body Shop therefore involves tracing product ingredients and packaging to assess their impact on the environment from sourcing, and on to re-use, recycling and disposal. Each item is given a numerical score based on approximately 100 environmental criteria. This means that the environmental characteristics of ingredients can be rated which will, in turn, influence day-to-day decisions in relation to formulations and purchasing decisions.

The Body Shop is also concerned to 'clear up its own mess' and conserve energy. In 1992 The Body Shop invested £500 000 in a wind farm to replace the electricity used by the company headquarters in Littlehampton. Environmental audit was introduced in 1993. On the main site, this involves all staff and managers in continuous data collection, frequent reviews of priorities and targets and an annual process of public reporting of results. The process extends to all retail outlets and is replicated in all overseas franchise operations.

A decentralized system of environmental management was also developed to ensure adequate implementation and achieve targets set out by the company's environment audit. A corporate team of environment, health and safety specialists acts as a central resource for networks of environmental advisers and coordinators in headquarters departments, subsidiaries, retail outlets and international markets. Environmental advisers and coordinators are dually part-time fulfilling their role in environmental communications and auditing alongside normal duties. In headquarter departments there is approximately one adviser for every 20 members of staff. Every individual department has at least one adviser as so does every retail outlet in the UK. The corporate EHS team serves to ensure that policies and guidelines are disseminated effectively, coordinates terms of reference for auditing and environmental management, and receives and collates data on relevant environmental indicators.

Auditing for sustainability, introduced since 1993, is committed to integrating environmental performance with wider issues of global ecology such as waste minimization, re-use and recycling. The Body Shop does not enclose every customer purchase in extraneous packaging, and where it is used, bags are made from recycled paper or biodegradable plastic. Internal distribution boxes are reused and the company carries out an internal waste audit. Mail-order catalogues are similarly made of recycled paper and positive efforts have been made to reduce the amount of paper used. The Body Shop is not putting an increased emphasis on life-cycle assessment and product stewardship within its environmental management and auditing framework.

The Body Shop has also committed itself to generating as much electricity from renewable resources as it consumes, and over the last two years has been introducing wind and solar energy sources at its Watersmead site. An agreement has been signed with National WindPower to develop a wind farm (Welford, 1995).

CAST STUDY 12.2: BT environmental management policy

British Telecommunications (BT) is the UK's largest company and its principal supplier of telecommunications services. BT is actively involved in the implementation of a comprehensive business-wide environmental management programme, which addresses all areas where the organization impacts upon the environment. The company publishes annually its company environmental performance report.

BT's environmental policy was introduced in March 1991. In the pursuit of its mission to provide world-class telecommunications and information products and services, BT asserts that it exploits technologies which are basically friendly to the environment. In the sense that use of the telecommunications network is often a substitute for travel or paper-based messages, BT is contributing positively to environmental well-being and conservation of resources. BT recognizes, however that in its day-to-day operations, the company inevitably impacts on the environment in a number of ways and wishes to minimize the potentially harmful effects of such activity where and whenever possible.

To this effect, the company has developed a comprehensive policy statement which will enable its management to set the targets by which efforts towards sustainable environmental improvement can be measured and monitored on a regular basis. In particular BT will:

- meet, and where appropriate, exceed the requirements of all relevant legislation – where no regulation exists, BT shall set its own exacting standards
- promote recycling and the use of recycled materials, while reducing consumption of materials wherever possible
- design energy efficiency into new services, buildings and products, and manage energy wisely in all operations
- wherever practicable reduce the level of harmful emissions
- minimize waste in all operations and product development
- work with BT suppliers to minimize the impact of their operations on the environment through a quality purchasing policy
- protect visual amenity by careful siting of buildings, structures and the deployment of operational plant in the local environment and respect wildlife habitats
- support through its community programme the promotion of environmental protection by relevant external groups and organizations
- include environmental issues in BT training programmes and encourage the implementation by all BT people of sound environmental practices
- monitor progress and publish an environmental performance report on an annual basis

(Quoted in Taylor and Welford, 1995, p. 62)

Environmental management development within BT is assigned between three groups: the environmental policy steering group, the environmental issues unit, and the environmental liaison panel.

- *Environmental policy steering group*   Members of this group include representatives from procurement, product design, product disposal, energy management, building services, external plant, and motor transport. The group meets on a quarterly basis and provides a forum in which issues concerning the implementation of environmental programmes and procedures for the whole organization can be discussed. BT deputy chairman as the chairman of this group, enables the EPSG to influence the adoption of the environmental programmes and procedures.
- *Environmental issues unit*   The primary function of this unit is to act as coordinating body for the programme on a day-to-day basis. Its other responsibilities and activities involve it in: monitoring and reporting on trends and changes in environmental legislation; acting as a company think-tank and providing a pool of expertise to develop new environmental

strategies consistent with BT activities. It undertakes environmental auditing of company sites and provides a communications channel between the company, stakeholders and the general public.

- *Environmental liaison panel* This panel is chaired by an independent environmental consultant, with members being drawn from a variety of backgrounds including representatives from the voluntary sector, organizations involved in energy policy, waste management and environmental auditing, those involved in undertaking and assessing research into climate change, sectors involved in teaching environmental skills, those concerned with the development of, and implementation of, corporate environmental strategies, organizations involved in community programmes, those concerned with the development and implementation of local government policy, and organizations representing youth groups. Representatives come from waste regulation authorities, local government and include school children. Representation on the environmental liaison panel is voluntary. Issues raised and discussed by the panel refer to policy statements and management systems, energy efficiency, waste management, environmental procurement standards, telephone directory recycling, environmental training needs and visual amenity.
- **Training programme** The company completed a full review of its environmental training requirement in 1993. Although special courses on broad environmental strategies have been developed for key personnel from each of the function units, the company extended training to the majority of staff. Attendance to BT's total quality management training programme entitled: 'Involving Everyone' is mandatory for all non-managerial staff.
- **Recycling** Schemes for promoting recycling have been introduced such as the Big-Bin Collection Programme for recycling confidential and general office waste, collection of drinks cans, aluminium collection points. Since 1993, BT purchases only aluminium cans for its drinks machines

(Taylor and Welford, 1995)

Various companies have carried out creative programmes that seeks to respond to environment expectations, such as The Body Shop and BT illustrated above. A list of actions that companies may wish to take to achieve environmental excellence has been summarized by Borchgrave (1993) as follows.

- **Monitor regulations** Comprehending existing legislation is not enough. Companies must also carefully monitor upcoming developments and their different effects. Regulatory monitoring is as important at the European level as at the member state level where a company does business.
- **Lobby** Active presence in the elaboration of policies at European and national levels is becoming a necessity for any organization wishing to stay abreast of events or to avoid having legislation imposed upon them that may, in extreme cases, threaten their existence.
- Create a function within the company to deal with environmental issues at a European level. The function should deal with the strategic aspects of environmental management, and the responsibility for it should be concentrated at a relatively high level within the company. Do not limit the function to public relations and legal issues. Financial and technical aspects must be dealt with as well.
- Understand the environmental problems your suppliers and clients face. One possible

approach is to assign to environmentally qualified staff the task of cooperating with the company's various commercial partners in identifying possible problems and solutions.

- Examine new resources. With the discovery of new raw materials and the invention of new production technology, companies must review the division of costs and carry out life-cycle analyses for both materials and products while examining the sources, costs and relative merits of different materials.
- View environmental management as a dimension of total quality in the organization. Provide all personnel with an understanding of the key environmental issues as it relates to the company's total quality management initiative.
- Market your company and products as environmentally friendly where possible. Publicize your environmental efforts and emphasize the greenness of your products in advertising and labelling in order to capture affluent, environmentally aware consumers.

For further assistance in drafting a possible environmental policy for your organization see Smith, (1995), also Winter (1995).

REVIEW QUESTIONS

1. Describe and evaluate the various strategies available for managing the environment. Illustrate where possible with real-life examples.
2. Identify and evaluate the main features of corporate environmental policy of a European company known to you.
3. Develop and describe the steps needed to design and implement an environmental management programme for a European firm with which you are familiar.
4. 'Business is often seen as the enemy of the environment, as the polluter. There is, however, a tide of change and it is now increasingly being seen as the essential partner, as part of the solution and not the problem, the provider of the wealth and the resources needed' (Peter Bright, Shell International Petroleum Co. Ltd., Chairman of the ICC Working Party on Sustainable Development). Discuss this claim, and identify the major factors that might have contributed to such a change in perceptions of business.

EXERCISE 12.1: The 'green' firm

Use the key elements which are likely to appear in any corporate environmental policy, to assist you in drawing up an environmental policy for a European firm with which you are familiar.

In drawing up your environmental policy, make sure you cover the following four key elements:

1. An overall statement about what the firm is trying to achieve – a integrative statement.
2. The principles it is aiming to adopt; sustainable development, equity with lesser developed countries or environmental leadership, for example.
3. Reference to the key issues relevant to the organization such as global warming, deforestation ozone depletion, or toxic waste disposal.
4. The specific impacts the organization has, for example, its energy usage, water usage, raw materials usage or its emissions to air, land and water.

FURTHER READING

Cairncross, F., *Green Inc. A Guide to Business and the Environment*, Earthscan Publ. Ltd, London, 1995.

George, W., *Blueprint for Green Management. Creating your Company's Own Environmental Action Plan*, McGraw-Hill, London, 1995.

Pollack, S., *Improving Environmental Performance*, Routledge, London, 1995.

Welford, R., *Cases in Environmental Management and Business Strategies*, Pitman, London, 1995.

Winter, G. (ed.), *European Environmental Law. A Comparative Perspective*. Dartmouth Publishing Co., Aldershot, 1996.

THIRTEEN
THE EAST EUROPEAN BUSINESS ENVIRONMENT

The upheavals which have taken place over the last decade in the countries of central and eastern Europe and the new independent states of the former USSR have had a significant impact on the European Union. The movement from centrally planned economies to democratic systems, with the declared objectives of establishing western style market economies represents the biggest change in Europe since the Second World War. The aim of this chapter is to help business managers obtain some understanding of the changes occurring in central and eastern Europe, and how these might affect opportunities for business development in the 'new' Europe.

LEARNING OBJECTIVES

- To identify potential business opportunities created by the liberalization and marketization process in central and eastern Europe
- To examine the problems and difficulties of doing business in central and east Europe
- To provide guidance on how to enter those markets, and how to overcome the many problems that may be encountered
- To provide an insight into contemporary transitions from central-planning economies to free-market economies in central and eastern Europe

BUSINESS OPPORTUNITIES IN CENTRAL AND EASTERN EUROPE

The collapse of the iron curtain released enormous commercial energy within central and eastern Europe. Eastern European economies are perceived to offer several advantages for business. The central and east European countries of the former communist bloc have a combined population of 400 million (including the former USSR) and there is excess demand for nearly every type of product.

Major consumer import markets are for the following products:

- food items
- house and home improvement goods
- demands for home furnishings, domestic appliances, DIY products, paint, wallpaper
- clothing and footwear – there is much interest in fashion goods, plus a willing growing ability to pay for them

- western computer hardware and software
- sales of automotive products
- video and other electronic equipment
- building materials and office equipment
- food processing equipment, medical supplies, machinery of all kinds
- items connected with environmental improvement
- telecommunications, distribution and transportation equipment
- pharmaceutical products
- industrial modernization
- hotel and restaurant equipment
- manpower training services, management consulting services, financial services, travel and tourism services

The potential of these markets is obviously considerable. Hungary appears to be the clear favourite among foreign investors, followed by the former Czechoslovakia and Poland. German companies are the most active, accounting for a third of the total number. Austrians have also moved quickly often re-establishing trading links with businesses that existed before communism took over. Further behind are retailers from the USA, Canada, the UK, France and Italy (*Euromonitor*, 1993, p. 21). A few examples are quite illustrative here. Pepsi-Cola in April 1990 signed the biggest ever trade agreement between the USA and Russia. The $3 million barter agreement enabled Pepsi to add 26 new plants to the 24 already operating throughout Russia (Holden and Peck, 1990, p. 29). In return for the new plants, the company received double the present quantity of vodka per year and ten 25 000–65 000 tonne freighters and oil tankers. Estee Lauder opened its first Soviet outlet in November 1989. Situated in Moscow's Gorky Street and with all goods priced in roubles, the merchandise has been hugely successful. During the first month of trading, crash barriers were erected to keep a permanent queue of up to 200 people off the road (Holden and Peck, 1990, pp. 26–31). Littlewoods had a similar success too in its early opening days and had to issue vouchers limiting purchases to five products per customer. Adidas sold its whole stock of famous striped sport shoes in one morning. In the first three months of its operation Lotus Development Corporation sold more than 1000 copies of its Lotus 1-2-3 personal computer software (Crummey, 1991, p. 25). US hoteliers have also competed fiercely for deals and properties in the eastern and central European markets. Hotel groups such as Marriott, Hyatt International Group, Sheraton and Hilton have all established hotels in the region. The Moscow Sheraton cost was estimated at $75 million. The USSR's first McDonald's restaurant also opened in Gorky Street as early as January 1990 with 200 seats outdoors, 700 more inside and 27 cash registers. It was the largest and the busiest of the nearly 12 000 McDonald's restaurants worldwide (Hume, 1990, pp. 16–51), serving 40 000–50 000 people a day. To service them, McDonald's had to build a 100 000 square foot distribution centre that included a meat plant, a bakery, a potato plant, a dairy and quality assurance laboratories, at a cost of $50 million (Foster, 1991, pp. 51–65). Ahold, the Dutch grocery chain operates in 11 Mana supermarkets in the Czech and Slovak republics. Billa, the Austrian conglomerate has plans for some 60 supermarkets in Prague in a joint venture with a local company. Delhaize operates 14 Hungarian supermarkets in a joint venture with a local wholesaler. GIB, the Belgian group operates five new supermarkets in Poland with local partners. Ikea operates a total of five stores in the region – Budapest, Warsaw, Poznan, Prague and Bratislava. K Shoes, a Clark-owned manufacturer and retailer set up a Polish joint venture and has opened three outlets to date. Littlewoods operates three outlets in Russia within the Gostinys Dvor department store in St Petersburg. This includes one local currency Littlewoods store, and separate Littlewoods and Index outlets that trade in hard currency (Retail Dynamics, 1994).

In the period since Poland's move to a market economy, a number of multinationals have made significant investments in Poland, either through equity participation in existing Polish companies or in 'green field' ventures. They include Alcatel, Asea Brown Boveri, AT&T, British Sugar, Coca-Cola, CPC Food, Curtis International, Epstein, Fiat, France Telecom, Gillette, Gerber, Henkel, Hewlett Packard, Ikea, International Paper Corporation, Levi Strauss, Lucchini Group, Marriott, Dr Oetker, Pepsi Co, Peugeot, Philips, Pilkington, Proctor & Gamble, RJ Reynolds, Siemens, Solco Basel, Thomson, Trust House Forte and Unilever (CBI, 1996, p. 446).

This euphoria that followed the dramatic changes since 1989 towards the establishment of a free-market economy, is now slowly dying down and we are beginning to see the challenges that lie ahead in the reconstruction of the eastern and central European market economies. The recession in the early 1990s adversely affected the growth of foreign investment, in addition to the enormous problems still remaining for western businesses wishing to exploit east European markets.

PROBLEMS AND DIFFICULTIES OF DOING BUSINESS IN CENTRAL AND EASTERN EUROPE

Some of the most critical issues impeding growth of foreign direct investment (FDI) in the region as a whole include:

The social costs of the transition

The particular focus on the mechanics of introducing privatization by simply concentrating on the techniques and tools needed for successful implementation of privatization has neglected consideration of whether or not the infrastructures do in fact exist for privatization to succeed in central and eastern Europe. For example the lack of capital, money markets, technology, know-how and so on. As a result, the adoption of western business ethics and business models in central and eastern Europe, contrary to the general expectations and experience of the workforce, have taken a long time to improve the local economy. Initially there were disastrous economic and social consequences at a tremendous human cost in growing unemployment and increased poverty (Pearce, 1990, pp. 43–47). All the economies of central and eastern Europe that are currently in transition from a command economy to a market-based system have experienced a rapid deterioration in economic performance and standards of living, and development is slow to emerge.

Risk

For many investors, the potential return is not high enough to offset the perceived economic and political risks of investing in central Europe. The devaluation of local currencies is often too frequent and unpredictable and makes it almost impossible to make accurate business forecasting. The absence of cost and financial accounting procedures make it difficult for investors in determining the true value of the assets of interest. Under the centrally planned economy there was little need for stringent accounting practices. In fact, according to Furhman, what scant accounting records did exist could be so replete with fraud from self-serving bureaucrats as to render them practically useless (Furhman, 1990). Some accounting errors include: revenues based on production rather than sales, non-existent inventory and accounts receivable records, and foggy notions of who actually owns the assets (Raiszadeh *et al.*, 1995, p. 17).

There is also too much red tape to deal with before getting approval for an FDI project. The process could be very lengthy and arbitrary. Even in countries with up-to-date legislation, and judicial system is still not capable of dealing with potential conflicts.

Operational environment and lack of managerial and business skills

S. De Bendern of Ernst & Young summed up the general situation in the area as follows:

> The east European countries who are now embracing the politics of the free market have been used to central planning for the past four to five decades. In a planned economy, state enterprises are used to receiving allotments of raw materials and funds, and have to produce enough goods to fulfil the plan that is imposed by a State Planning committee. If they fall short of the plan, state subsidies are increased to help boost the output. If they surpass the plan, the surplus is reabsorbed by the state. Concepts such as profit, loss, cost accounting and marketing played no role in the functioning of the state enterprise. Whatever the end results, the status quo within the enterprise remains the same.
>
> (De Bendern, 1990, p. 27)

Consequently eastern European managers have no concept of competitive markets, quality control or worker's participation in decision making. They need technical advice on how to structure their internal organization, how to create new departments such as procurement, finance, personnel and marketing, and how to introduce new technology. During his business trip to eastern Europe in April and May 1991, Sir John Harvey Jones visited Krosno, the first company to be privatized in Poland. He found that one of the seven factories of Krosno was still maintaining the same level of glass production despite the lack of demand for its product. The unsold glassware was simply stacked in a large warehouse, costing the company around $1 million in interest charges. The factory was overmanned, and management was simply not allowed either to slowdown or even stop production. When asked about their costing systems, the company had no record of their profit and loss accounts, but kept a simple record of their stock inventory (Jones, 1991).

Since state-owned factories were traditionally overstaffed because of the policy of life employment, foreign investors in negotiating their investments were required to maintain certain employment levels for two or three years and suffered badly from low productivity.

The information gap

Marketing and customer service were also unknown concepts in central and eastern Europe and are only now becoming established. Market information has only been properly compiled for the last few years. Enterprises simply worked according to a plan which usually ignored demand and market needs entirely. Under the central planning, the customer did not exist. People took what they could get and waited hours, days or weeks for it. Changing priorities to suit customer needs were unknown. Plans were made on a yearly basis and then followed. For example, under the conditions of a centrally planned economy the term brand had not much sense. In a socialist society, where by definition no competition between the producers operating on the market exists, where in fact only one big producer – the state – exists, and where there is practically no 'real' advertising, the brands have simply no chance to be established.

...Everybody who lived here at that time remembers well the way of doing shopping under such conditions. Standing in long lines, hunting all over the city for products in more or less constant short supply. You were going into a shop asking: is there any cheese? The only differentiation made perhaps between white (cottage cheese) and yellow (ordinary cheese). You saw a line, you took a place at the end of it, asked the person in front of you what are they selling? or the even more characteristic: what are they giving? Were happy to hear that 'they' are 'giving' washing powder, or chocolate bars or maybe toilet paper, and hoping your waiting will not be in vain (the chocolate box, bar or roll being sold to the person in front of you). In such a situation there was no place for a deliberate choice of one producer over another, for a reflection about specific features of products made by the one or the other company.

(Fratczak-Rudnicka, 1995, p. 258)

Another problem of branding is linguistic difficulty. The Polish equivalent of the term 'brand' does not have one clearly established meaning. It might mean the 'brand' name, the produce name, and the name of the company being the producer of the product. Additionally it is also a synonym for quality and a name of a currency as illustrated in the following case.

CASE STUDY 13.1: Demoskop

In August last year Demoskop asked its respondents in a national representative survey, some questions concerning their understanding of the word brand (Polish *marka*). The first was an open-ended question where the respondents were asked to say how they understood the word brand. The largest number of respondents – 49 per cent – gave their understanding of the word as 'quality' and eight per cent identified the word with 'something good, valued', and a further five per cent with 'fame, prestige, esteem or tradition' which all also come close to the meaning of 'quality'. Forty per cent of the respondents identified the brand with the 'producer or company name', 13 per cent identified it with the product, seven per cent identified it with the product name, five per cent with the trade mark. Finally two per cent each understood the brand as the price, the packaging or the country of origin. In total, quality and quality-related meanings were ascribed to the word 'brand' by 63 per cent of the respondents; company, producer, product-related meanings were ascribed by 65 per cent, and other meanings were ascribed by 12 per cent, each understood the brand as the price, the packaging or the country of origin...

(Source: Fratczak-Rudnicka, 1995, p. 258)

Advertised goods furthermore, are generally suspected to be products of such low quality, that despite the general lack of goods on the market, no one wanted to buy them.

Lack of raw materials and well-established distribution infrastructure

Under the centrally planned regime, over 90 per cent of all orders to factories were placed, priced and distributed by the state (de Bendern, 1990, pp. 26–30). The state also chose suppliers and determined prices and wage levels. Foreign investors will have problems with local suppliers and may even have to provide funds for capital investment and extensive worker training to ensure a consistent raw material input in sufficient quantities. McDonald's for example, which opened two Moscow restaurants in 1989, had to overcome direct material procurement difficulties by setting up its own greenhouses and factories to grow and process ingredients. Such grandiose ventures would probably exceed the capabilities of smaller investors (Raiszedeh *et al.*, 1995, p. 16).

Cultural differences

State planning resulted in unique societal norms. Realizing these differences and knowing what to expect is crucial for a successful venture in eastern Europe. There are considerable problems with attitudes from the communist past. Russian managers' motivation, for example, has been reshaped by historical forces that are different from western experience, causing western managers to wonder whether their Russian counterparts can survive in the global market economy. Puffer explains the native of Russian managerial motivation as follows (Puffer, 1993, pp. 473–478):

1. *Achievement*   While in the USA, high achievers have been found to gain satisfaction from performing challenging tasks, meeting high standards, and finding better ways of doing things, achievement orientation was not fostered in traditional Russian society. In a rural communal society, the norm was for people to blend into the groups, and not to challenge the standard way of doing things. Group harmony was maintained by having everyone work at the same level. Consequently there was little motivation to strive to meet higher standards. The lack of incentives for innovation and productivity were also largely due to the remote possibility of firing an employee for non-performance. After completing their education, most Soviet citizens were assigned to a job from which they could not be fired, with little possibility of promotion or salary increase. The lack of incentive to work and to earn money was also related to the lack of consumer goods to buy. Managers during the communist period had to meet unrealistic deadlines and to manufacture products specified according to a plan. Instead of the opportunity to find better ways of doing this, they had to improvise methods to meet the plan based on insufficient resources (Puffer, 1993, p. 472).
2. *Ambition*   In Russia, ambition is a dirty word. For centuries ambitious people have typically been viewed with resentment, suspicion, and envy (Puffer, 1993, p. 472). According to egalitarian principles, no one was supposed to sink too low, or rise too high. People who strived to be better than others were violating social norms, and were seen as taking away the rightful share of others (Connor, 1991). Under communism, ambitious people'...had to cloak their ambition in service to the party and advancement of the common good of the organisation. Their success depends both on talent and political factors' (Puffer, 1993, p. 573). As former *New York Times* Moscow correspondent Felicity Barringer put it: 'In America, it's a sin to be a loser, but if there's one sin in Soviet society, it's being a winner' (Barringer, 1989).
3. *Destiny*   Many east Europeans believe that their destiny, reinforced by the teachings of the Russian Orthodox Church, is to endure suffering as a means to a brighter future (Puffer, 1993, p. 477).
4. *Tenacity*   The Russian people's ability to endure hardship and survive harsh conditions is a hallmark of their character. Over the centuries they have preserved through brutality harsh winters, the ravages of war, and severe shortages of basic materials, goods, and comforts that the western world takes for granted. During the communist period, managers had to work under adversity and fulfil company plans in spite of shortages of materials, resources and facilities. A number refused to be defeated by bureaucracy and found ways to get the job done.
5. *Initiative*   Under the centrality planned economy, there was no need to take any responsibility. There was always a government procedure, and managers were simply expected to follow rules unquestioningly: meeting fixed deadlines, provide regular feedback, and the importance and urgency of accomplishing the task. Initiative was discouraged.

Different work and business ethics

The state-run economies have instilled in people a specific behaviour and work culture, radically different from that in the west (Reinsch, 1991, pp. 13–14). As Shekshnia Stanislav (1994, p. 303) explains:

> Westerners have lived under conditions of more or less perfect markets for many years, have enjoyed civil and human rights for at least two hundred years and experienced the strong influence of the Protestant Work Ethic, with its emphasis on hard work and honesty. Most of these things are still foreign to Russia which has never had democracy, but was governed by authoritarian rule, whose economy was for centuries based on forced labour, and its main religion Orthodoxy emphasizes suffering on the Earth and joy in Heaven.

Furthermore, keeping the job for Russian workers is more important than their performance. Salary in their eyes is attached to the position, not to the performance. Values such as friendship, social contacts, entertainment, equality therefore become much more important than work and they come to work thinking about friends, contacts. This does not mean they cannot work hard, but it means that their work should be organized differently from the work of westerners.

BUSINESS STRATEGIES FOR DOING BUSINESS IN CENTRAL AND EASTERN EUROPE

There are many ways in which international business managers can take advantage of the opening up of the eastern and central European markets, provided they bear in mind the underlying difficulties and problems outlined briefly in the previous section.

Historically the most effective method of doing business in eastern Europe was the cultivation of contacts in ministries and foreign trade organizations (FTOS). But western companies nowadays have turned to franchising as the least risky and most effective way of investing in the east. That method is sometimes the only way to sidestep chaotic state distribution systems, which have no incentive to deliver products on time, if at all. Quality and price can be controlled more effectively.

Cooperative agreements are also becoming popular with foreign investors in eastern Europe. There are various forms of cooperative agreements available. One type is when a western firm agrees to provide an eastern European company with advanced production equipment, technical documentation, and training. The eastern European company begins production and sells products domestically or to foreign countries stipulated in the contract, and pays the western vendor with products produced or with other goods that it obtains locally. In other agreements, the western company may provide know-how and documentation in exchange for products produced. Co-production between a western company and one in eastern Europe is another form of cooperative agreement where each company produces components or sub-assemblies which go into a final product that will be marketed by both sides. This form of an agreement will become more common as eastern European companies become more adept at marketing internationally. Another type of cooperative agreement is when two partners agree to jointly finance the engineering and prototyping of an entirely new product, as well as its eventual manufacture. A western firm might fund research by an eastern European company in exchange for the right to use the research results. Finally, co-production could be achieved through a simple swap of technical licences, documentation and training programmes between the western and eastern European firm (Engholm, 1993, pp. 116–127).

A Western company considering a cooperative venture in central and eastern Europe must first of all conduct an 'audit' of the business opportunities available.

The first step is to understand the political behaviour of each of the eastern European nations considered. Information needs to be extracted about whether reforms will continue and if so in what direction. Although there have been multi-party elections in a number of eastern and central European countries, some still have a substantial communist component in their governments. The opposition within these countries is still too weak to offer any real opposition at the present time.

The second step is to find out whether the organizations with which you want to do business are likely to be competitive on an international basis.

The third step consists of assessing the difference that technology transfer can make to an eastern European organization, which activities it can affect and what values this will add. Transport and telecommunications infrastructures within eastern Europe are a major problem area for many western investors. As a fourth step, it is important to establish the sources of raw materials. Distribution problems and the failure of the centralized systems produced chronic shortages of raw materials. Western manufacturers may have to import their own raw materials if the requirements cannot be met in the local markets. The best way to find out is by making an initial visit as a member of a trade mission. Details of trade missions and joint visits can be obtained from the Chamber of Commerce or from the Eastern European Trade Council.

The fifth step relates particularly to dealing with the local language. Language is proving to be a greater barrier than anticipated in eastern and central Europe. Excellent translators are available, but the problem is that in the Slavic languages the vocabulary needed to describe many of the new concepts of business simply does not exist.

The sixth step in making decisions about investing in central and eastern Europe is for investors to be aware of the levels of debt that exist between eastern European companies, particularly in Russia. Before making any investment decisions, western investors need therefore to have reliable financial information. They will have to spend a great deal of time and effort finding out about the credit-worthiness of some companies. But the availability of such information is a problem in itself.

The seventh step for potential investors is to be aware of the lack of legal protection for their goods and investments in central and eastern Europe. The protection of intellectual property rights is inadequate compared to that in the west, even though central and eastern European countries are signatories of the Paris Convention of 1883 regarding the protection of industrial property.

Finally, business people should not only take account of the many problems involved in trading with eastern and central Europe, they should also be aware of the changes occurring in the region, and how these might affect opportunities for business development. An understanding of the process of liberalization and marketization taking place within eastern and central Europe is therefore essential. Investors should be very cautious when evaluating the region. There is no typical eastern European economy, or one set of characteristics which holds true for all localities. Some generalizations could be made across all central and eastern European countries, for example, the Independent States that replaced the same number of Soviet socialist republics at the end of 1991 (Armenia, Azerbaijan, Belarus, Georgia, Kazakhstan, Turkistan, Moldova, Russia, Tajikistan, Turkmenistan, the Ukraine and Uzbekistan) do share a similar heritage. All were subject to Soviet rule from 40 to 70 years, all inherited the Soviet economic and political system and they had very close and intensive trade and other economic relationships within the Soviet Union. However, it is important to note that these 15 states differ in many other respects: in geographical location, cultural heritage, size, natural resources, degree of economic development, industrial structure and education level of their populations. Central European countries such as Albania, Bulgaria, Czech Republic, Estonia, Hungary, Latvia, Lithuania, Poland, Romania, Slovakia and Slovenia do differ significantly from the new independent states. A general overview of the recent changes being introduced in eastern and central Europe is provided in the following section.

THE MOVEMENT TOWARDS A FREE MARKET ECONOMY

Central and eastern European countries are currently experiencing a 'seemingly' dramatic transition from centrally planned systems to free-market economies. Four key periods in the development of eastern European countries can be identified since the Second World War (Eszes and Muhlemann, 1993, p. 12).

The first period is that of classical, rigid central planning. During this period, all companies were owned by the state and all strategic decisions were made centrally. Local decision making was minimal, with the primary objective being to execute centrally determined plans.

The second period is known as the era of reformed central planning. During this period, as the central control on the economy weakened, the independence of companies grew, and a semi-market economy emerged.

The third period is currently one of a transition to market economy with the aim of developing political systems close to the western democratic model. However, there are still significant economic difficulties: high inflation, high unemployment, huge national debts, poor infrastructure and energy problems.

The fourth period, still to arrive, is the emergence of a real market economy, but it is very difficult to predict when this will be achieved, if ever.

The World Bank has been influential in the transition movement in central and eastern European countries because the investment capital supplied by the World Bank for infrastructure projects has been dependent on the recipient countries continued progress towards macro-economic stability established by the World Bank programme. This programme relies heavily on establishing reform in four main areas (Summers, 1992, quoted in Foley, 1996, p. 24).

1. Macro-economic stabilization and the tightening of fiscal and credit policies, and addressing internal and external imbalances.
2. Price stability and market reform – removing price controls, liberalizing trade, and creating competitive factor markets.
3. Enterprise reform and restructuring – development of private sector, establishing and clarifying property rights, facilitating entry and exit of firms, restructuring of enterprises.
4. Institution reform – redefining the role of the state, legal and regulatory reform, social safety net and reform of government institutions.

Following the World Bank recommendations, economic reforms on a massive scale in central and east European countries have been implemented to varying degrees, with the ultimate hope of achieving the membership of the European Union. However, as Merritt (1991) comments: 'What has taken ten years in Poland and 14 months in Hungary took only ten weeks in Germany, ten days in former Czechoslovakia and ten hours in Rumania'. An insight into these reforms is necessary to understand the problems of transition and identity the business opportunities now available in those countries.

The first 'free-trade zone area' was introduced in Russia in November 1990 to increase foreign economic cooperation, promote foreign investment and to serve as a laboratory for developing new economic forms during the period of transition (Torbet, 1991, pp. 16–18). The 'Shatalin Plan' or the 500-day plan for installing capitalism represented another drive by Gorbachev for the full restoration of market relations in the USSR. The Shatalin Plan included:

- The slashing of the budget deficit from 100 billion roubles to 5 billion roubles in 100 days
- the establishment of a stock exchange
- the privatization of 40 per cent of industry (including 50 per cent of construction and 60 per cent of the industry) by the 400th day
- the sale of collective farms to peasants, and the elimination of state subsidies on many foods and properties
- the deregulation of prices
- the recognition of trade unions, and the opportunity for the workforce to 'buy-out' their factories via share issues, and to operate them as private companies

(Hibbert, 1991; Lindsay, 1989)

In 1991, a further shock therapy approach was introduced in Russia by the Yeltsin government based on the following:

- price liberalization
- privatization
- establishing a legal and institutional framework supportive of a market economy
- the opening-up of the Russian economy to free trade
- the unification of the exchange rate
- tight monetary policy

(Dent, 1994, p. 15)

As part of the general reform programme, Russia abolished the state monopoly over foreign trade, and by January 1992 all firms were allowed to trade directly. The price liberalization of January 1992 was followed by a gradual freeing of the rate of exchange. In a number of steps during 1992 the pre-existing system of multiple exchange rates was unified, and the foreign exchange price of the rouble was determined in an open daily auction. However, although the exchange rate was free to float according to market forces, the Central Bank of Russia maintained the power to intervene, an option that it has frequently used since the middle of 1992.

Around 82 000 enterprises were privatized between 1992 and 1993 in Russia. By mid-1993 2300 medium to large-sized enterprises had been auctioned into the private sector. Sectors targeted have been: consumer goods, retailing, catering, food processing, health care, agriculture, machine engineering, automobiles, construction and general services. Almost all small business have been privatized, and many new ones have been established. Furthermore, the majority of large-scale enterprises have been privatized. According to official data, nearly 80 per cent of all employees in industry were employed by private enterprises by the fall of 1994 (Government of the Russian Federation, 1994, p. 7). The privatization programme based on vouchers and auctions, was almost completed in the summer of 1994 and a new stage of direct cash sales is now being prepared. The voucher system was introduced and distributed the rights of the Russian citizenship to become shareholders in the newly privatized companies. Auctions were utilized to sell off the larger old state enterprises. Managers and workers were permitted to buy up to 51 per cent of the share capital, with at least 30 per cent offered to the public with the state normally retaining the remainder.

After the break-up of the former USSR, the developing legislation regarding foreign investment varied from republic to republic. By 1993 many of the new republics embraced a foreign investment policy in which most forms of foreign investment are allowed, including joint ventures, wholly owned subsidiaries and in some cases portfolio investment. But it is expected that laws will be frequently revised. As far as the repatriation of profits is concerned, in all the former USSR the opening of rouble accounts for non-residents is now permitted, although the transfer of balances overseas is not guaranteed in any republic, including Russia, and the use of counter-trade, the long-accepted route to profit repatriation remains. Although the newly independent states are all committed to currency convertibility, problems still exists with new currencies in the former USSR.

Market-oriented policies have also been fiercely pursued in central and eastern Europe, particularly in the Czech Republic, Slovakia, Hungary, Poland, and to a certain extent in Bulgaria.

The former Czechoslovakia embarked on economic reforms in early 1991. Cornerstones of the reforms were a 'big bang' liberalization of prices and external trade, large-scale privatization, and a rigorous macro-economic stabilization policy. Small-scale privatization got off to a quick start in 1991 and large-scale privatization started in May 1992. State industrial assets estimated at $148.7 billion have all been put up for privatization. Vouchers or coupon books were issued in October 1991 and distributed to Czechoslovakian citizens to allow them to buy equity in the companies that appealed to them (Ash, 1991, pp. 511–514). This coupon scheme was a success, transferring ownership of firms to citizen and investment funds.

In Hungary, economic reforms included the privatization of half the current 90 per cent state-owned enterprises in four years (Szegedi, 1989–1990, pp. 109–120), the demonopolization of foreign trade (Newbery, 1991, pp. 571–580), and a three-year reform programme including the development of new laws on banking, insurance, mutual funds and bankruptcy, and full liberalization of foreign trade by the end of 1992 (Nutti, 1991, p. 62). The Foreign Investment Act of 1988 became effective on 1 January 1991 (*Euromonitor*, 1993, pp. 48–49). The Act provides full guarantee to all investments of foreign entities and individuals in Hungary. All losses suffered as a result of nationalization, expropriation, or similar measure will be compensated to the foreign investor in full and without delay (*Euromonitor*, 1993). To increase further the attractiveness of the business environment the Act also allows foreign firms wishing to invest in Hungary to:

- establish a 100 per cent foreign ownership
- to enter into a joint venture with one or more Hungarian or foreign partners by either: setting up a company or acquiring a stake in an existing Hungarian company
- to be treated in the same way as normal Hungarian companies in all respects
- to enter into joint ventures with private and state-owned Hungarian companies of any size
- to use dividends from one venture as capital for another
- to hold their capital contribution in any joint venture in hard currency which may be freely used for acquisition of the means of production (plant, machinery, equipment) durable goods and spare parts, and for paying costs incurred in hard currency

Western investors are also guaranteed the right to repatriate dividends and royalty payment in hard currency whether or not the enterprise has generated the currency itself.

The first phase was successfully implemented, with prices stabilized and balance of payments pressures contained. The predicted recovery, however, failed to materialize in 1992. Output fell sharply and declined by 40 per cent in 1990–1992, while GDP declined by 16 per cent in 1991 alone. Public consumption stagnated, personal consumption was reduced by one-third, and net investment became negative. Exports have been redirected away from CMEA and towards EC markets, and the trade balance has come into surplus. Industrial production declined by 11 per cent in 1992. Unemployment was rapidly rising to 14 per cent by the end of the year and reached 20 per cent in 1993. The fall in private consumption became the main driving force in the recession. Inflation declined to 22 per cent in 1992 down from 35 per cent in 1991 and industrial producer prices rose only by half the rate of consumer prices. Two major problems appeared during 1992: overshooting of the budget deficit, which halted IMF supports, and problems in the privatization programme. The private-sector growth has been largely due to the rapid expansion of new enterprises and the inflow of foreign capital, with little help from the privatization of state-owned companies. Multinational firms had taken over the most promising enterprises but left about 1000 smaller and less attractive firms on the government's books. Fiscal revenues fell significantly and caused the budget crisis. Hungary also faces tensions with its minority population of more than 500 000 and externally strained relations especially with the new Slovakia.

In Poland, the Mazowiecki government, determined to achieve a full-fledged market economy, introduced in January 1990 a series of provisions which could be called, because of their extreme austerity, a shock treatment to stabilize the economy, bring about market equilibrium and to lower inflation (Adam, 1992, p. 55). The stabilization package introduced to achieve a free market included the abolition of subsidies and the reduction of the budget deficit to one per cent of GNP (down from eight per cent in the previous year), an increase in real interest rates, almost complete price liberalization, trade liberalization, 32 per cent devaluation of the zloty (made convertible), and the setting up of a stock exchange where Polish state assets could be sold and retraded (Grosfeld, 1990).

Under the Foreign Investment Act of 1991 (*Euromonitor*, 1993, p. 51) foreign investors:

- may participate in a wholly owned company, or they may enter into a joint venture with other foreign or Polish parties
- may establish a representative office, which may be a technical information office, a supervision office or a commercial branch office
- may conduct foreign trade activities through an agency or by dealing direct with a Polish principal

Foreign banks may also operate in Poland with the permission of the National Bank of Poland and the Finance Ministry, provided the required minimum capital contribution of US $6 million is met. Banks can establish a presence by setting up a joint-stock company, by buying shares in an existing Polish bank through the privatization process, or through a branch of a representative office.

Other changes introduced by the 1991 Foreign Investment Act include:

- the absorption of the Foreign Investment Agency created in 1988 into the Ministry of Privatization
- An increase in the discretion of the minister of finance to grant tax exemptions
- The liberalization of restrictions on the repatriation of profits
- The abolition of minimum financial requirement for foreign investment and minimum participation requirements for joint ventures
- The automatic protection of foreign investments

Furthermore, in respect of the repatriation of profits, the Foreign Investment Act 1991 released restrictions on profit repatriation for foreigners who are now able to purchase and transfer abroad foreign currency to the full extent of tax-paid profits without the need for a separate foreign exchange licence.

The privatization of some companies (over 7000) started in September 1990. The Act on the Privatization of State Owned Enterprises (*Euromonitor*, 1993, p. 121) was approved in July 1990 allowing foreign investors to purchase state company shares, subject to an overall ceiling of 10 per cent. The Act was amended in November 1991 to include:

- the creation of a Ministry of Ownership Changes, since renamed as the Ministry of Privatization – to oversee and regulate the privatization process
- the transfer of ownership of 'small' state assets – such as shops, restaurants and apartments – to local authorities which are responsible for their privatization
- the privatization of state-owned enterprise can be initiated by its management and workers' council, or by the ministry in charge of a company in agreement with the management and the council. It can also be initiated at the request of the prime minister, or on the advice of the minister of privatization
- before offering the shares to third parties an economic and financial study must be prepared in order to evaluate the assets and establish whether there is a need for strategic or organisational changes

The new amended Polish privatization law also provided that employees of the privatizing state enterprise are entitled to buy up to 20 per cent of the shares on a preferential basis – at 50 per cent discount compared with the price set for Polish citizens.

In June 1993 privatization legislation approved in April came into force. Under these provisions 600 enterprises were to be denationalized.

Thus Poland's radical stabilization measures introduced since January 1990 aimed for full price liberalization, an end to subsidies, currency devaluation, full convertibility, wage controls and a reduction of the budget deficit. The stabilization programme helped to reduce hyper-inflation from 64 per cent in 1989 to less than 40 per cent in 1992. However, Poland experienced a deep recession with output declining by more than 34 per cent in 1990–92 and unemployment rising above 14 per cent on average and to over 20 per cent in the northern regions. By the second half of 1992; macro-economic indicators signalled considerable improvement and an end to the recession. Poland's economic performance in 1992 was considered the best in the region. The industrial sector is now showing signs of recovery. The turnaround has been driven primarily by the country's strong export performance. Poland's exports to the EC rose from 32 per cent of total exports in 1989 to 56 per cent in 1991 (Euromonitor, 1993).

Bulgaria started economic reform only in 1990 but has managed to administer a quick progress towards creating the necessary legislative basis, establishing democratic institutions and promoting market reform (*Investor's Guide*, 1996). The Act on Economic Activity by Foreign Persons and the Protection of Foreign Investment was introduced in January 1992. Its main provisions are as follows:

- Foreign individuals and companies have the same rights to acquire shares in companies or undertake business activity as Bulgarian citizens and companies, unless specifically prohibited by the Act.
- Foreign persons can acquire ownership rights over buildings and limited property rights over immovable property, although neither foreign persons nor companies, nor Bulgarian

companies with more than 50 per cent for foreign participation, can acquire ownership of farmland.

- Details of foreign investments must be registered with the Ministry of Finance within 30 days of being put into effect, and foreign investments made under previous legislation are also required to be registered. Failure to comply with this requirement, or making a false declaration, means that foreign investor will be fined-one tenth of the value of the unregistered investment.
- Specific permission must be obtained from various authorities if a company over which a foreign person has effective control is intending to engage in any of the following activities:
  - manufacture or trade in arms
  - permission required from a special government commission
  - banking or insurance
  - acquisition of real estate in certain geographic areas
- Protection of investment in cases of nationalization or expropriation and deals with various currency issues.

(*Euromonitor*, 1993, p. 48–49)

Bulgaria's Article 10 of Laws on Foreign Investment also provides that expropriation can only occur by order of the Ministry of Finance when important national needs cannot be met in any other way. In such cases, compensation equal to the market value of the property on the day of expropriation, according to the article, will be paid. Protection against nationalization is offered by the constitution, which states that nationalization and restriction of the rights of ownership may only be made by law in the public interest and only if compensation is paid.

As far as the convertibility of the currency is concerned, in Bulgaria, trade in hard currency has been liberalized and is now permitted between banks, companies and private individuals. A rate of exchange for the level is now fixed daily by the National Bank for the purpose of accounting, statistics, customer appraisals and remittance. Foreign investors can also easily repatriate all income in Bulgaria paying the withholding tax of 15 per cent unless reduced by relevant tax treaties. If profits are reinvested, no further tax is due. The prevailing tax rate is 40 per cent on the net income of corporations (European Bank for Reconstruction and Development, 1996, p. 7).

Furthermore, the Transformation and Privatization of State-Owned and Municipal Enterprises (TPSMEA) was adopted by Parliament in April 1992 and was amended in June 1994 to include necessary changes for launching the so-called 'mass' privatization due to start at the beginning of 1996. The Foreign Investment Agency (FIA) was created in March 1995 by a Decree N 54 of the Council of Ministers for the promotion and monitoring of foreign investment.

All these reforms, as well as the fact that inflation which was almost 300 per cent in 1991 slowed down to 35 per cent in 1995 (European Bank for Reconstruction and Development, 1996, p. 6), and interest rates cut down from 72 per cent in March 1995 to 34 per cent in August 1995 (European Bank for Reconstruction and Development, 1996, p. 6), improve considerably the attractiveness of the Bulgarian business environment for foreign investment.

PROSPECTS FOR THE EASTERN ENLARGEMENT

The overriding priority of the Czeck Republic, Slovakia, Hungary, and Poland is to achieve full membership in the EU as soon as possible. They are claiming that they fulfil the basic criteria for entry: stable democracies and growing market economies. But no timetable for membership has yet been provided. The EU governments put forward five arguments for keeping them waiting (Fratzscher, 1994, pp. 228–230). Fratzscher summarizes them as follows:

1. Membership is a question of financial means. Budget transfer from the EC's regional fund (accounting for 25 per cent of the EC budget) plus expenditures for supporting farmers under the Common Agricultural policy (accounting for 50 per cent of the EU budget). Rich countries strictly refuse to carry the extra burden and poor countries strongly resist sharing their benefits with even poorer central and eastern European countries. On the other hand, substantial benefits may develop when the central and eastern European countries (CECs) are integrated into the EU, in particular through increased exports of the EU to CECs markets and through improved growth potential. Moreover the cost of the alternative of closing the door may far outweigh the costs of opening the door. Once political stability in CECs is quantified as an asset for the EU, the alternative cost in case of political turmoil in eastern Europe becomes an important part of the calculation.
2. Second, membership is a question of domestic politics as well. Large exports in sensitive products into the EC may hurt the German steel-maker, the French farmer, and the Portuguese textile worker and this perceived threat shapes domestic politics. Trade in these products has already been severely restricted in the association agreements, and long transitional periods will be required in the case of membership.
3. Third, a more long-term concern, the EU allows free movement of people within its borders. Membership of the CECs may increase incentives for their workers to migrate in a westward direction to highly paid jobs. This argument is unlikely to hold since membership treaties usually impose transitional restrictions on migration and since workers in CECs may prefer to stay in a prosperous and growing environment at home.
4. Fourth, early membership in the EU may hurt the CECs, since they may need longer transitional periods to transform their economies than widely expected. Entire sectors may be crushed by import competition if they do not establish a competitive position before EU integration.

The attitude of the European Union government towards enlargement is further explained by Euromonitor in the following terms (*Euromonitor*, 1993, p. 7):

> All the former eastern bloc countries are poor, they have bigger populations than the potential west European members, and they depend more heavily on agriculture. The average GDP per capita of Bulgaria, former Czechoslovakia, Hungary, Poland and Romania is only about 13 per cent of the EU average and no more than 60 per cent of Portugal's which is the EU's poorest member. This combination of low income, large populations and a big farming sector means that east European members would be large net recipients of EU aid, both from the structural fund and from the common agricultural policy (CAP).

Consequently, the main barriers to EU membership are:

1. Each country depends heavily on agriculture and hence would immediately qualify for huge amounts of EU agricultural subsidies and support.
2. East European countries are poor and hence would absorb most of the Union's regional development budget.
3. The low wages costs of enterprises could give them a competitive advantage against EU firms. Average per capital income of Bulgaria, Hungary, Poland, Romania and the Czech and Slovak Republics is about 12 per cent of the average in the EU and just 60 per cent of the capita GDP of Portugal – the EUs poorest member state.

4. Extension of free movement of labour to east European countries would almost certainly lead to large-scale migrating of technically well-qualified workers from east to west, possibly causing stresses and strains in west European labour markets.

(Bennett, 1994, p. 95)

At the moment, the former Czechoslovakia, Hungary, and Poland, has association agreements with the EU. These are meant to regulate trade and investment relations in the following areas:

- *Trade*   The EU removed quotas in early 1992 and will reduce tariffs over 2–5 years. The east Europeans have promised to phase out tariffs and quotas over 4–10 years. To be granted duty-free status, goods exported by the associate members must have at least 60 per cent local content.
- *Sensitive products*   The EU has removed very few of its restrictions on imports of food, textiles, steel and coal but these will eventually be phased out.
- *Competition policy*   The east Europeans must begin to apply EU anti-trust law within three years but can give state aid to backward industries.
- *Labour*   The agreements do not allow more workers into the EU but those already there will enjoy equal social benefits.

(*Euromonitor*, 1993, p. 8)

The four countries also formed a club known as the Visegrad Group in February 1991, in the hope of securing more effective concessions from the EU. This regional trading zone called the Visegrad was further developed as the Central European Free Trade Area (CEFTA) in the Cracow Treaty of December 1992. The CEFTA constitutes Europe's third trading bloc with 64 million consumers, and came into effect in March 1993. Under this pact, tariffs on goods traded among the four members will be reduced to the levels applied to EU goods. Intra-regional tariffs will be reduced in stages and should be eliminated entirely by 2001. The pact is likely to reduce government revenues and it will force further restructuring of industries and services within the EFT countries (Schipke, 1994, pp. 172–189, also pp. 208–209). It is also hoped that this pact will strengthen the bargaining power of the four CECs in negotiating their full membership with the EU.

The EU recognizing the importance of the desire of the countries of central Europe to move away from centrally planned to market economies has established different programmes to help them rejoin the mainstream of European development through future membership of the European Union.

Phare programme

At the Arch Summit held in Paris from 14–16 July 1989, the heads of state and government of the G7 countries (Germany, France, Italy, the UK, Canada, the USA and Japan) expressed their willingness to help the countries of the east transform their economies, improve their environment and establish truly democratic forms of government. In response to the G7 initiative, the 24 countries comprising G24 (the 12 member states of the EU, Austria, Finland, Iceland, Norway, Sweden, Switzerland, Turkey, the USA, Canada, Australia, Japan and New Zealand) decided on 9 and 10 July 1990 to launch a concerned action to provide economic aid for the countries of central and eastern Europe, and for historical and geographical reasons, to give the European Commission a mandate to coordinate the programme.

Thus, in 1990 the Poland and Hungary Assistance for the Reconstruction of the Economy, known as the PHARE programme was launched. Originally designed to assist Poland and Hungary as its name indicates PHARE now involves 11 central and eastern European countries: Poland, Hungary, Albania, Bulgaria, Estonia, Lithuania, Latvia, the Czech Republic, the Slovak Republic, Romania and Slovenia (PHARE, European Commission, 1994).

In its first five years of operation to 1994 PHARE has made available ECU 4.248 million to 11 partner countries, making PHARE the largest assistance programme of its kind. The key areas include restructuring of state enterprises including agriculture, private-sector development, reform of institutions, legislation and public administration, reform of social services, employment, education and health, development of energy, transport and telecommunications infrastructure, environment, and nuclear safety. To encourage foreign investment in central and eastern Europe, PHARE offered to help ministries and other bodies in designing and using good investment promotion policies. Foreign Investment Agencies (FIA), 'one-stop-shops' have been established to help investors, – from finding a local partner to dealing with local red tape (PHARE, 1994, p. 13). The following Foreign Investment Agencies have been established with PHARE support.

- CzechInvest
- Estonian Foreign Investment Agency
- Hungary Investment and Trade Development Agency
- Latvian Development Agency
- Lithuania Investment Promotion Agency
- Poland State Foreign Investment Agency
- Romanian Development Agency
- Slovakia Slovak National Agency for Foreign Investment and Development
- Slovenia Bureau for Foreign Investment Promotion and Trade Development

These FIA provide the following services: strategy elaboration, institutional assessment, advisory support, help with marketing, research and drafting of strategy studies, training and the supply of equipment. The exception is Latvia, where the training element was provided by the UK's Know-How-Fund rather than by PHARE (PHARE, 1994, p. 17).

CASE STUDY 13.2: PHARE and Philips

Philips is a typical case of what can be achieved with skilful use of PHARE support. The Dutch multinational first met CzechInvest at a trade fair in Germany. Philips, looking for investment opportunities in central and eastern Europe, was sufficiently impressed by the first contact to ask CzechInvest for help in scouting out possible locations for a plant, in identifying investment opportunities and in negotiating local regulation and institutions. This relationship eventually resulted in Philips setting up Philips Mecoma Ceske SRO in Ceske Budejovice. The company is using the buildings of a former Tesla factory and the new plant is supplying parts for use both inside and outside the company. By 1995 over 1120 people were employed there.

TACIS programme

The Technical Assistance for the Commonwealth of Independent States (TACIS) programme is a European Union initiative. The equivalent of PHARE but set up in 1991 to speed up the process of economic reform and transition to democracy currently underway in the new independent states of the former Soviet Union and to strengthen their democratic societies. It provides support in the form of grant finance to foster the exchange of knowledge and expertise through partnerships, links and networks at all levels of society. TACIS support activities in the following fields: energy, human resource development, nuclear safety, food production and distribution, transport, telecommunications and company services.

Essential tips on business etiquette in central and eastern Europe

Eastern European society is formal in communication, behaviour, negotiating, and attire (Engholm, 1993, pp. 265–291). First impressions in the east start with punctuality. Eastern Europeans are generally very punctual. Clothing is conservative and suit and tie are essential for all business meetings. As far as the use of names and titles, eastern Europeans use fairly elaborate courtesies in addressing business contacts. Family names preceded by the title are often used. Translated business cards are required when introducing yourself at a company or government office. As far as meetings are concerned, these are rarely held in offices. Conference and boardrooms are usually the place for meetings with foreigners, conducted around a rectangular conference table, with eastern Europeans on one side and foreigners on the other. Eastern European negotiators are typically under enormous pressure to sell an enterprise and may suddenly become impatient. They might lay all their cards on the table at the outset and then become frustrated if you need time to consider a deal. Using a lawyer in eastern Europe business negotiations is crucial. Eastern Europeans avoid the direct use of the word 'no' out of politeness and formality. 'A Russian will never tell you the truth', writes A. Craig Copetas. 'He will also never lie to you. He will tell you what you want to hear. Russians do this to live'. Don't take yes for an answer anywhere in the region without verification and cross-checking to ensure that the yes you may have heard was not a polite yes that really means no or maybe.

REVIEW QUESTIONS

1. Many argue that the current reforms in the former Eastern Bloc countries provide the greatest opportunity to improve east–west business relations, which the west must not waste. Others see the developments in central and eastern Europe as welcome but no reason for euphoria. The results so far of the limited reform programmes in central and eastern Europe are uncertain, and serious setbacks are inevitable. Discuss the issues involved in these different views.
2. Under the central planning system, all internal and external trade was mapped out and imposed on enterprises by the central plan. Quantities, prices, buyers and suppliers were all predetermined. Participation in the global trading system was also minimal. The emphasis was on economic self-sufficiency for the bloc as a whole. Enterprises were completely isolated from foreign trade and global markets. What are the subsequent problems that foreign investors might face when doing business in that region. How might these be overcome?
3. In the light of the problems and opportunities of doing business in eastern and central

Europe which business techniques or methods would you recommend as most appropriate and why?
4. Discuss the reasons why European business might diversify into the central and eastern European countries and the problems it might face.

EXERCISE 13.1: Western support programmes towards central and eastern Europe

Aim   European and international organizations have frequently been criticized for the lack of support they have actually provided to the central and eastern European countries in their transition to market economies. The aim of this exercise is to familiarize students with various western support programmes and financial aid programmes so far developed.

Assignment   Students are allocated one of the following organizations to research:

- the German Treuhand
- the European Agreements
- partnership and cooperation agreements (PCA)
- the European Investment Bank
- The G24 nations
- the International Monetary Fund
- the World Bank
- the European Bank for Reconstruction and Development

Format   Each group is asked to conduct an in-depth research of one of the above mentioned organizations. Students should consider the following points when preparing for their class presentation:

- brief historical background of the European or international organization selected
- overview of the programmes developed so far to support central and eastern European countries
- evaluation of their role in the transition movement from a centrally planned economy to a free-market economy
- assessment of their support and financial contribution

Sources

Students should use the Internet to collect information for this assignment. Most international organizations now have a web page on the World Wide Web (WWW) providing detailed information about their work to the general public.

FURTHER READING

Engholm, C., *The Other Europe. A Complete Guide to Business Opportunities in Eastern Europe*, McGraw-Hill, New York, 1993.

European Bank for Reconstruction and Development, *Investor's Guide to Privatization with Debt-Swaps in Bulgaria*, Price Waterhouse, Sofia, 1996.

Jolly, A. (ed.), *CBI European Business Handbook*, Kogan Press, London, 1996.

Raiszadeh, F.M.E., Helms, M. and Varner, M.C., Critical issues to consider when developing business operations in Eastern bloc countries, *European Business Review*, **95** (6), 1995, pp. 12–20.

Schipke, A., *The Economics of Transformation. Theory and Practice in the New Market Economies*, Springer-Verlag, Berlin Heidelberg, 1994.

FOURTEEN

WOMEN IN THE EUROPEAN LABOUR MARKET

Suzanne Tieze

This chapter is divided into two sections and will deal with the role of women in the labour force in countries of the European Community and in countries of central and eastern Europe. Even though there are signs that Europe is growing more closely together, there are still differences that necessitate a distinction between the two areas. In particular, trends around modes of employment (e.g. part-time, temporary work, etc.), occupational segregation, gender pay gaps, childcare, and social security systems shall be discussed. Commonalties and differences between countries shall be examined and explained. Additionally, case study material will be used to highlight some of these topics.

LEARNING OBJECTIVES

- To define the position of women in the labour force in EU countries and to establish some trends in all EU countries
- To identify various elements that contribute to women's particular situation in certain countries of the EU
- To provide examples of initiatives promoting women in the workplace in EU countries
- To define the role of women in the workforce in east and central European countries before 1989 and to define the role of women in the workforce in the newly emerged capitalist/democratic systems (post 1989)
- To discuss the reasons for the changed role of women in the workforce
- To show how companies are trying to facilitate the integration of women into their organizations

WOMEN IN THE LABOUR FORCE

The EU has supported the ideal of an equal role for women in society from its very inception. Article 119 of the founding Treaty of Rome (1957) states that:

> Each member state shall during the first stage ensure and subsequently maintain the application of the principle that men and women should receive equal pay for equal work (...). Equal pay without discrimination based on sex means: that pay for the same work at piece rates shall be calculated on the basis of the same unit of measurement; that pay for work at time shall be the same for the same job.

However, equality as some critics claim remains a mere theory and the principles of Article

119 are interpreted not so much as a stance on equal opportunity policies, but 'rather it [Article 119] was inspired by the desire to ensure equal competition between states' (Buckley and Anderson, 1988, p. 10).

THE SUPPLY OF FEMALE LABOUR

More and more women participate in the labour market. The reasons for this can be attributed to various occurrences in modern societies: a shortage of skilled labour, greater marital instability, rising educational standards, increasing awareness of women's rights backed up by relevant political support, are all contributing to the trend of an increasing female labour force (Cooper and Davidson, 1992). Whether the current labour market is actually providing a 'window of opportunity' for women (Ninon and Williamson, 1993, p. 111) shall be discussed in the following sections.

Between 1979 and 1988 female economic activity grew in every single state. 'The latest Labour Force Survey (EUROSTAT, 1993) shows the following picture for 12 member states. There are 282.3 million persons aged 15 years and more, of which 51.9 per cent are female.

137.5 million persons are *in employment* of which 41.0 per cent are female. A *part-time* job was held by 21.2 million persons of which 81.8 per cent are female. 14.8 million people of which 84.2 per cent are female are not available for full-time jobs and 3.8 million people, 73.4 per cent female, are seeking full-time employment. Currently, 116.3 million persons are in *full-time employment*, 33.6 per cent of which are female. Out of this group 18.8 million (21.6 per cent female) are *self-employed*, 2.0 million (67 per cent female) are *family workers* and 95 million (35.1 per cent female) are *employees*. Finally, of the 95 million employees 85.1 million (34.6 per cent female) have a *permanent* job and 9.1 million (40 per cent female) have a *temporary* job.

What do these statistics tell us? First, that women play a significant part in the European labour force, that they work part-time most of the time, even though of those people (3.8 million) available for a full-time job, 73.4 per cent are female. With regards to full-time jobs only 33.6 per cent are held by women – with in terms of per cent less women than men are self-employed or working as employees, but more are working as family workers.

The darker side of employment is *unemployment*. Large-scale unemployment is one of the gravest economic and social problems facing the EU and each of its member states. In 1977 there were 5 million unemployed in EU countries, in 1986 14.6 million and in 1989 12.7 million (EUROSTAT, 1993a). Unemployment leads to economic hardship, loss of social status and sense of purpose and social integration. In 1994 of a total of 282.3 million persons, 17.7 million were unemployed. 47.7 per cent of these were female. The long-term unemployed (one year or longer) count at 8.4 million (49.2 per cent female) of which 6.7 million (45.1 female) are looking for a full-time job, 1.0 million (84.4 per cent female) are looking for a part-time job.

Those unemployed less than a year count at 9.1 million (46.4 per cent female) of which 7.3 million (40.7 per cent female) are looking for a full-time job, 1.2 million (83.5 per cent female) for a part-time job. Different tensions have led to different experience of unemployment for women and men. The uninterrupted linear work-pattern is still regarded as the male 'norm', women move in and out of the labour force according to their domestic responsibilities. However, more and more women are as attached to their paid work as men and with changing patterns of household structure, women are taking on 'breadwinner' status and have the same expectations of their paid labour as has been traditionally expected of men.

Finally, a third category of *non-active persons* needs to be taken into account: 127.1 million

(64.3 per cent female). 104.8 million do not want to have work, 7.1 million (66.3 per cent female) would like to have work, but are not seeking it. 1.7 million (57.2 per cent female) are seeking employment, but cannot find any.

Although the activity rates of women have not reached those of men, figures are indicating an increase of female participation in the labour force markets. Forecasts suggest that the trend will be continuing in the next decades. Accepting these figures and forecasts at face value is, however, misleading. Occupational segregation is pervasive and a persistent characteristic of all labour markets and needs to be taken into account in employment analysis – as do part-time and temporary employment forms and the usually less well-protected employment status that is connected with them.

Occupational segregation

Rubery and Fagan (1993) used data from EUROSTAT to compare percentages of employed women in seven major occupational groups (professional, managerial, clerical, sales, service agriculture, production, armed forces) in some European countries (Belgium, Denmark, Germany, Greece, Spain, France, Ireland, Luxembourg, Netherlands, Portugal, and the UK). The most salient factor is the overall low concentration in the armed forces and the managerial field (NB: There is no one accepted definition for what constitutes 'managerial' work in each country. Therefore other surveys might deliver different results). The armed forces can be viewed as a traditionally male-oriented occupation into which women have only recently gained access. In all countries fewer than one per cent of women in employment work for the armed forces, the highest score (0.2 per cent) occurs in Belgium and France. The highest participation rate in the managerial field occurs in the UK with 3.8 per cent, followed by Belgium with 1.7 per cent, Denmark, Germany and Ireland with 1.6 per cent, the Netherlands with 1.3 per cent and Portugal (1 per cent), Greece and Spain (0.5 per cent) and Luxembourg (0.3 per cent).

Women are increasingly working in the professions with teaching being a major source of employment for qualified women (Netherlands: 27.2 per cent Denmark 35.5, per cent Belgium 29.1 per cent, Ireland 23.2 per cent and the other countries between 11 and 19 per cent). Clerical work is an important source of work for women in all EC states (Luxembourg 35.0 per cent, lowest score Greece 15.6 per cent), with slightly higher concentration in the northern countries compared to the southern countries (Greece, Spain, Portugal). Sales jobs have proven quite stable over the 1980s in most countries – between 15.2 per cent (Spain) and 8.7 per cent (Denmark) of women are employed in this sector. Similarly, the service sector has been stable throughout the 1980s. Women have begun to dominate this sector since the early 1980s, with five countries having over 20 per cent participation rates (Spain, France, Luxembourg, Netherlands, UK). The agriculture and related occupation category accounts for more employment in some countries than in others. It accounts for 30.3 per cent in Greece, 22.6 per cent in Portugal and 10 per cent in Spain – a fact attributable to the relatively late onset of industrial development in those countries. Although the importance of clothing and textiles in Portugal is reflected by the 22.6 per cent participation figure which is by far the highest score in the production category, in all other countries the female participation rate has remained stable or declined in this field (in Luxembourg and the Netherlands it account for little more than 5 per cent of female employment, in all other countries, but Portugal it accounts for 10–15 per cent of female employment). Whereas 35–48 per cent of European men work in production-related jobs.

Part-time work, temporary employment, homeworking

Technological advances have meant the decline of employment in manufacturing and the growing dominance of the service industries. This general change in industry structures 'favours' women in so far, as they more easily find employment in the service sector. Many of the newly created service jobs are part-time and temporary positions.

As has been stated at the beginning of this chapter, of 137.5 million people in employment in the EC, 21.1 million are working part-time, 81.8 per cent which are female. Part-time work can be a source of great personal and organizational flexibility, benefiting both parties of the employment contract. However, there is emerging evidence that an increasing number of female employees accept part-time work and temporary work out of necessity rather than choice. Hammond and Holton (1991) argue that the disadvantages outweigh the benefits with women working part-time being less likely to receive training, the rates of hourly pay being lower compared to those of male employees. However, part-time workers have traditionally been vulnerable with less employment protection, worse working conditions and lower pay than those employees working full-time. Since women tend to be disproportionately concentrated in this employment form, it is suggested that this is indicative of 'the presence of a form of indirect discrimination against women in pay for this type of work' (Rubery and Fagan, 1994, p. 2).

Part-time work suits many women and it is the natural preference which allows them to combine family and job responsibilities. However, in most countries fixed-term contracts are accepted by necessity rather than by choice, indicating that job security is an important, though neglected, element in employment contracts. In 1987 the majority of women working part-time was working so by preference, rather than by obligation (e.g. Belgium 24.2 per cent work part-time, 17.1 per cent by preference, 7.1 per cent by obligation – figures for other European countries are slightly different, but reveal the same trend) (Source: Women in the EC, 1992). However, of those working on fixed-term contracts the majority does so by obligation, rather than by preference: in Greece of 15 per cent working on a fixed-term contract, 2.5 per cent do so by preference, 12.5 per cent by obligation; in Portugal of those (16.1 per cent) working under fixed-term contracts 4.8 per cent do so by preference, 11.3 per cent by obligation. This pattern is similar for Spain, Ireland, Italy, the Netherlands, but slightly reversed (i.e. the majority prefers to work fixed term) in Belgium, Denmark, Luxembourg, and the UK.

Women's vulnerability to low-pay systems is associated with the segregation of the employment system and work in 'atypical' forms such as part-time, temporary and homeworking, which are frequently excluded from wage protection systems or eligibility for social security or employment benefits. Recent research on low pay in the EU has confirmed that women are generally more vulnerable to low pay then men – whether in full-time or in part-time employment. The continued integration of women into paid employment over the last decade has had little effect on their pay relative to men. Women are still overrepresented among low-paid workers. Though this gap is closing, progress is still slow. Low pay is obviously not exclusively a women-only issue (low pay = 66 per cent of national median level of earnings), however, women to their particular situation are at greater risk at being low paid. Low pay is more frequent where wage regulations are weakest (*Bulletin on Women and Employment in European Countries*, 1994).

In the Netherlands, the Homework Support Centre estimates that 97 per cent of homeworkers are women. In the UK, local surveys have found 95 per cent to be women. In France, research carried out in 1978–80 showed that the majority of homeworkers were women. In Greece, 85 per cent are women. In a study conducted in Valencia, Spain, the typical homeworker is described as a middle-aged women who is married to an industrial worker and also does the domestic work. In Italy, homework is usually associated with women. (Source: Tate, 1993)

Education

Meulders, Plasman and Vander Stricht (1993) observe that the level of educational attainment is decisive for the participation of women in the labour market, with qualifications being equally important. Highly qualified women are engaged frequently in uninterrupted careers. However, young people aged 15–24 tend to leave educational systems at very different ages according to their country: in Belgium, Denmark, France, the Netherlands, and Germany young people stay longer in the education system than in the UK, Ireland, Greece and Spain. In higher education, the number of female students are approaching, and in some countries, even exceeding the numbers of male students. Though, on the whole women students tend to attend shorter courses in higher education and leave the system earlier than their male counterparts.

With regards to vocational training, slightly fewer women than men receive vocational training. Other than in Belgium, Greece and Portugal, slightly fewer women than men receive initial vocational training.

Generally speaking, women receive training on all levels. However, the level of education and training does not translate itself into senior positions in the professional, managerial or industrial fields. Cooper and Davidson (1992) contribute this lack of female senior postholders despite a pool of talent, ambition and education to the existence of a 'glass ceiling' that prevents women from pushing through into the corridors of senior responsibility and power.

Motherhood and economic activity

Naturally, a link between motherhood and economic activity can be established. The dual responsibility of bringing up a family and to contribute financially to the family can be difficult to combine for both women and men. However, it has been shown that women carry the burden of raising children and doing housework to a much greater extent than men.

In all member states the economic activity rate declines with the number of children at a given age. A decline of activity proportionate to the number of children looks very different from country to country, though the activity rates for women without children are very similar in each country at least up to the age of 40. In some countries the activity rate is only slightly reduced by the presence of one child or even two children, but severely reduced by the presence of a third child.

Social protection

As has been shown the structure of the family impacts upon activity rates of women in the labour market. There might be an argument that the existence of social protection programmes and sufficient childcare facilities help women to combine the strains of motherhood and economic activity. Throughout Europe there is wide disparity concerning social protection programmes. Each member state has its own regulations and the systems governing expenditure on maternity, family allowances and subsidising childcare facilities are extremely varied. (For further details, see EUROSTAT, 1993a. *Rapid Reports: Population and Social Conditions, 1992*).

CASE STUDY 14.1: The glass-ceiling breakers

The following examples show how companies and individuals are chipping away at old traditional labour and marketplace structures. In light of the 'demographic timebomb companies act in enlightened self-interest if they regard Europe's 165 million women as an important resource' (Robert Horton, BP chairman).

Education and training
1. At Goldolphin School in Salisbury, UK, an all-girls school, technology training is firmly established in the school's syllabus. Girls are not pushed into established career structures, but can prove themselves in any field and go anywhere.
2. Moulinex in France established a pilot scheme that allowed 100 women who had so far been working at the assembly line, to go on training courses. Martine Doleans, a former assembly-line worker, is now a qualified electrician. She had to train at college for one day a week for 1.5 years and one year full-time in order to achieve her current position of higher pay and better prospects. The scheme proved so successful that over 1000 employees are now participating.
3. NMB Bank in Amsterdam, Holland, enabled Yvonne Bos-Middlebeck via the possibility of a job share to combine career and domestic life. She started as an office junior 'making coffee' and now holds a managerial position as consumer adviser.
4. The Dutch 'Women and Trade Union Initiative' works under the auspices of Europe's IRIS network (good training practice network). Their mothers returning to work scheme can boast a success rate of 90 per cent. This is made possible by funding provided by the EC and the Dutch government and the flexible training conditions provided by the Initiative, thus allowing women to attend courses when their children are at school.

Childcare
1. Schering Chemicals, Berlin, Germany, turned the top floor of their car park into a giant playground and nursery. Rita Ackermann, a public financial consultant works for 30 hours a week. She can bring her little son for breakfast at 8.30am to the nursery, where he will stay all day. Also, Schering operates parental leave arrangements, which allows fathers to stay at home and be entitled to the same job if they wish to return.
2. Blue Arrow, an employment agency, in the UK, gives childcare vouchers (£20 a week) to its employees. They can then buy their own childcare, be it from a registered nanny or a family member.

Changing attitudes
1. Frau Erika Korner is the assistant manager at the Deutsche Bank, Germany. She consciously acts as a role model to younger women, who aspire to senior roles, but who meet difficulties. She stresses the importance of attitudes, which need to change – a long and slow process. Happiness in her opinion needs to be found in both work and private life and one needs to strike a happy medium.
2. Fleur and Mariam Bergamin share the responsibility of bringing up their two young children. Fleur is a computer manager at the NMB bank in Holland. He takes one day per week off to look after his children. Mariam is a biology technician at a university and takes two days per week off. Both agree that this is the best way for them to combine family and work. Also, Fleur has been promoted twice while he was working under this scheme. This

is possible because both Fleur and Mariam work for family-friendly, sympathetic employers.

(Source: adapted from: *The Glass Ceiling Breakers* (1992), Equal Opportunity film produced for the European Commission, sponsored by Unilever)

There are a plethora of action programmes, networks and initiatives on a European level. If any of these activities are to have any real effect, they need to be translated into everyday practice (Collins, 1992). Employers in various countries react differently to these challenges – depending on their own national context, which might favour either voluntary, company-based activities as is the case in the UK or a more strongly regulated framework within which companies are obliged to implement equal opportunity policies.

CASE STUDY 14.2: Opportunity 2000

Companies in the UK operate in the 'voluntary framework', i.e. there is little legislation concerning equal opportunities. In 1991 a campaign was launched by the charity BITC (Business in the Community) which encourages its members (there were 61 members in 1991, 188 in 1993 and 275 in autumn 1994) to make a public commitment to improving prospects for women at work by setting goals for improving women's representation at all levels in the workplace and devising action plans for achieving them. Its mission statement reads:

> (. . .) The purpose of Opportunity 2000 is to encourage companies to take up the challenge and set programmes and goals necessary for improvement.
> Campaign members accept that in the long term their companies will be best served by a balance of women and men in their workforce in all areas and at all levels, especially in management, that reflects the abilities of the labour force as a whole.
> As a first step, campaign companies will voluntarily set their own goals for increasing opportunities for women in the workforce by the year 2000. Each company's goals will be based on its own particular starting point, its specific circumstances and business needs with progress monitored regularly and reported on. Above all, the goals will clearly signal a public commitment to ensure that in all areas and at all levels, women have the opportunity to make progress according to their abilities. (. . .)

Each year a report to monitor progress in equal opportunities and promote examples of best practice is filed. Examples concerning family friendly initiatives in 1994 include: *Rank Xerox* introduced five days of paid leave a year for emergency childcare. *Home Office* opened a second interdepartmental nursery in central London. It subsidises 50 per cent of the cost of a place. *BBC Engineering* introduced a 12-month pilot scheme for child-care vouchers.
Also, members of Opportunity 2000 offer more non-member paternity leave.

(Source: Opportunity 2000. Information Pack. Third Year Report (1994)

CASE STUDY 14.3: The Danish context: in-company training for adult women

The Danish context of equal opportunities and implementation is strongly regulated. Employers' obligations to treat men and women equally on employment, transfer and promotion, working conditions and access to vocational and continuing training, right for maternity/paternity leave, equal pay for equal work are firmly anchored in the law. There is an Equal Status Council that falls under the competence of the prime minister's department and promotes equality in society and the labour market. It also encourages the social partners to increase efforts to achieve equality and it coordinates the work related to the government's Action Plan on Equal Opportunities.

The rate of unionization is high: 80 per cent of employees belong to trade unions, 90 per cent are covered by collective agreements. Collective bargaining is strong. However, the labour market is segregated according to sex: women work primarily in the public sector and the service industries as well as office workers.

The nine companies who participated in the study represent eight different industries: the commercial and clerical sectors: transport and storage; electronics; textiles and wearing apparel; plastics; insurance; banks and saving banks; and the public sector. They include seven private enterprises, one semi-public and one public enterprise. Two of them employ 1–100 persons, one between 100–200, four between 200–600, one between 4000–5000 and one over 20 000 persons.

The female share of employees is between 40 and 60 per cent, but considerable sex bias still exists at the individual job levels and in individual job areas. All enterprises have an operation committee which actively takes a stand on development requirements and strategies. The enterprise represent a broad range of strategic thinking reflecting the varied demands that small and large enterprises are facing in various industries.

However, all of them faced an increasingly competitive environment, in particular in export markets, pressure for increased productivity and quality, the necessity to create a flexible organization and thus the necessity for the employees to be ready to change and development-oriented.

Training was viewed as one major way to achieve this and women were identified as one group to be targeted. The need to promote women in the workforce was not viewed primarily as an equal opportunity exercise, but as a strategic necessity. The intensified demands on competitiveness make it necessary for all enterprises to optimize their use and development of human resources. Concrete problems were poor working environment, high wastage rate, high sickness absence, high staff turnover rate, many production bottlenecks, employees' lack of qualifications, gossip and intrigues.

Training needs were identified through interview surveys, questionnaire surveys, analysis, mapping exercises, employee conferences, and then specified and translated into a training plan.

In companies 1 and 2 women in administrative jobs with vocational training and many years' work experience were targeted. Traditionally, this group has not previously been the focus of attention as regards training. However, the information technology revolution has made the need for job development a priority. A training course of six months to support vocational and personal clarification and a targeted action plan for future job opportunities was implemented.

Companies 3, 4, 5 and 6 targeted women in production, who are typically unskilled. New technology, changed work organization and new payroll systems require other vocational and personal qualifications. Process-oriented training and vocationally oriented training courses were introduced. Each focused on areas of importance ranging from word processing, control technology, languages, team-building, quality awareness, process technology, safety, storage and transport to somewhat surprisingly Danish – up to 33 per cent of all employees were not able to read and write to the extent required by their future jobs.

Companies 7, 8 and 9 targeted women who were potential managers, but who needed support in their career planning. Methods included personal clarification and targeted action through confrontation with the individual's own resources. A personal action plan formed the basis of training and development activities.

All companies distinguished between the following short-term and long-term results:

Short term:
- increase in productivity was much higher than expected; between 20 and 50 per cent
- the wastage rate was reduced
- sickness absence dropped significantly
- staff turnover rate was minimized: 0–25 per cent
- increase in working pace
- improved communications and cooperation

Long term:
- improvement in the physical working environment
- increased flexibility: increased rotation, greater responsibility
- a steady increase in the share of the female managers (one per cent per year)

  (*Source:* Valbjorn, L. and Hansen, M. (1993) *Looking Back. Planning for the Future* (report prepared for the European Commission, Diretorate-General V), V/401/94-EN)

WOMEN IN THE LABOUR MARKET OF EAST AND CENTRAL EUROPE

The year 1989 was to be a watershed for east and central European countries: transformational changes saw the collapse of the communist regimes (though some communist governments have been restored recently) and the consequent substitution of centralized planned economies by market driven forms of capitalism and democracy. The position of women in the labour force is closely linked to the problems associated with the marketization of the economies (e.g. changed social policies regarding provision of childcare, etc.). It is therefore necessary to investigate the position of women in the labour force pre and post the change period in order to assess whether their role in the economy had changed and if so, in which regards.

The method of data collection for this part was quite difficult and various sources were used. Whereas most of the data for part 1 was provided by EC sources and provided a relatively reliable basis for comparison between countries, no such institution exists for central and east European countries. Exact comparison therefore remains difficult to make and renders anything but the establishment of general trends impossible.

Before the watershed

Everyday life was very different for people living in a communist state before 1989. Deacon (1993) provides a checklist balancing the advantages and disadvantages of the pre-1989 systems in terms of their welfare agenda. Advantages include: job security for many, workers' wages were a high percentage of average wages, free health services (but oiled with bribes and gifts), three-year childcare grants for working women and the right to return to work (especially in the GDR and Hungary), highly subsidised flats, state organized social security pension and sick pay systems, party/workplace paternalism. On the disadvantage side he ranks: inadequate or absent unemployment pay, hidden privileges of party/state bureaucrats, underdevelopment of preventative approach to health, high mortality/morbidity rates, obligations upon women to work and care, sexist division of labour, maldistribution of flats, so better off live in the most heavily subsidised, inadequate social aid, absence of rights to articulate social needs autonomously from below.

The main difference between EU countries and east and central European countries in terms of gender participation rates in the economy was the sheer number of working women. Working age women who are economically active were 70.1 per cent in Hungary (1990), 65 per cent in Poland (1988), 83.2 per cent in the GDR (1988) compared to 55.4 per cent in FRG (1987) and 59.2 per cent in France (1989). Also, the norm of east and central European countries was to work full-time rather than part-time (data taken from Einhorn, 1993, p. 266). This was made possible by the high amount of job security, backed by ample state-financed childcare systems (e.g. the so-called 'baby-year' in the GDR, three years partially paid leave in Hungary, or supply of nursery and kindergarten places). According to Einhorn (1993) Hungary provided 10.1 per cent of 0–3 year olds and 77.9 per cent of 5 to 6 year olds with creche or kindergarten places in 1980, 2.3 per cent and 87.8 per cent in 1995, the GDR provided 61.2 per cent and 92.2 per cent of these age groups with places in 1980, 72.7 per cent and 94 per cent in 1985 and 80.2 per cent and 95.1 per cent in 1989 – whereas the FRG provided 3.0 per cent and 76.5 per cent similar places in 1989, the Netherlands 2.0 per cent and 52.5 per cent respectively and France 2.0 per cent and 37.5 per cent in the same year.

The right to work was generally written into the constitution (however, this led quite often to the phenomenon of 'hidden unemployment' and resulted in large-scale redundancies during the transition time from communist to capitalist regimes), being equally applicable to men and women alike. For several generations it was the norm for women to be in full-time employment and bring up a family. At a superfluous glance, these circumstances seem to be ideal, allowing men and women to develop their potential both in their professional and private life. In order to gain a balanced view, it is necessary to consider not only participation rates of women in the economy, but also occupational segregation, pay rates and, in particular, the duality of the right to work versus the obligation to work.

The dual role

In all Central and East European countries the level of female labour force participation was very high in comparison with west Europe. The problems for women lay in the fact that they were legislatively defined as workers and mothers. There was no equivalent definition of men as workers and fathers (UN proceeding, 1992, p. 15). So women remained their carer for the children, the (unpaid) domestic workers and additionally the contributor to the family income. Some figures taken from a UN publication (1992b) highlight the role of women as the major domestic worker in various countries: UN surveys compared the distribution (in per cent) between women and men of unpaid housework. In Bulgaria women did 70 per cent of the housework in 1965, men did 30 per cent. In 1988 this had barely changed: 69 percent vs. 31 per cent. The former GDR shows a similar pattern. In 1966 women did 75 per cent of this work, men 25 per cent. Hungary and Poland read for 1965: 84 per cent vs. 16 per cent and 76 per cent vs. 24 per cent. Little has changed by 1976: 73 per cent vs. 27 per cent (Hungary) and by 1984 78 per cent vs. 22 per cent (Poland). For a comparison some data with regards to western Europe is provided. Federal Republic of Germany (1965) 80 per cent vs. 20 per cent, the Netherlands in 1975: 79 per cent vs. 21 per cent and the same figures for 1980, in the UK in 1961 the situation is as follows: 88 per cent vs. 12 per cent vs. 16 per cent in 1975 and 72 per cent vs. 28 per cent in 1984.

The most striking fact of these tables are not so much the national differences, but the similar patterns in east and west – in so far that the traditional roles of the women being in charge of family and home is the shared model in use and how little has changed in a period of approximately 20 years. Even though some of the data provided goes back to the 1970s, there is more recent evidence that traditional attitudes still prevail: Winkler's study (1990) showed that three per cent of women and 43 per cent of men in the former GDR believed that women should make career compromises for the sake of their family and young children. Only three per cent of women and one per cent of men made the same demand for men.

Unsurprisingly, many women suffered from severe stress and felt over-burdened and the right to work was often felt to be an unwelcome obligation.

CASE STUDY 14.4: New federal states (former GDR) of Germany

The former GDR (German Democratic Republic) was annexed and merged into a western-style economy almost overnight. In 1989 the Berlin Wall fell, an event that finally accumulated in the unification of both German parts in October 1990. Since the fall of the Wall birth rates have dropped dramatically in the NFS of Germany. East Germany had a population of 16 million in 1990. The population now stands at around 15 million – and is expected to fall by another two million in the next 15 years (emigration from east to west can only be held responsible for a small proportion of the decline). Economic instability and the abandonment of the comprehensive childcare system are certainly factors to be taken into account when investigating the so-called 'womb strike'; however, on the upside there are a whole new range of possibilities for young east Germans in terms of travel and career development which contribute to the changed average age of having children. It used to be 21 (compared to 28 in the west). This gap is now beginning to close.

(*Source:* Münz and Ulrich (1993/94), Humboldt University, Berlin)

Occupational segregation and pay

Stories of female crane or tractor drivers were used to promote an ideologically inspired stereotype of the truly emancipated woman among the population – but also to demonstrate to the western countries the superior achievements of the socialist states. Did women achieve economic independence, better social positions and greater autonomy leading to an improved self-image? Women did enter into traditionally male sectors such as heavy industry, construction and mining, though they were more strongly presented in industries such as chemicals, clothing, food processing and textiles, the retail and the service sector (Einhorn, 1993). Furthermore, within these sectors women were primarily employed in lower-status, low-pay jobs. Similarly professional women did not proceed to the top of the hierarchy and were under-represented in the e.g. managerial positions. Statistics made available after the end of the old regimes showed substantial discrepancies in wages between men and women in all sectors of the economy: 'in most countries women earned on average between 66 and 75 per cent of men's wages' (UN report, 1992a, p. 19).

The position of women in the labour force since 1989

The profound reforms of the transition process from a planned to a market economy affected both men and women. However, it is necessary to investigate if and how the role of women in the labour force has changed and whether these reforms provide opportunity or can only be achieved at high cost.

Industrial restructuring is still taking place – entire industries are closed down (brown coal in former Czechoslovakia, Eastern Germany). Technical obsolescence of plants and 'hidden unemployment' resulted in large-scale redundancies. Unemployment has risen sharply in all countries, with a tendency for women to form the majority of the unemployed (46 per cent of total unemployed in Slovenia, 1990; 51 per cent in Poland, 1990; 54 per cent of ex GDR in January 1991; 69.4 per cent in Bulgaria in 1990 (Einhorn and Mitter, 1992).

If western employment trends will repeat themselves, there will be future employment opportunities in particular in the service sector. In the short term, however, female unemployment will increase. It is suggested that redundancy is accepted by women more easily as an opportunity to enjoy a rest from the double-burden of work and domestic responsibilities. The downside of this is the danger of long-term unemployment and a missing out of training opportunities. The reduction of childcare facilities by enterprises and the abandonment of social security support measures for mothers support the trend of a return of women to purely domestic responsibility. This seems to suggest that in spite of the achievements in terms of female employment in the former communist states, the traditional role stereotypes were in existence all the time and the patriarchal structures of thinking run deeper than 40 years of decreed emancipation.

A segregated workforce is thus, not so much a national, but a European (even global) phenomenon with women concentrated in certain occupations and low-paid work. Nevertheless, the shared socialist experience of women in central and eastern European countries resulted in some differences compared to developments in EU countries: women went out to work, mostly full-time. This was only possible because of the existence of childcare facilities and a system of state benefits. Though the duality of mother and worker did have an impact on personal (stress factor) and professional lives: women more often than men remained at the lower end of (organizational) hierarchies and thus in lower paid positions. Occupational pay segregation formed part of women's socialist experience as well.

Establishing European trends can only be achieved at the cost of neglecting country-specific differences. Parts of this chapter – and indeed any deeper analysis – have shown, that enormous differences between countries remain. Historical developments and cultural expectations play an important part in determining the role of both men and women in society in general and in the labour force in particular.

If it is accepted that occupational segregation and the linked low-pay situation are undesirable, this raises the question how the status quo can be changed. There are various recommendations on how to tackle this situation – ranging from the 'liberal individualist' stance (i.e. little or no regulations and laws) promoted in countries such as the UK (and the USA) and the strongly regulated framework as promoted in countries such as Denmark (and Sweden). There is conflicting evidence which one is the more successful. Even in a social model country such as Sweden, where a high proportion of women work, segmentation of the labour market persists despite financial inducements to employers to take positive action to improve the situation. Whereas in the USA, a higher proportion of women reach senior management positions in both the public and private sector. In the UK, though female participation in the labour force is strong, breaking through the 'glass ceiling' into senior managerial positions has not happened.

In the light of the evidence provided it seems adequate to suggest that traditional gender stereotypes and behaviour patterns are underlying today's societies and that cultural expectations of what constitutes women's work are remarkably resilient and might be the main factor determining the position of women in society and at the workplace.

Business reaction to women's employment in Europe

A recent EU report (*Employment in Europe*, 1996) confirms the findings of this chapter that women have accounted for the major part of growth in the EU's labour force and are likely to continue to do so in the future. Segregation trends and associated low pay together with job insecurity combine to create a smaller likelihood of women reaching senior positions in organizations. However, if female labour is regarded as an important resource for companies, it begs the question what companies are doing to integrate women into their workforce and what companies can contribute in order to assist women in coping with the twin demands of career/mother and provider/breadwinner. Some of the cases provided in this chapter give examples of how individual companies or institutions are endeavouring to achieve this integration. However, to what extent are women and family-friendly policies put into practice on a large scale and have strategies with regards to human resource planning and development been implemented to realize these policies by more than just a minority of well-known employers?

A Price Waterhouse/Cranfield project (1990) about women and employment practices in France, Germany, Spain, Sweden and the UK sought answers to questions such as 'to what extent do employers target women?', 'what measures do employers use to attract women?', 'what are the essential skills the workforce will need in future?', 'what training initiatives are provided to cater for them?'. Most of the answers provided are country-specific, although generally speaking demographic changes in the make up of the respective workforces (e.g. decline of 16–24 year olds) have encouraged many employers to see women more actively as a potential source of labour. In Germany and the UK about two-fifths of all organizations target women for special attention. In Sweden, were equal opportunity policies have already taken stronger effect, the targeting is much more selective and in Spain, employers are only just beginning to see women as an important source of skilled labour. In terms of the measures used to attract women, the most popular ones were offering part-time work, job sharing or flexible working. In all countries twice as many public sector organizations compared to private sector companies offer part-time work or job sharing as recruitment incentives. In the UK the number of employers offering training for women returners is highest among the countries surveyed (a quarter of British firms offer it).

Training (for women and men) is the most important strategic issue in all countries, with people management skills and new technology being identified as the most crucial training areas. Overall, the design of training strategies and their assessment remains unsystematic and inconsistent. The report concludes that overall 'policies designed to encourage women to play a more active and advanced role at the workplace lack consistency and coherence in order to achieve their well-intended objectives' (quoted in *Women and Training News*, 1990:2).

More recent research into the same area comes to similar conclusions. A collection of country-specific papers (presented at a research workshop about, Families, Labour Markets and Gender Roles in Dublin 1995), drew together current research on the concepts of family, gender and reconciling family and working life in European countries. The workshop confirms that women have gained employment in most member states mainly in the growing service sector, often in part-time jobs and as homeworkers: positions that are more likely linked to low pay, lack of access to training and poor opportunities for promotion. Country-specific differences in tradition and state policies determine the differences in employers' commitment to integrating women into their labour force. Dutch companies, for example, often offer facilities to working parents such as maternity and paternity leave, informal arrangements for flexi-time, part-time work, emergency leave and priority for parents and holiday leave. Denmark offers very extensive childcare provisions, but individual companies vary in their efforts to provide family-friendly policies. In Germany, institutional childcare gaps are increasingly addressed by grassroots initiatives by parents, often supported by churches and local authorities, with firms offering referral services provided by agencies as well as financial support to improve childcare facilities. However, no common picture emerges and what constitutes good practice is often context- and nation-specific.

Overall, the conclusion was drawn that 'this presentation of research and exchange of experiences within different member states and cultures provides informative, if somewhat negative, indicators of how family-friendly initiatives are perceived, particularly by managers/employers (who are mainly men). The clear signal for women which tends to emerge across member states is that, unlike their male counterparts, in order to balance work and family, women must choose' (Families, Labour Markets and Gender Roles. A Report of a European Research Workshop, 1995).

Similar evidence emerges form a workshop in Berlin (1996), which concentrated entirely on aspects of European approaches to (continuing) vocational training for female employees. A contribution (Joy-Matthews and Newey, 1996) about the UK (region Yorkshire), for example, found that practical barriers such as lack of childcare facilities, inflexible working hours and career patterns, together with covert barriers such as gender blindness, psychological barriers, stereotyping and prejudice (Cassell and Walsh, 1992) kept women from participating in training schemes. However, these were counterbalanced by examples of good practice implemented by individual employers. The Midland Bank branches, for example, are reputed to have the most comprehensive drive towards employer-based nursery care. In 1994, they had 113 nurseries and partnerships with around 60 playschemes. Also, they offer career-break schemes and facilitate the return into their workforce for women wishing to take time out for family reasons. Other companies mentioned were: Yorkshire Bank, British Gas, British Petroleum, IBM, and Shell. Similarly, the importance of mentor networks for women and leadership training for women was stressed by other reports (Ripke and Sulzbacher, 1996), although these initiatives remain only patchy.

In conclusion it seems that stereotypical catergorization of the labour force continue to exist. In particular, the stereotype of the male executive (works unlimited overtime, highly mobile) is still in force today. Drawing all data together, it is not possible to claim that a clear picture for all countries emerges: 'country-specific traditions and legislation determine how intensively companies are implementing equal opportunity policies. Also, not all countries have been researched to a similar degree with regards to the implementation of equal opportunity policies. Thus, making exact comparisons remains difficult. However, an overall trend can be observed, that despite equal opportunity legislation and much rhetoric, current efforts remain on the level of good practice as followed by individual companies, grass root activities and *pockets of inspiration* (Joy-Matthews and Newey, 1996), which facilitate only very gradual progress for both the female and male parts of the workforce. This is, in particular, evident in private companies. The continuing difficulties of combining the twin demands of career and provider are particularly observable in senior management positions, where relatively little change has been recorded, despite increasing participation rates of women in the workforce (Harris, 1993). Some researchers claim (Okanlawon, 1994) that unless women have realistic chances to enter decision-making positions in organizations, little real progress will be made with regards to the above matters, despite the slowly spreading practices which seek to implement family-friendly policies.

REVIEW QUESTIONS

1. What are the major features of women's employment in the EC?
2. What were the major features of women's employment in central and east European

countries before the watershed year 1989? What were the major changes taking place after 1989?

3. Which factors influence the changing pattern of female work?
4. Are there significant differences concerning female part-time employment between the different member states of the EC?
5. Which roles have national governments to play in the promotion of women in the workforce?
6. What constitutes the ideological ideal of women in society in communist states? What was the reality?
7. Why should employers be concerned about training and developing their female workforce?
8. In how far is it correct to say that both west and central/eastern European countries share the same patriarchal structures of society?
9. To what extent are European firms trying to integrate women into their workforces? Illustrate your answer with examples.

EXERCISE 14.1: The position of women in the European workforce

Aim   This exercise should assist students in familiarizing themselves with the factors contributing to the particular situation of women in the labour force, enable students to take particular national systems into account when assessing these factors, raise student awareness about the different assumptions about the role of women in different socio-economic systems, develop students' research skills in locating relevant material and country-specific information.

Assignment   Students are to work in small groups of four to six. They will then form subgroups of two to three. Each group will then choose either a state of the European community or a central/east European state of particular interest to them and fully research it in terms of its education system, industrial relation system, political and economic system, religious/societal and cultural expectations. They are then to relate their findings to the positions of women in the labour force of this particular country and assess how the national framework helps or hinders the promotion of women in the workplace.

Format   A presentation in class time introduces the country audits and how they relate to the position of women in the workforce; examples are used to illustrate the findings.

In a plenum discussion at the end of the session the findings of the groups can be compared.

Sources

Opportunity 2000
8 Stratton Street
UK London W1X 5FD

EUROSTAT
Information Office
Rue Alcide de Gasperi
L 2920 Luxembourg

United Nations Publications
DC-2-0853 Dept 798
New York 10017
USA

W.I.S.H. *The International Handbook of Women's Studies.* Harvester, Wheatsheaf, London, 1993.
A worldwide reference guide to women's organizations, study courses, centres, research and contacts.

FURTHER READING

Adler, J.N. and Izraeli, D.N. (eds), *Competitive Frontiers. Women Managers in a Global Economy*, Blackwell, Oxford, 1994.

Cooper, C.L. and Davidson, M.J. (eds.) *European Women in Business and Management*, Paul Chapman Publ., London, 1993.

Deacon, B. *et al.*, *The New Eastern Europe. Social Policy. Past, Present and Future*, Sage, London, 1992.

Jones, C., *New Perspectives on the Welfare State in Europe*, Routledge, London, 1993.

Meulders, D., Plasman, R. and Vander Stricht, V., *Position of Women on the Labour Market in the European Community*, Dartmouth Publishing Ltd. Hampshire, 1993.

Moghadam, V.M., *Privatization and Democratization in Central and Eastern Europe and the Soviet Union: The Gender Dimension*, WIDER Institute of the United Nations University, Helsinki, 1992.

BIBLIOGRAPHY

Adams, D., The monkey and the fish: cultural pitfalls of an educational advisor, *International Development Review*, 2(2), 1969.

Adam, J., The possible new role of market and planning in Poland and Hungary, in Anders, A. (ed.), *Market Socialism or the Restoration of Capitalism*, Cambridge University Press, Cambridge, 1992.

Ash, N., Czechoslovakia. Fulfilling in the new state plan, *Euromoney*, June, 1991.

Asheghian, P. and Ebrahimi, B., *International Business: Economics, Environment and Strategies*, Harper Collins, New York, 1990.

Badaracco, J., *The Knowledge Link: How Firms Compete through Strategic Alliances*, Harvard Business School Publications, 1991.

Barnes, I. and Barnes, P., *The Enlarged European Union*, Longman Group, Essex, 1995.

Barringer, F., Comment on the conference: Chautaugua at Pittr. The Fifth General Chautaugua Conference on US and Soviet Relations, 30 October 1989, cited in Smith, H., *The New Russians*, Random House, New York, 1990, p. 203.

Beamish, P.W., Killing, J.P., Lecraw, D.J., and Crookell, H. (eds.), *International Management: Text and Cases*, Irwin, Homewood Il, 1991.

Bennett, R., *Prospects for Business in the European Union*, Croner Publications Ltd, London, 1994.

Bennett, R., *International Business*, Pitman, London, 1996a.

Bennett, R., Doing business in a single European currency, *International Small Business Journal*, **2**(14), 1996b, pp. 27–34.

Bleeke, J. and Ernst, D., Is your strategic alliance really a sale?, *Harvard Business Review*, January/February, 1995, pp. 97–105.

Bleeke, J. and Ernst, D. (eds.), *Collaborating to Compete. Using Strategic Alliances and Acquisitions in the Global Marketplace*, McKinsey and Co. Inc, London, 1993.

Bloom, H., Calori, R. and de Woot, P., *European Management. A New Style for the Global Market*, Kogan Page, London, 1994.

Body Shop International (The), Environmental Policy, Company Profile fact sheet, 1993.

Borchgrave, R., It is not easy being green. Developing an EC environmental strategy, *The Journal of European Business*, January/February, 1993, pp. 48–53.

Brash, J., Export Management Companies, *Journal of International Business Studies* **9**(1), Spring/Summer, 1978.

Brooks, H. and Gulle, B.R. Overview, in Gulle, B.R. and Brooks, H. (eds), *Technology and Global Industry: Companies and Nations in the World Economy*, National Academy Press, Washington DC, 1987, pp. 1–15.

Brown, R., *Managing in the Single European Market*, Butterworth, Oxford, 1995.

Brown, L. and McDonald, M., *Competitive Marketing Strategy for Europe*, Macmillan, Basingstoke, 1994.

Buckley, N., Only Ronald strides the frontier, *Financial Times*, 4 January, 1993, p. 8.

Buckley, M. and Anderson, M. (eds), *Women, Equality and Europe*, Macmillan, Basingstoke, 1988.

Bulletin of the European Communities, No. 3, 1985, p. 101.

Bulletin on Women and Employment in the EU, October, 1994.

Burke, T., *The Green Capitalists*, Victor Gollancz, London, 1989.

Burke, T. and Hill, J., *Ethics Environment and the Company: A Guide to Effective Action*, Institute of Business Ethics, 1990.

Burton, J., Partnering with the Japanese: threat or opportunity for European businesses?, *European Management Journal*, **13**(3), 1995, pp. 304–315.

Business Week International, The battle for Europe, 3 June, 1993. Caetora, P., *International Marketing*, 8th edition, Irwin, Homewood, Il, 1993.

Cairncross, F., *Green Inc. A Guide to Business and the Environment*, Earthscan Publ. Ltd. London, 1995.

Calori, R. and Lawrence, P. *The Business of Europe: Managing Change*, Beverly Hills CA, 1991.

Calori, R. and de Woot, P., *A European Management Model. Beyond Diversity*, Prentice-Hall, London, 1994.

Carter, M., Britain's Bavarian bulldog, *Director*, January, 1996, pp. 29–32.

Cassell, C. and Walsh, S., Being seen, not heard: Barriers to women's equality in the workplace, *The Psychologist*, March, pp. 65–69, 1992.

Cecchini, P., *1992: The European Challenge. The Benefits of the Single Market*, The Cecchini Report, Wildwood House, Aldershot, 1989.

Chaudhry, P., Dacin, P. and McManus, J.R., The pharmaceutical industry and European Community integration, *European Management Journal*, **12**(4), December, 1994, pp. 442–453.

Chesnais, O.F., Science, technology and competitiveness, *Science Technology Industry Review*, **1**, 1986.

Child, J., Culture, contingency and capitalism in the cross-national study of organizations, in Staw, B.M. and Cummings, L.L. (eds), *Research in Organizational Behaviour*, JAI Press, Greenwich, 1981.

Cocks, R., Towards a Marxist theory of European integration, *International Organization*, Winter, 1980.

Collins, H., *Equality Matters; Equal Opportunities in the '90s: Background and Current Issues*, Library Association Publishing, London 1992.

Commission Report, *Intergovernmental Conference 1996*, European Commission, Luxembourg, 1995.

Commission of the EC, *Communication on Industrial Competitiveness and Protection of the Environment*, COM 92, 1986.

Commission of the EC, *Completing the Internal Market*, European Documentation, 1989.

Commission of the EC, *Fifth Environmental Action Program*, COM (92)23 final, Luxembourg, 1992.

Commission of the EC, *Report on Reinforcing the Effectiveness of the Internal Market*, COM (93) 256, 1993.

Confederation of British Industry, *Environmental Technology; Competing in a Growing Market*, 1991.

Confederation of British Industry, European Business Handbook: The Essential Guide to Trading and Investment in the New Europe, 1996.

Connor, W.D., Equality of opportunity, in Jones, A., Connor, W.D. and Powell, D.E. (eds) *Soviet Social Problems*, Boulder, Co., Westview, 1991, pp. 296–318.

Cooper, C.L. and Davidson, M.J., *Shattering the Glass Ceiling*, Paul Chapman Publishing Ltd, London, 1992.

Cooper, C.L. and Davidson, M.J. (eds), *European Women in Business and Management*, Paul Chapman Publishing Ltd, London, 1993.

Coopers and Lybrand, *Barriers to Takeovers in the European Community*, Her Majesty's Stationery Office, London, 1989.

Copland, L. and Crigges, L., *Going International*, Random House, New York, 1985.

Costabile, M., Ostillio, M., with Valdami, L. Nescafé Italy: Global brand, local culture in Montana, M. (ed.), *Marketing in Europe. Case Studies*, Sage Publications, London, 1994.

Council of the European Union, *Declaration of the Council on Social Policy, Consumers, Environment, Distribution of Income*, Annex 2, Edinburgh, 1992.

Crummey, S., Adventures in the Soviet market place, *Computer World*, **15**(18), 16 May, 1991.

Culpan, R., *Multinational Strategic Alliances*, International Business Press, Birmingham, New York, 1993.

Daniels, J.D. and Radebaugh, L.H., *International Business*, Addison-Wesley, Reading, MA, 1992.

Daniels, P. and Schwartz, C. (eds), *Encyclopedia of Associations: National Organizations of the United States*, **1**(2) (28th edition) Detroit, Gale Research, 1994.

Danton de Rouffignac, P., *Europe's New Business Culture*, Pitman, London, 1991.

Davies Arnold Cooper Solicitors, *Turning the Green Worm: Costing environmental compliance in the EC*, A report to industry from Davies Arnold Cooper Solicitors, October 1992.

Davison, L.M. and Fitzpatrick, E., 'Reviewing the EC merger control regulation: present experience and practice and future directions, *European Business Review*, **96**(2), 1996, pp. 11–17.

Deacon, B., Developments in east European social policy in Jones, C. (ed.), *New Perspective on the Welfare State in Europe*, Routledge, London, 1993, pp. 177–198.

De Bendern, S., Eastern Europe towards the millennium. Economic miracle or Weimar Year 2000?, *Economic Situation Report*, CBI, **21**(3), summer, 1990.

Dedman, M.J., *The Origins and Development of the European Union 1945–1995. A History of European Integration*, Routledge, London, 1996.

Delors, J., *EC Commission on Economic and Monetary Union in the European Community*. European Commission, 1989.

Dent, C., The business environment in Russia. An overview, *European Business Review*, **94**(3), 1994, pp. 15–21.

Department of Trade and Industry, *Europe open for Professionals*, 2nd edition, DTI Publications, 1991.

Department of Trade and Industry, *Brussels, Can you hear me? Influencing decisions in the EC*, DTI publications, 1992.

Department of Trade and Industry, *Country Profile: Sweden*, DTI Publications, 1993.

Department of Trade and Industry, *The Single European Market. Making it work*, DTI Publications, September, 1994a.

Department of Trade and Industry, *Country Profile: Austria*, DTI Publications, 1994b.

Department of Trade and Industry, *Euro Manual. Linking EC legislation to UK business functions: Volume 1, How business functions are affected*, DTI Publications, 1995.

Department of Trade and Industry, European Manual, DTI Publications, 1996.

Dicken, P., *Global Shift. Industrial Change in a Turbulent World*, 2nd edition, Paul Chapman, London, 1992.

Dijck, J. van, Transnationalization of economic and social life in Europe, in van Dijck, J. and Wentick, A.G, (eds.), *Transnational Business in Europe. Economic and Social Perspectives*, Tilburg University, 1992.

Donaldson, J., *Business Ethics. A European Casebook*, Academic Press, London, 1992.

Doz, Y., Partnerships in Europe: The 'Soft restructuring' option? in Lars-Gunnar, M. and Bengt, S. *Corporate and Industry Strategies for Europe: Adaptations to the European Single Market in a Global Industrial Environment*, Elsevier Science, Amsterdam, 1991, pp. 303–326.

Drew, J., *Doing Business in the European Community*, 3rd edition, Whurr, London, 1992.

Drucker, P., *Management*, Harper & Row, New York, 1974.

Dudley, J., *1992, Strategies for the Single Market*, Kogan Page, London, 1990.

Duff, A., Pinder, J. and Pryce, R. (eds), *Maastricht and Beyond. Building the European Union*, Routledge, New York, 1995.

Earl-Slater, A., Recent developments in regulating the pharmaceutical business in the EU, *European Business Review*, **96**(1), 1996, pp. 17–25.

Economist, Edith the First, 18 May, 1991, p. 52.

Economist, 11 July 1992, pp. 12–39.

Economist, How to shift the goal-posts: Economic and monetary union. New Hope for the Euro, 20 April, 1996.

Economist Intelligence Unit, *A Strategic update on Ford of Europe* in *European Motor Business*, 1st quarter 1995, EIU Ltd, London, 1995, pp. 68–87.

Economist Intelligence Unit, *The EIU European Yearbook 1994–1995*, Research Report, EIU Ltd, London, March, 1995a.

Economist Intelligence Unit, *EIU Country Profile: France*, EIU Ltd, 1995–1996.

Egan, C. and McKiernan, P., *Inside Fortress Europe. Strategies for the Single Market*, Addison-Wesley, London, 1993.

Einhorn, B., *Cinderella goes to Market. Citizenship, Gender and Women's Movements in East Central Europe*, Verso, London, 1993.

Einhorn, B. and Mitter, S., A comparative analysis of women's industrial participation during the transition from centrally-planned to market economies in East-Central Europe in The Impact of Economic and Political Reform on the Status of Women in Eastern Europe, *Proceedings of a United Nations Regional Seminar*, UN Publications, New York, 1992, pp. 15–26.

Emerson, M. and Huhne, C., *The ECU Report*, Pan, London, 1991.

Employment in Europe, EC report, 1996.

Engholm, C., *The Other Europe. A Complete Guide to Business Opportunities in Eastern Europe*, McGraw-Hill, New York, 1993.

Equal Opportunity through New European Approaches to Continuing Vocational Training for Female Employers, **1,** International Leonardo Workshop, at FHW Berlin, 1996.

ESOMAR, Number attitudes and brand images in a newly established market (Poland), in 2nd E.S.O.M.A.R. East and Central European Conference: Towards a market Economy: Beyond the point of no return, Warsaw, Poland, 23–26 April, 1995. ESOMAR Publications, The Netherlands, 1995. pp. 257–266.

Eszes, L. and Muhlemann, A., Manufacturing management in Hungary: a perspective, *European Business Review*, **93**(5), 1993, pp. 12–19.

Euromonitor, *East European Business Handbook,* Euromonitor plc, London, 1993.

Euromonitor, *European Marketing Data Statistics*, 31st edition, Euromonitor plc, London, 1996.

European Bank for Reconstruction and Development, *Private Investment in Central and Eastern Europe: Survey Results*, Working Paper No. 7, London, 1993.

European Bank for Reconstruction and Development, *Investor's Guide to Privatisation with Debt-Swaps in Bulgaria*, January, 1996. (Edited by Price Waterhouse, Sofia)

European Commission, European Union, ECS-EC-EAEC, Brussels, Luxembourg, 1994.

European Commission, European Economy, *Annual Economic Report for 1996*, Directorate-General for Economic and Financial Affairs, No. 16, 1996.

European Documentation, The ECU, *The European Documentation Series*, No. 31, 1987.

European File, The Removal of Technical Barriers to Trade, Commission for the European Community, European Documentation, November 1988a.

European File, A European financial area: the liberalization of capital movements, Commission for the European Communities, European Documentation, June/July 1988b.

European File, Towards a big internal market in financial services, Commission for the European Communities, European Documentation, November 1988c.

European File, Community Charter of Fundamental Social Rights for Workers, Commission for the European Communities, European Documentation, May 1990.

European Perspective Series, The European Monetary System: Origins, Operations and Outlook, 1985.

European Treaty, Second paragraph, Article 130r.

European Union, Reference Services, Central Office of Information, HMSO publication, 1994.

EUROSTAT, *Rapid reports. Population and Social Conditions*, Office for Official Publications of the European Communities, Luxembourg, 1993a.

EUROSTAT, *Unemployed women in the EC*, *Statistical Facts*, Office for Official Publications of the European Communities, Luxembourg, 1993b.

European Motor Business, 1st quarter, 1995.

Eykmans, S., The wheels are finally starting to turn at the EMEA, *Materials Management*, January, 1995, pp. 33–36.

Families, Labour Markets and Gender Roles. A Report on a European Research Workshop, European Foundation for the Improvement of Living and Working Conditions, Dublin, 1995.

Faulkner, D., *International Strategic Alliances: Corporate Compete*, McGraw-Hill, London, 1995.

Financial Times, Who gets what from maternity provisions? 19 October, 1994.

Foley, P., Hutchinson, J., Kondej, A. and Mueller, J., Economic development in Poland: a local perspective, *European Business Review*, **96**(2), 1996, pp. 23–31.

Foster, P., McDonald's excellent Soviet venture, *Canadian Business*, **64**(5), May, 1991.

Fratczak-Rudnicka, B., Problems connected with studying brandbloc countries, *European Business Review*, **95**, 1995, p. 258.

Fratzscher, O., European integration: lessons from the south and prospects for the east, in Schipke, A. and Taylor, A.M. (eds), *The Economics of Transformation*, Springer Verlag, Berlin, 1994, pp. 171–231.

Freidheim, D., The demise of the global firm, *The Economist*, 6 February, 1993.

Freidheim, A, The ascent of Everest, *Financial Times*, 16 January, 1992.

Furhman, P., Doing business in the dark, *Forbes*, 19 February, 1990, pp. 50–54.

Garland, F.T. (ed.), *International Dimensions of Business Policy*, PWS Kent, Boston, 1991.

Gittleman, M. and Graham, E., quoted in Mason, D.T. and Tunay, A.M., *Japan, NAFTA and Europe. Trilateral Cooperation and Confrontation*, St Martin's Press, New York, 1994, p. 155.

Gibbs, P., *Doing Business in the European Community*, Kogan Page, London, 1990.

Gibbs, P., *Doing Business in the European Community*, 3rd edition, Kogan Page, London, 1994.

The Glass Ceiling Breakers. Equal Opportunity film produced for the European Community, sponsored by Unilever, 1992.

Gold, M., EC Social and Labour Policy: An Overview and Update, ESRC Single European Market Initiatives, Working paper No. 11, National Institute of Economic and Social Research, London, 1992.

Goldstein, I., Europe after Maastricht, *Foreign Affairs*, Winter, 1992–1993.

Goodhard, D., Opting out and crashing in, *Financial Times*, 28 February, 1992, p. 16.

Gore, C., Murray, K. and Richardson, B., *Strategic Decision-making*, Cassell, London, 1992.

Government of the Russian Federation, *Russian Economic Trends: Monthly Update*, December, London Whurr Publishers, 1994.

Gray, R., *Accounting for the Environment*, ACCA, 1992.

Grayson, L., *Environmental Auditing. A Guide to Best Practice in the UK and Europe*, British Library Science and Information Service, Oxford, 1992.

Griffiths, B., *Morality and the Market Place. Christian Alternatives to Capitalism and Socialism*, Hodder and Stoughton, London, 1982.

Grosfeld, I., Prospects for privatization: Poland, *European Economy*, No. 43, Brussels, March, 1990.

Guianluigi, G., Implementing a Pan European Marketing Strategy, *Long Range Planning*, **24**(5), 1991, pp. 23–33.

Guy, V. and Mattock, J., *The New International Manager – An action guide for Cross-Cultural Business*, Kogan Page, London, 1991.

Habib, G.M. and Burnett, J.J., An assessment of channel behaviour in an alternative structural arrangement. The international joint venture, *International Marketing Review*, **6**(3), 1989.

Hamel, G. and Prahaland, C.K., Do you really have a global strategy? *Harvard Business Review*, July–August, 1985.

Hammond, V. and Holton, V., *A Balanced Workforce – Achieving Cultural Change for Women: A Comparative Study*, Ashbridge Management College, Ashbridge, 1990.

Harper, T., Pulling the Right Strings – Selecting a Site in Europe, *Manufacturing Systems*, February, 1993, pp. 19–23.

Harrigan, K., *Strategies of Joint Ventures*, Lexington Book, Lexington MA, 1983.

Harris, H., Women in international management. Opportunity or threat, *Women in Management Review*, **8**(5), pp. 9–14, 1993.

Harris, N., *European Business*, Macmillan, Basingstoke, 1996.

Harris, P. and McDonald, F., *European Business and Marketing Strategic Issues*, Paul Chapman Publishing, London, 1994.

Harrop, K., *The Political Economy of Integration in the European Community*, Edward Elgar, Aldershot, 1989.

Hayashi, E., Franchising fever: the growth business of the 1990s, *Export Today*, April 1989.

Heitger, B. and Stehn, J., Japanese direct investment in the EC – responses to the internal market, *Journal of Common Market Studies*, **29**(1), 1991.

Hibbert, N., *Soviet Managers*, European Training Agency, Coventry University, June, 1991.

Hilderbrand, D., Lawyers and Marketers, *European Business Journal*, **2**(6), 1994, pp. 45–54.

HMSO, Searching the Potential, Cmnd 2250, HMSO, London, 1993.

Hofstede, G., *Culture's Consequences: International Dimensions in Work-Related Values*, Sage, Beverly Hills CA, 1980.

Hofstede, G., Managerial Values: The Business of International Business in Culture in Terence Jackson (ed.), *Cross-cultural Management,* Butterworth-Heinemann, Oxford, 1995.

Holden, L. and Peck, H., Perestroika, Glasnost, management and trade, *European Business Review*, **2**(90), 1990.

Hoult, T. and Porter, M. How global companies win out, *Harvard Business Review*, September/October, 1982, pp. 98–108.

Hume, S., How Big Mac made it to Moscow, *Advertising Age*, **61**(4), 22 January, 1990.

Hunter, M., 'How to get your way with the EC: lobbying Brussels', *Business Month*, August 1989, p. 43.

Huszagh, S.M. and Huszagh, F.W., Barter and countertrade, *International Marketing Review*, Summer, 1986.

Investor's Guide: Privatization with swaps in Bulgaria, European Bank, 1996.

Jacek, H. 'The American Organization of Firms', in Greenwood, J. (ed.) *European Casebook on Business Alliances*, Prentice-Hall, New York, 1995.

Jelassi, T. and Figon, O., Competing through EDI at Bruno Passot: Achievements in France and Ambitions for the Single European Market, *MIS Quarterly*, December 1994, pp. 337–352.

Jensen, W.G., *Common Market*, Foulis, London, 1967.

Johnson, M. and Moran, R.T., *Robert T. Moran's Cultural Guide to doing Business in Europe*, Butterworth-Heinemann, Oxford, 2nd edition, 1992.

Jolly, A. (ed.) *CBI European Business Handbook*, Kogan Press, London, 1996.

Jones, C., Hungary. Everything for sale, *Business*, **141**(785), July 1991.

Joy-Matthews, J. and Newey, Y., The UK Equal Opportunity Research Project, contribution to 1, International Leonardo Workshop, London, 1996.

Kashani, K., *Managing Global Marketing*, PWS Kent, Boston, A, 1992.

Kemp, D., *Global Environmental Issues: a climatological approach*, Routledge, 1994.

Khambata, D. and Ajami, R., *International Business: Theory and Practice*, Macmillan, New York, 1992.

Killing, J.P., How to make global joint venture work. *Harvard Business Review*, May–June, 1982.

Killing, J.P., Understanding alliances: their role of task and organization complexity in Contractor, F. and Lorange, P. (eds), *Cooperative Strategies in International Business*, Lexington Books, New York, 1992, pp. 57–75.

Kirkbride, P.S. (ed.), *Human Resources Management in Europe. Perspectives for the 1990s*, Routledge, London, 1994.

Knowlton, C., Europe cooks up a cereal bowl, *Fortune*, 3 June, 1991, p. 61.

Korah, V., *An Introduction Guide to EC Competition Law and Practice*, 5th edition, Sweet and Maxwell, London, 1994.

Kossoff, J., Europe: up for sale, *New Statesman and Society*, 1988, pp. 43–44.

Kotler, P., *Marketing Management: Analysis, Planning and Control*, 5th edition, Prentice-Hall, Englewood Cliffs NJ, 1984.

Kramer, L., The elaboration of EC environmental legislation, in Winter, G. (ed.), *European Environmental Law. A Comparative Perspective*, Dartmouth Publishing Co., Aldershot, 1996, pp. 297–316.

Kramer, L., *EEC Treaty and Environmental Protection*, Sweet and Maxwell, London, 1990.

Lei, D. and Slocum, J.W., Jr., Global strategic alliances: payoffs and pitfalls, *Organization Dynamics*, Winter, 1991.

Levitt, T., The globalization of markets, *Harvard Business Review*, May–June, 1983a, pp. 92–102.

Levitt, T., *The Marketing Imagination*, The Free Press, New York, 1983b.

Lindsay, M., *International Business in Gorbachev's Soviet Union*, Pinter, London, 1989.

Lipgens, W., *A History of European Integration, vol. 1. 1945–47*, Clarendon Press, Oxford, 1982.

Lorange, P. and Ross, J., *Strategic Alliances. Formation, Implementation and Evolution*. Blackwell, Oxford, 1995.

Lynch, R. (ed.), *Cases in European Marketing*, Kogan Page, London, 1993.

Lynch, R., *European Business Strategy: An Analysis of Europe's Top Companies*, Kogan Page, London, 1990.

Manser, W., *Control from Brussels*, Addison-Wesley, London, 1994.

Mazey, S., *European Community Social Policy: Development and Issues*, European Dossier, Series No. 14, 1989.

Mazio, C., Appendix – The transition to a single European currency. The institutional steps involved, in Banca Nazionale del Lavoro, *Quarterly Review, The European Monetary Union: The Problems of the Transition to a Single Currency*, Special Issue, March, 1996, pp. 178–184.

McDonald, F. and Dearden, S., (eds), *European Economic Integration*, 2nd edition, Longman Group Limited, Harlow, Essex, 1995.

McIntyre, J.R., Europe 1992 and Japan's relations with western Europe, in Mason, D.T. and Turay, A.M., *Japan, NAFTA and Europe. Trilaterial Cooperation or Confrontation?* St Martin's Press, New York, 1994, pp. 58–92.

McKenna, R., *Relationship Marketing*, Addison-Wesley, London, 1991.

Mehnert-Meland, R.J., *ECU in Business. How to Prepare for the Single Currency in the European Union*, Graham and Trotman, London, 1994.

Merritt, G., *Eastern European and the USSR: The Challenge of Freedom*, Kogan Page, London, 1991.

Meulders, D., Plasman, R. and Vander Stricht, V., *Position of Women on the Labour Market in the European Community*, Dartmouth Publishing Company Ltd, Hampshire, 1993.

Milward, A., *The Reconstruction of Western Europe 1945–1951*, Methuen, London, 1984.

Mole, J., *Mind your Manners. Managing Culture Clash in the Single European Market*, Nicholas Brealey Publishing, London, 1993.

Monnet, J., *A Grand Design for Europe*, Commission of the European Community, European Documentation 5/1988, Brussels.

Montana, J. and Trell, M., SEAT on Europe. A strategy for survival in Montana, J. (ed.), *Marketing in Europe. Case Studies*, Sage Publications, London, 1994.

Morgan, S., *Marketing Management. A European Perspective*, Addison-Wesley, London, 1995.

Morrison, D., 'Mastering the system. How disparities within the European Union contribute to Japan's lobbying success', in Greenwood, J., (ed.), *European Casebook on Business Alliances*, Prentice-Hall, London, 1995.

Moss Kanter, R., Collaborative advantage, *Harvard Business Review*, July–August, 1994, pp. 96–108.

Munro-Faure, L., Munro-Faure, M. and Bones, E., *Achieving the New International Quality Standards*, Pitman Publishing. London, 1995.

Münz, R. and Ulrich, R., Demographische Entwicklungen in Ostdeutschland und in ausgewählten Regionen, *Zeitschrfit für Bevölkerungswissenschaft*, Jg. 19-4, 1993–1994, special edition, pp. 475–515.

Murray, J.A. and Fahy, J., The marketing environment, in Nugent, N. and O'Donnell, R. (eds), *The European Business Environment*, Macmillan, Basingstoke, 1994, pp. 183–198.

Myers, A., Kakabadse, A., McMahon, T. and Spony, G., Top management styles in Europe: implications for business and cross-national teams, *European Business Journal*, 1985, pp. 7–17.

Newbery, D., Netherlands, *European Economic Review*, **35**(2) April, 1991.

Nicoll, W., and Salmon, T., *Understanding the New European Community,* Harvester, Wheatsheaf, London, 1994.

Ninon, J. and Williamson, V., Returner and retainer policies for women. Short-term or long-term gains?, in Jones, C. (ed.), *New Perspectives on the Welfare State in Europe*, Routledge, London, 1993, pp. 108–129.

Nutti, M., Privatization of socialist economies: general issues and the Polish case in transformation of planned economies, in Bloommestein, C. and Marrese, M., (eds), *Property Rights, Reform and Micro-Economic Stability*, OECD, 1991.

Official Journal of the European Community, L168, 10 July, 1993.

Ohmae, K., *The Mind of the Strategist. Business Planning for Competitive Advantage*, Penguin, London, 1983.

Ohmae, K., *Traid Power: The Coming Shape of Global Competition,* The Free Press, New York, 1985.

Ohmae, K., *The Borderless World. Power and Strategy in the interlinked economy*, Collins, London, 1990.

Ohmae, K., Managing in a borderless world, in *Going Global. Succeeding in World Markets*, Harvard Business Books, 1991.

Okanlawon, G., Women as strategic decision makers: A reflection on organizational barriers, *Women in Management Review*, **9**(4), pp. 25–32, 1994.

Opack, J.H., Likeness of Licensing franchising, *Les Nouvelles*, June, 1977.

Opportunity 2000, *Information Pack*.

Organization for Economic Co-operation and Development, *OECD Economic Surveys: Austria*, Paris, 1992.

Palmer, J., *Trading Places*, Mackays of Chatham Ltd, London, 1988.

Pearce, D., *Blueprint, Capturing Global Environmental Value*, Earthscan Publications Ltd, London, 1995.

PHARE. Sector paper on investment promotion, export development and tourism, published by the European Commission, 1994.

Pentland, C., *International Theory and European Integration*, Faber and Faber, London, 1973.

Perlmutter, H.V. and Heenan, D.A., Thinking ahead. Cooperate to compete globally, in *Going Global. Succeeding in World Markets*, Harvard Business Books, 1991, pp. 63–68.

Perry, K., *Business and the European Community*, Butterworth-Heinemann, Oxford, 1994.

Piggot, J., Cook, M. (eds), *International Business Economics: A European Perspective*, Longman Group, Harlow, Essex, 1993.

Pinder, M., *Personal Management for the Single European Market*, Pitman, London, 1990.

Pollack, S., *Improving Environmental Performance*, Routledge, London, 1995.

Porter, M. *Competitive Strategy: Techniques for analyzing industries and competitors*, Free Press, New York, 1980.

Porter, M., *The Competitive Advantage of Nations*, Macmillan, Basingstoke, 1990.

Porter, M., *America's Green Strategies*, *Scientific America*, 1991.

Portes, R., EMS and EMU after the Fall, *The World Economy*, **16**(2), January, 1993.

Puffer, R., A riddle wrapped in an enigma: demystifying Russian managerial motivation, *European Management Journal*, **11**(4), December, 1993.

Quelch, J., Kashani, K. and Vandermerwe, S., *European Cases in Marketing Management*, Irwin, Homewood, Il, 1994.

Raiszedeh, F.M.E., Helms, M.M. and Varner, M.C., Critical issues to consider when developing business operations in Eastern bloc countries, *European Business Review*, **95**(6), 1995, pp. 12–20.

Randlesome, C., *Business Cultures in Europe*, Butterworth-Heinemann, Oxford, 1993.

Randlesome, C., Brierley, W., Bruton, K., Gordon, C., King, P. *Business Cultures in Europe*, 2nd edition, Butterworth-Heinemann, Oxford, 1993.

Reinsch, R., Doing Business in the Soviet Union, *Europe*, 305, April 1991.

Retail Dynamics, European superstore decisions, Spring, 1994, pp. 14–20.

Ricks, D., *Big Business Blunders: Mistakes in Multinational Marketing*, Irwin Dow Jones, Homewood, Il, 1983.

Ripke, M. and Sulzbacher, B., *Betriebliche Massnahmen zur Verbessurung der Chancengleichheit*, contribution to 1. International Leonardo Workshop, 1996.

Romero, F., Migration as an issue in European interdependence and integration: The case of Italy, in Milward, A., Lynch, F., Romero, F. and Ranieri, R. (eds), *The Frontier of National Sovereignty: History and Theory 1945–1992*, Routledge, London, 1993.

Rubery, J. and Fagon, C., Occupational Segregation of Women and Men in the European Community, *Report for Directorate-General for Employment, Industrial Relations and Social Affairs, Social Europe*, Supplement, 3/93, 1993.

Rubery, J. and Fagan, C., Wage Determination and Sex Segregation in Employment in the European Community, *Report for Directorate-General for Employment, Industrial Relations and Social Affairs, Social Europe*, Supplement, 4/94, 1994.

Rugman, A., *International Business*, McGraw-Hill, New York, 1995.

Saghafi, M.M., Sciglimpaglia, D. and Withers, B.E., Strategic Decisions for American and European Industrial Marketers in a Unified European Market, Industrial Marketing Management, 24, 1995, pp. 9–81.

Salier, J.E., The General Mills Board and Strategic Planning, Harvard Business School Case, 1991.

Schlesinger, H., By invitation. Money is just the start, *Economist*, 21 September, 1996.

Schipke, A., The political economy of privatization, in Schipke, A. and Taylor, A.M. (eds.) *The Economics of Transformation. Theory and Practice in the New Market Economies*, Springer-Verlag, Berlin Heidelberg, 1994.

Schneider, S., National corporate culture: implications for human resource management, *Human Resource Management*, **27**(2), 1993, pp. 231–246.

Sellers, P., Coke's brash new European strategy, *Fortune*, 13 August, 1990.

Shekshnia, S., Managing People in Russia: Challenges for Foreign Investors, *European Management Journal*, **12**(3), September, 1994.

Simpson, T., quoted in Littler, D., and Schlieper, K. The development of the Eurobrand, *International Marketing Review*, **12**(2), 1993, pp. 23–37.

Smith, H., *The New Russians*, Random House, New York, 1990.

Solvell, O. and Zander, I., European myopia in Mattsson, I.G. and Stynme, B. (eds), *Corporate and Industry Strategies for Europe*, North-Holland Elsevier Science Publishers B.V., Amsterdam, 1991, pp. 353–378.

Sparrow, P. and Hiltrop, J.M., *European Human Resource Management in Transition*, Prentice-Hall, London, 1994.

Stanislav, S., Managing people in Russia. Challenge for foreign investors, *European Management Journal*, **12**(3), September, 1994.

Stone, I. United Kingdom in Somers, F. (ed.) *European Community Economies, A comparative study*, Longman Group, Harlow, Essex, 1995.

Stephenson, A., Changing Rover Group through its employees, *Management Services*, February, 1994, pp. 6–10.

Stitt, H.J. and Baker, S., *The Licensing and Joint Venture Guide*, Ministry of Industry, Trade and Technology, Toronto, 1985.

Stopford, J., Strange, S. and Henley, J., *Rival States, Rival Firms. Competition for World Market Shares*, Cambridge University Press, Cambridge, 1991.

Summers, L., The next decade in central and eastern Europe in Clague, C. and Rausser, G. (eds), *The Emergence of Market Economies in Eastern Europe*, Basil Blackwell, London, 1992, pp. 25–34.

Szegedi, A., The economy and international business in Hungary, *Journal of Business Administration*, Canada, **19**(112), 1989–1990.

Tate, J. Homeworking in the EC, Report for Directorate General for Employment, Industrial Relations and Social Affairs, Doc Ref V/7173/93-EN.

Taylor, A., New ideas from Europe's automakers, *Fortune*, December, 1994, pp. 73–78.

Taylor, G. and Welford, R., A commitment to environmental improvement: The case of British Telecommunications, in Welford, R., *Cases in Environmental Management and Business Strategies*, Pitman, London, 1995, pp. 60–76.

Terpestra, V. (ed.), *The Cultural Environment of International Business*, South Western, Cincinnati, 1985.

Terpestra, V. and Sarathy, R., *International Marketing*, 5th edition, Dryden, New York, 1991.

Thomson, K., France, A comparative study in Somers, F. (ed.), *European Community Economies. A Comparative Study*, 2nd edition, Longman Group Limited, Essex, 1995.

Torbet, P., First Soviet free-zone will give firm access to Pacific Basin markers, *East Asia Executive Reports*, **13**(3), 1991.

Treaty of Rome, Annexes 85 and 86 contains Article 85 and 86 on Competition Policy.

Tsoukalis, L., *The New European Economy: The Politics and Economics of Integration*, 2nd revised edition, Oxford University Press, Oxford, 1993.

Turner, C., Trans-European corporate networks: the rise of carrier-based telecommunications outsourcing, *European Business Review*, **96**(2), 1996, pp. 18–22.

Tyson, S., Lawrence, P., Poirson, P., Manzolini, L. and Vicente, C.S., *Human Resource Management in Europe. Strategic Issues and Cases*, Kogan Page, London, 1993.

United Nations. *The Impact of Economic Political Reform on the Status of Women in Eastern Europe*, Proceedings of a United Nations Regional Studies Seminar, UN Publications, New York, 1992a.

United Nations, *The World's Women 1970–1990. Trends and Statistics*, UN Publications, New York, 1992b.

Valbjorn, L. and Hansen, M., Looking Back: Planning for the Future. A Code of Good Practice in Promoting Continuing Training and Career Development for Women – Based on Danish in-company Experiences, *Report for the European Commission, Directorate-General for Employment, Industrial Relations and Social Affairs*, Doc. Ref:V/401/94-EN, 1993.

VanderMerwe, S. and L'Huillier, M., Euro-consumers in 1992, *Business Horizons*, January/February, 1989, pp. 34–40.

Venturini, P., *The Social Charter. Potential Effects of the Internal Market*, ECSC, Brussels, 1988.

Walley, N. and Whitehead, B., It is not easy being green, *Harvard Business Review*, May–June, 1994.

Walker, P., *Taking your Business into Europe*, Hawkmere, London, 1989.

Waltz, K. *Theory of International Politics*, Addison-Wesley, Reading MA, 1979.

Weale, A. and Williams, A., The Single Market and Environmental Policy in Furlong, P. and Cox, A. (eds), *The European Union at the Crossroads. Problems in Implementing the Single Market Project*, Earlsgate Press, Lincolnshire, 1995, pp. 131–159.

Weber, M., *The Protestant Ethics and the Spirit of Capitalism*, Allen & Unwin, London, 1952.

Weihrich, H., The TOWS matrix – A tool for situational analysis, *Long Range Planning*, **15**(2), April, 1982. pp. 54–66.

Welford, R., *Cases in Environmental Management and Business Strategy*, Pitman, London, 1994.

Welford, R., *Environmental Strategy and Sustainable Development. The Corporate Challenge for the 21st Century*, Pitman, London, 1995.

Welford, R. and Gouldson, A., *Environmental Management and Business Strategy*, Pitman, London, 1993.

Welford, R. and Prescott, K., *European Business*, 3rd edition, Pitman, London, 1996.

Welsh, M., *Europe United? The European Union and the Retreat from Federalism*, Macmillan, Basingstoke, 1996.

Williams, A., *The European Community*, 2nd edition, Blackwell, Oxford, 1995.

Winkler, G., Sozailreport 90, Berlin Verlag Die Wirtshaft, 1990.

Winter, G., *Blueprint for Green Management. Creating your Company's Own Environmental Action Plan*, McGraw-Hill, London, 1995.

Winter, G. (ed.), *European Environmental Law. A Comparative Perspective*, Dartmouth Publishing Co. Ltd, Aldershot, 1996.

Women in the European Community, Office for Official Publications of the European Communities, Luxembourg, 1992.

INDEX

CHESTER COLLEGE LIBRARY